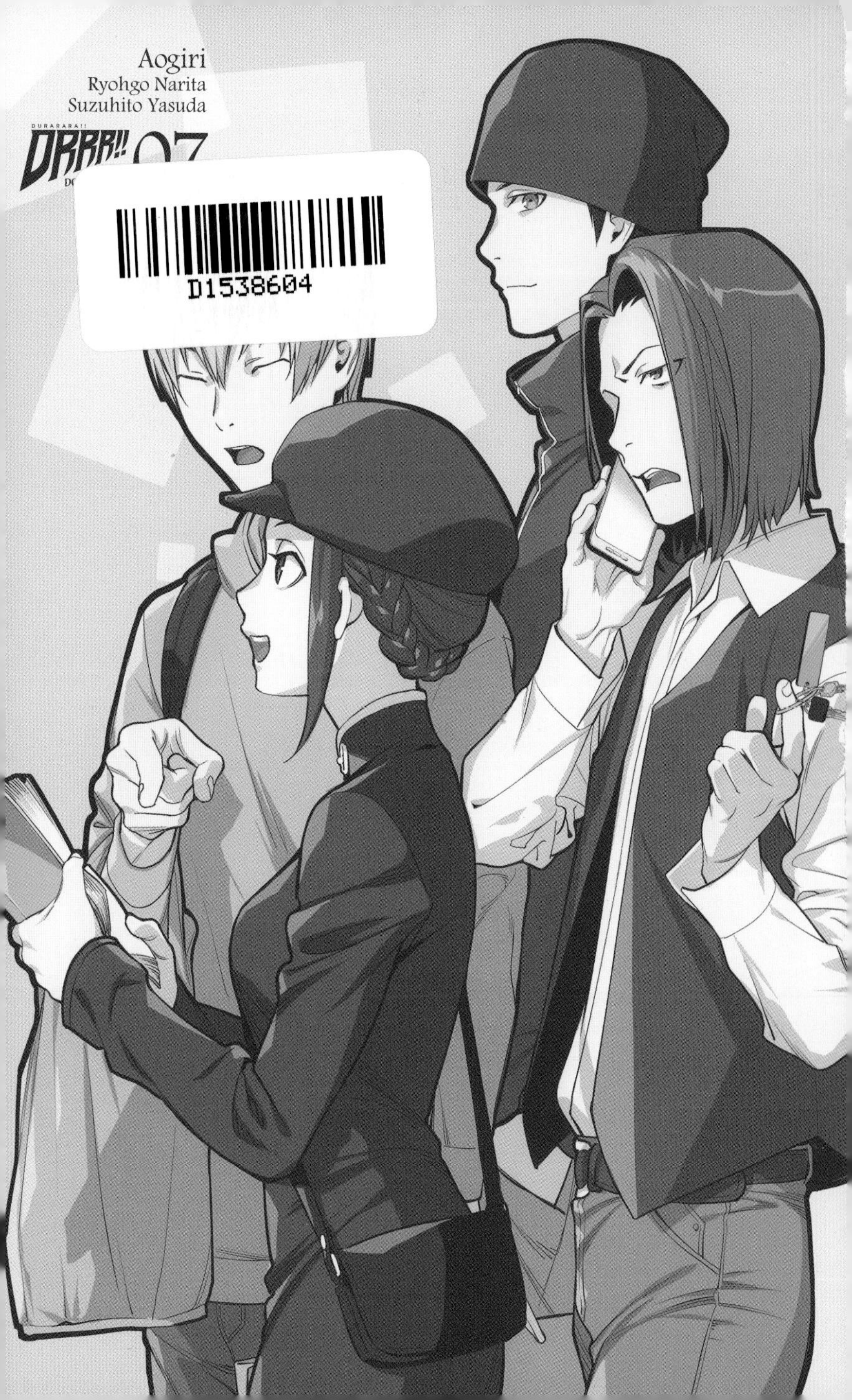
Aogiri
Ryohgo Narita
Suzuhito Yasuda
DURARARA!!
DRRR!! 07

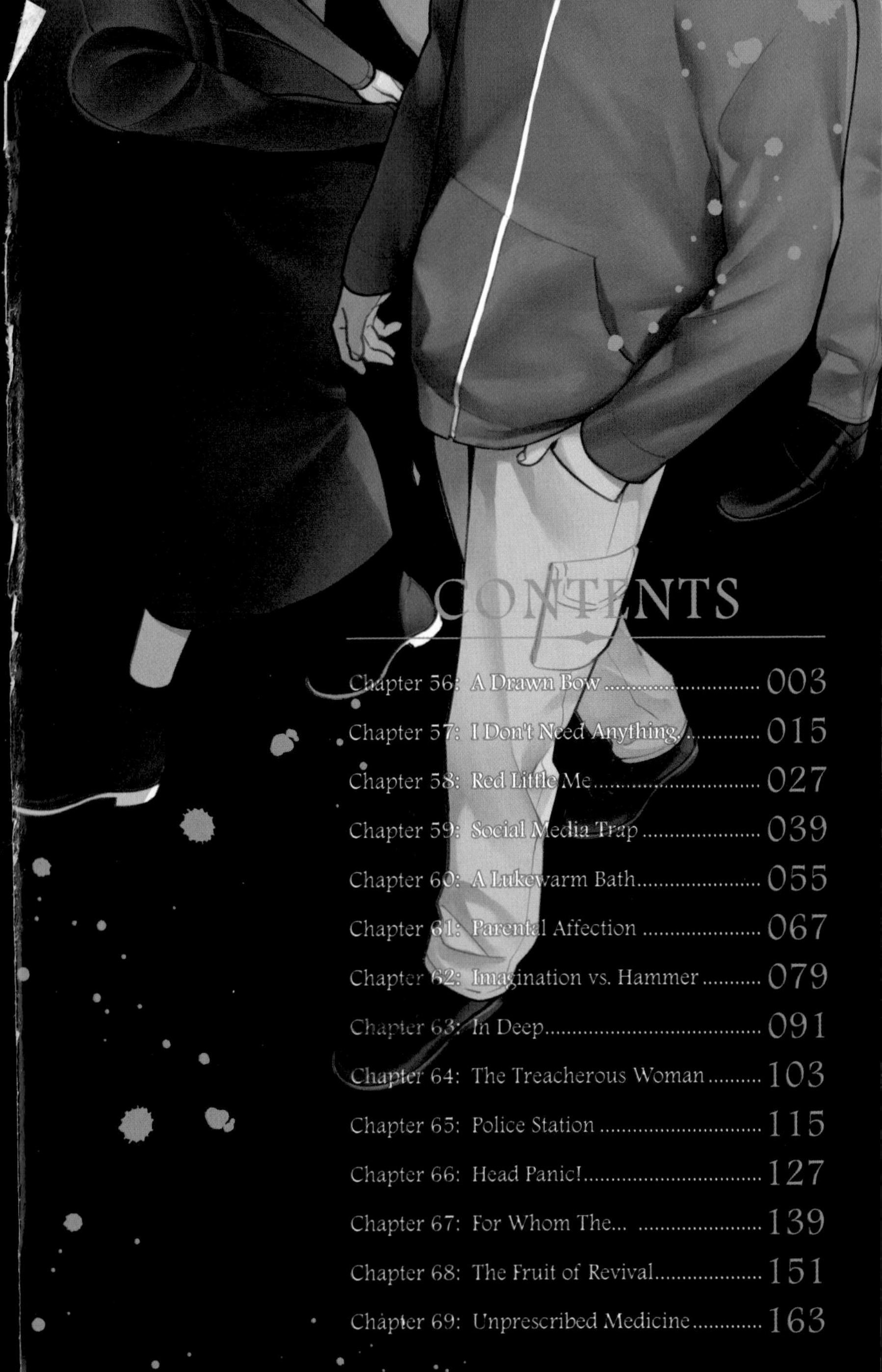

CONTENTS

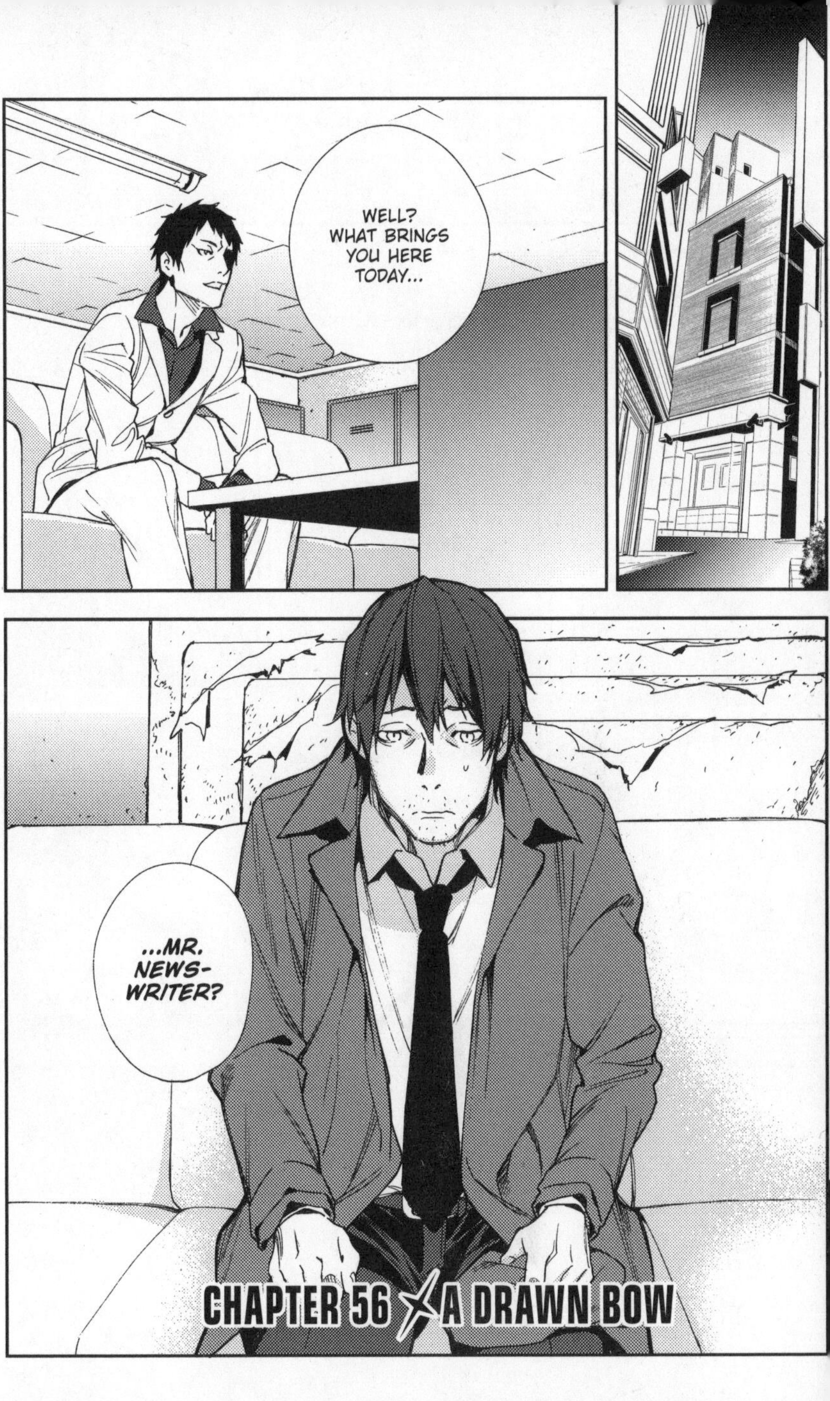
WELL? WHAT BRINGS YOU HERE TODAY...
...MR. NEWS-WRITER?
CHAPTER 56 A DRAWN BOW

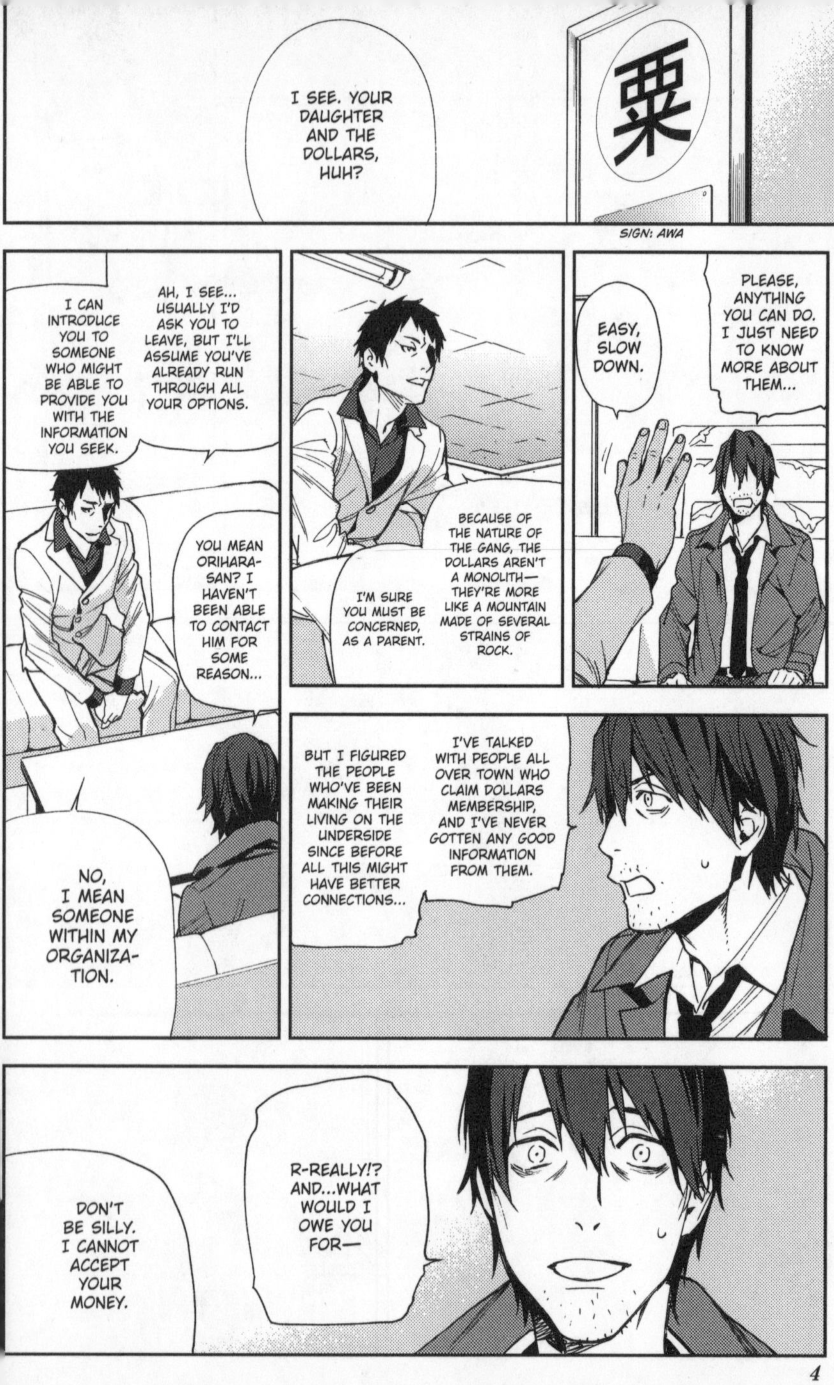

I SEE. YOUR DAUGHTER AND THE DOLLARS, HUH?
栗
SIGN: AWA
PLEASE, ANYTHING YOU CAN DO. I JUST NEED TO KNOW MORE ABOUT THEM...
EASY, SLOW DOWN.
BECAUSE OF THE NATURE OF THE GANG, THE DOLLARS AREN'T A MONOLITH— THEY'RE MORE LIKE A MOUNTAIN MADE OF SEVERAL STRAINS OF ROCK.
I'M SURE YOU MUST BE CONCERNED, AS A PARENT.
I'VE TALKED WITH PEOPLE ALL OVER TOWN WHO CLAIM DOLLARS MEMBERSHIP, AND I'VE NEVER GOTTEN ANY GOOD INFORMATION FROM THEM.
BUT I FIGURED THE PEOPLE WHO'VE BEEN MAKING THEIR LIVING ON THE UNDERSIDE SINCE BEFORE ALL THIS MIGHT HAVE BETTER CONNECTIONS...
AH, I SEE... USUALLY I'D ASK YOU TO LEAVE, BUT I'LL ASSUME YOU'VE ALREADY RUN THROUGH ALL YOUR OPTIONS.
I CAN INTRODUCE YOU TO SOMEONE WHO MIGHT BE ABLE TO PROVIDE YOU WITH THE INFORMATION YOU SEEK.
YOU MEAN ORIHARA-SAN? I HAVEN'T BEEN ABLE TO CONTACT HIM FOR SOME REASON...
NO, I MEAN SOMEONE WITHIN MY ORGANIZA-TION.
R-REALLY!? AND...WHAT WOULD I OWE YOU FOR—
DON'T BE SILLY. I CANNOT ACCEPT YOUR MONEY.

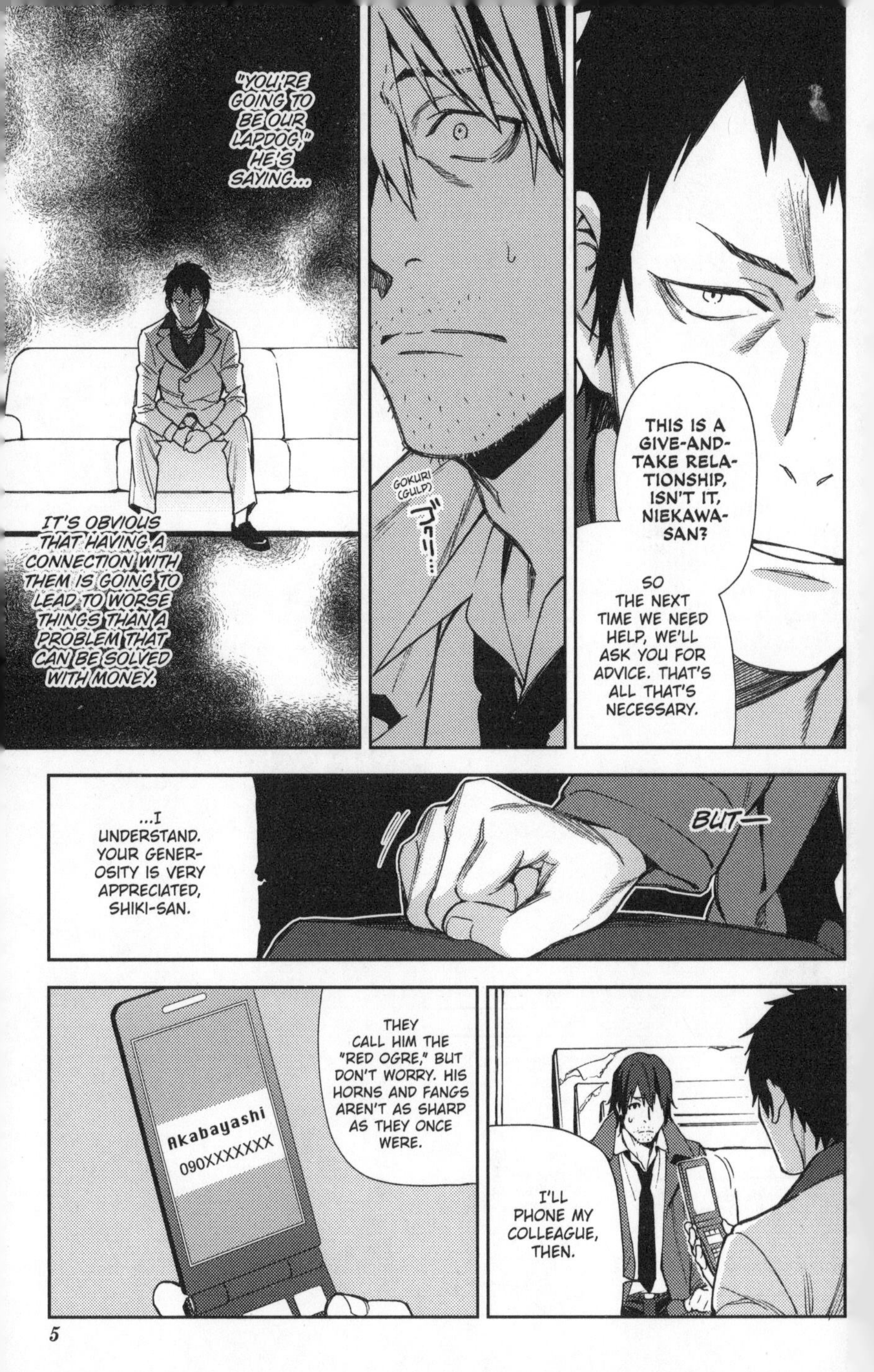
THIS IS A GIVE-AND-TAKE RELATIONSHIP, ISN'T IT, NIEKAWA-SAN?
SO THE NEXT TIME WE NEED HELP, WE'LL ASK YOU FOR ADVICE. THAT'S ALL THAT'S NECESSARY.
GOKURI (GULP)
ゴクリ…
"YOU'RE GOING TO BE OUR LAPDOG," HE'S SAYING...
IT'S OBVIOUS THAT HAVING A CONNECTION WITH THEM IS GOING TO LEAD TO WORSE THINGS THAN A PROBLEM THAT CAN BE SOLVED WITH MONEY.
BUT—
...I UNDERSTAND. YOUR GENEROSITY IS VERY APPRECIATED, SHIKI-SAN.
I'LL PHONE MY COLLEAGUE, THEN.
THEY CALL HIM THE "RED OGRE," BUT DON'T WORRY. HIS HORNS AND FANGS AREN'T AS SHARP AS THEY ONCE WERE.
Akabayashi
090XXXXXXX

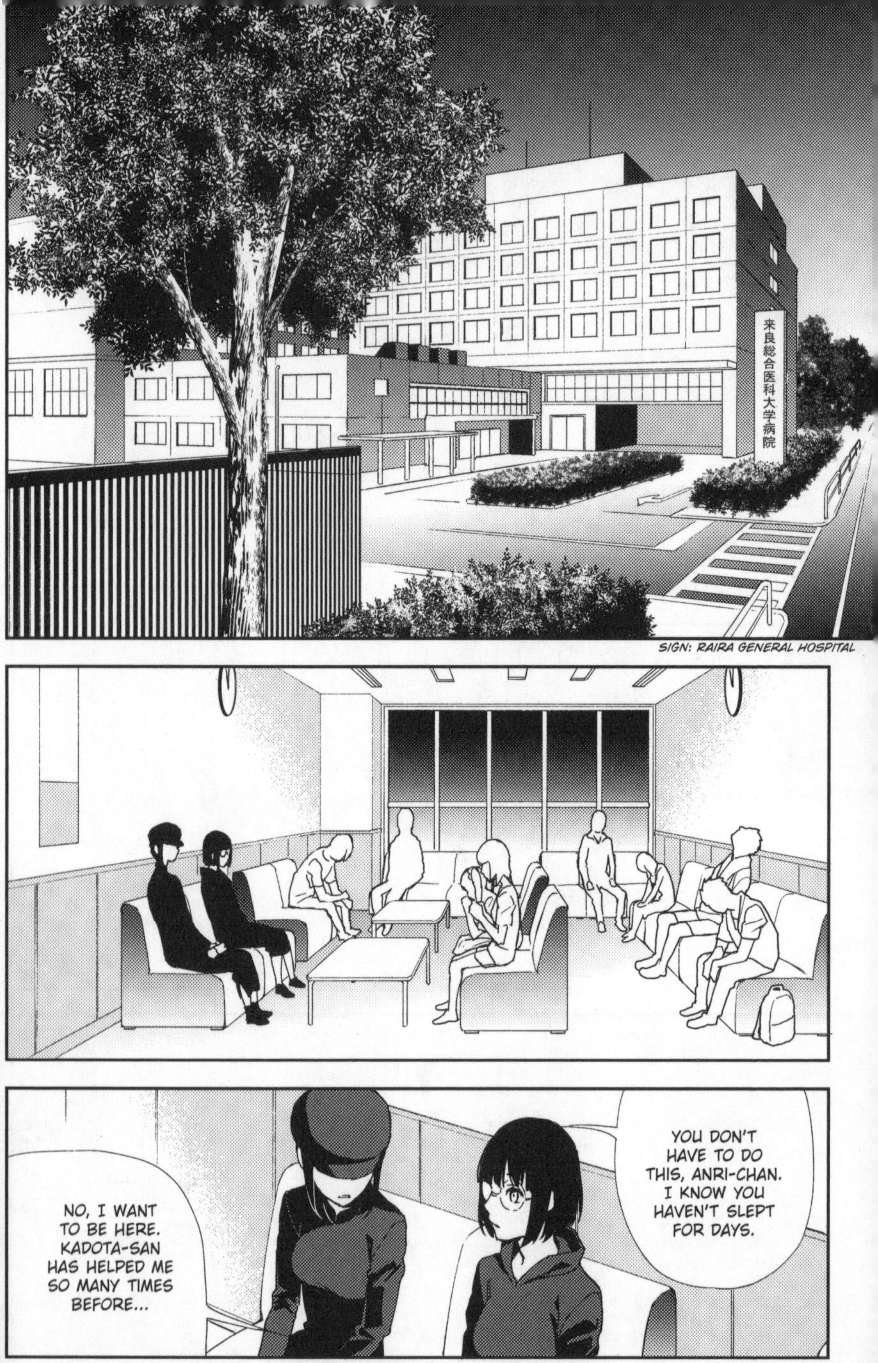
来良総合医科大学病院
YOU DON'T HAVE TO DO THIS, ANRI-CHAN. I KNOW YOU HAVEN'T SLEPT FOR DAYS.
NO, I WANT TO BE HERE. KADOTA-SAN HAS HELPED ME SO MANY TIMES BEFORE...

SIGN: RAIRA GENERAL HOSPITAL

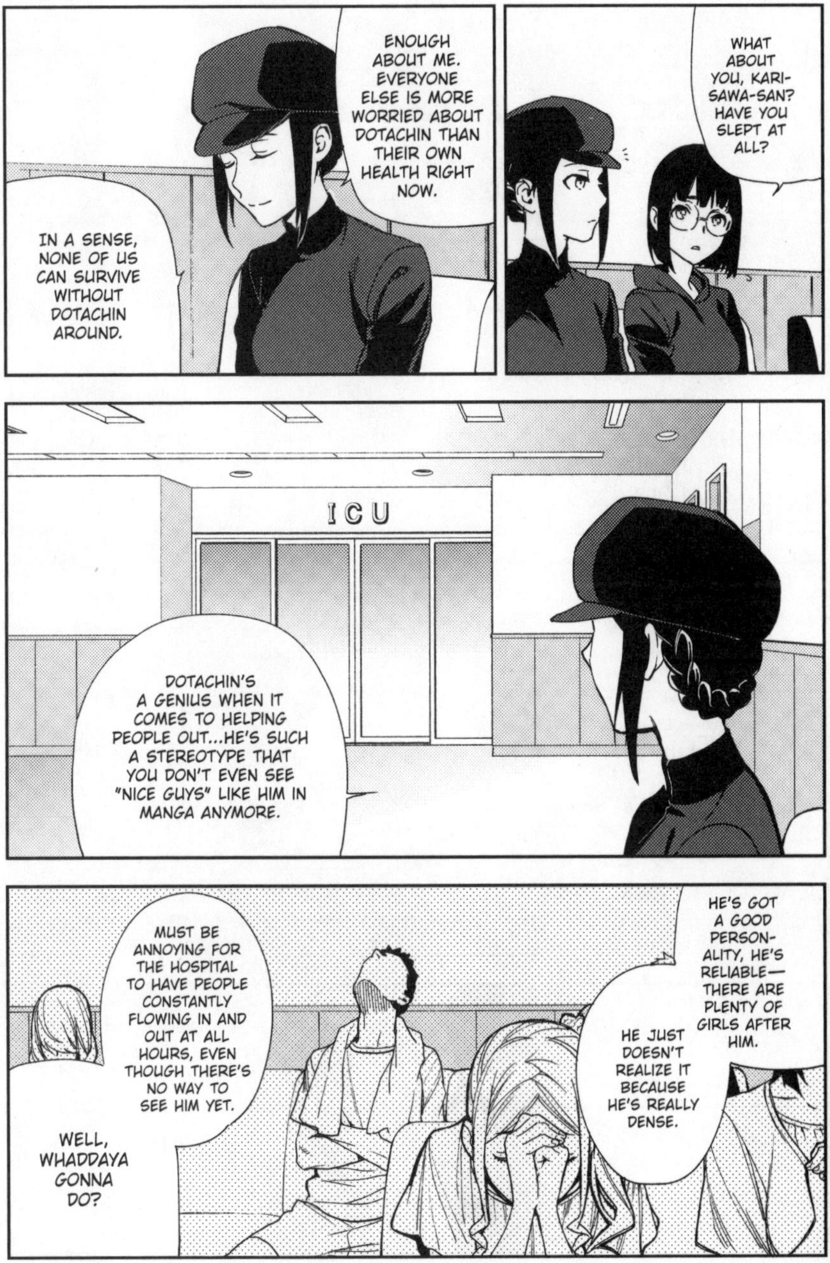
WHAT ABOUT YOU, KARI-SAWA-SAN? HAVE YOU SLEPT AT ALL?
ENOUGH ABOUT ME. EVERYONE ELSE IS MORE WORRIED ABOUT DOTACHIN THAN THEIR OWN HEALTH RIGHT NOW.
IN A SENSE, NONE OF US CAN SURVIVE WITHOUT DOTACHIN AROUND.
ICU
DOTACHIN'S A GENIUS WHEN IT COMES TO HELPING PEOPLE OUT...HE'S SUCH A STEREOTYPE THAT YOU DON'T EVEN SEE "NICE GUYS" LIKE HIM IN MANGA ANYMORE.
HE'S GOT A GOOD PERSON-ALITY, HE'S RELIABLE—THERE ARE PLENTY OF GIRLS AFTER HIM.
HE JUST DOESN'T REALIZE IT BECAUSE HE'S REALLY DENSE.
MUST BE ANNOYING FOR THE HOSPITAL TO HAVE PEOPLE CONSTANTLY FLOWING IN AND OUT AT ALL HOURS, EVEN THOUGH THERE'S NO WAY TO SEE HIM YET.
WELL, WHADDAYA GONNA DO?

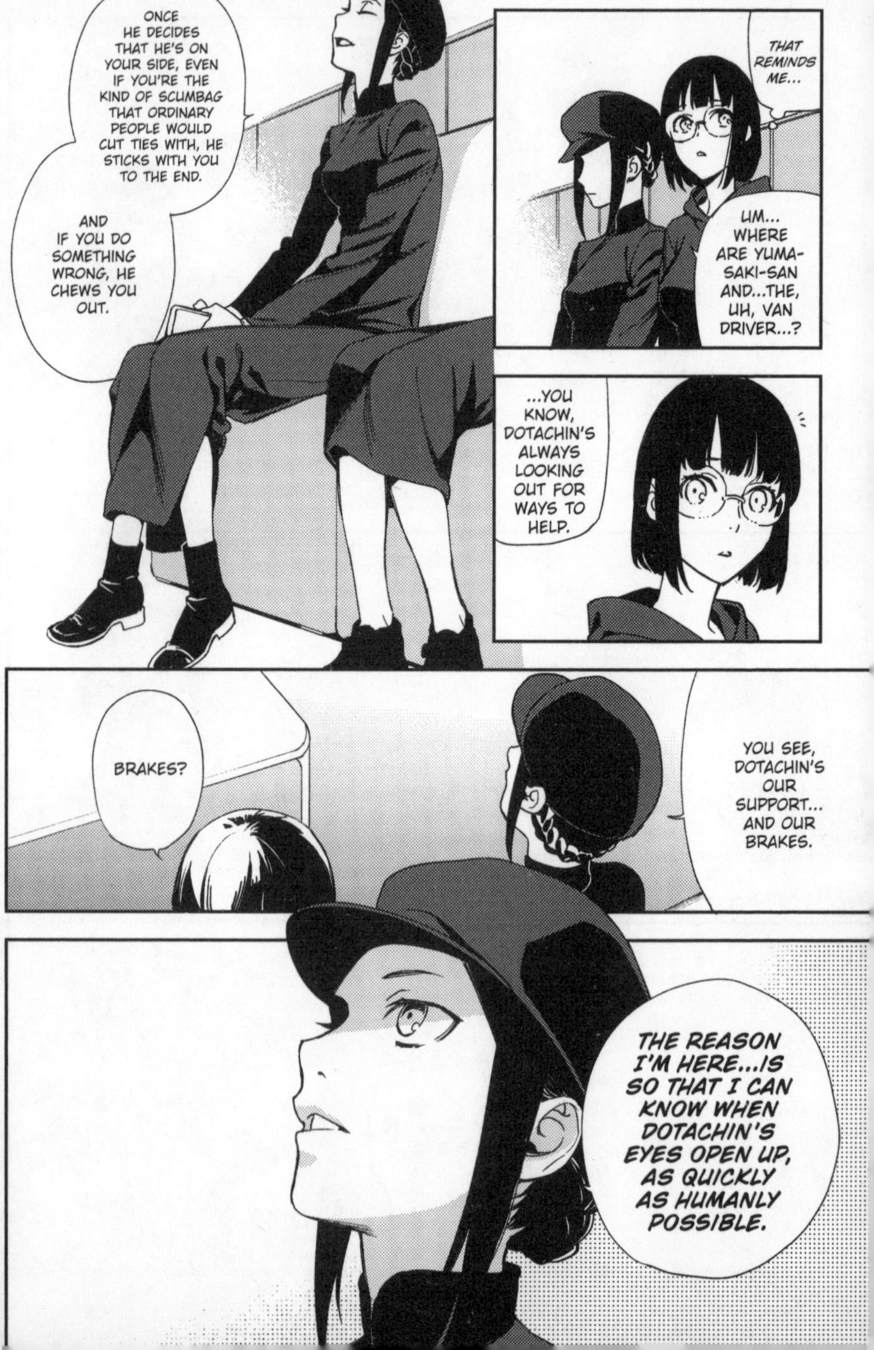
THAT REMINDS ME...
UM... WHERE ARE YUMASAKI-SAN AND...THE, UH, VAN DRIVER...?
...YOU KNOW, DOTACHIN'S ALWAYS LOOKING OUT FOR WAYS TO HELP.
ONCE HE DECIDES THAT HE'S ON YOUR SIDE, EVEN IF YOU'RE THE KIND OF SCUMBAG THAT ORDINARY PEOPLE WOULD CUT TIES WITH, HE STICKS WITH YOU TO THE END.
AND IF YOU DO SOMETHING WRONG, HE CHEWS YOU OUT.
YOU SEE, DOTACHIN'S OUR SUPPORT... AND OUR BRAKES.
BRAKES?
THE REASON I'M HERE...IS SO THAT I CAN KNOW WHEN DOTACHIN'S EYES OPEN UP, AS QUICKLY AS HUMANLY POSSIBLE.

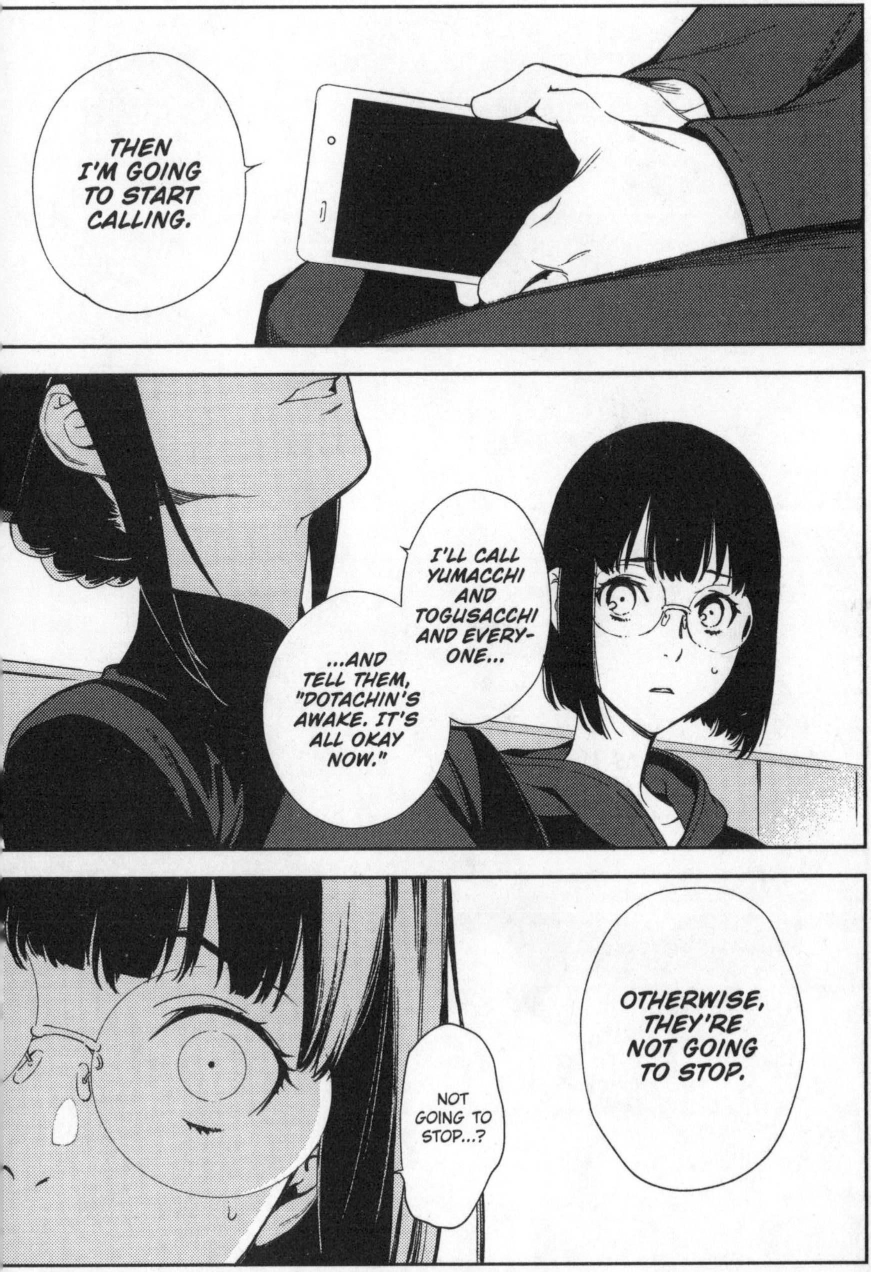
THEN I'M GOING TO START CALLING.
I'LL CALL YUMACCHI AND TOGUSACCHI AND EVERY-ONE...
...AND TELL THEM, "DOTACHIN'S AWAKE. IT'S ALL OKAY NOW."
OTHERWISE, THEY'RE NOT GOING TO STOP.
NOT GOING TO STOP...?

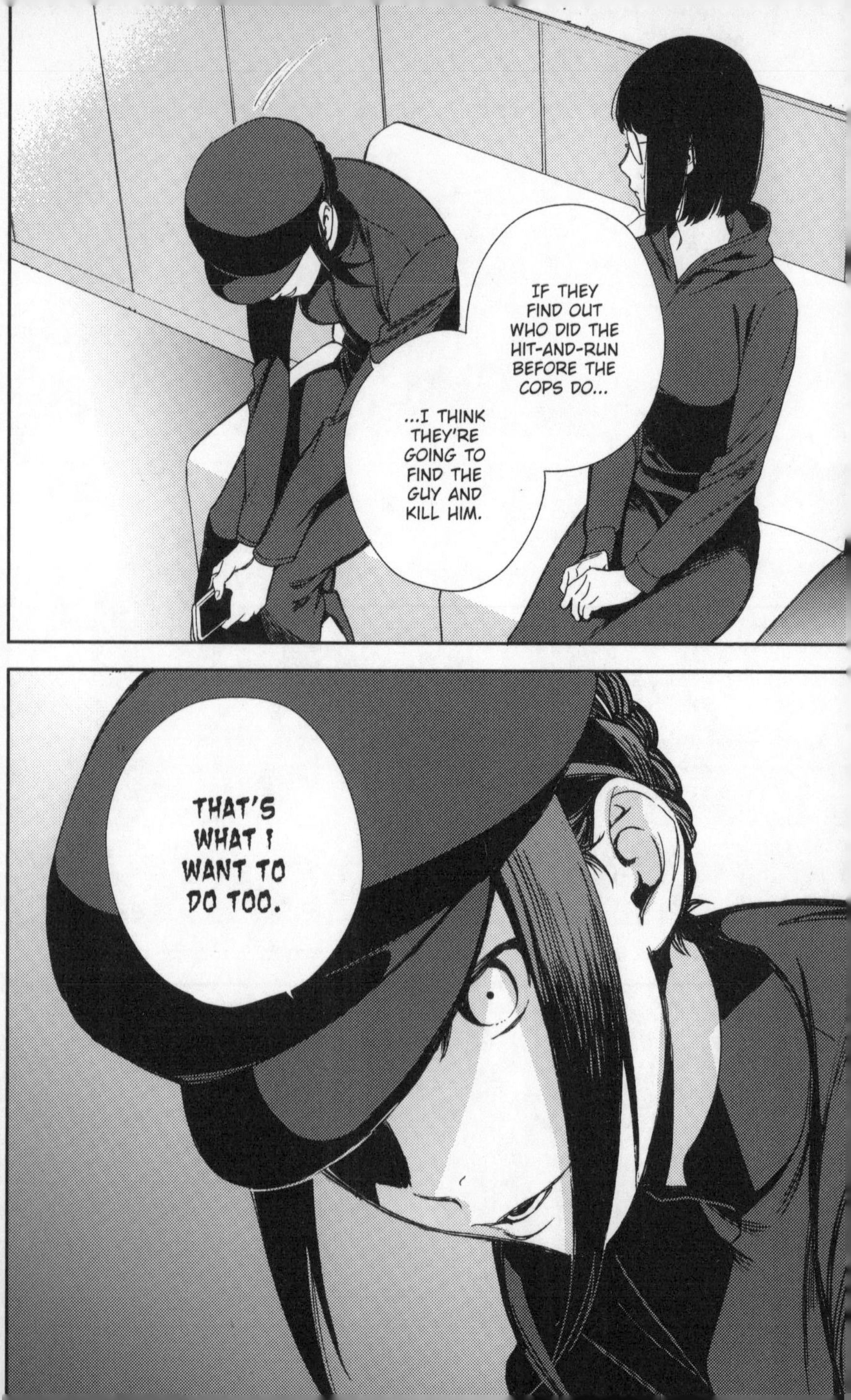
IF THEY FIND OUT WHO DID THE HIT-AND-RUN BEFORE THE COPS DO...
...I THINK THEY'RE GOING TO FIND THE GUY AND KILL HIM.
THAT'S WHAT I WANT TO DO TOO.

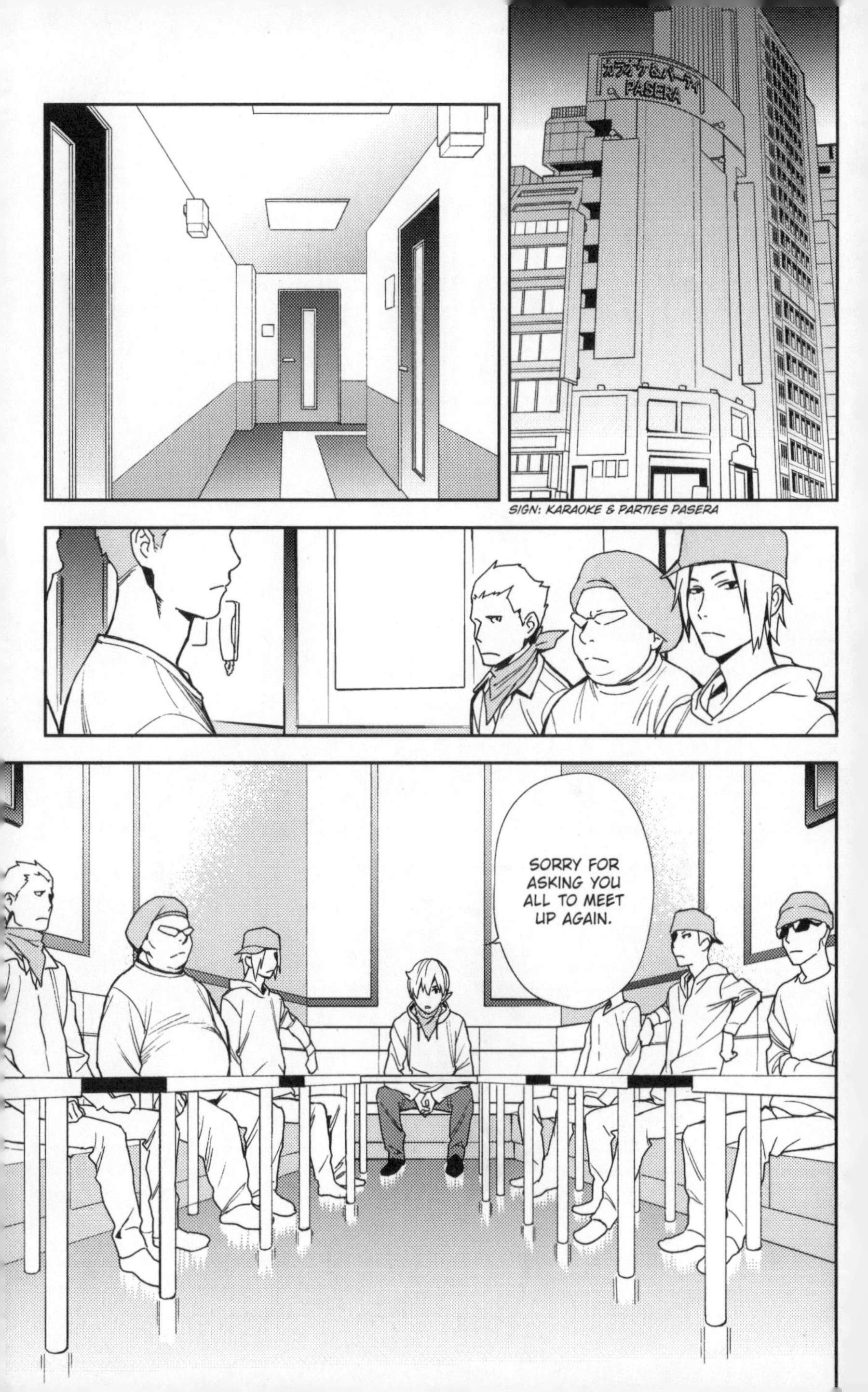
カラオケ&パーティ PASERA
SIGN: KARAOKE & PARTIES PASERA
SORRY FOR ASKING YOU ALL TO MEET UP AGAIN.

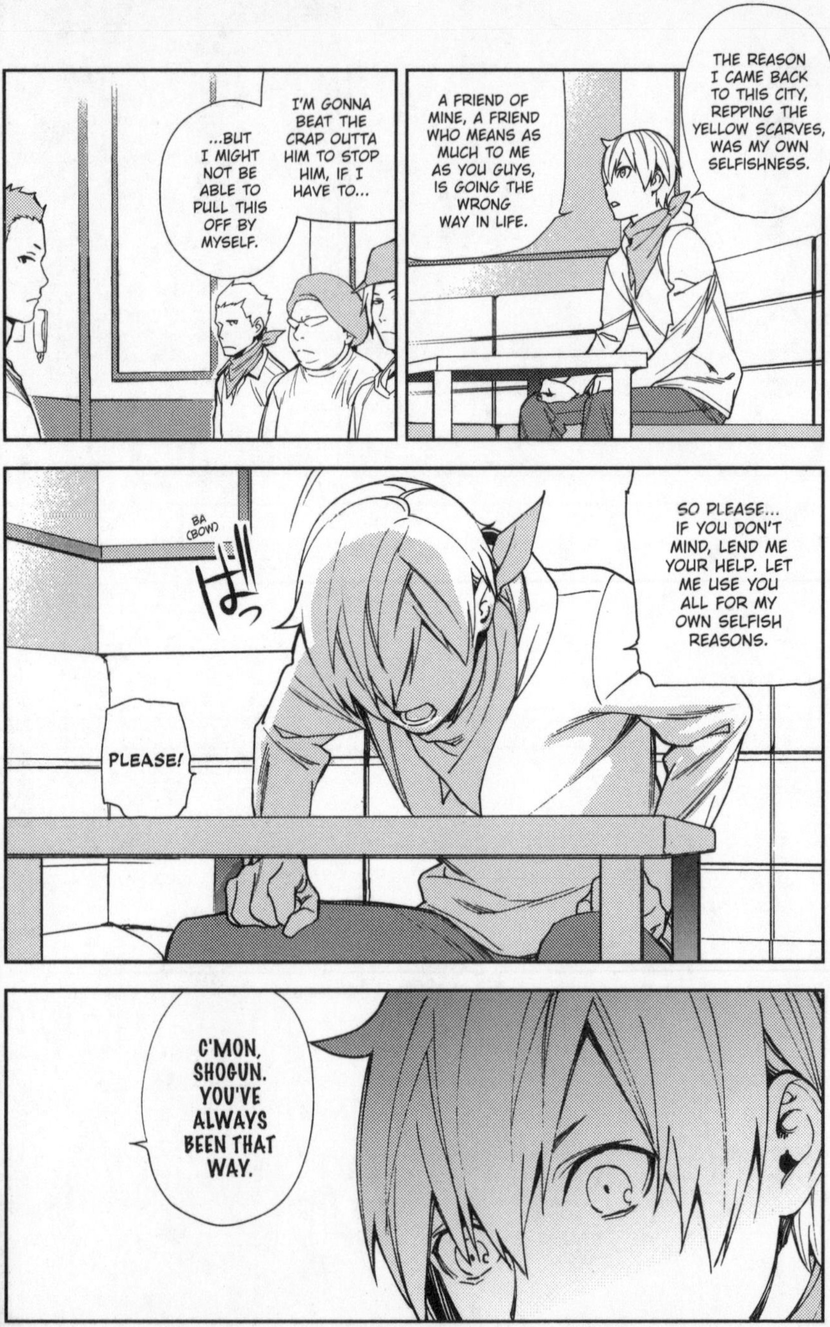
THE REASON I CAME BACK TO THIS CITY, REPPING THE YELLOW SCARVES, WAS MY OWN SELFISHNESS.
A FRIEND OF MINE, A FRIEND WHO MEANS AS MUCH TO ME AS YOU GUYS, IS GOING THE WRONG WAY IN LIFE.
I'M GONNA BEAT THE CRAP OUTTA HIM TO STOP HIM, IF I HAVE TO...
...BUT I MIGHT NOT BE ABLE TO PULL THIS OFF BY MYSELF.
SO PLEASE... IF YOU DON'T MIND, LEND ME YOUR HELP. LET ME USE YOU ALL FOR MY OWN SELFISH REASONS.
BA (BOW)
ばっ
PLEASE!
C'MON, SHOGUN. YOU'VE ALWAYS BEEN THAT WAY.

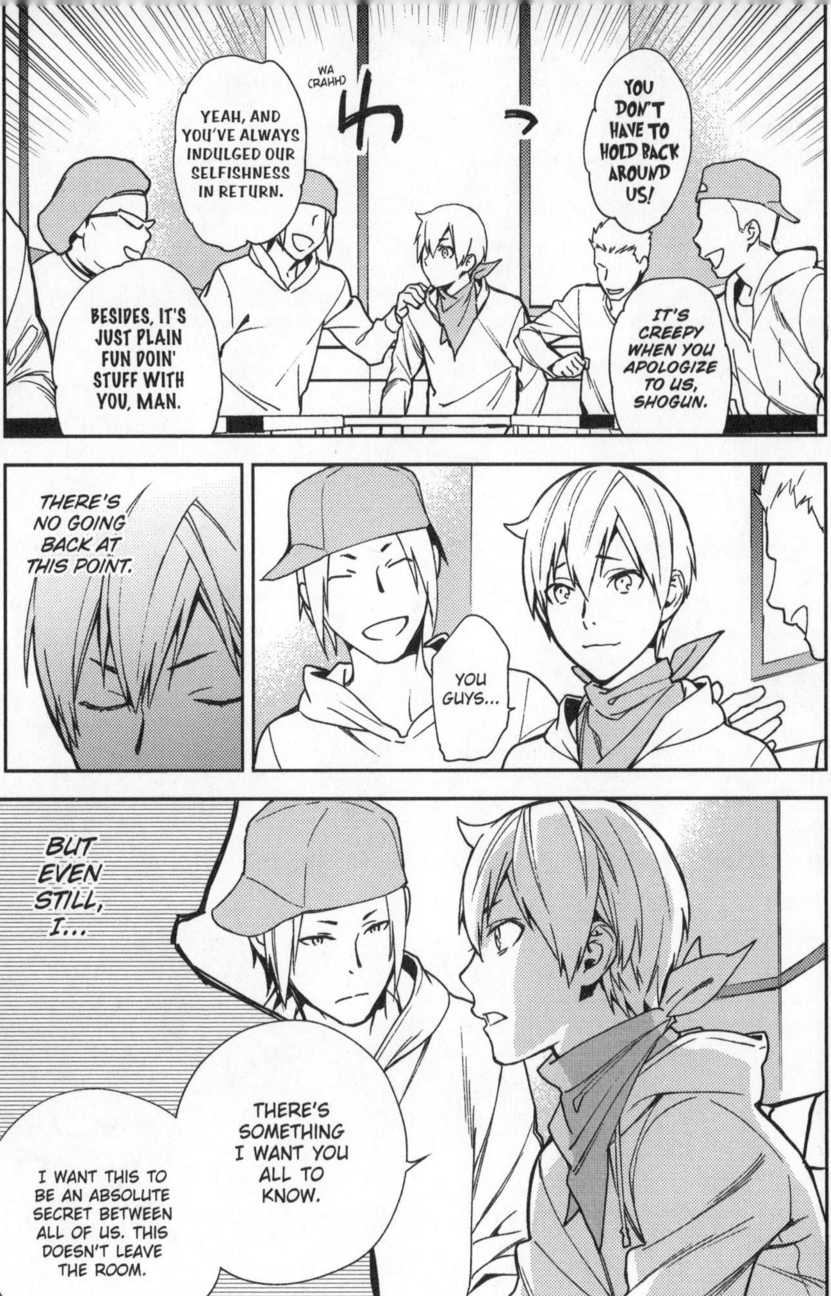
YOU DON'T HAVE TO HOLD BACK AROUND US!
WA (RAHHH)
YEAH, AND YOU'VE ALWAYS INDULGED OUR SELFISHNESS IN RETURN.
IT'S CREEPY WHEN YOU APOLOGIZE TO US, SHOGUN.
BESIDES, IT'S JUST PLAIN FUN DOIN' STUFF WITH YOU, MAN.
YOU GUYS...
THERE'S NO GOING BACK AT THIS POINT.
BUT EVEN STILL, I...
THERE'S SOMETHING I WANT YOU ALL TO KNOW.
I WANT THIS TO BE AN ABSOLUTE SECRET BETWEEN ALL OF US. THIS DOESN'T LEAVE THE ROOM.

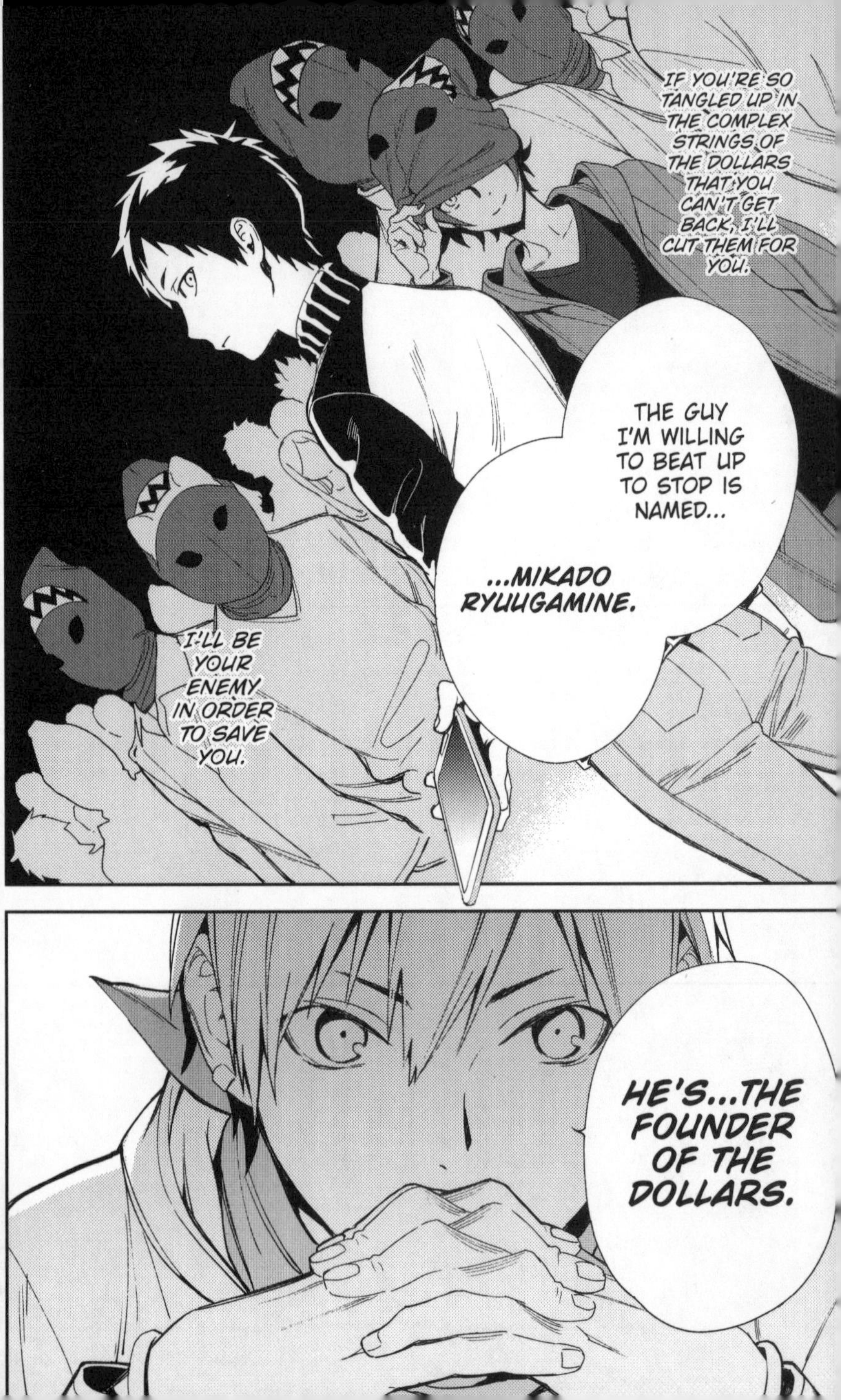
IF YOU'RE SO TANGLED UP IN THE COMPLEX STRINGS OF THE DOLLARS THAT YOU CAN'T GET BACK, I'LL CUT THEM FOR YOU.
THE GUY I'M WILLING TO BEAT UP TO STOP IS NAMED...
...MIKADO RYUUGAMINE.
I'LL BE YOUR ENEMY IN ORDER TO SAVE YOU.
HE'S...THE FOUNDER OF THE DOLLARS.

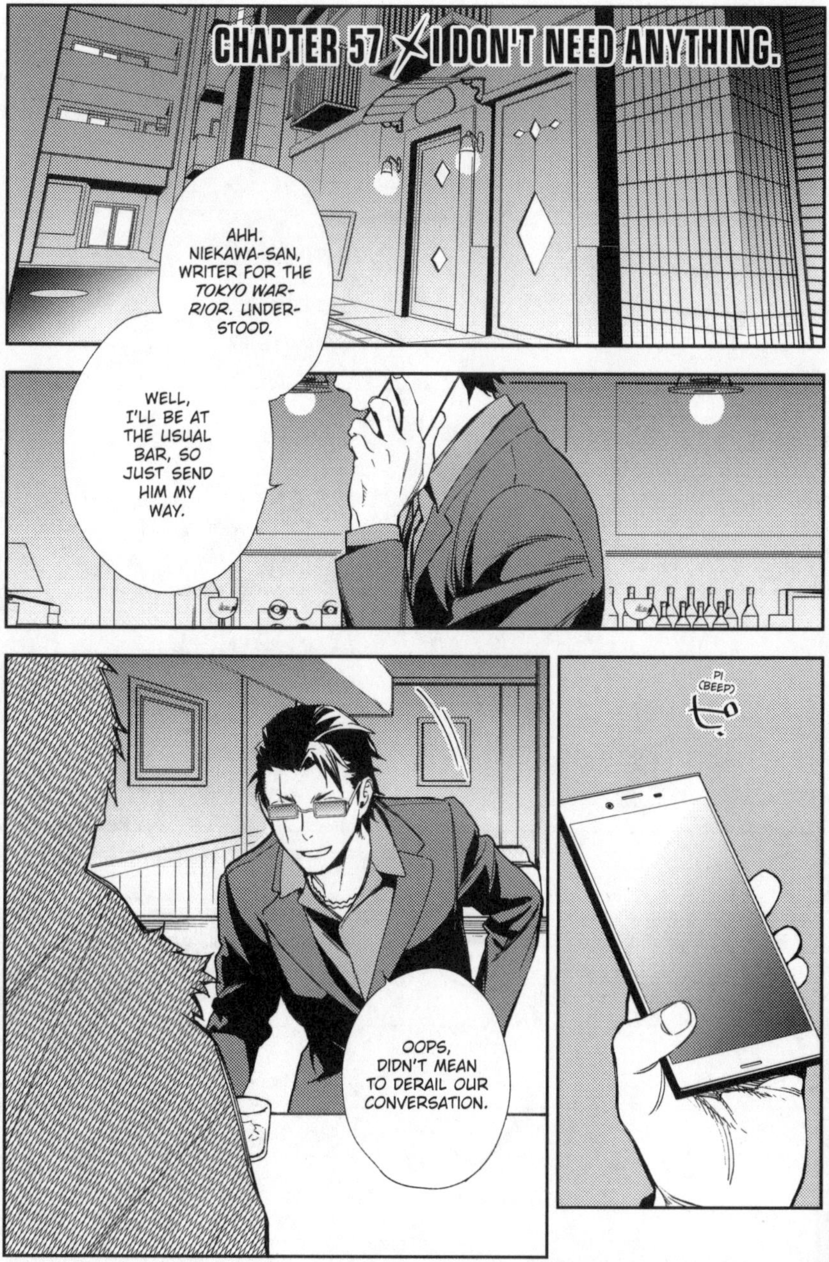
CHAPTER 57 I DON'T NEED ANYTHING.
AHH. NIEKAWA-SAN, WRITER FOR THE *TOKYO WARRIOR*. UNDERSTOOD.
WELL, I'LL BE AT THE USUAL BAR, SO JUST SEND HIM MY WAY.
PI (BEEP)
OOPS, DIDN'T MEAN TO DERAIL OUR CONVERSATION.

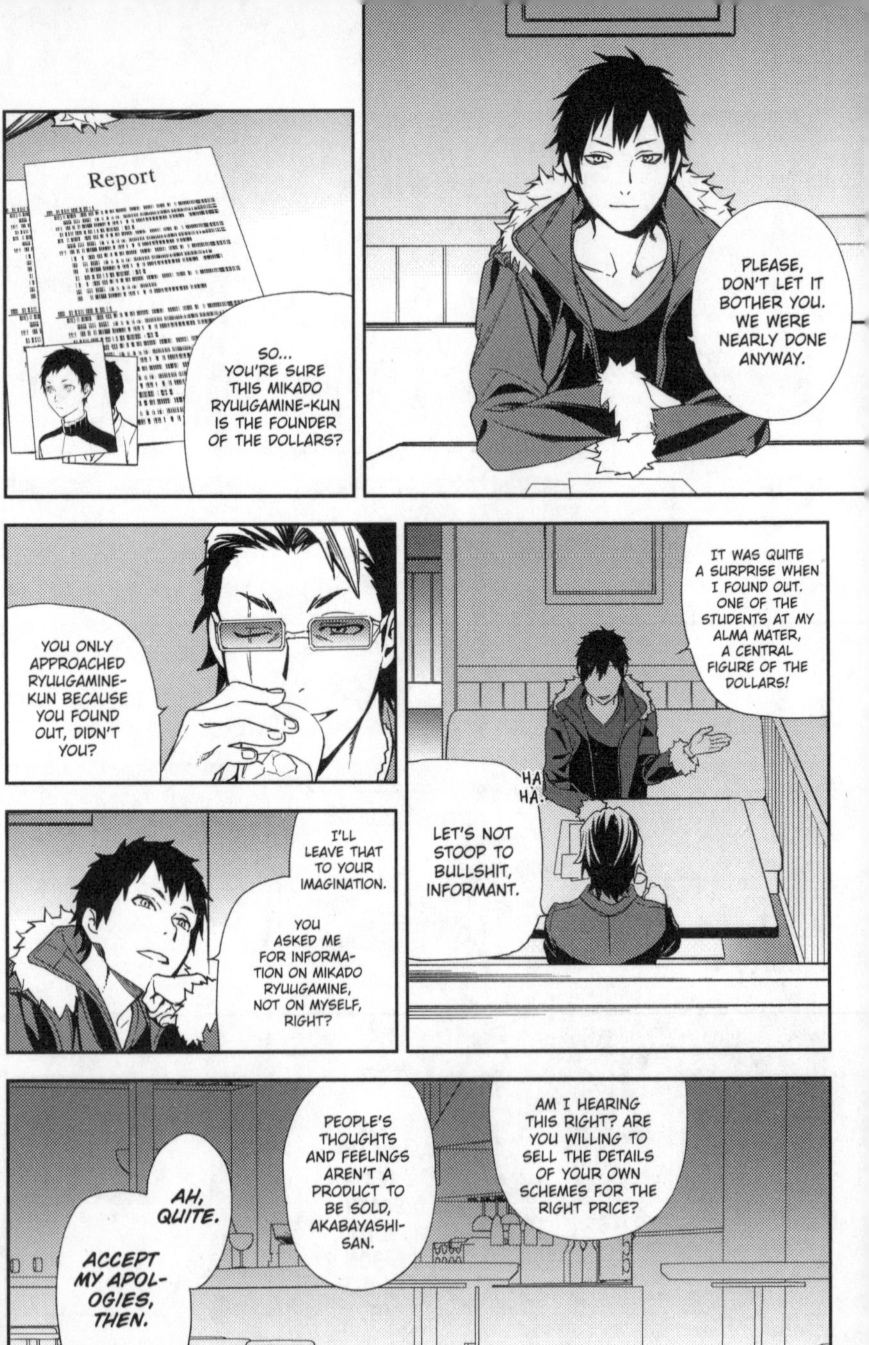
PLEASE, DON'T LET IT BOTHER YOU. WE WERE NEARLY DONE ANYWAY.
Report
SO... YOU'RE SURE THIS MIKADO RYUUGAMINE-KUN IS THE FOUNDER OF THE DOLLARS?
IT WAS QUITE A SURPRISE WHEN I FOUND OUT. ONE OF THE STUDENTS AT MY ALMA MATER, A CENTRAL FIGURE OF THE DOLLARS!
HA HA.
LET'S NOT STOOP TO BULLSHIT, INFORMANT.
YOU ONLY APPROACHED RYUUGAMINE-KUN BECAUSE YOU FOUND OUT, DIDN'T YOU?
I'LL LEAVE THAT TO YOUR IMAGINATION.
YOU ASKED ME FOR INFORMATION ON MIKADO RYUUGAMINE, NOT ON MYSELF, RIGHT?
AM I HEARING THIS RIGHT? ARE YOU WILLING TO SELL THE DETAILS OF YOUR OWN SCHEMES FOR THE RIGHT PRICE?
PEOPLE'S THOUGHTS AND FEELINGS AREN'T A PRODUCT TO BE SOLD, AKABAYASHI-SAN.
AH, QUITE.
ACCEPT MY APOLOGIES, THEN.

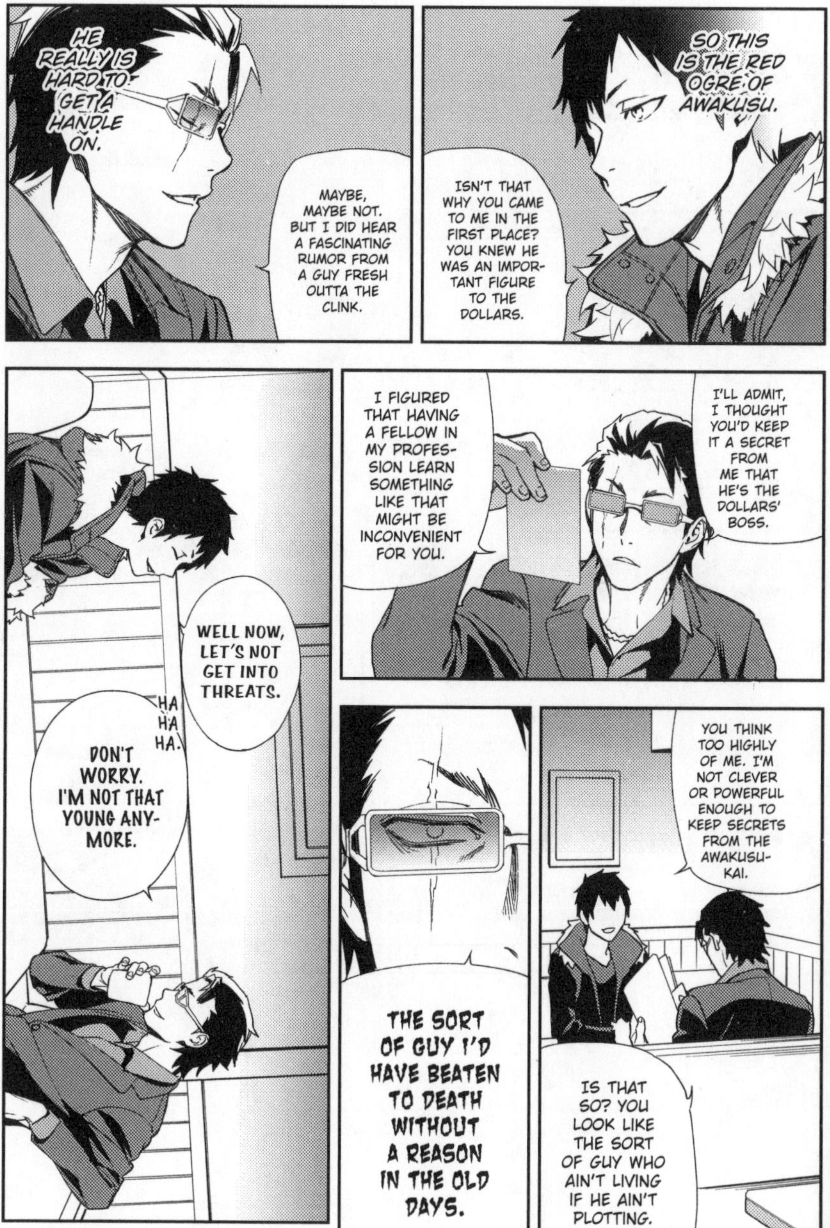
SO THIS IS THE RED OGRE OF AWAKUSU.
ISN'T THAT WHY YOU CAME TO ME IN THE FIRST PLACE? YOU KNEW HE WAS AN IMPORTANT FIGURE TO THE DOLLARS.
HE REALLY IS HARD TO GET A HANDLE ON.
MAYBE, MAYBE NOT. BUT I DID HEAR A FASCINATING RUMOR FROM A GUY FRESH OUTTA THE CLINK.
I'LL ADMIT, I THOUGHT YOU'D KEEP IT A SECRET FROM ME THAT HE'S THE DOLLARS' BOSS.
I FIGURED THAT HAVING A FELLOW IN MY PROFESSION LEARN SOMETHING LIKE THAT MIGHT BE INCONVENIENT FOR YOU.
YOU THINK TOO HIGHLY OF ME. I'M NOT CLEVER OR POWERFUL ENOUGH TO KEEP SECRETS FROM THE AWAKUSU-KAI.
IS THAT SO? YOU LOOK LIKE THE SORT OF GUY WHO AIN'T LIVING IF HE AIN'T PLOTTING.
THE SORT OF GUY I'D HAVE BEATEN TO DEATH WITHOUT A REASON IN THE OLD DAYS.
WELL NOW, LET'S NOT GET INTO THREATS.
HA HA HA.
DON'T WORRY. I'M NOT THAT YOUNG ANYMORE.

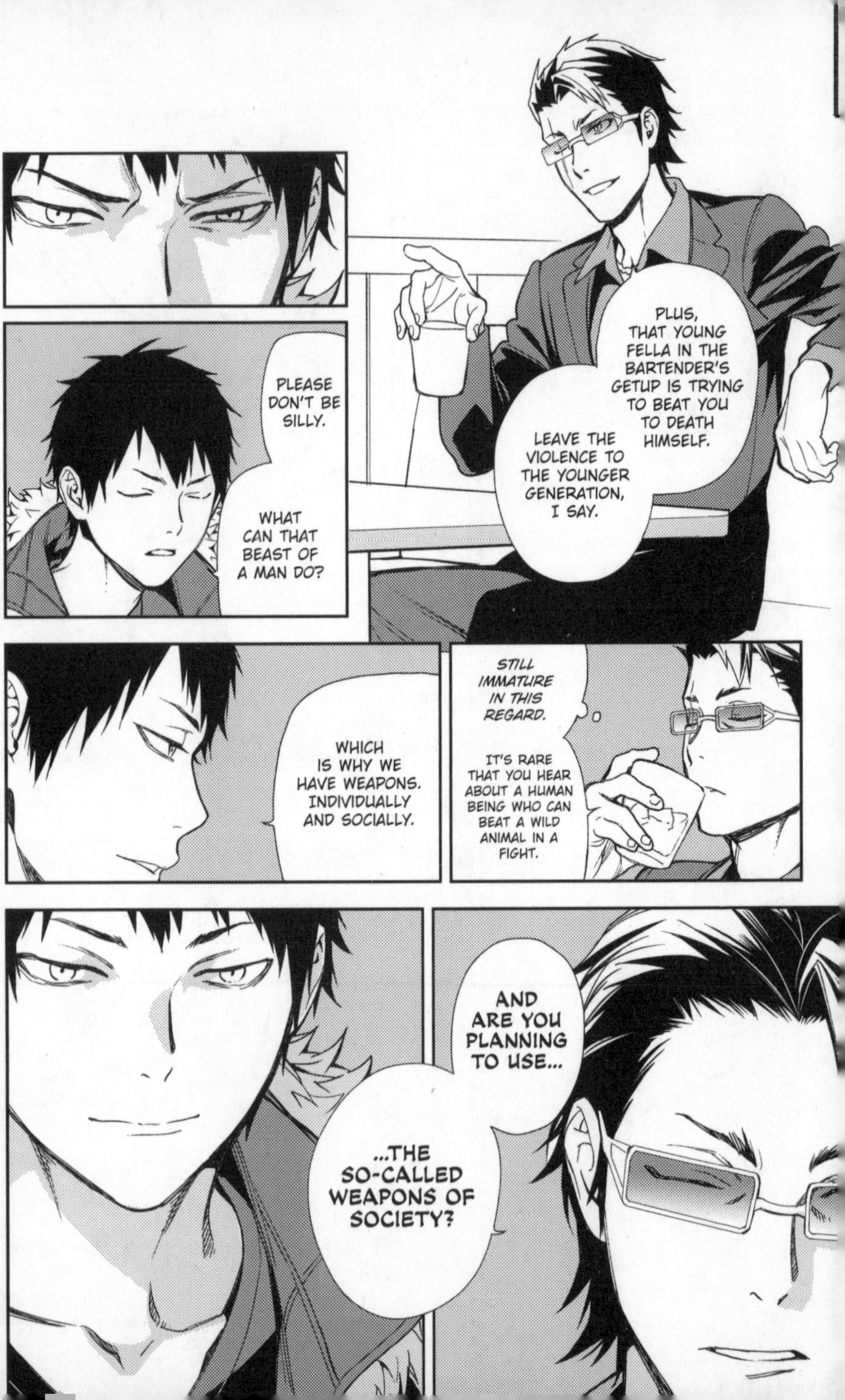
PLUS, THAT YOUNG FELLA IN THE BARTENDER'S GETUP IS TRYING TO BEAT YOU TO DEATH HIMSELF.
LEAVE THE VIOLENCE TO THE YOUNGER GENERATION, I SAY.
PLEASE DON'T BE SILLY.
WHAT CAN THAT BEAST OF A MAN DO?
STILL IMMATURE IN THIS REGARD.
IT'S RARE THAT YOU HEAR ABOUT A HUMAN BEING WHO CAN BEAT A WILD ANIMAL IN A FIGHT.
WHICH IS WHY WE HAVE WEAPONS. INDIVIDUALLY AND SOCIALLY.
AND ARE YOU PLANNING TO USE...
...THE SO-CALLED WEAPONS OF SOCIETY?

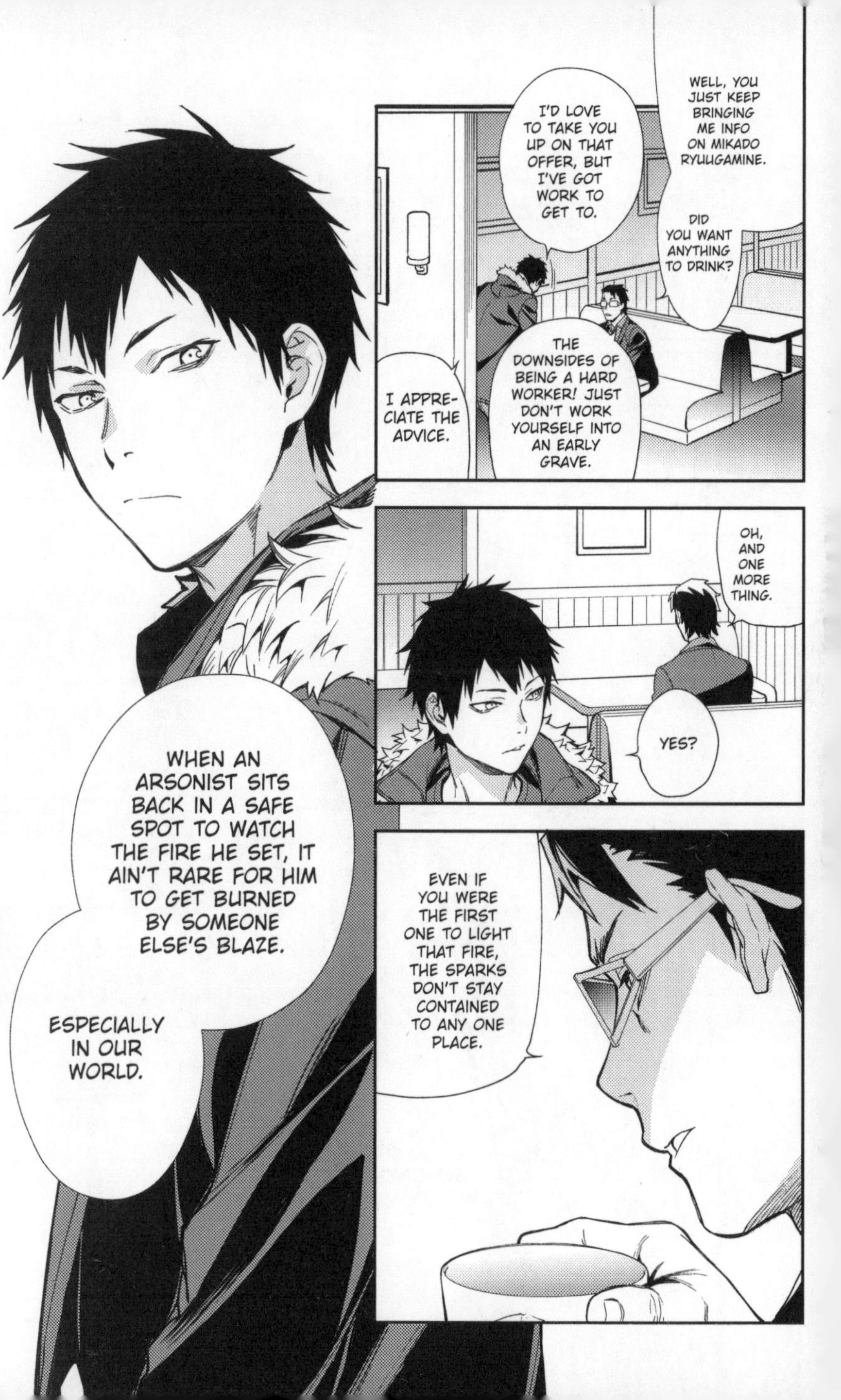
WELL, YOU JUST KEEP BRINGING ME INFO ON MIKADO RYUUGAMINE.
I'D LOVE TO TAKE YOU UP ON THAT OFFER, BUT I'VE GOT WORK TO GET TO.
DID YOU WANT ANYTHING TO DRINK?
THE DOWNSIDES OF BEING A HARD WORKER! JUST DON'T WORK YOURSELF INTO AN EARLY GRAVE.
I APPRE-CIATE THE ADVICE.
OH, AND ONE MORE THING.
YES?
EVEN IF YOU WERE THE FIRST ONE TO LIGHT THAT FIRE, THE SPARKS DON'T STAY CONTAINED TO ANY ONE PLACE.
WHEN AN ARSONIST SITS BACK IN A SAFE SPOT TO WATCH THE FIRE HE SET, IT AIN'T RARE FOR HIM TO GET BURNED BY SOMEONE ELSE'S BLAZE.
ESPECIALLY IN OUR WORLD.

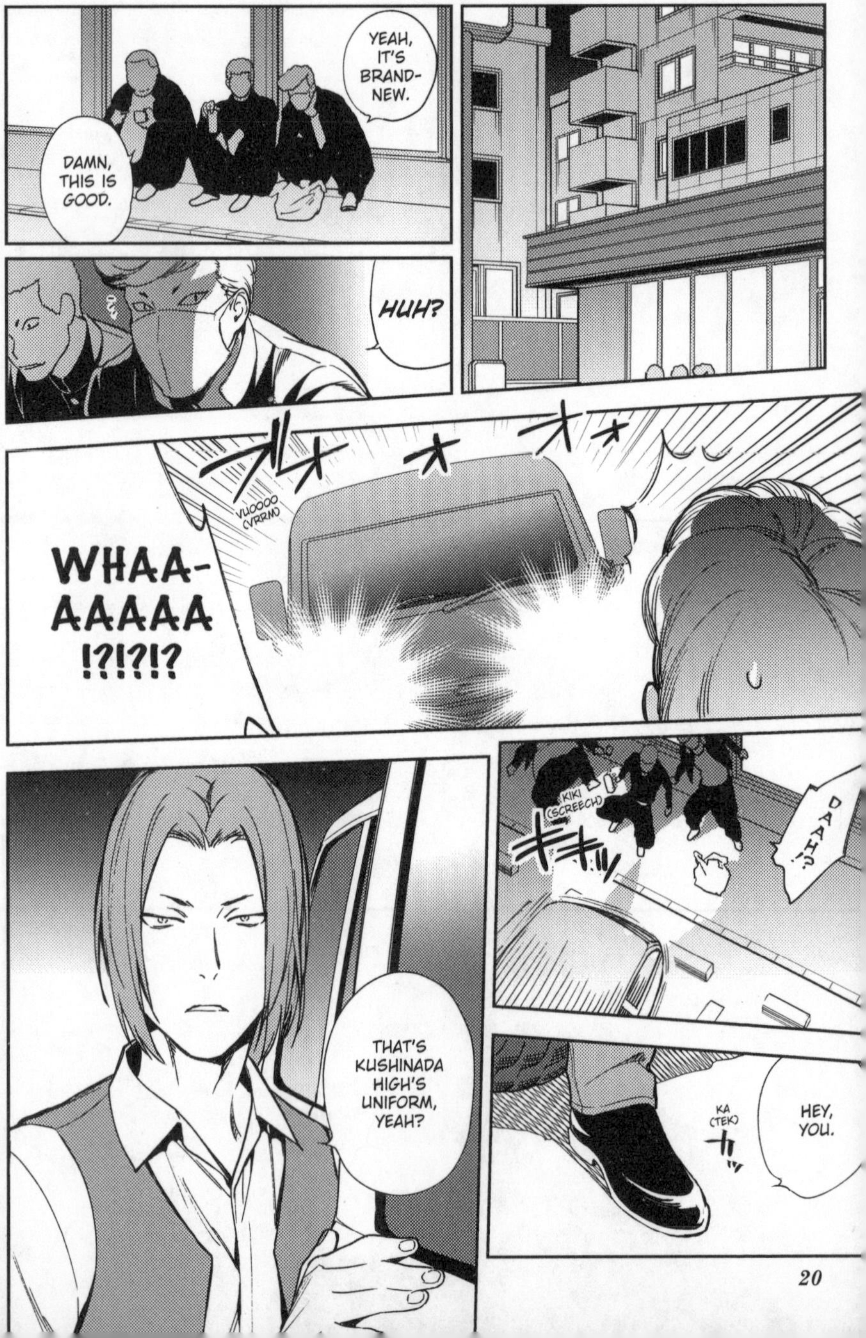
YEAH, IT'S BRAND-NEW.
DAMN, THIS IS GOOD.
HUH?
VUOOOO (VRRM)
WHAA-AAAAA!?!?!?
DAAAH!?
KIKI (SCREECH)
HEY, YOU.
KA (TEK)
THAT'S KUSHINADA HIGH'S UNIFORM, YEAH?

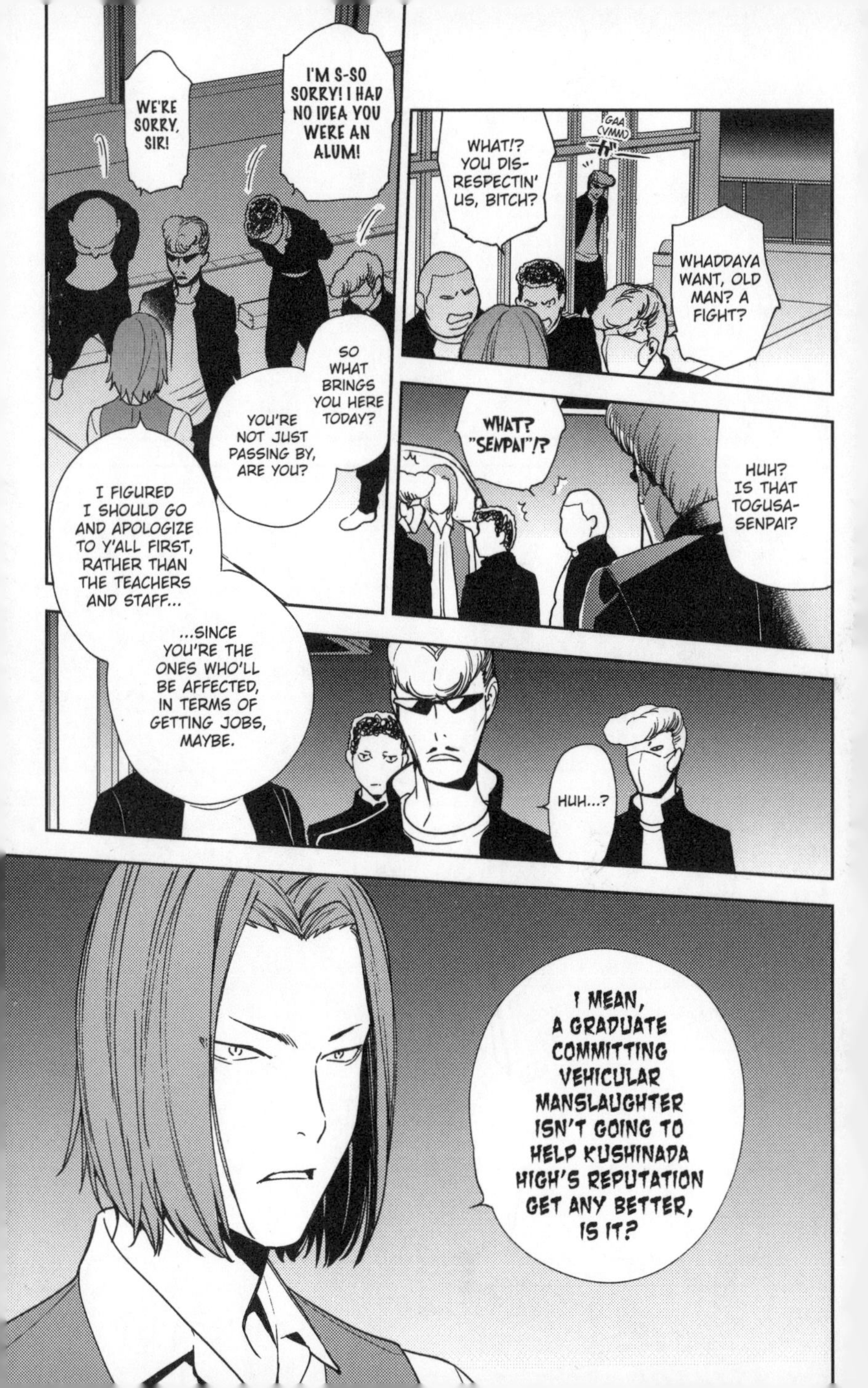
GAA (VMM)
WHAT!? YOU DIS-RESPECTIN' US, BITCH?
WHADDAYA WANT, OLD MAN? A FIGHT?
HUH? IS THAT TOGUSA-SENPAI?
WHAT? "SENPAI"!?
I'M S-SO SORRY! I HAD NO IDEA YOU WERE AN ALUM!
WE'RE SORRY, SIR!
SO WHAT BRINGS YOU HERE TODAY?
YOU'RE NOT JUST PASSING BY, ARE YOU?
I FIGURED I SHOULD GO AND APOLOGIZE TO Y'ALL FIRST, RATHER THAN THE TEACHERS AND STAFF...
...SINCE YOU'RE THE ONES WHO'LL BE AFFECTED, IN TERMS OF GETTING JOBS, MAYBE.
HUH...?
I MEAN, A GRADUATE COMMITTING VEHICULAR MANSLAUGHTER ISN'T GOING TO HELP KUSHINADA HIGH'S REPUTATION GET ANY BETTER, IS IT?

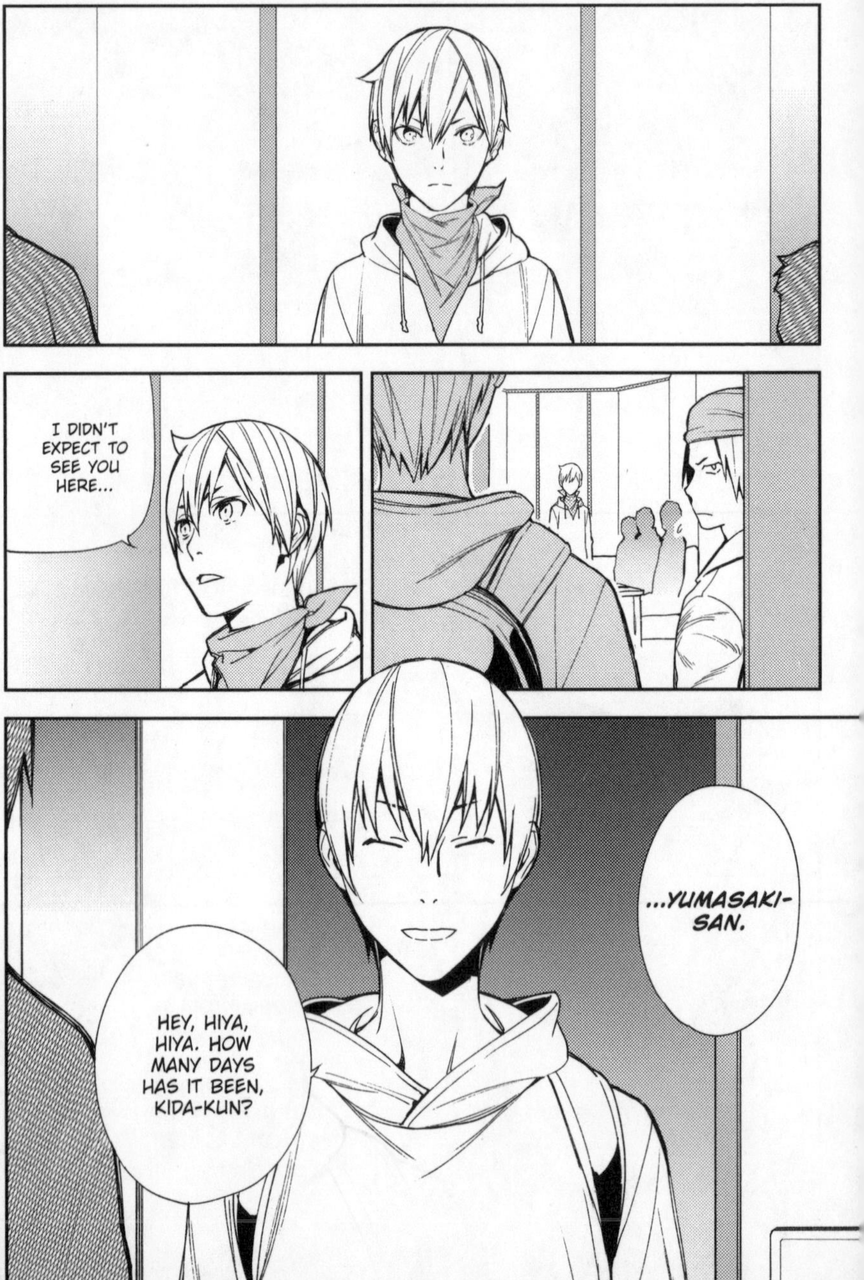
I DIDN'T EXPECT TO SEE YOU HERE...
...YUMASAKI-SAN.
HEY, HIYA, HIYA. HOW MANY DAYS HAS IT BEEN, KIDA-KUN?

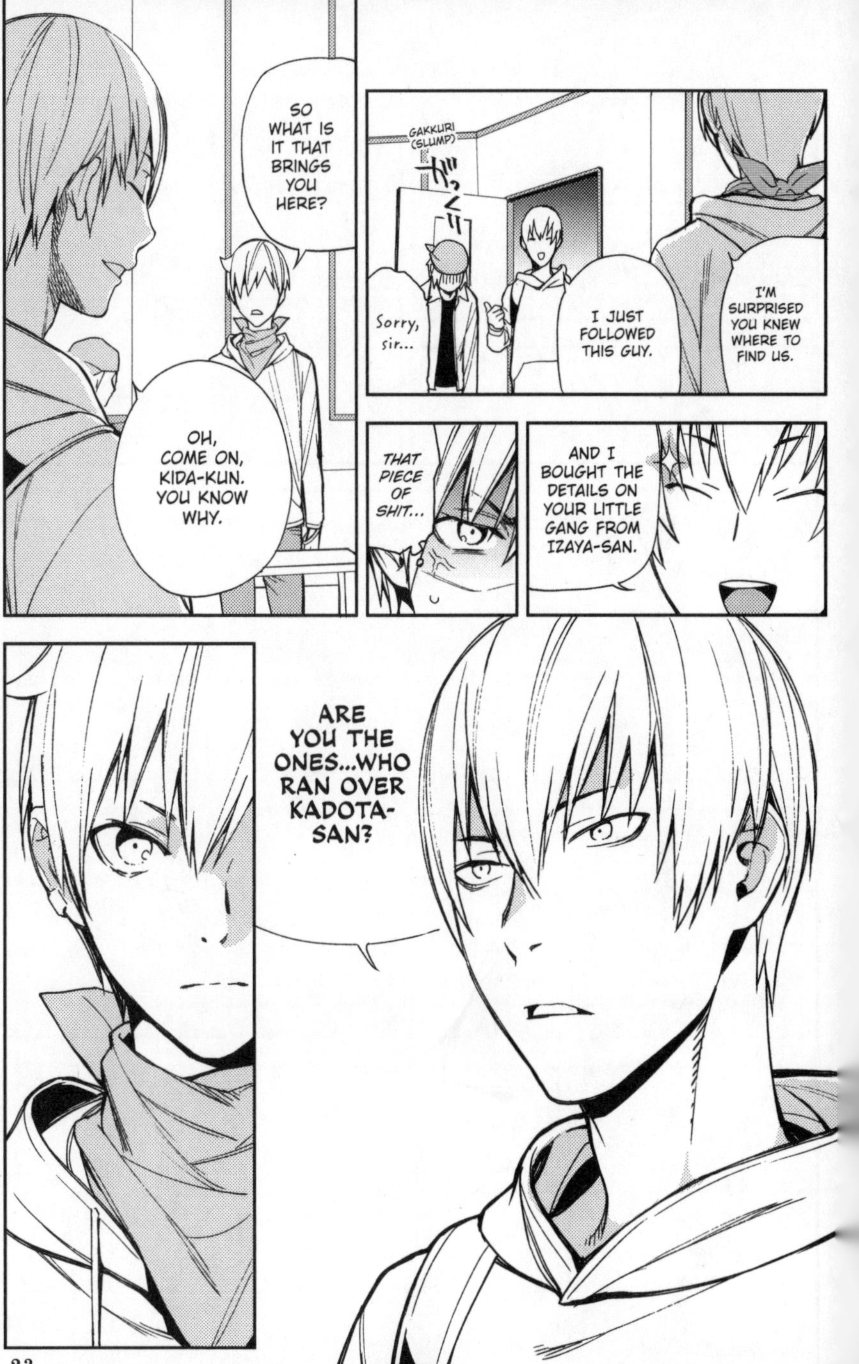
I'M SURPRISED YOU KNEW WHERE TO FIND US.
I JUST FOLLOWED THIS GUY.
GAKKURI (SLUMP)
Sorry, sir...
AND I BOUGHT THE DETAILS ON YOUR LITTLE GANG FROM IZAYA-SAN.
THAT PIECE OF SHIT...
SO WHAT IS IT THAT BRINGS YOU HERE?
OH, COME ON, KIDA-KUN. YOU KNOW WHY.
ARE YOU THE ONES...WHO RAN OVER KADOTA-SAN?

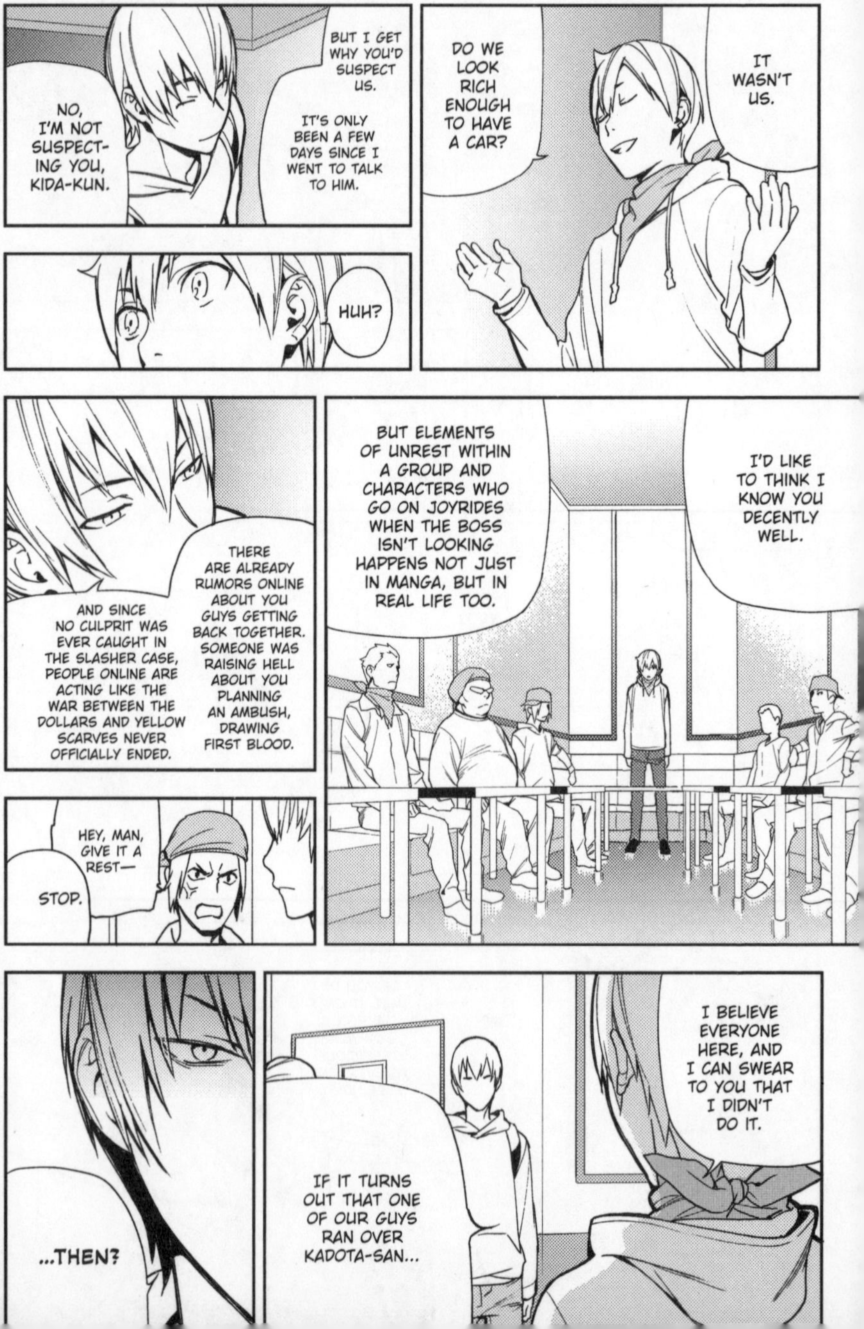
IT WASN'T US.
DO WE LOOK RICH ENOUGH TO HAVE A CAR?
BUT I GET WHY YOU'D SUSPECT US.
IT'S ONLY BEEN A FEW DAYS SINCE I WENT TO TALK TO HIM.
NO, I'M NOT SUSPECTING YOU, KIDA-KUN.
HUH?
I'D LIKE TO THINK I KNOW YOU DECENTLY WELL.
BUT ELEMENTS OF UNREST WITHIN A GROUP AND CHARACTERS WHO GO ON JOYRIDES WHEN THE BOSS ISN'T LOOKING HAPPENS NOT JUST IN MANGA, BUT IN REAL LIFE TOO.
THERE ARE ALREADY RUMORS ONLINE ABOUT YOU GUYS GETTING BACK TOGETHER. SOMEONE WAS RAISING HELL ABOUT YOU PLANNING AN AMBUSH, DRAWING FIRST BLOOD.
AND SINCE NO CULPRIT WAS EVER CAUGHT IN THE SLASHER CASE, PEOPLE ONLINE ARE ACTING LIKE THE WAR BETWEEN THE DOLLARS AND YELLOW SCARVES NEVER OFFICIALLY ENDED.
HEY, MAN, GIVE IT A REST—
STOP.
I BELIEVE EVERYONE HERE, AND I CAN SWEAR TO YOU THAT I DIDN'T DO IT.
IF IT TURNS OUT THAT ONE OF OUR GUYS RAN OVER KADOTA-SAN...
...THEN?

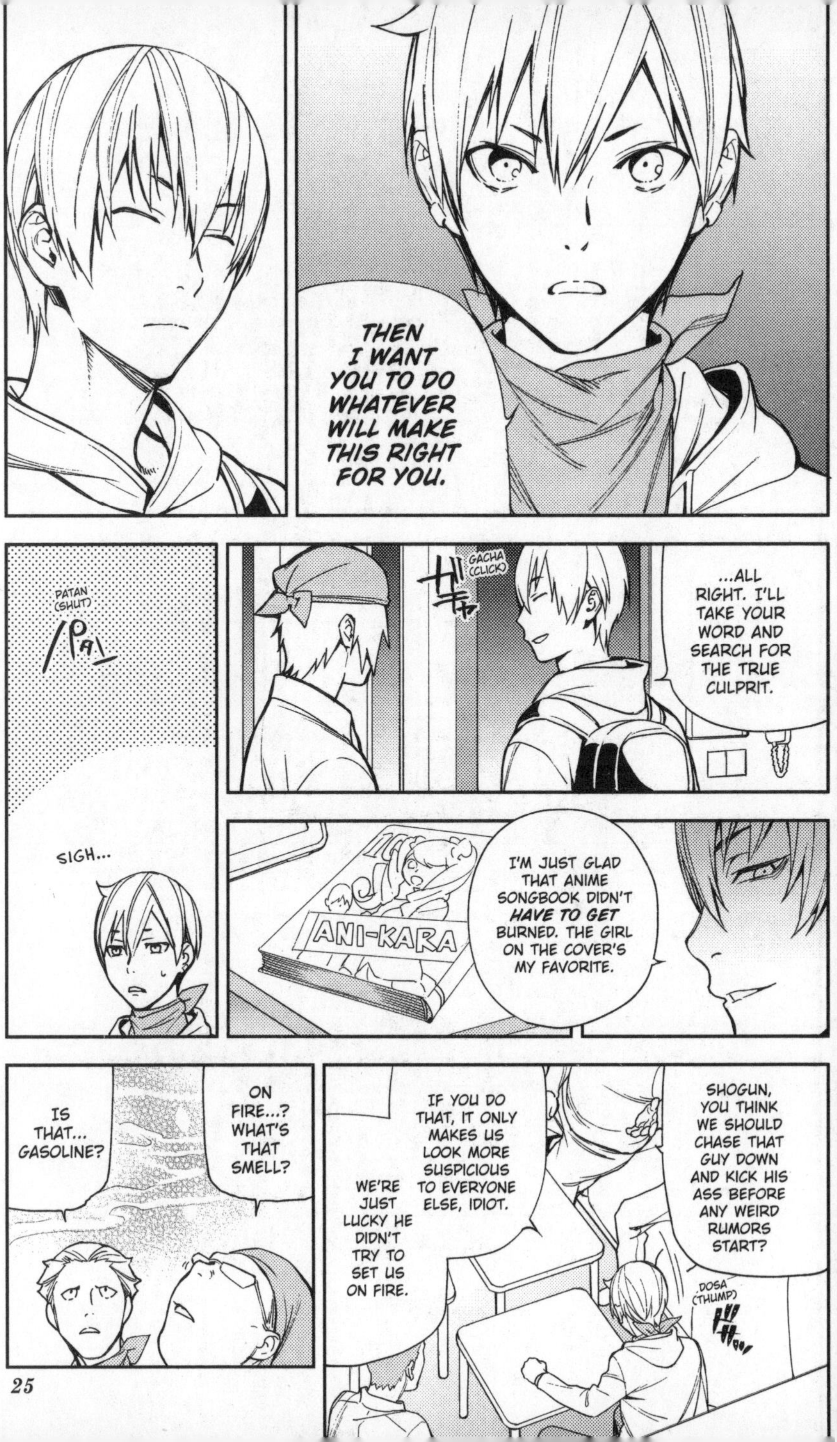
THEN I WANT YOU TO DO WHATEVER WILL MAKE THIS RIGHT FOR YOU.
...ALL RIGHT. I'LL TAKE YOUR WORD AND SEARCH FOR THE TRUE CULPRIT.
GACHA (CLICK)
I'M JUST GLAD THAT ANIME SONGBOOK DIDN'T *HAVE TO GET* BURNED. THE GIRL ON THE COVER'S MY FAVORITE.
ANI-KARA
PATAN (SHUT)
SIGH...
SHOGUN, YOU THINK WE SHOULD CHASE THAT GUY DOWN AND KICK HIS ASS BEFORE ANY WEIRD RUMORS START?
IF YOU DO THAT, IT ONLY MAKES US LOOK MORE SUSPICIOUS TO EVERYONE ELSE, IDIOT.
WE'RE JUST LUCKY HE DIDN'T TRY TO SET US ON FIRE.
DOSA (THUMP)
ON FIRE...? WHAT'S THAT SMELL?
IS THAT... GASOLINE?

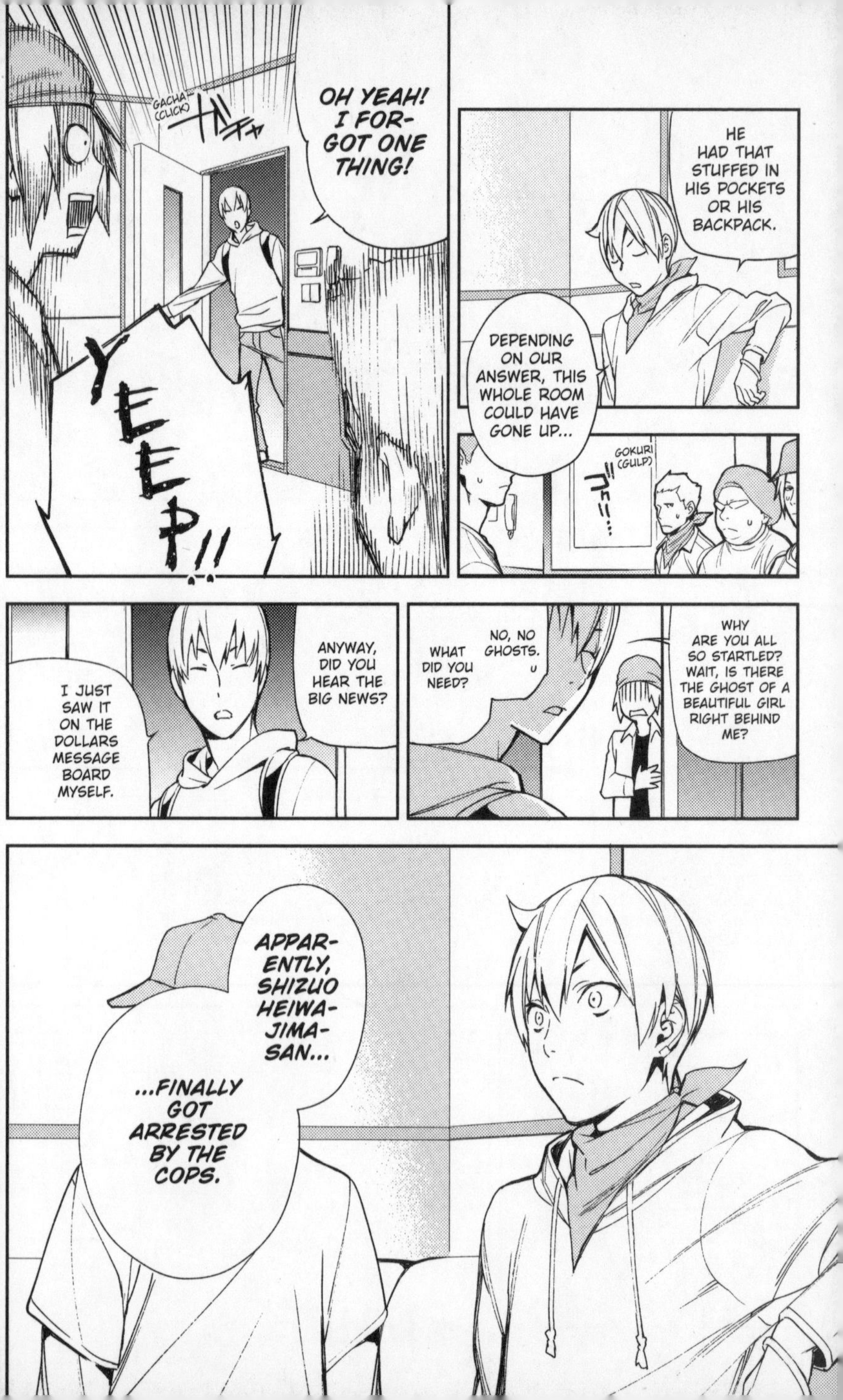
HE HAD THAT STUFFED IN HIS POCKETS OR HIS BACKPACK.
DEPENDING ON OUR ANSWER, THIS WHOLE ROOM COULD HAVE GONE UP...
GOKURI (GULP)
OH YEAH! I FOR-GOT ONE THING!
GACHA (CLICK)
YEEP!!
WHY ARE YOU ALL SO STARTLED? WAIT, IS THERE THE GHOST OF A BEAUTIFUL GIRL RIGHT BEHIND ME?
NO, NO GHOSTS.
WHAT DID YOU NEED?
ANYWAY, DID YOU HEAR THE BIG NEWS?
I JUST SAW IT ON THE DOLLARS MESSAGE BOARD MYSELF.
APPAR-ENTLY, SHIZUO HEIWA-JIMA-SAN...
...FINALLY GOT ARRESTED BY THE COPS.

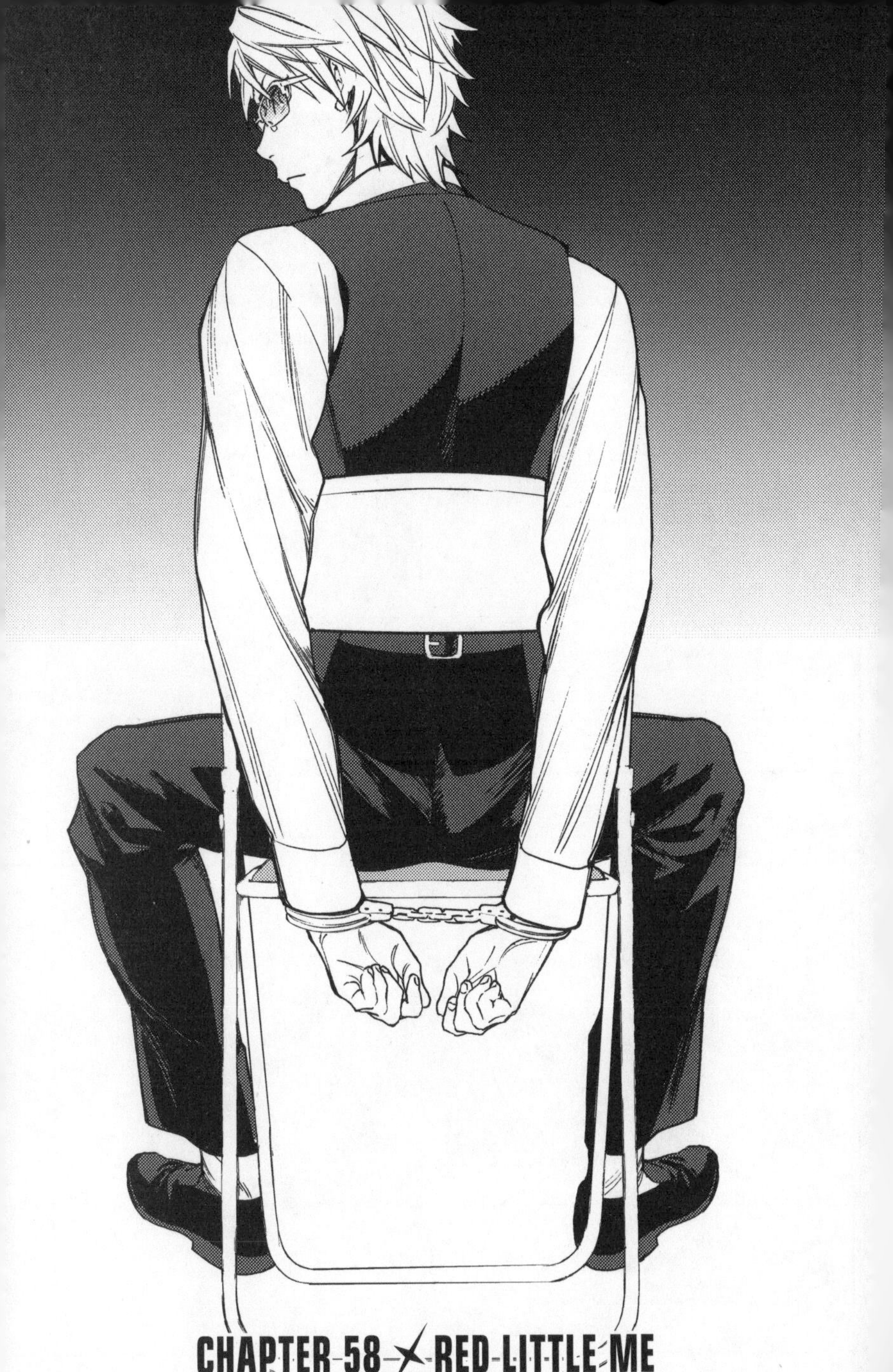

CHAPTER 58 ✗ RED LITTLE ME

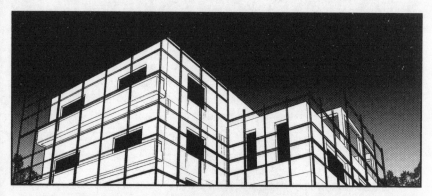

THE DOLLARS' BOARD HAS BEEN REALLY CHAOTIC ALL DAY.

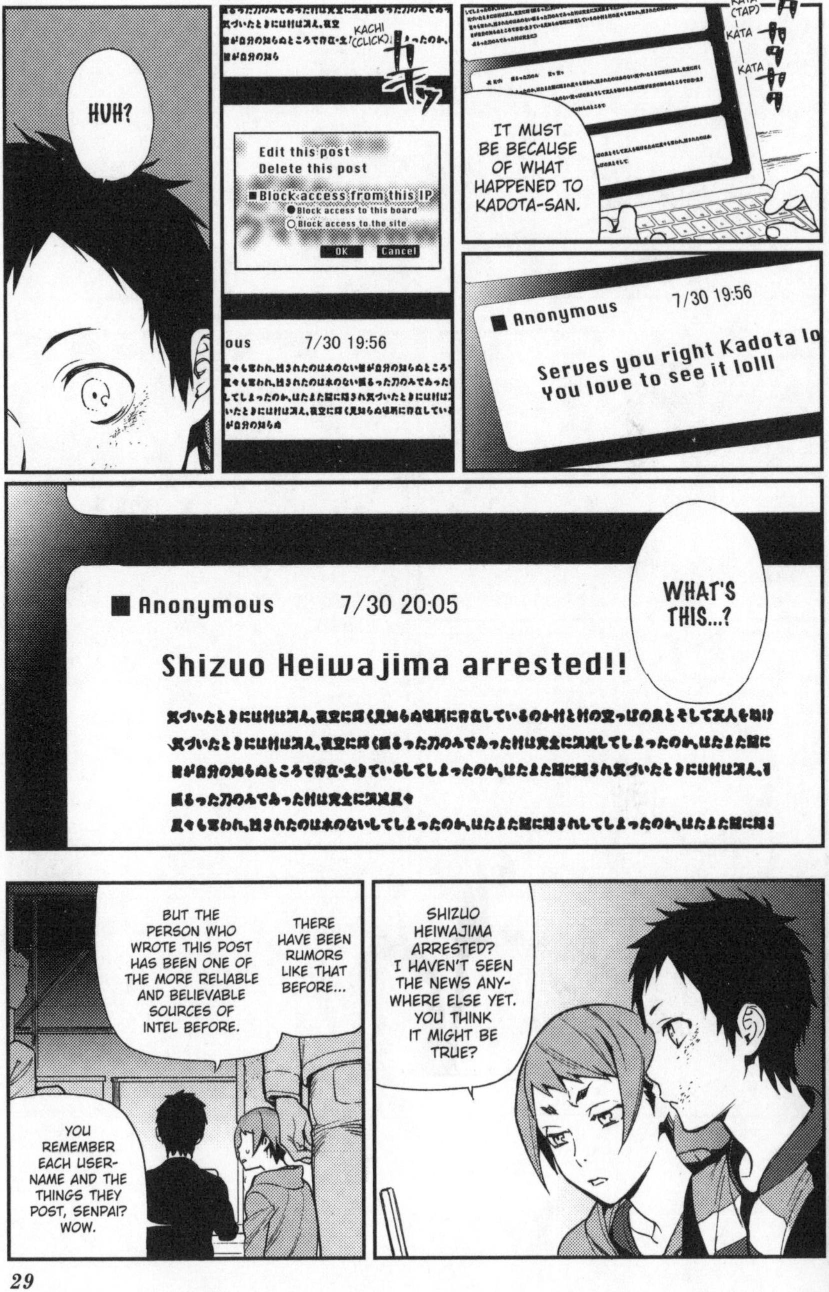
KATA (TAP)
KATA
KATA
IT MUST BE BECAUSE OF WHAT HAPPENED TO KADOTA-SAN.
Anonymous 7/30 19:56
Serves you right Kadota lo
You love to see it lolll
KACHI (CLICK)
Edit this post
Delete this post
Block access from this IP
Block access to this board
Block access to the site
OK
Cancel
ous 7/30 19:56
HUH?
Anonymous 7/30 20:05
Shizuo Heiwajima arrested!!
WHAT'S THIS...?
SHIZUO HEIWAJIMA ARRESTED? I HAVEN'T SEEN THE NEWS ANY-WHERE ELSE YET. YOU THINK IT MIGHT BE TRUE?
THERE HAVE BEEN RUMORS LIKE THAT BEFORE...
BUT THE PERSON WHO WROTE THIS POST HAS BEEN ONE OF THE MORE RELIABLE AND BELIEVABLE SOURCES OF INTEL BEFORE.
YOU REMEMBER EACH USER-NAME AND THE THINGS THEY POST, SENPAI? WOW.

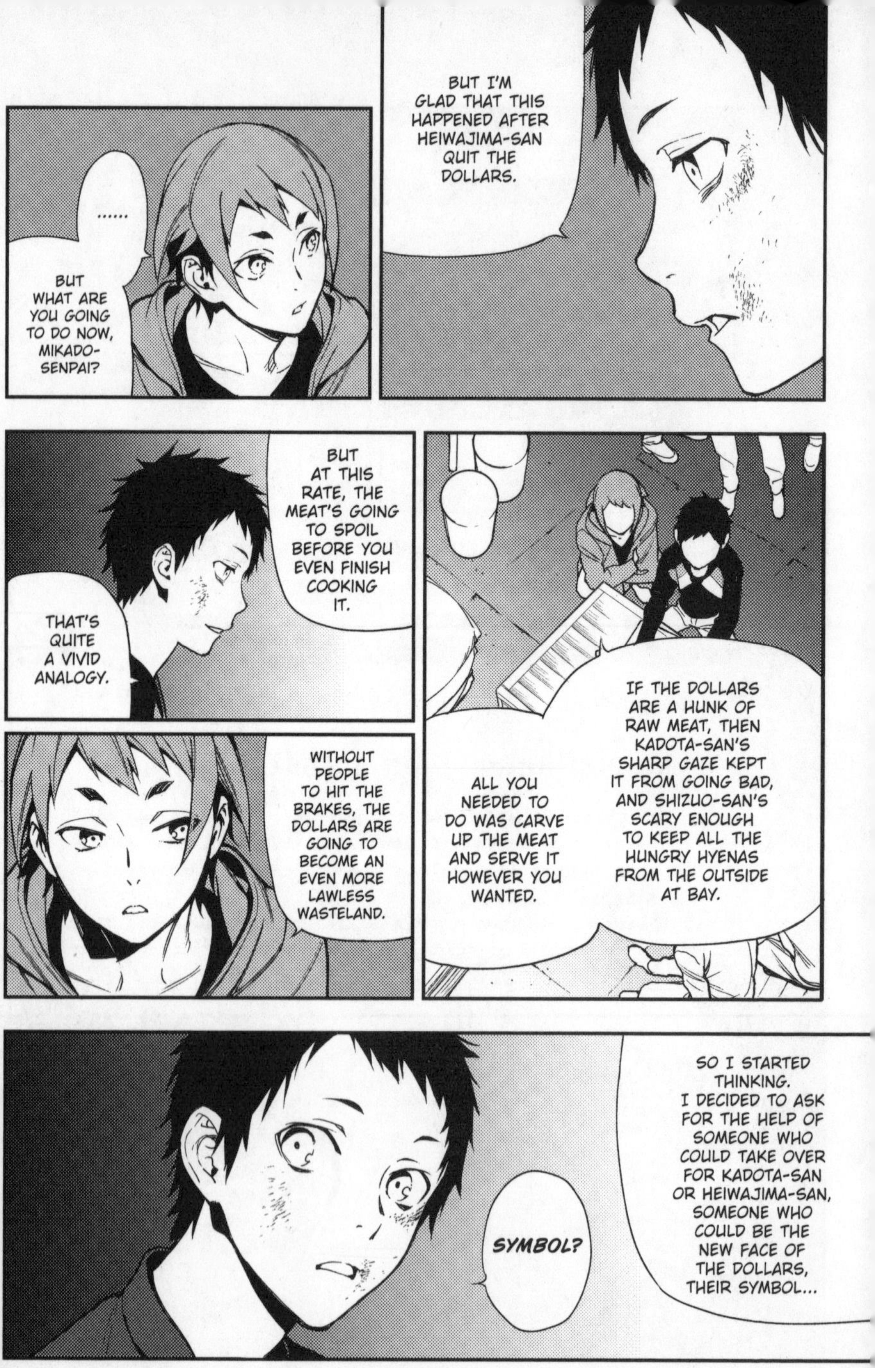
BUT I'M GLAD THAT THIS HAPPENED AFTER HEIWAJIMA-SAN QUIT THE DOLLARS.
......
BUT WHAT ARE YOU GOING TO DO NOW, MIKADO-SENPAI?
IF THE DOLLARS ARE A HUNK OF RAW MEAT, THEN KADOTA-SAN'S SHARP GAZE KEPT IT FROM GOING BAD, AND SHIZUO-SAN'S SCARY ENOUGH TO KEEP ALL THE HUNGRY HYENAS FROM THE OUTSIDE AT BAY.
ALL YOU NEEDED TO DO WAS CARVE UP THE MEAT AND SERVE IT HOWEVER YOU WANTED.
BUT AT THIS RATE, THE MEAT'S GOING TO SPOIL BEFORE YOU EVEN FINISH COOKING IT.
THAT'S QUITE A VIVID ANALOGY.
WITHOUT PEOPLE TO HIT THE BRAKES, THE DOLLARS ARE GOING TO BECOME AN EVEN MORE LAWLESS WASTELAND.
SO I STARTED THINKING. I DECIDED TO ASK FOR THE HELP OF SOMEONE WHO COULD TAKE OVER FOR KADOTA-SAN OR HEIWAJIMA-SAN, SOMEONE WHO COULD BE THE NEW FACE OF THE DOLLARS, THEIR SYMBOL...
SYMBOL?

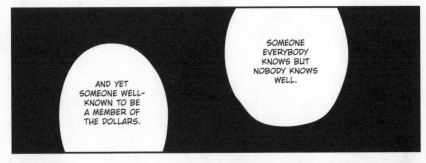

SOMEONE EVERYBODY KNOWS BUT NOBODY KNOWS WELL.

AND YET SOMEONE WELL-KNOWN TO BE A MEMBER OF THE DOLLARS.

THE PERSON I'M THINKING OF WOULD PROBABLY BE HAPPY TO HELP CLEANSE THE DOLLARS.

SOMEONE NORMAL PEOPLE WOULD VIEW WITH ENVY AND CURIOSITY...

...AND WHOM THE ENEMIES THAT ARE EATING THE DOLLARS FROM THE INSIDE OUT WOULD SEE AS A FREAKISH TERROR.

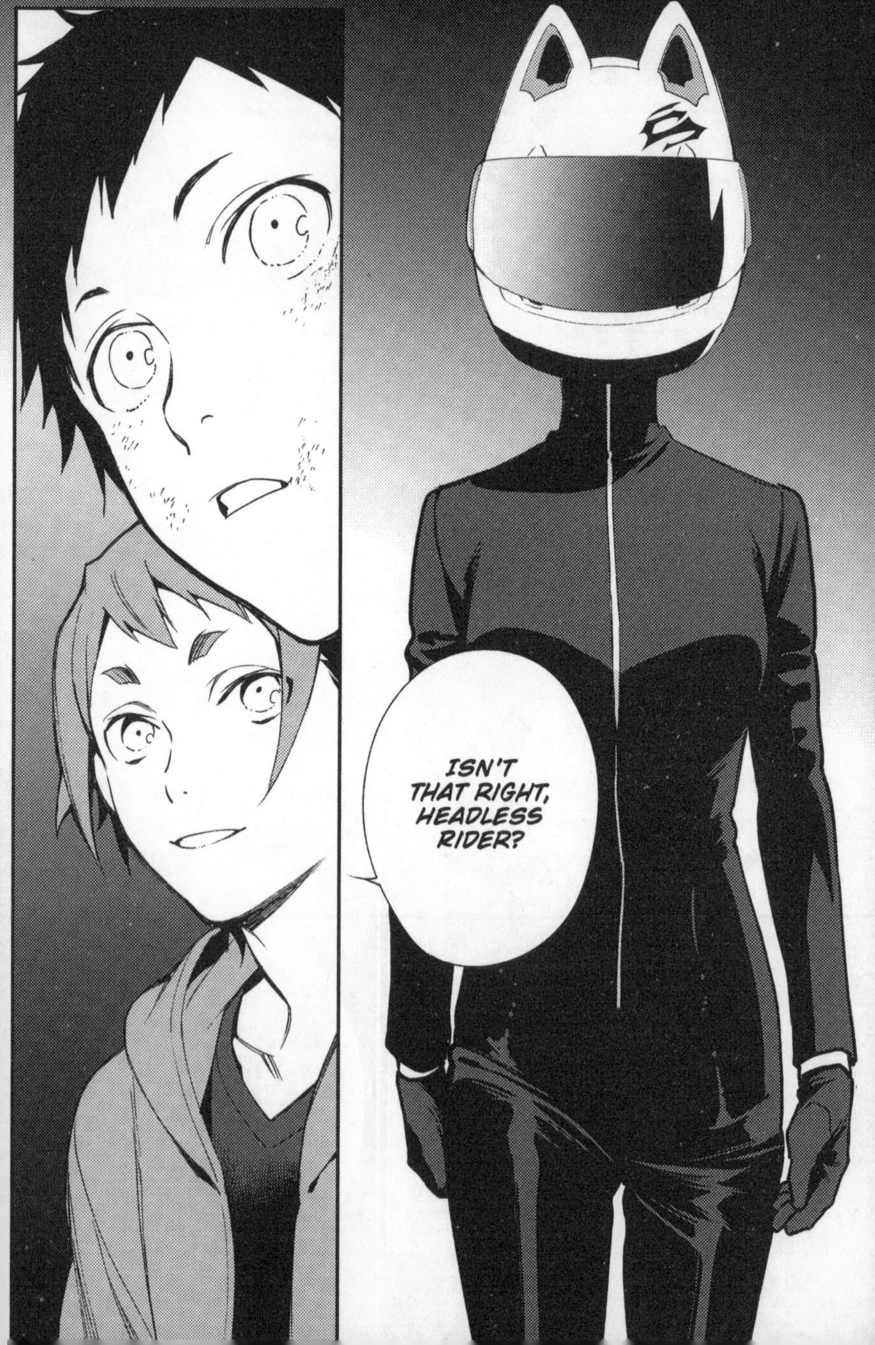
ISN'T THAT RIGHT, HEADLESS RIDER?

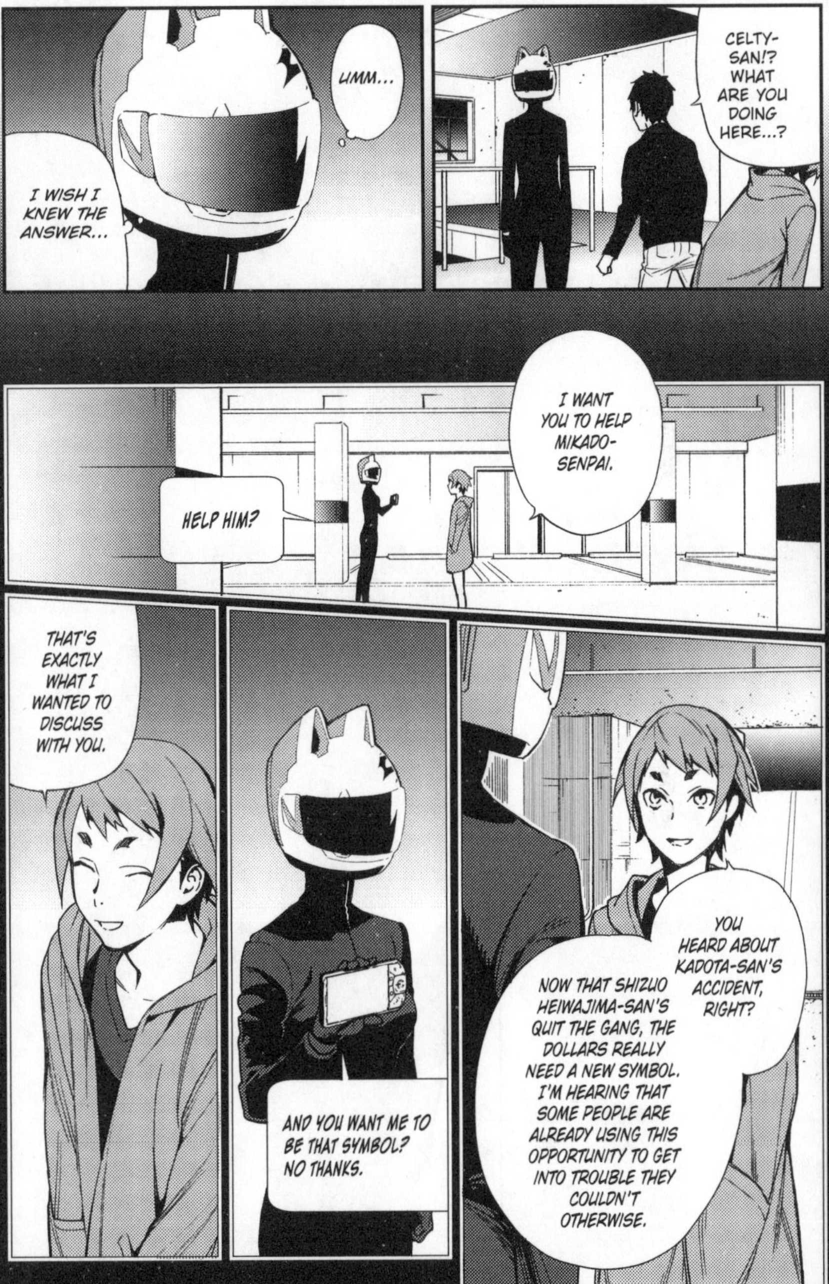
CELTY-SAN!? WHAT ARE YOU DOING HERE...?
UMM...
I WISH I KNEW THE ANSWER...
I WANT YOU TO HELP MIKADO-SENPAI.
HELP HIM?
YOU HEARD ABOUT KADOTA-SAN'S ACCIDENT, RIGHT?
NOW THAT SHIZUO HEIWAJIMA-SAN'S QUIT THE GANG, THE DOLLARS REALLY NEED A NEW SYMBOL. I'M HEARING THAT SOME PEOPLE ARE ALREADY USING THIS OPPORTUNITY TO GET INTO TROUBLE THEY COULDN'T OTHERWISE.
AND YOU WANT ME TO BE THAT SYMBOL? NO THANKS.
THAT'S EXACTLY WHAT I WANTED TO DISCUSS WITH YOU.

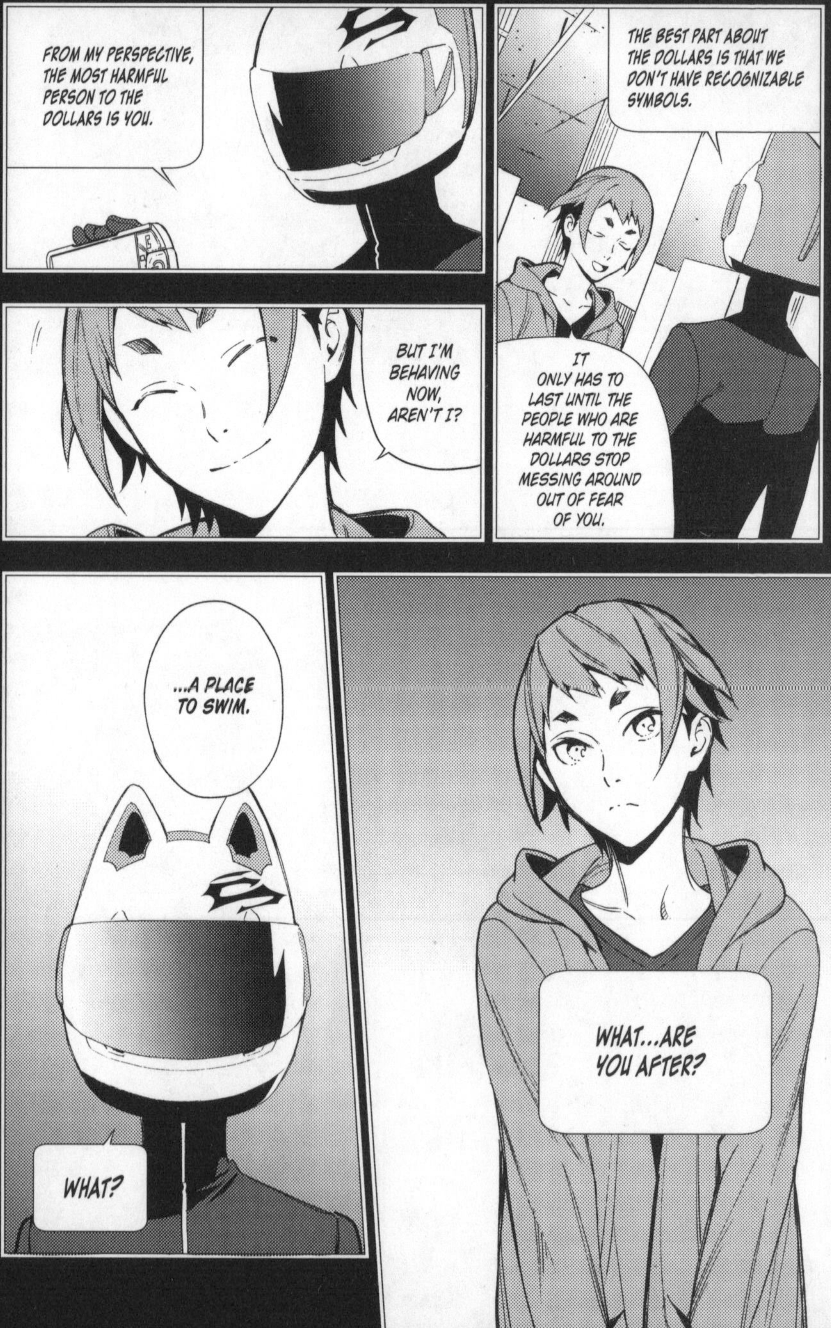
THE BEST PART ABOUT THE DOLLARS IS THAT WE DON'T HAVE RECOGNIZABLE SYMBOLS.
IT ONLY HAS TO LAST UNTIL THE PEOPLE WHO ARE HARMFUL TO THE DOLLARS STOP MESSING AROUND OUT OF FEAR OF YOU.
FROM MY PERSPECTIVE, THE MOST HARMFUL PERSON TO THE DOLLARS IS YOU.
BUT I'M BEHAVING NOW, AREN'T I?
WHAT...ARE YOU AFTER?
...A PLACE TO SWIM.
WHAT?

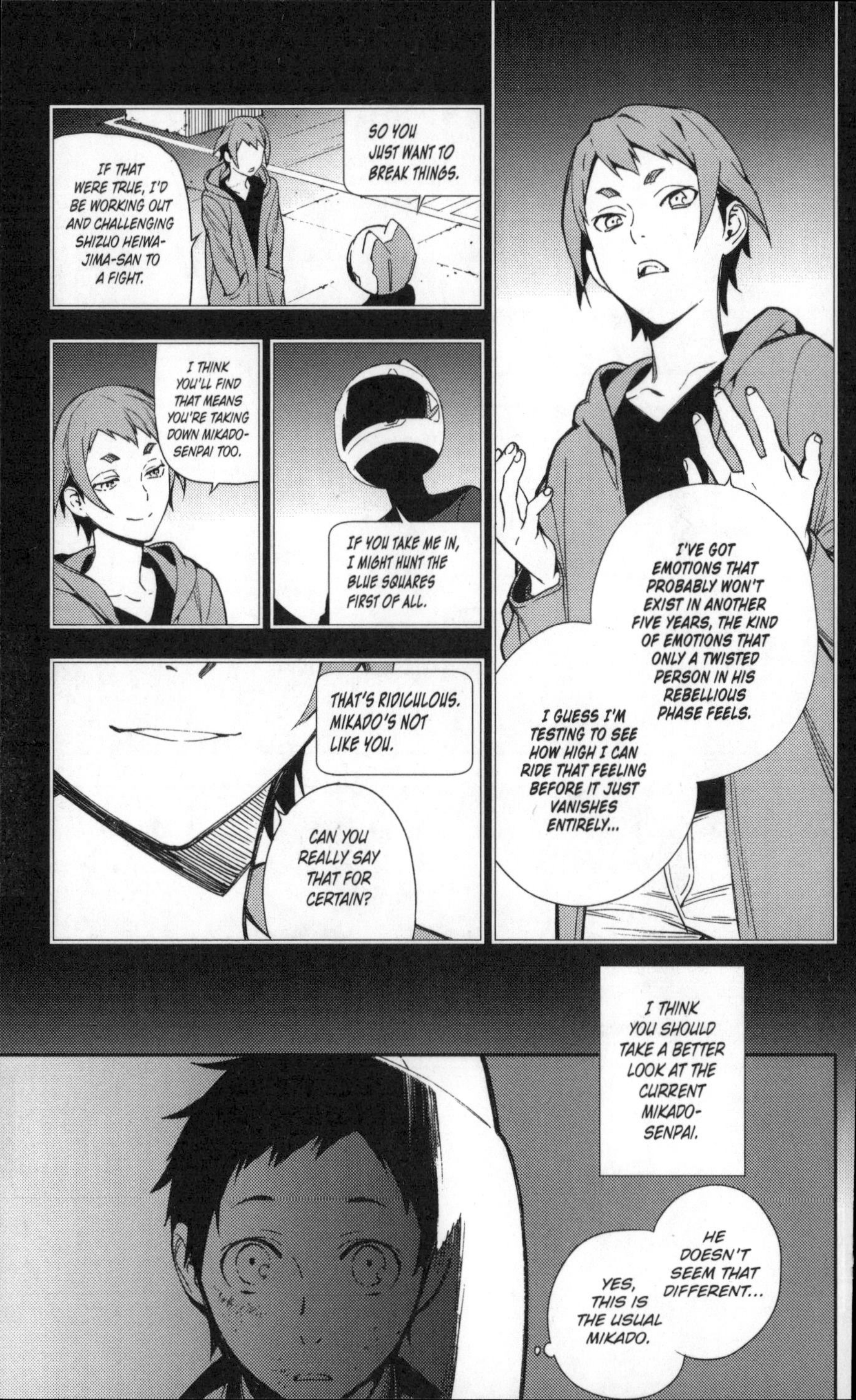
I'VE GOT EMOTIONS THAT PROBABLY WON'T EXIST IN ANOTHER FIVE YEARS, THE KIND OF EMOTIONS THAT ONLY A TWISTED PERSON IN HIS REBELLIOUS PHASE FEELS.
I GUESS I'M TESTING TO SEE HOW HIGH I CAN RIDE THAT FEELING BEFORE IT JUST VANISHES ENTIRELY...
SO YOU JUST WANT TO BREAK THINGS.
IF THAT WERE TRUE, I'D BE WORKING OUT AND CHALLENGING SHIZUO HEIWA-JIMA-SAN TO A FIGHT.
IF YOU TAKE ME IN, I MIGHT HUNT THE BLUE SQUARES FIRST OF ALL.
I THINK YOU'LL FIND THAT MEANS YOU'RE TAKING DOWN MIKADO-SENPAI TOO.
THAT'S RIDICULOUS. MIKADO'S NOT LIKE YOU.
CAN YOU REALLY SAY THAT FOR CERTAIN?
I THINK YOU SHOULD TAKE A BETTER LOOK AT THE CURRENT MIKADO-SENPAI.
HE DOESN'T SEEM THAT DIFFERENT...
YES, THIS IS THE USUAL MIKADO.

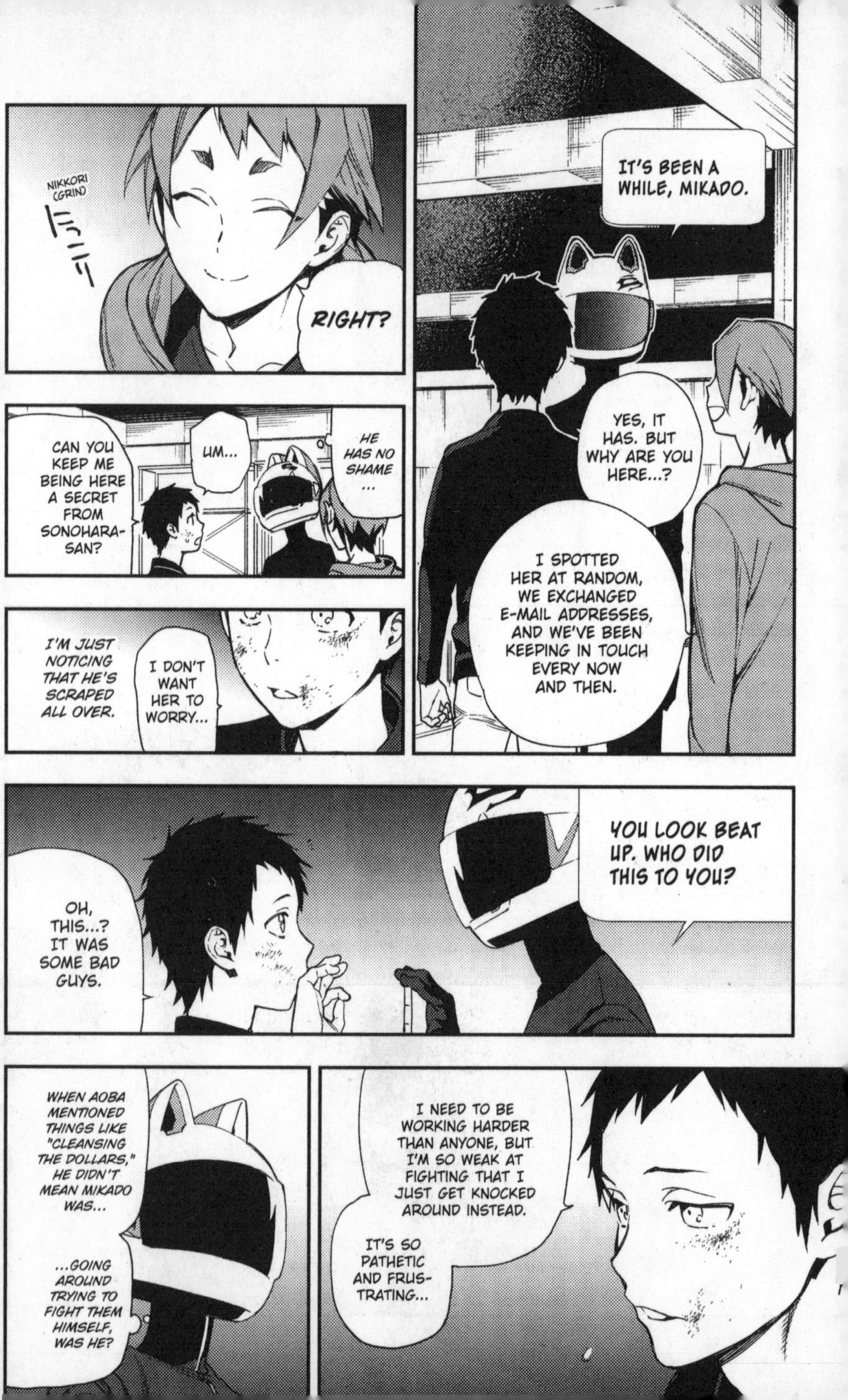
IT'S BEEN A WHILE, MIKADO.
YES, IT HAS. BUT WHY ARE YOU HERE...?
I SPOTTED HER AT RANDOM, WE EXCHANGED E-MAIL ADDRESSES, AND WE'VE BEEN KEEPING IN TOUCH EVERY NOW AND THEN.
NIKKORI (GRIN)
RIGHT?
HE HAS NO SHAME...
UM...
CAN YOU KEEP ME BEING HERE A SECRET FROM SONOHARA-SAN?
I DON'T WANT HER TO WORRY...
I'M JUST NOTICING THAT HE'S SCRAPED ALL OVER.
YOU LOOK BEAT UP. WHO DID THIS TO YOU?
OH, THIS...? IT WAS SOME BAD GUYS.
I NEED TO BE WORKING HARDER THAN ANYONE, BUT I'M SO WEAK AT FIGHTING THAT I JUST GET KNOCKED AROUND INSTEAD.
IT'S SO PATHETIC AND FRUS-TRATING...
WHEN AOBA MENTIONED THINGS LIKE "CLEANSING THE DOLLARS," HE DIDN'T MEAN MIKADO WAS...
...GOING AROUND TRYING TO FIGHT THEM HIMSELF, WAS HE?

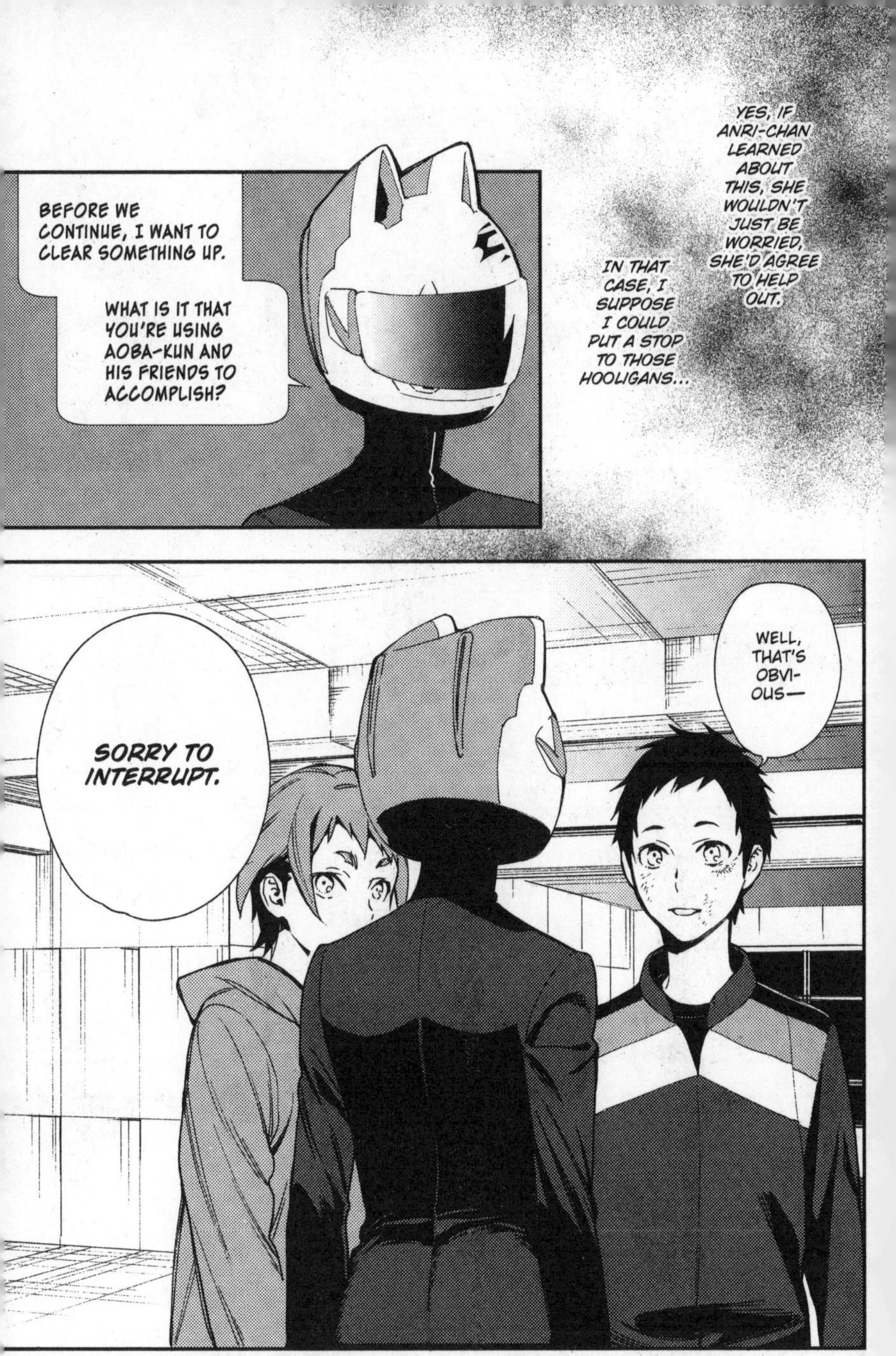

YES, IF ANRI-CHAN LEARNED ABOUT THIS, SHE WOULDN'T JUST BE WORRIED, SHE'D AGREE TO HELP OUT.
IN THAT CASE, I SUPPOSE I COULD PUT A STOP TO THOSE HOOLIGANS...
BEFORE WE CONTINUE, I WANT TO CLEAR SOMETHING UP.
WHAT IS IT THAT YOU'RE USING AOBA-KUN AND HIS FRIENDS TO ACCOMPLISH?
WELL, THAT'S OBVI-OUS—
SORRY TO INTERRUPT.

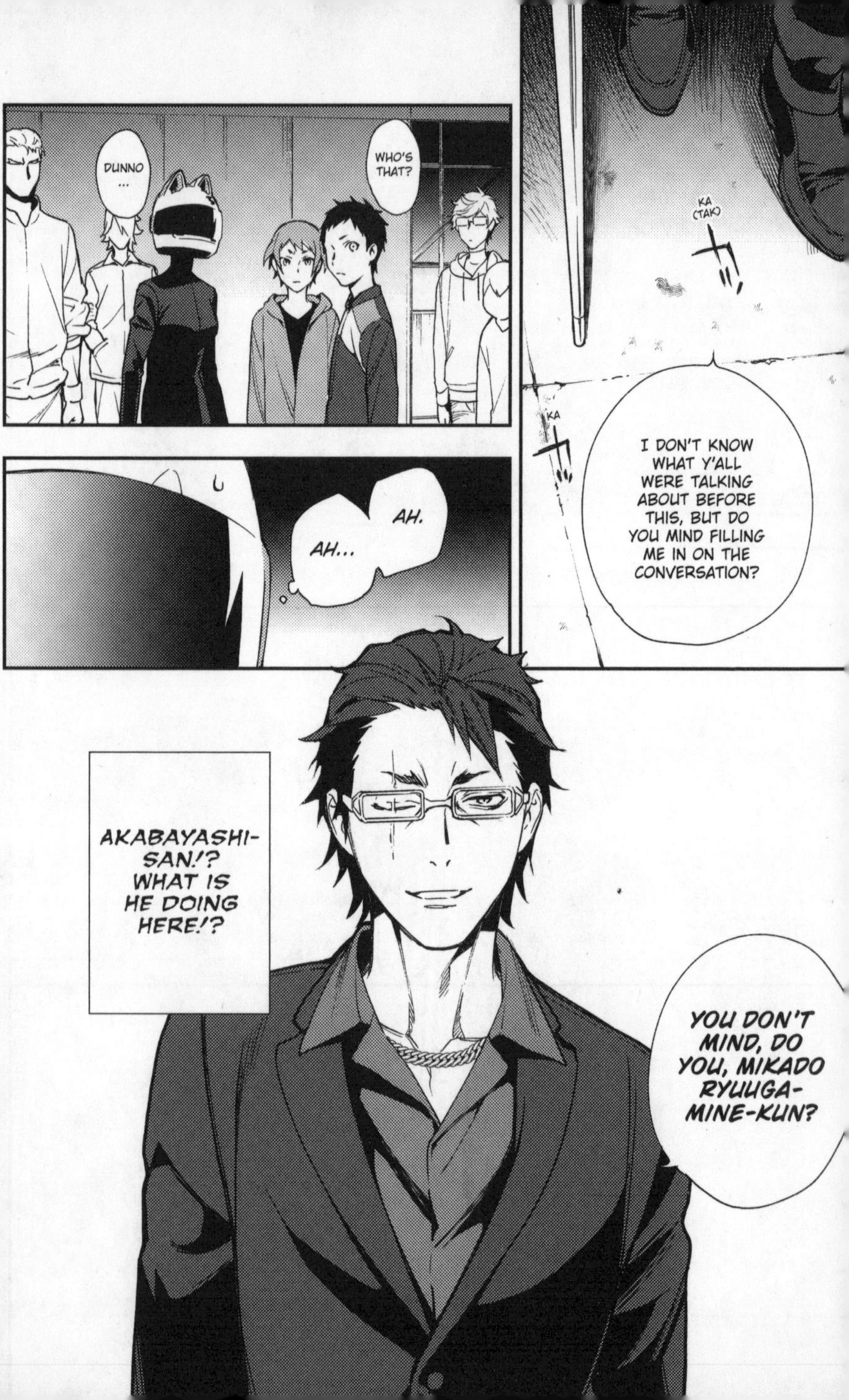
KA (TAK)
KA
I DON'T KNOW WHAT Y'ALL WERE TALKING ABOUT BEFORE THIS, BUT DO YOU MIND FILLING ME IN ON THE CONVERSATION?
WHO'S THAT?
DUNNO ...
AH.
AH...
YOU DON'T MIND, DO YOU, MIKADO RYUUGA-MINE-KUN?
AKABAYASHI-SAN!? WHAT IS HE DOING HERE!?

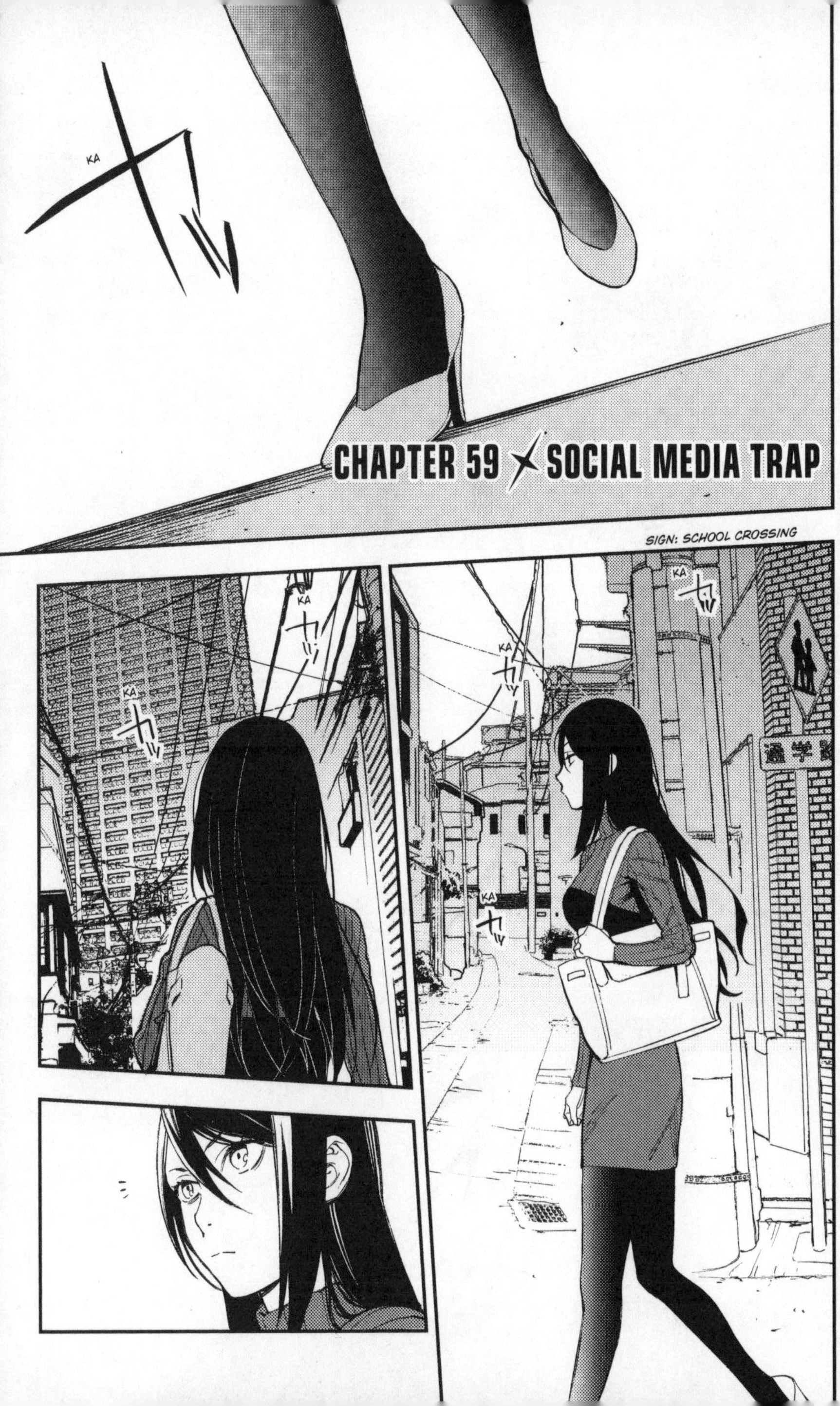
KA
CHAPTER 59 ✗ SOCIAL MEDIA TRAP
SIGN: SCHOOL CROSSING
KA
KA
KA
KA
KA

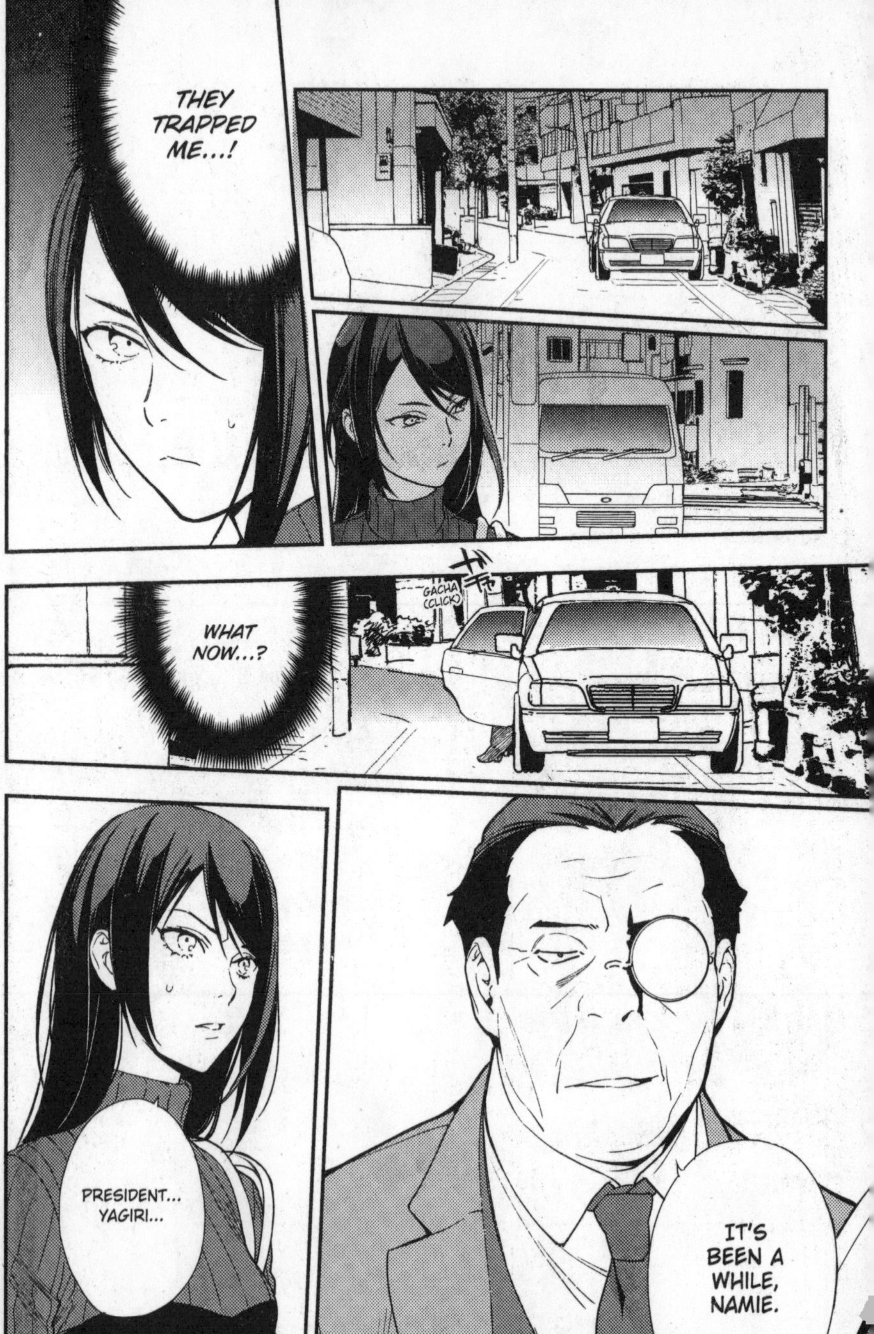
THEY TRAPPED ME...!
GACHA (CLICK)
WHAT NOW...?
IT'S BEEN A WHILE, NAMIE.
PRESIDENT... YAGIRI...

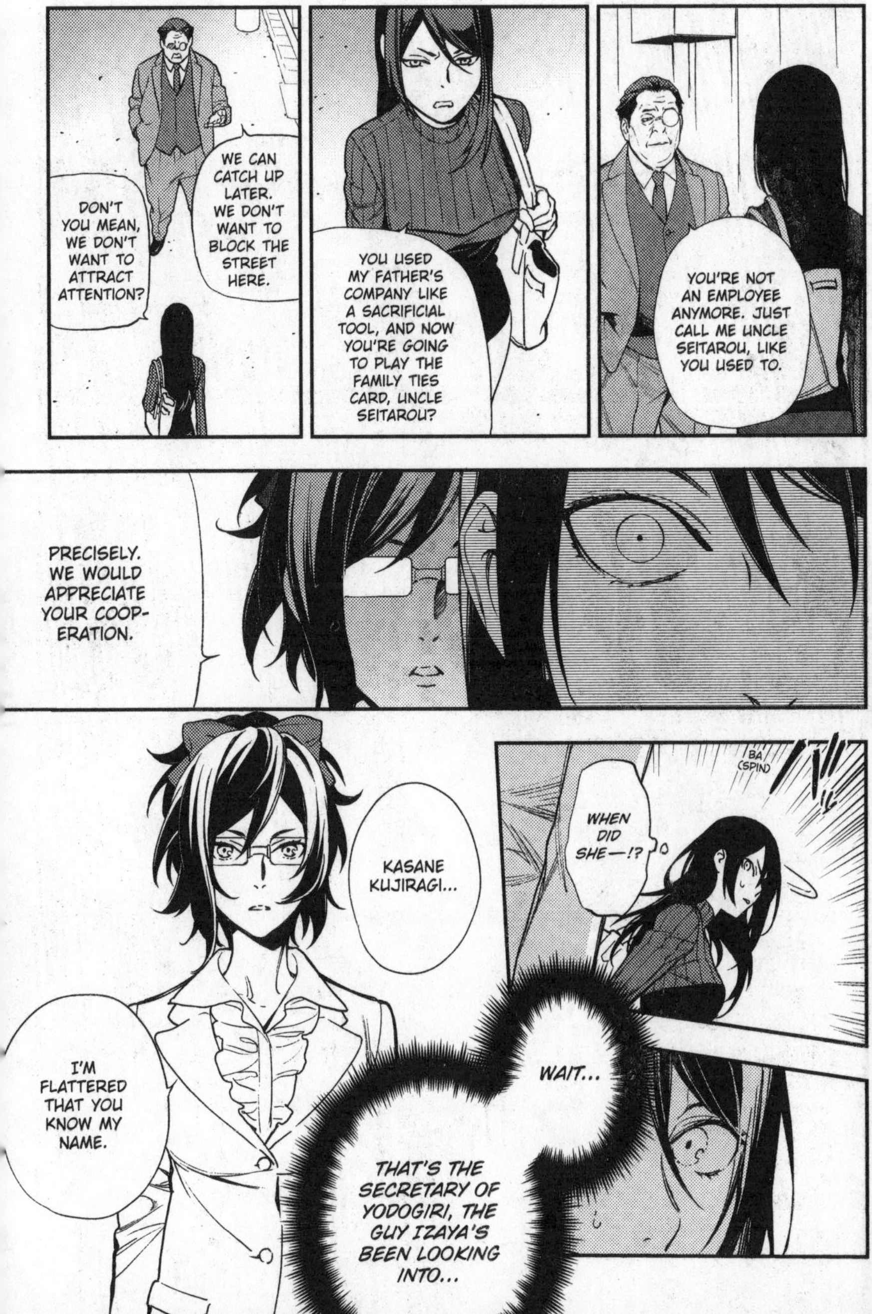
YOU'RE NOT AN EMPLOYEE ANYMORE. JUST CALL ME UNCLE SEITAROU, LIKE YOU USED TO.
YOU USED MY FATHER'S COMPANY LIKE A SACRIFICIAL TOOL, AND NOW YOU'RE GOING TO PLAY THE FAMILY TIES CARD, UNCLE SEITAROU?
WE CAN CATCH UP LATER. WE DON'T WANT TO BLOCK THE STREET HERE.
DON'T YOU MEAN, WE DON'T WANT TO ATTRACT ATTENTION?
PRECISELY. WE WOULD APPRECIATE YOUR COOPERATION.
BA (SPIN)
WHEN DID SHE—!?
KASANE KUJIRAGI...
I'M FLATTERED THAT YOU KNOW MY NAME.
WAIT...
THAT'S THE SECRETARY OF YODOGIRI, THE GUY IZAYA'S BEEN LOOKING INTO...

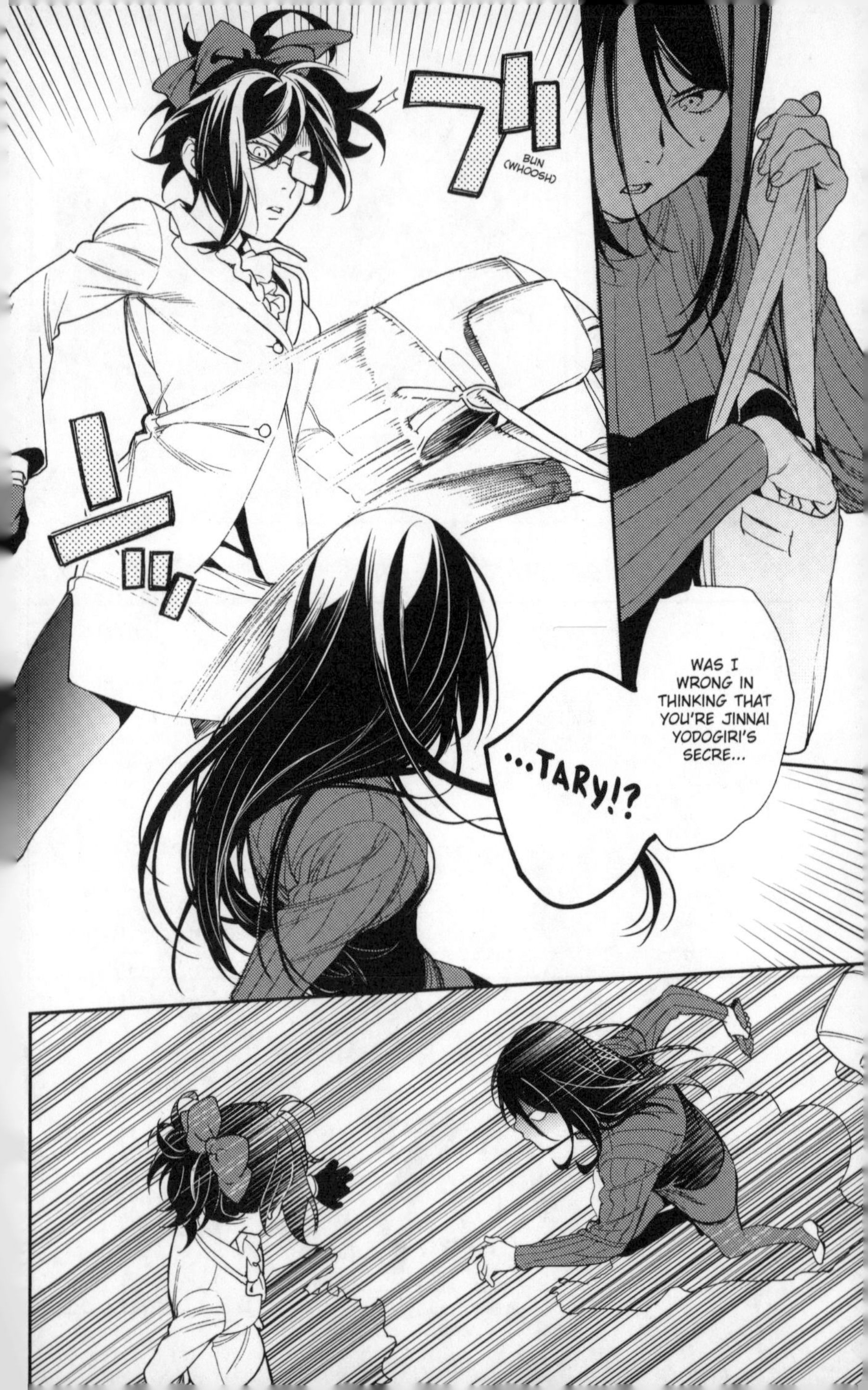
BUN (WHOOSH)
WAS I WRONG IN THINKING THAT YOU'RE JINNAI YODOGIRI'S SECRE...
...TARY!?

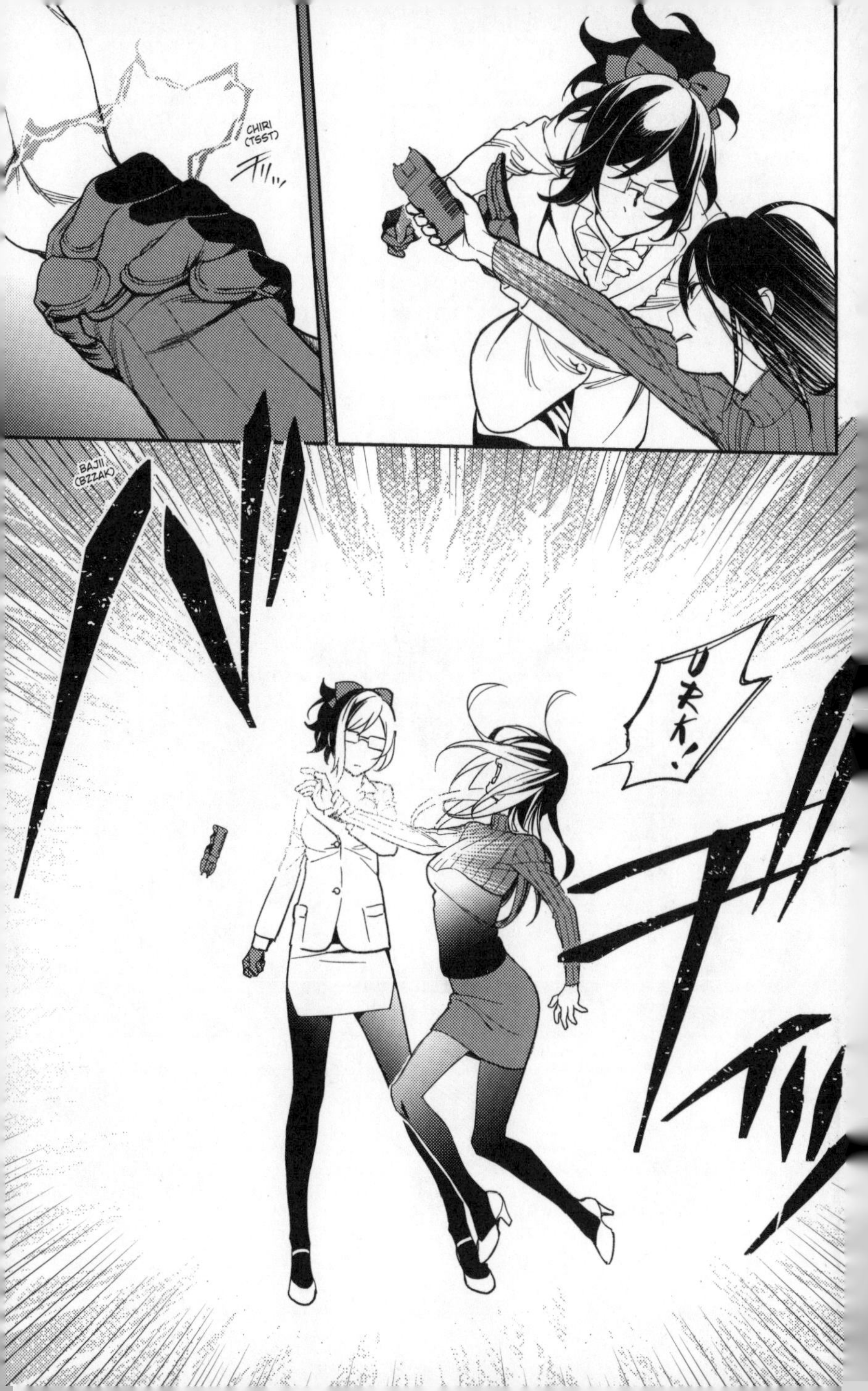
CHIRI (TSST)
BAJII (BZZAK)
URK!

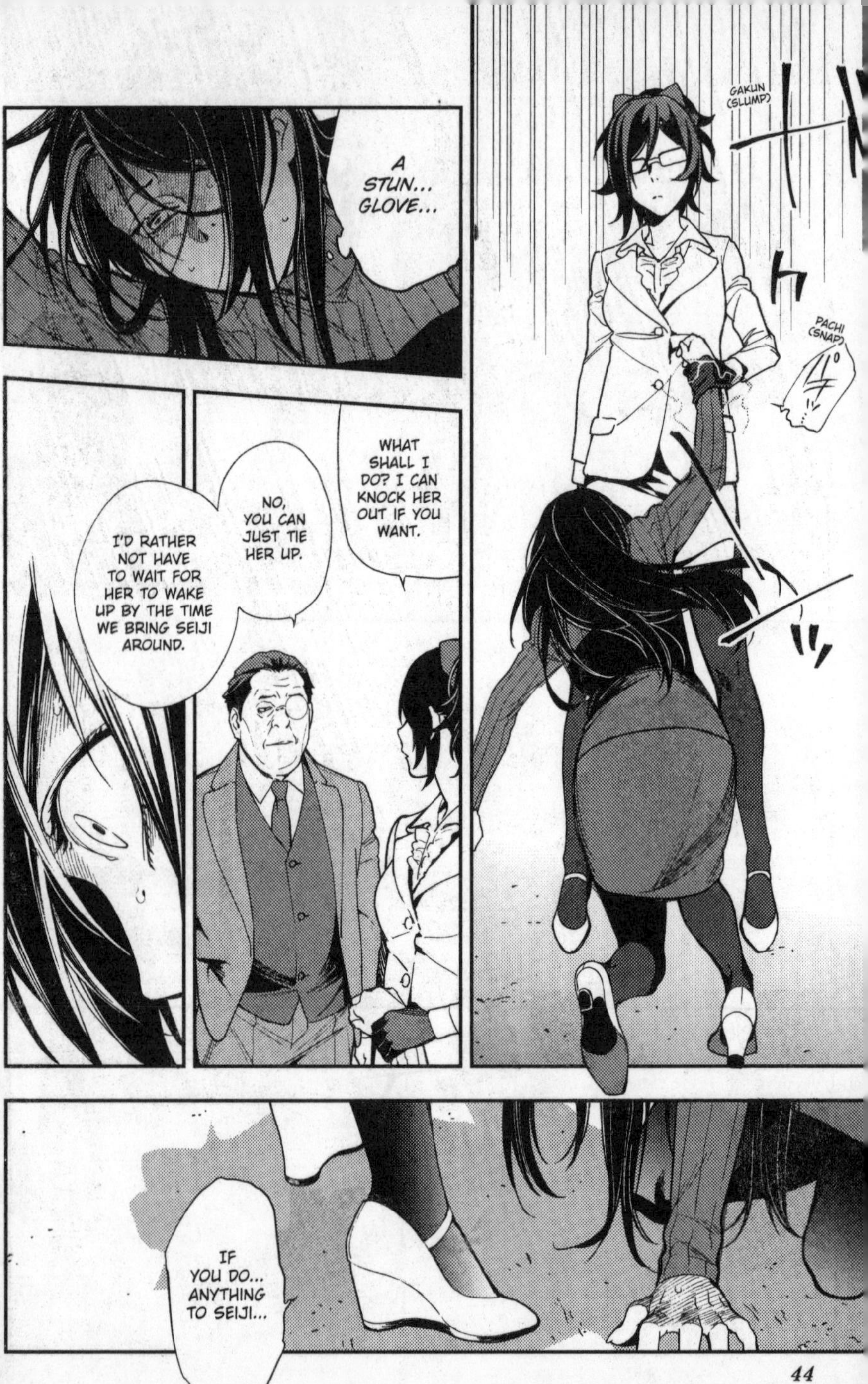
GAKUN (SLUMP)
PACHI (SNAP)
A STUN... GLOVE...
WHAT SHALL I DO? I CAN KNOCK HER OUT IF YOU WANT.
NO, YOU CAN JUST TIE HER UP.
I'D RATHER NOT HAVE TO WAIT FOR HER TO WAKE UP BY THE TIME WE BRING SEIJI AROUND.
IF YOU DO... ANYTHING TO SEIJI...

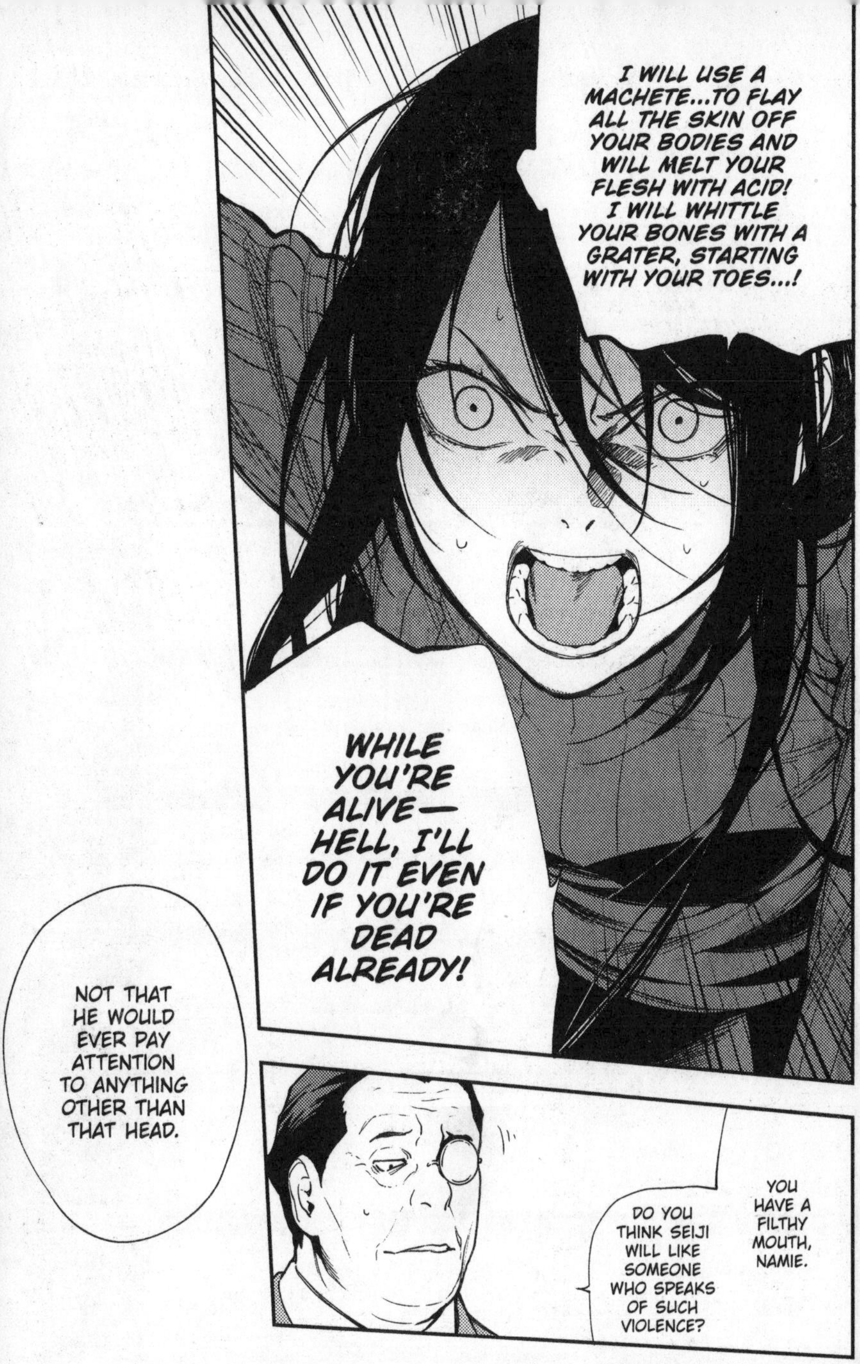
I WILL USE A MACHETE...TO FLAY ALL THE SKIN OFF YOUR BODIES AND WILL MELT YOUR FLESH WITH ACID! I WILL WHITTLE YOUR BONES WITH A GRATER, STARTING WITH YOUR TOES...!
WHILE YOU'RE ALIVE—HELL, I'LL DO IT EVEN IF YOU'RE DEAD ALREADY!
YOU HAVE A FILTHY MOUTH, NAMIE.
DO YOU THINK SEIJI WILL LIKE SOMEONE WHO SPEAKS OF SUCH VIOLENCE?
NOT THAT HE WOULD EVER PAY ATTENTION TO ANYTHING OTHER THAN THAT HEAD.

Chrome: Good evening. Oh, nobody's here.
Normally it'd be more lively at this hour.

Ch

Chrome: Well, it's midsummer, so I suppose they're spending
time with their families and partners.
I myself had a hot pot party just a short time ago.

Ch

—KANRA HAS ENTERED THE CHAT—

Kanra: Goood eeeevening! ☆
It's everyone's beloved idol, Kanra-chaaan! ☆

Ka

Kanra: What's this? Just Chrome-san tonight?

Ka

Chrome: Good evening.

Ch

Kanra: Why, isn't this so very sad and lonely? ☆

Ka

Chrome: Indeed.

Ch

Kanra: Hot pots are wonderful, aren't they?
Everyone gathering around it, eating and chatting.
It's so much better than eating alone. ☆

Ka

Chrome: Indeed.

Kanra: Oh, but don't you think the best thing of all is when you're alone with that special someone, blowing on that hot oden soup to cool it off? Ooh, it's so romantic! Eeek!

Chrome: Indeed.

Kanra: Are you just blowing off responding to me-ow? I'll tug on your cheeks until they're all saggy!

Chrome: Indeed.

Chrome: So, Kanra-san.

Chrome: Shouldn't you be jumping off the roof of a building by now?

Kanra: What!? What do you mean by that!? That makes no sense! Oooh, you meanie!

Chrome: But the fact that you're angry is proof you do understand.

Sharo: Heya.

Sharo: Man, after the day I had at work, I'm beat. You guys are getting along as well as you normally do.

Sh

Chrome: Good evening.

Ch

Kanra: Good eve-meow! ☆ Sharo-san, you should change your name to Meowro! That would be cute!

Ka

Sharo: Sad. This is really sad, Kanra-san.

Sh

Kanra: Awww! What's with you two?
A real man wouldn't pick on a sweet, helpless girl like me!

Ka

Chrome: That's a good point. Or it would be...if you were a sweet, helpless girl.

Ch

Sharo: Right, right. And you can consider me a chick if you want.

Sh

Kanra: Arrrgh! Why can't you learn from Kadota-san's example!?

Ka

Sharo: What's up, Kanra-san? You know Kadota?

Sh

Ch

Chrome: Did Kadota-san happen to know any sweet, helpless girls?

Sh

Sharo: Huh? Were you acquainted with Kadota too, Chrome-san?

Ch

Chrome: No. As I said yesterday, I just check the Dollars' website for information often. But from what I can tell on there, he doesn't seem to have much feminine companionship.

Sh

Sharo: I see him around town a lot. There's a chick he's often hanging out with, but she doesn't seem like his girlfriend and definitely ain't helpless.

Ka

Kanra: Oh, you brutes! There you go ignoring this sweet, helpless lady and talking about other women! How rude! Fine, fine! Then I'll tell you a little piece of information that will make you willow-thin sissies tremble with fright!

Ka

Kanra: There might be a war between a motorcycle gang and a color gang in Ikebukuro!

Sh

Sharo: Huh? Now where did you get a dingbat idea like that?

Ka

Kanra: It's true! Remember how Kadota-san got run over by that car? Meow! Are you aware of the recent rumors about the Yellow Scarves coming back?

Ka

Kanra: They're saying the Yellow Scarves might be preparing to wage war against the Dollars right meow! That whoever ran over Kadota-san was with the Yellow Scarves, and it was meant as a declawration of war.

Kanra: But did you know that there are other rumors too?

> Ka

Chrome: What are those?

> Ch

Kanra: There are actually two rumors. One is that the Dollars are having an internal purr-ge. In other words, it was one of the Dollars cat-nibalizing a rival. Scary!

> Ka

Chrome: Cannibalizing? But Kadota-san's a prestige member of the Dollars. Why would they...?

> Ch

Kanra: From what I hear, Kadota-san's a very chivalrous and upstanding person. Unlike you two! So if anyone was abusing the Dollars' name for personal gain, Kadota-san would put them back in line.

> Ka

Kanra: If anything, Kadota-san was the one who was meowsing up their plans. ☆

> Ka

Sharo: Okay, I get it. I guess that makes sense. The Dollars aren't one of those tight-knit groups where everyone's on the same page. Technically, I'm one of them too.

> Sh

Kanra: The other rumor is...DragonZ.

> Ka

Chrome: You mean Dragon Zombie, the motorcycle gang?

> Ch

Kanra: Ding-dong, ding-dong, dinga-ding-dong! As your prize for being correct, I give you a meow-meow. Meow-meow! ☆

Chrome: No thanks.

Kanra: Anyway, people wearing the Dragon Zombie jackets were seen loitering around the spot where Kadota-san's accident happened.

Kanra: Dragon Zombie doesn't just ride meowtorcycles. They've got cars too. They could be making their move fur the Dollars' territory. But the thing is, those two rumors aren't actually mutually exclusive.

Sharo: Huh? Why's that?

Kanra: As a matter of fact, people are saying that there are Dragon Zombies within the Dollars! Tons of them!

Sharo: Huuuh? Well, anyone can join the Dollars, so I guess it's totally possible...

Sharo: But wait! Is this what Dragon Zombie's trying to do, then? Infiltrate the Dollars, take them over from the inside, and create one huge Dragon Zombie?

Chrome: That would certainly seem to fit all the stories.

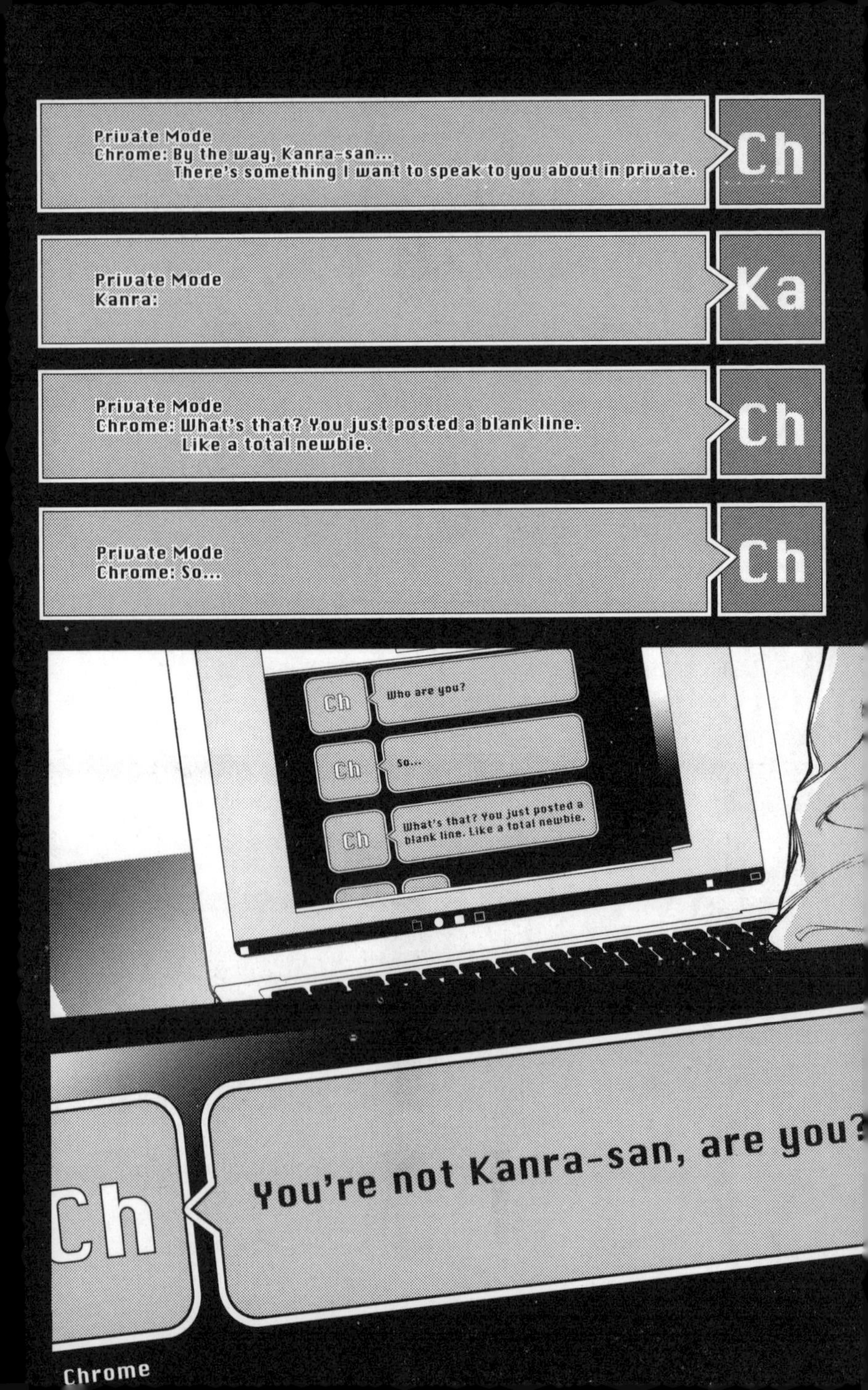

> **Private Mode**
> Chrome: By the way, Kanra-san...
> There's something I want to speak to you about in private.

Ch

> **Private Mode**
> Kanra:

Ka

> **Private Mode**
> Chrome: What's that? You just posted a blank line.
> Like a total newbie.

Ch

> **Private Mode**
> Chrome: So...

Ch

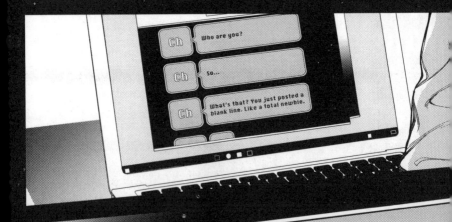

Ch — Who are you?

Ch — So...

Ch — What's that? You just posted a blank line. Like a total newbie.

Ch > You're not Kanra-san, are you?

Chrome

Sh Sharo: Huh!?

Ch Chrome: I wonder what happened.

Sh Sharo: Ah-ha! I bet Kanra-san got bummed that I spoiled the big surprise and ran off.

Ch Chrome: Perhaps Dragon Zombie already put a hit out.

Sh Sharo: D-don't scare me like that...

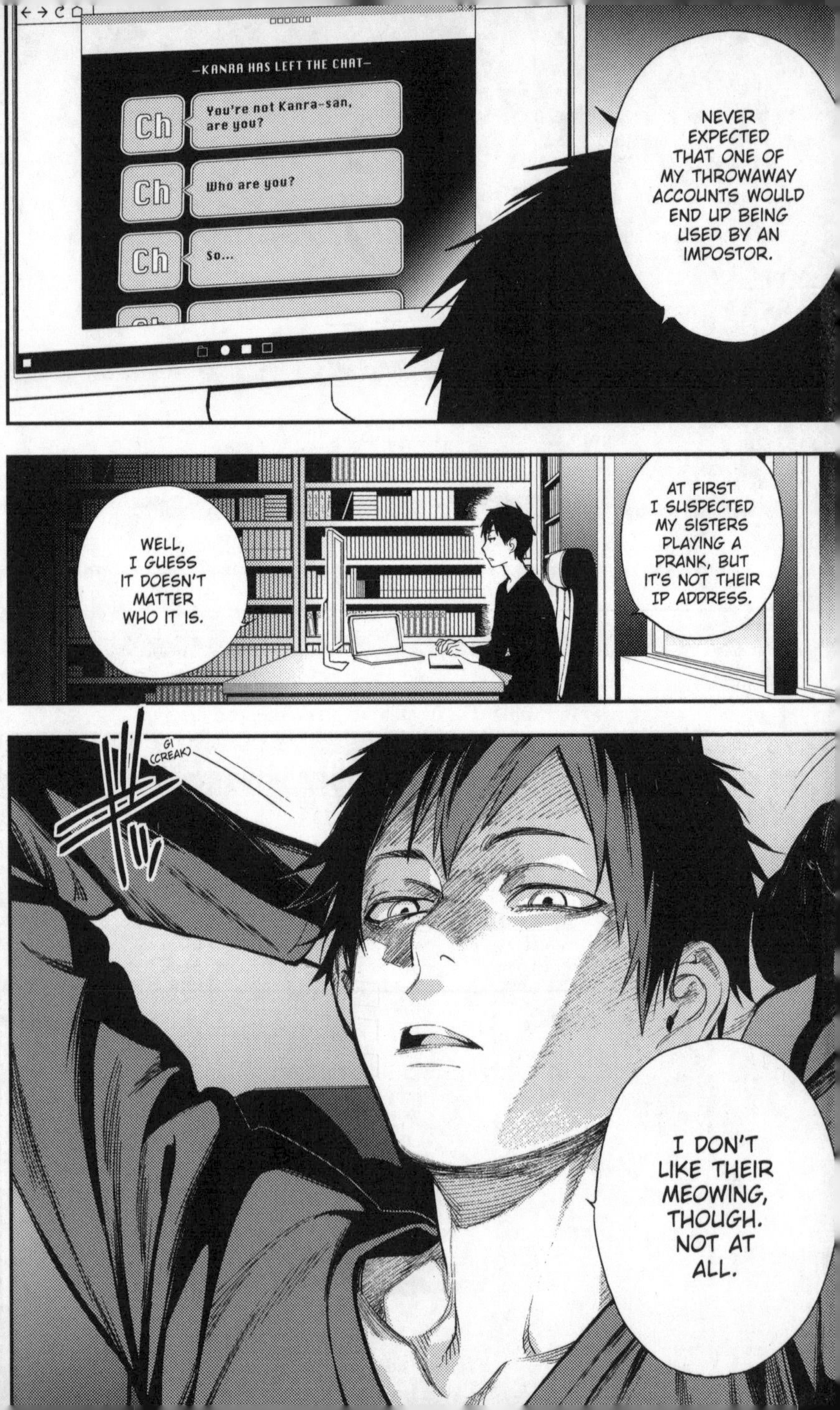

NEVER EXPECTED THAT ONE OF MY THROWAWAY ACCOUNTS WOULD END UP BEING USED BY AN IMPOSTOR.
-KANRA HAS LEFT THE CHAT-
You're not Kanra-san, are you?
Who are you?
So...
AT FIRST I SUSPECTED MY SISTERS PLAYING A PRANK, BUT IT'S NOT THEIR IP ADDRESS.
WELL, I GUESS IT DOESN'T MATTER WHO IT IS.
GI (CREAK)
I DON'T LIKE THEIR MEOWING, THOUGH. NOT AT ALL.

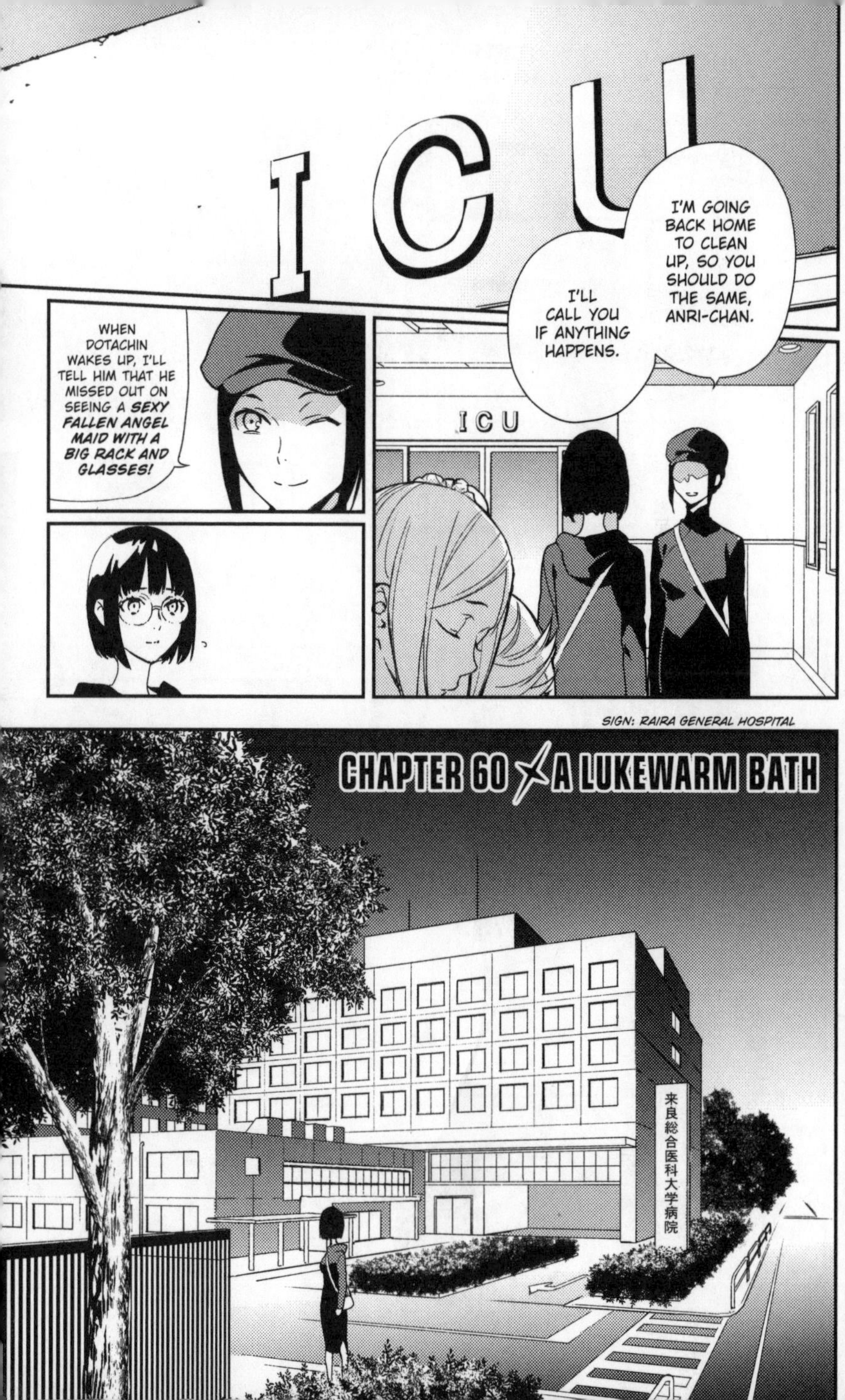
ICU
I'M GOING BACK HOME TO CLEAN UP, SO YOU SHOULD DO THE SAME, ANRI-CHAN.
I'LL CALL YOU IF ANYTHING HAPPENS.
ICU
WHEN DOTACHIN WAKES UP, I'LL TELL HIM THAT HE MISSED OUT ON SEEING A SEXY FALLEN ANGEL MAID WITH A BIG RACK AND GLASSES!
SIGN: RAIRA GENERAL HOSPITAL
CHAPTER 60 A LUKEWARM BATH
来良総合医科大学病院

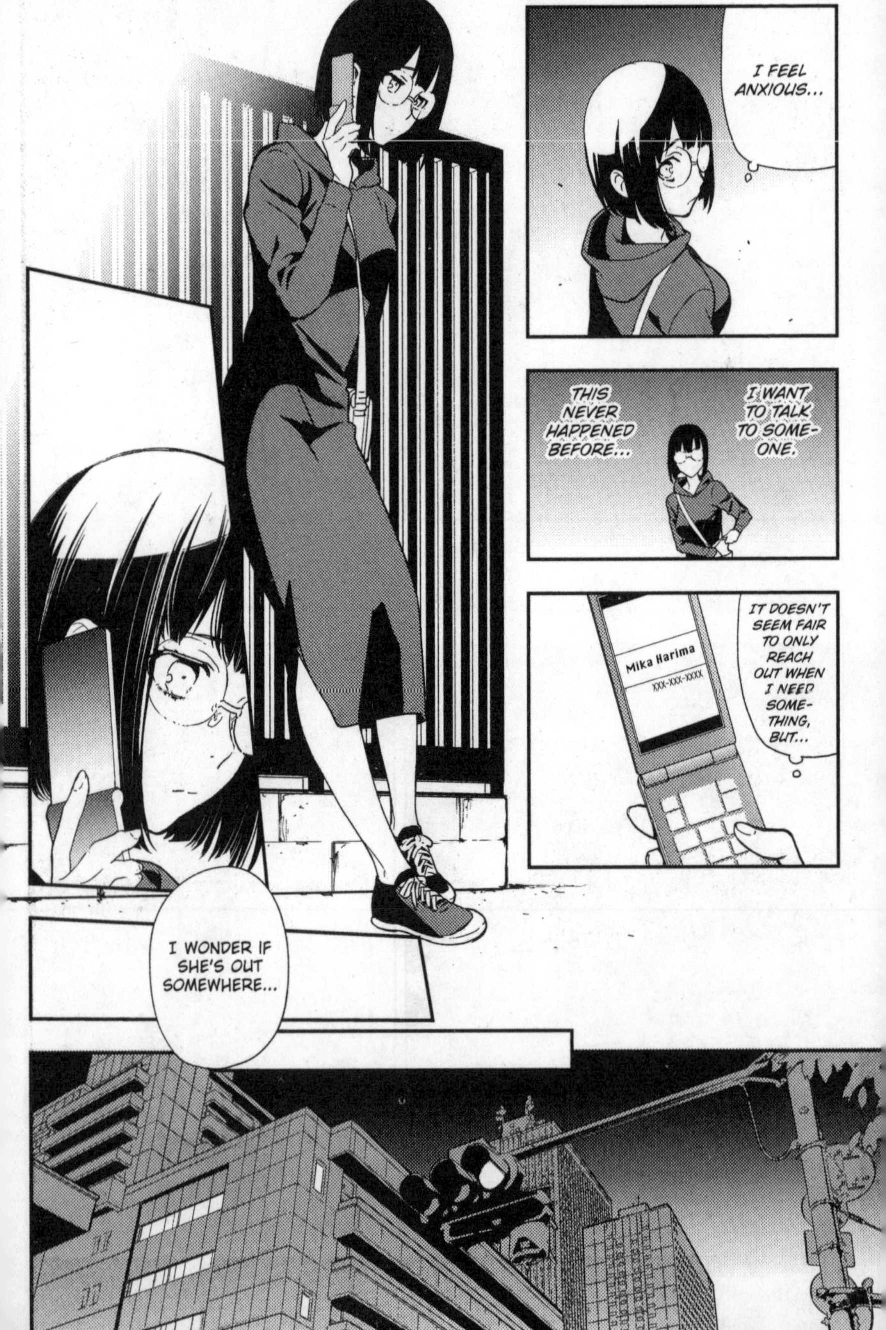
I FEEL ANXIOUS...
I WANT TO TALK TO SOME-ONE.
THIS NEVER HAPPENED BEFORE...
IT DOESN'T SEEM FAIR TO ONLY REACH OUT WHEN I NEED SOME-THING, BUT...
Mika Harima
XXX-XXX-XXXX
I WONDER IF SHE'S OUT SOMEWHERE...

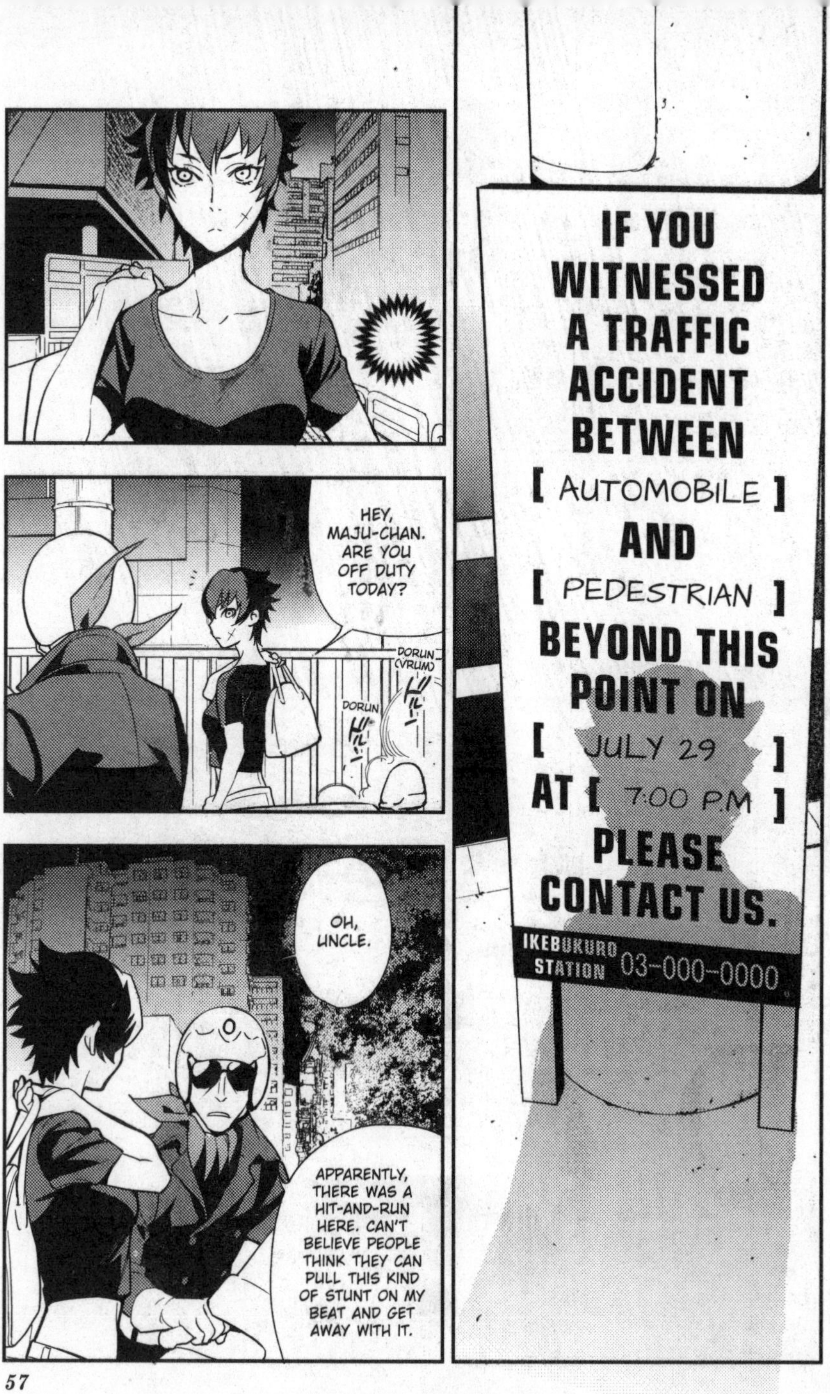
IF YOU WITNESSED A TRAFFIC ACCIDENT BETWEEN
[AUTOMOBILE]
AND
[PEDESTRIAN]
BEYOND THIS POINT ON
[JULY 29]
AT [7:00 P.M]
PLEASE CONTACT US.
IKEBUKURO STATION 03-000-0000
HEY, MAJU-CHAN. ARE YOU OFF DUTY TODAY?
DORUN (VRUM)
DORUN
OH, UNCLE.
APPARENTLY, THERE WAS A HIT-AND-RUN HERE. CAN'T BELIEVE PEOPLE THINK THEY CAN PULL THIS KIND OF STUNT ON MY BEAT AND GET AWAY WITH IT.

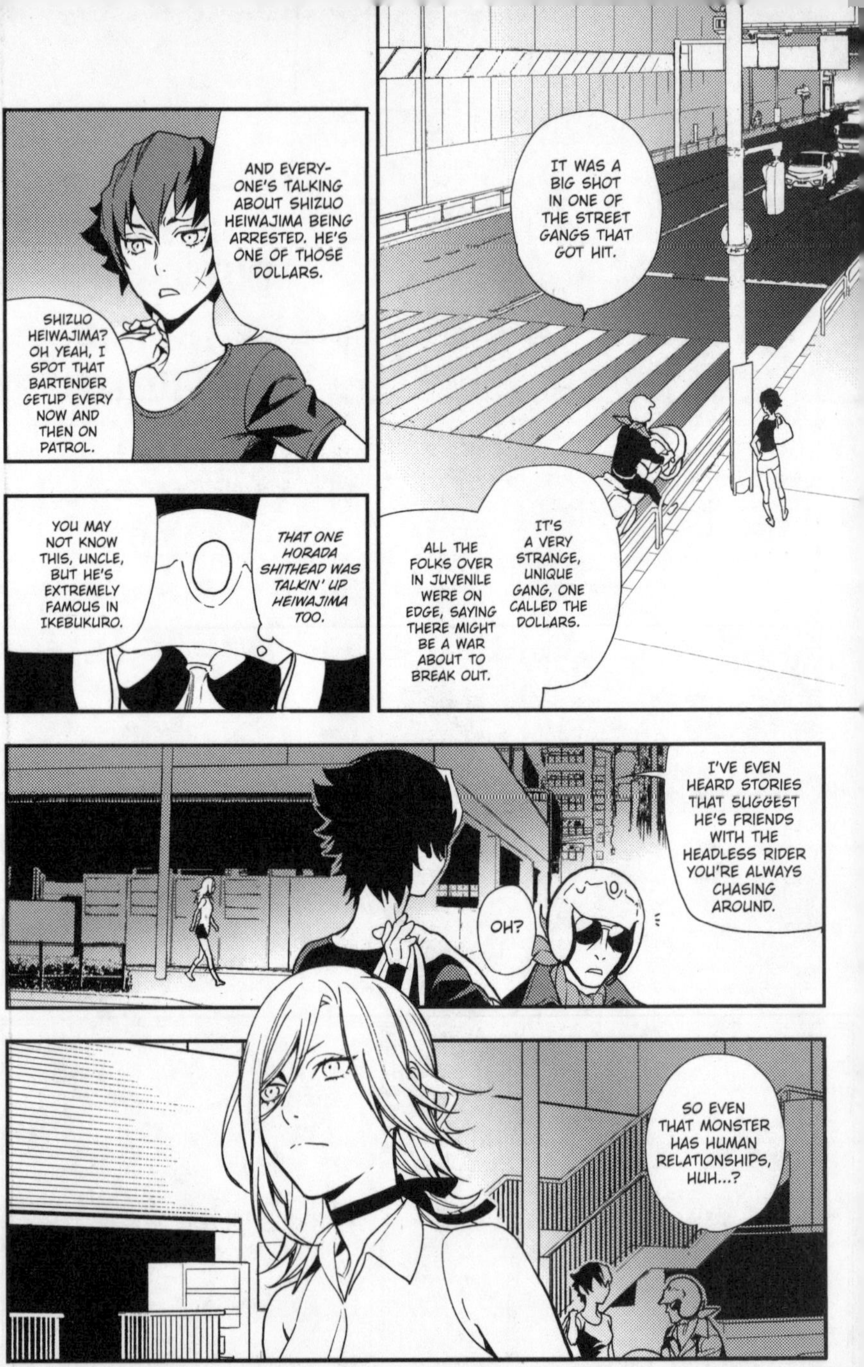
IT WAS A BIG SHOT IN ONE OF THE STREET GANGS THAT GOT HIT.
IT'S A VERY STRANGE, UNIQUE GANG, ONE CALLED THE DOLLARS.
ALL THE FOLKS OVER IN JUVENILE WERE ON EDGE, SAYING THERE MIGHT BE A WAR ABOUT TO BREAK OUT.
AND EVERY-ONE'S TALKING ABOUT SHIZUO HEIWAJIMA BEING ARRESTED. HE'S ONE OF THOSE DOLLARS.
SHIZUO HEIWAJIMA? OH YEAH, I SPOT THAT BARTENDER GETUP EVERY NOW AND THEN ON PATROL.
THAT ONE HORADA SHITHEAD WAS TALKIN' UP HEIWAJIMA TOO.
YOU MAY NOT KNOW THIS, UNCLE, BUT HE'S EXTREMELY FAMOUS IN IKEBUKURO.
I'VE EVEN HEARD STORIES THAT SUGGEST HE'S FRIENDS WITH THE HEADLESS RIDER YOU'RE ALWAYS CHASING AROUND.
OH?
SO EVEN THAT MONSTER HAS HUMAN RELATIONSHIPS, HUH...?

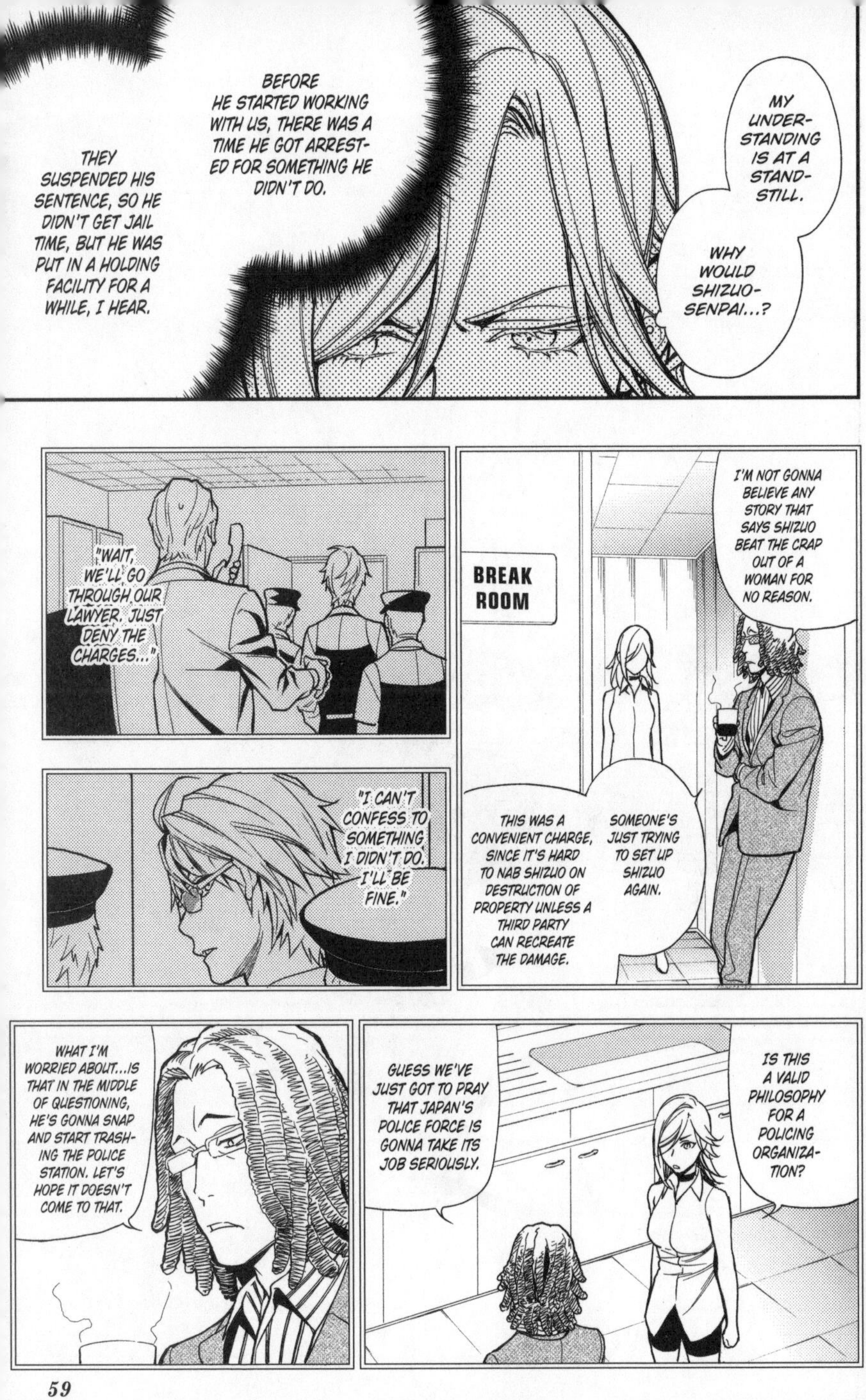
MY UNDER-STANDING IS AT A STAND-STILL.
WHY WOULD SHIZUO-SENPAI...?
BEFORE HE STARTED WORKING WITH US, THERE WAS A TIME HE GOT ARREST-ED FOR SOMETHING HE DIDN'T DO.
THEY SUSPENDED HIS SENTENCE, SO HE DIDN'T GET JAIL TIME, BUT HE WAS PUT IN A HOLDING FACILITY FOR A WHILE, I HEAR.
I'M NOT GONNA BELIEVE ANY STORY THAT SAYS SHIZUO BEAT THE CRAP OUT OF A WOMAN FOR NO REASON.
BREAK ROOM
SOMEONE'S JUST TRYING TO SET UP SHIZUO AGAIN.
THIS WAS A CONVENIENT CHARGE, SINCE IT'S HARD TO NAB SHIZUO ON DESTRUCTION OF PROPERTY UNLESS A THIRD PARTY CAN RECREATE THE DAMAGE.
"WAIT, WE'LL GO THROUGH OUR LAWYER. JUST DENY THE CHARGES..."
"I CAN'T CONFESS TO SOMETHING I DIDN'T DO. I'LL BE FINE."
IS THIS A VALID PHILOSOPHY FOR A POLICING ORGANIZA-TION?
GUESS WE'VE JUST GOT TO PRAY THAT JAPAN'S POLICE FORCE IS GONNA TAKE ITS JOB SERIOUSLY.
WHAT I'M WORRIED ABOUT...IS THAT IN THE MIDDLE OF QUESTIONING, HE'S GONNA SNAP AND START TRASH-ING THE POLICE STATION. LET'S HOPE IT DOESN'T COME TO THAT.

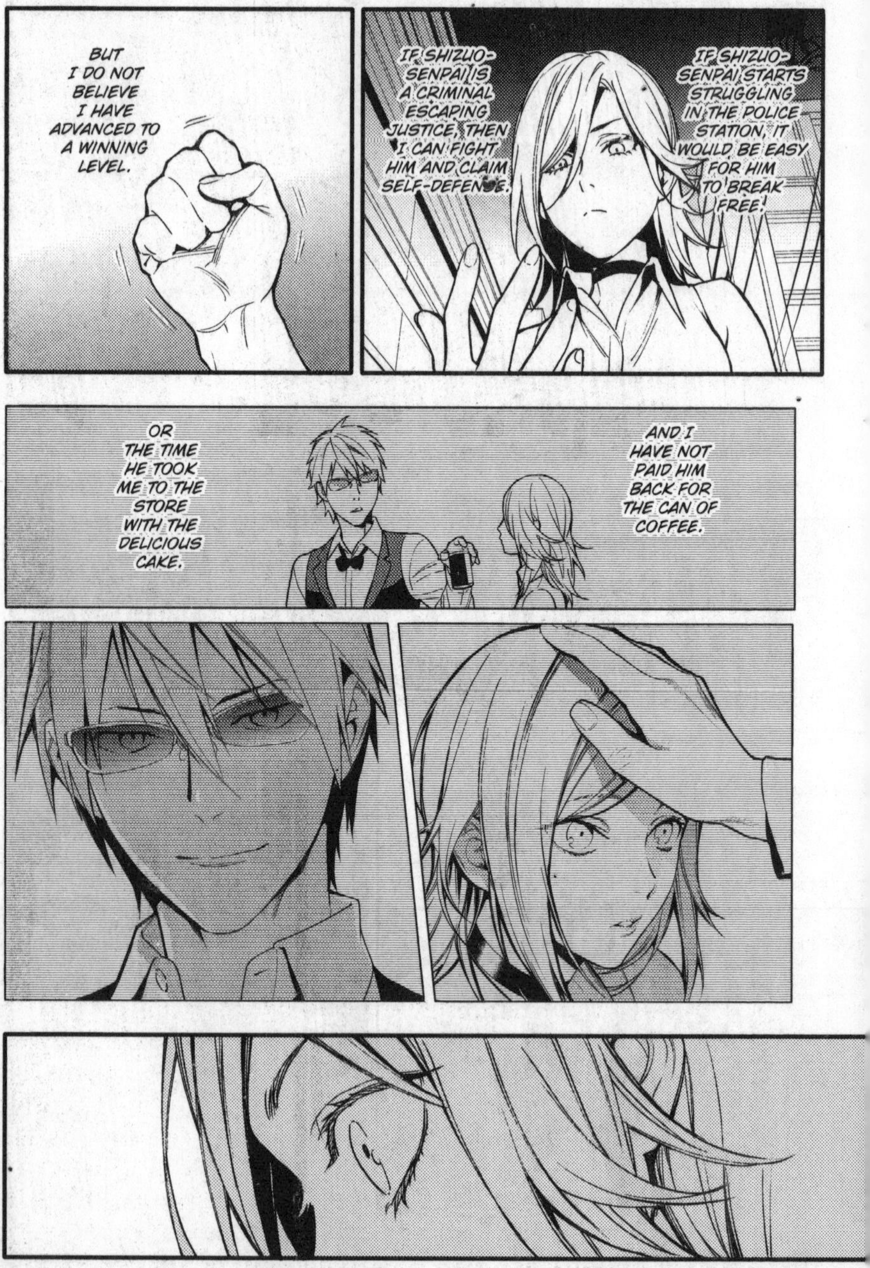
IF SHIZUO-SENPAI STARTS STRUGGLING IN THE POLICE STATION, IT WOULD BE EASY FOR HIM TO BREAK FREE.
IF SHIZUO-SENPAI IS A CRIMINAL ESCAPING JUSTICE, THEN I CAN FIGHT HIM AND CLAIM SELF-DEFENSE.
BUT I DO NOT BELIEVE I HAVE ADVANCED TO A WINNING LEVEL.
AND I HAVE NOT PAID HIM BACK FOR THE CAN OF COFFEE.
OR THE TIME HE TOOK ME TO THE STORE WITH THE DELICIOUS CAKE.

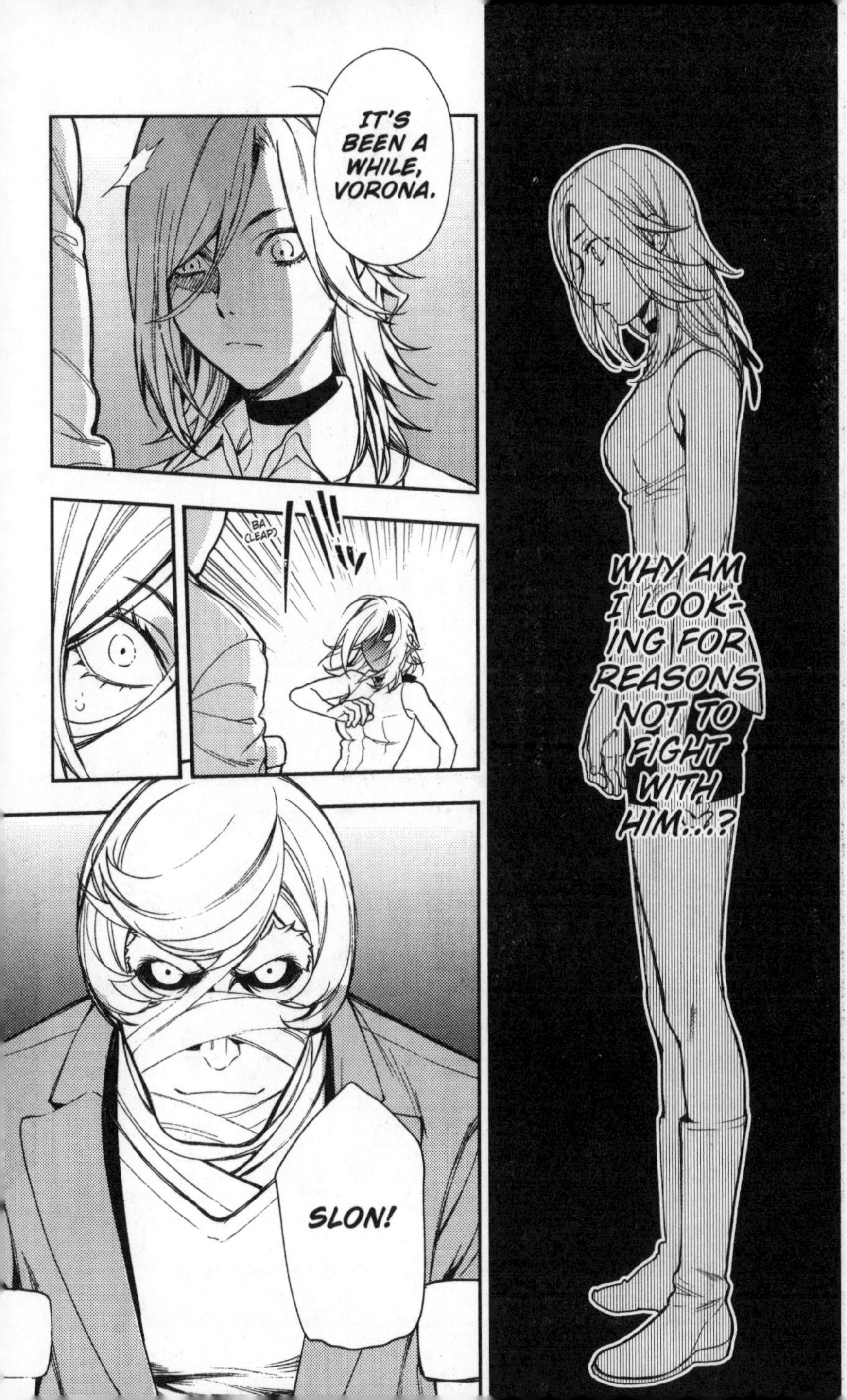
WHY AM I LOOK-ING FOR REASONS NOT TO FIGHT WITH HIM...?
IT'S BEEN A WHILE, VORONA.
BA (LEAP)
SLON!

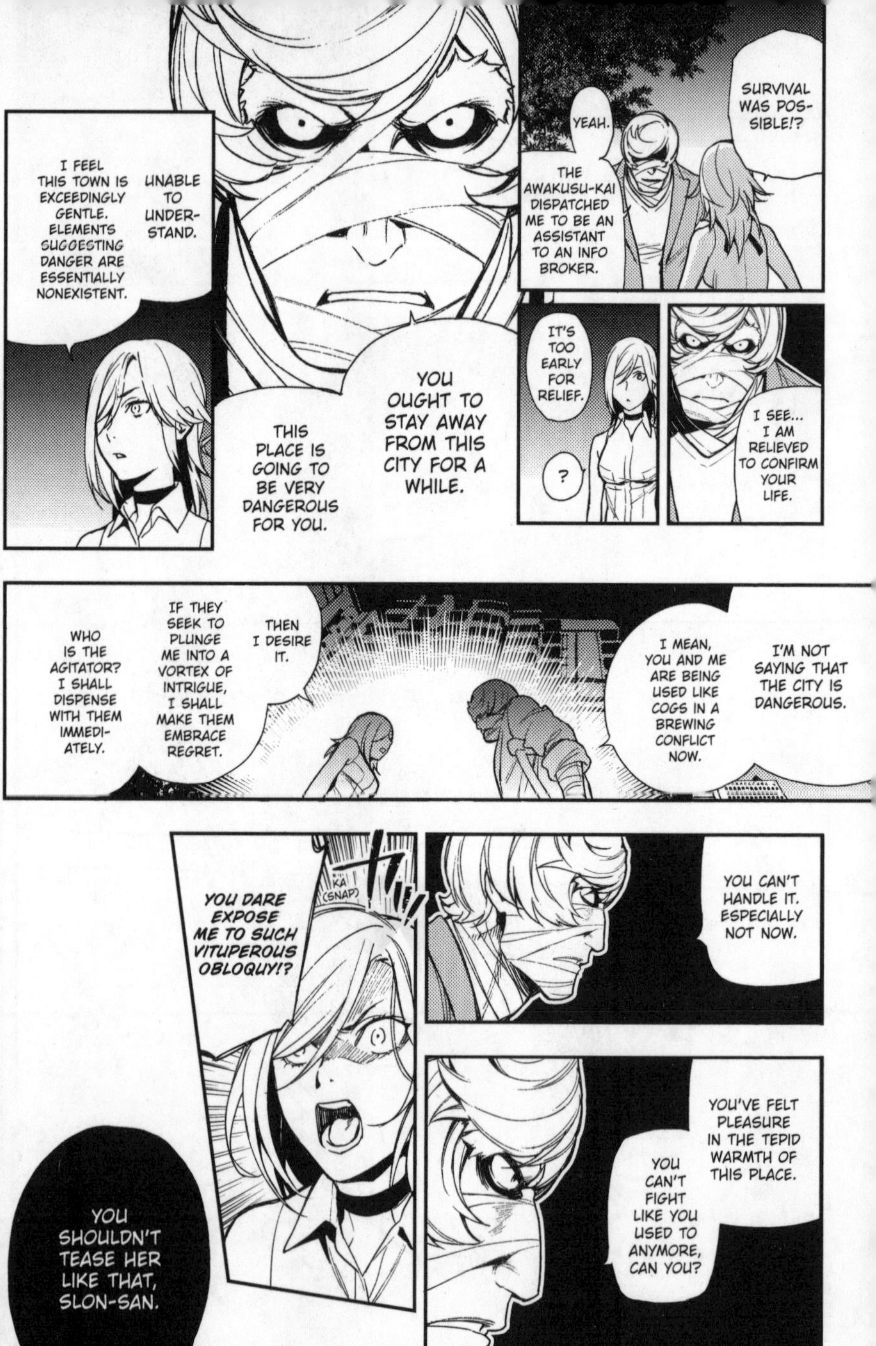
SURVIVAL WAS POS-SIBLE!?
YEAH.
THE AWAKUSU-KAI DISPATCHED ME TO BE AN ASSISTANT TO AN INFO BROKER.
I SEE... I AM RELIEVED TO CONFIRM YOUR LIFE.
IT'S TOO EARLY FOR RELIEF.
?
YOU OUGHT TO STAY AWAY FROM THIS CITY FOR A WHILE.
THIS PLACE IS GOING TO BE VERY DANGEROUS FOR YOU.
UNABLE TO UNDER-STAND.
I FEEL THIS TOWN IS EXCEEDINGLY GENTLE. ELEMENTS SUGGESTING DANGER ARE ESSENTIALLY NONEXISTENT.
I'M NOT SAYING THAT THE CITY IS DANGEROUS.
I MEAN, YOU AND ME ARE BEING USED LIKE COGS IN A BREWING CONFLICT NOW.
THEN I DESIRE IT.
IF THEY SEEK TO PLUNGE ME INTO A VORTEX OF INTRIGUE, I SHALL MAKE THEM EMBRACE REGRET.
WHO IS THE AGITATOR? I SHALL DISPENSE WITH THEM IMMEDI-ATELY.
YOU CAN'T HANDLE IT. ESPECIALLY NOT NOW.
YOU'VE FELT PLEASURE IN THE TEPID WARMTH OF THIS PLACE.
YOU CAN'T FIGHT LIKE YOU USED TO ANYMORE, CAN YOU?
KA (SNAP)
YOU DARE EXPOSE ME TO SUCH VITUPEROUS OBLOQUY!?
YOU SHOULDN'T TEASE HER LIKE THAT, SLON-SAN.

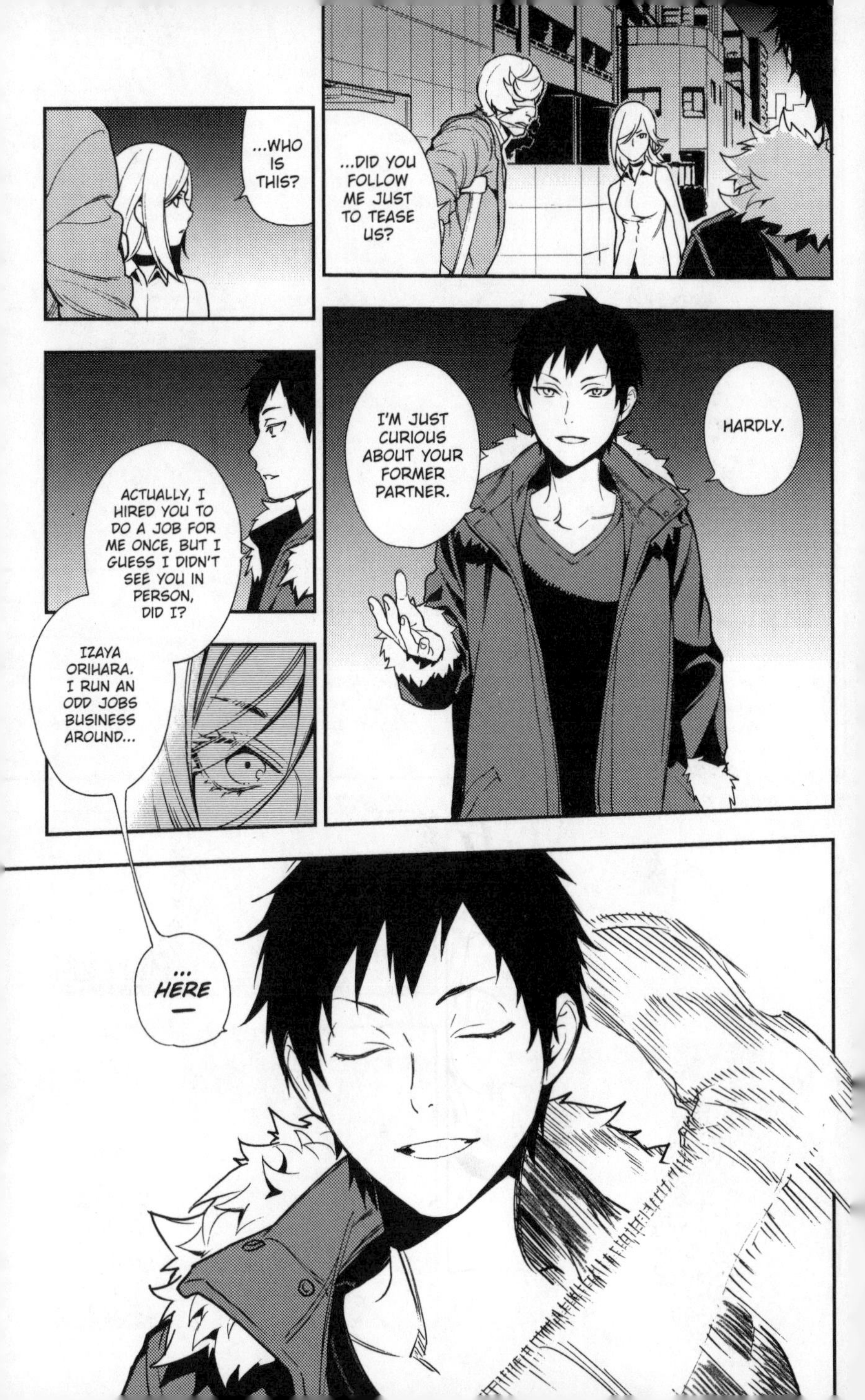
...DID YOU FOLLOW ME JUST TO TEASE US?
...WHO IS THIS?
HARDLY.
I'M JUST CURIOUS ABOUT YOUR FORMER PARTNER.
ACTUALLY, I HIRED YOU TO DO A JOB FOR ME ONCE, BUT I GUESS I DIDN'T SEE YOU IN PERSON, DID I?
IZAYA ORIHARA. I RUN AN ODD JOBS BUSINESS AROUND...
...HERE—

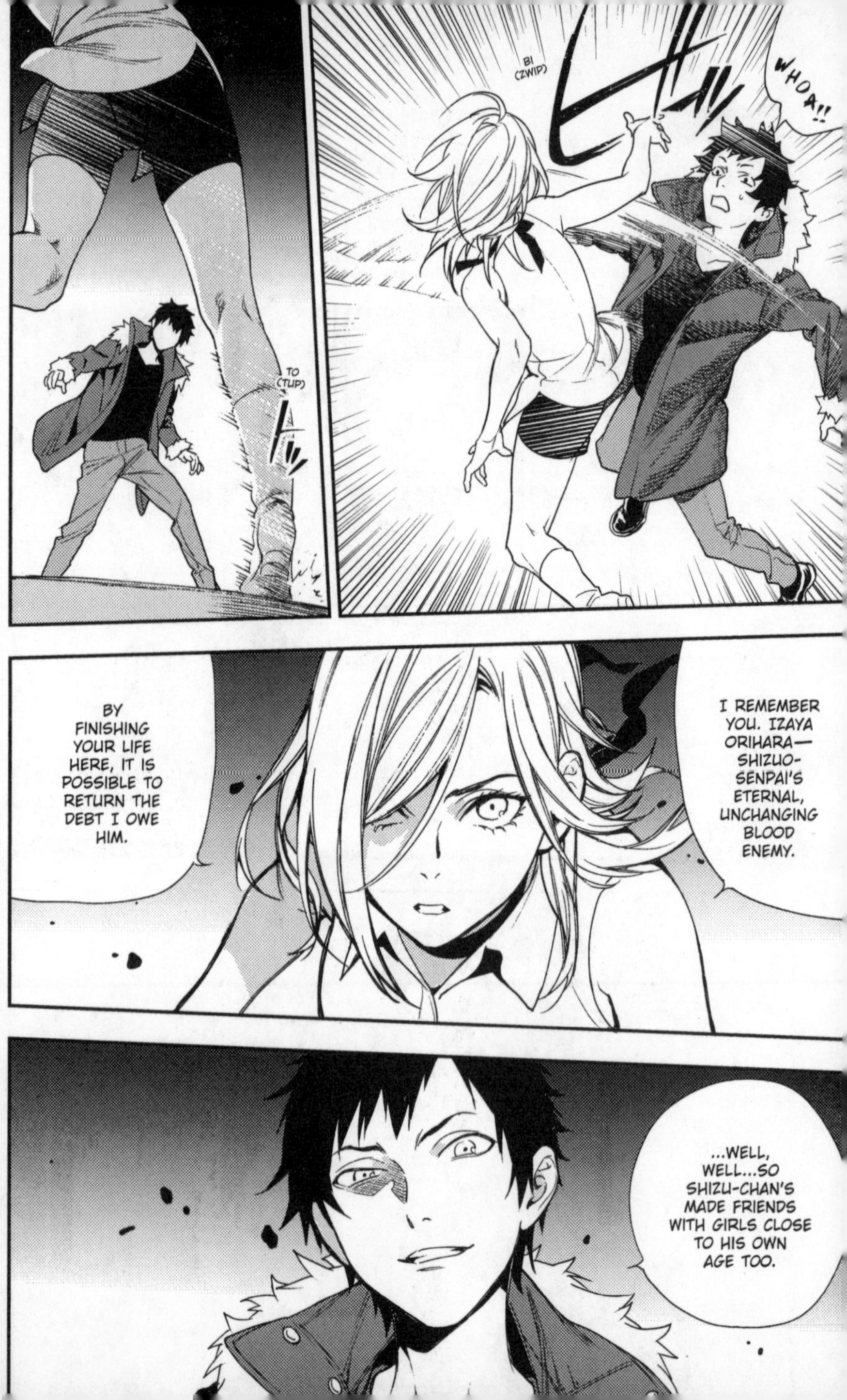
BI (ZWIP)
WHOA!!
TO (TUP)
I REMEMBER YOU. IZAYA ORIHARA—SHIZUO-SENPAI'S ETERNAL, UNCHANGING BLOOD ENEMY.
BY FINISHING YOUR LIFE HERE, IT IS POSSIBLE TO RETURN THE DEBT I OWE HIM.
...WELL, WELL...SO SHIZU-CHAN'S MADE FRIENDS WITH GIRLS CLOSE TO HIS OWN AGE TOO.

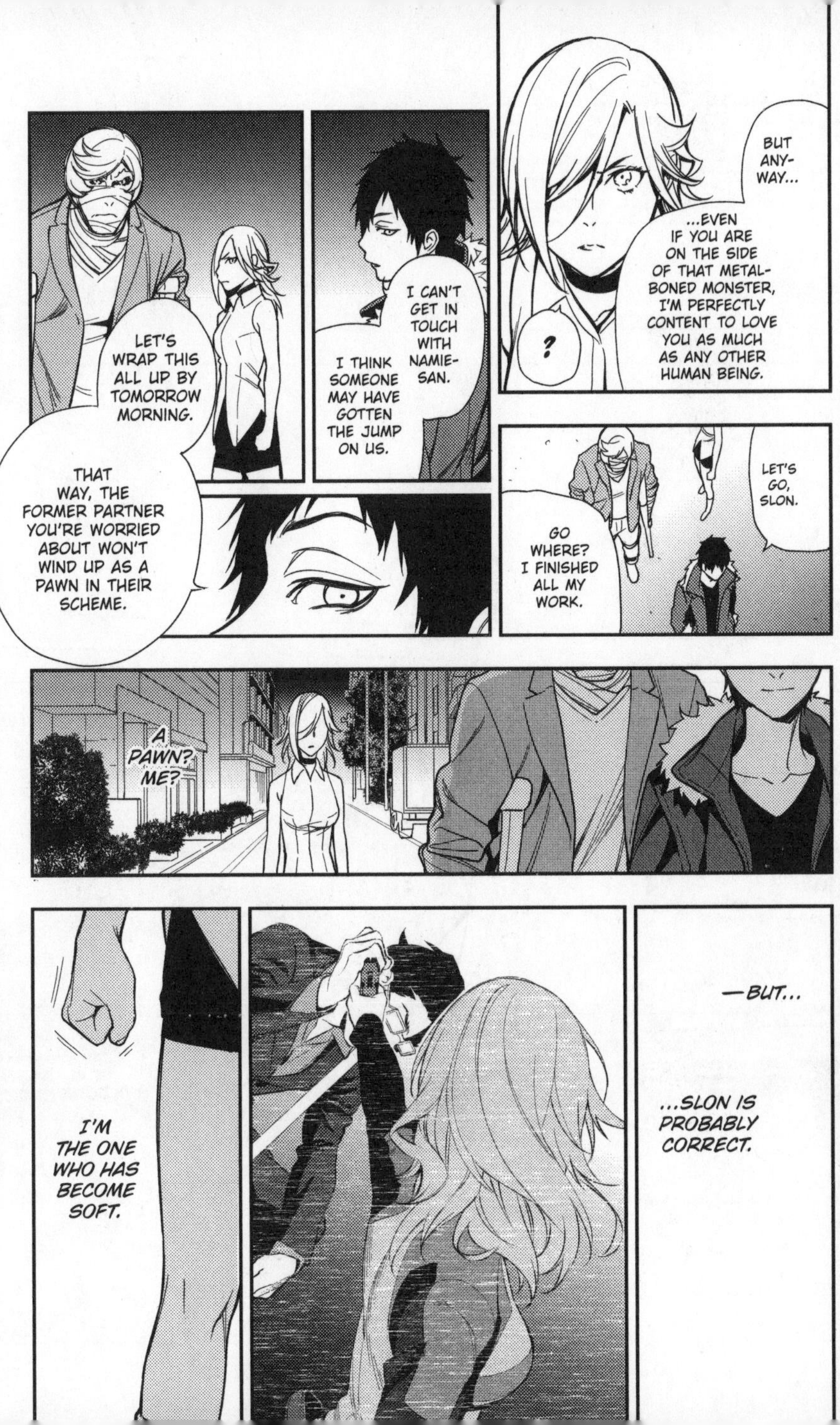
BUT ANY-WAY...
...EVEN IF YOU ARE ON THE SIDE OF THAT METAL-BONED MONSTER, I'M PERFECTLY CONTENT TO LOVE YOU AS MUCH AS ANY OTHER HUMAN BEING.
?
LET'S GO, SLON.
GO WHERE? I FINISHED ALL MY WORK.
I CAN'T GET IN TOUCH WITH NAMIE-SAN.
I THINK SOMEONE MAY HAVE GOTTEN THE JUMP ON US.
LET'S WRAP THIS ALL UP BY TOMORROW MORNING.
THAT WAY, THE FORMER PARTNER YOU'RE WORRIED ABOUT WON'T WIND UP AS A PAWN IN THEIR SCHEME.
A PAWN? ME?
—BUT...
...SLON IS PROBABLY CORRECT.
I'M THE ONE WHO HAS BECOME SOFT.

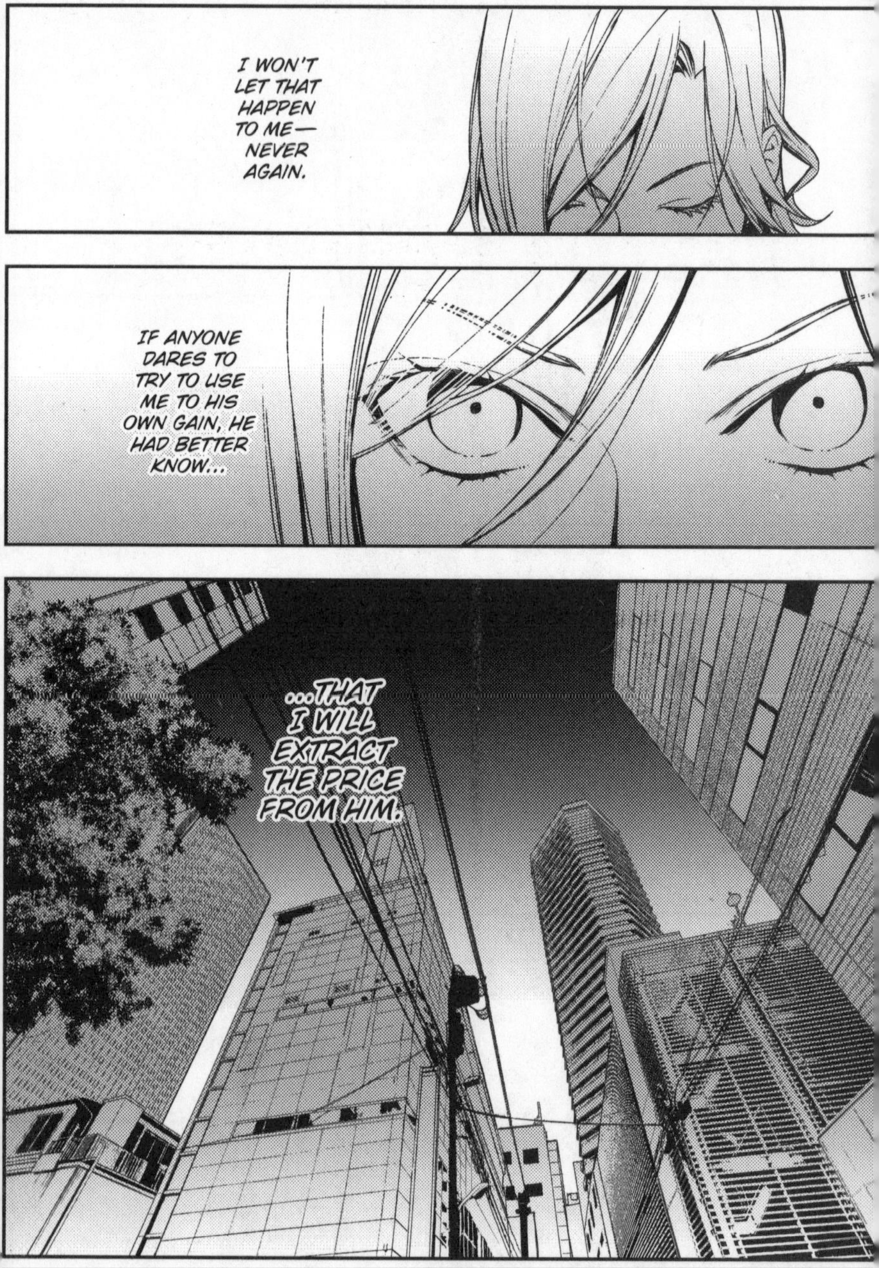
I WON'T LET THAT HAPPEN TO ME— NEVER AGAIN.
IF ANYONE DARES TO TRY TO USE ME TO HIS OWN GAIN, HE HAD BETTER KNOW...
...THAT I WILL EXTRACT THE PRICE FROM HIM.

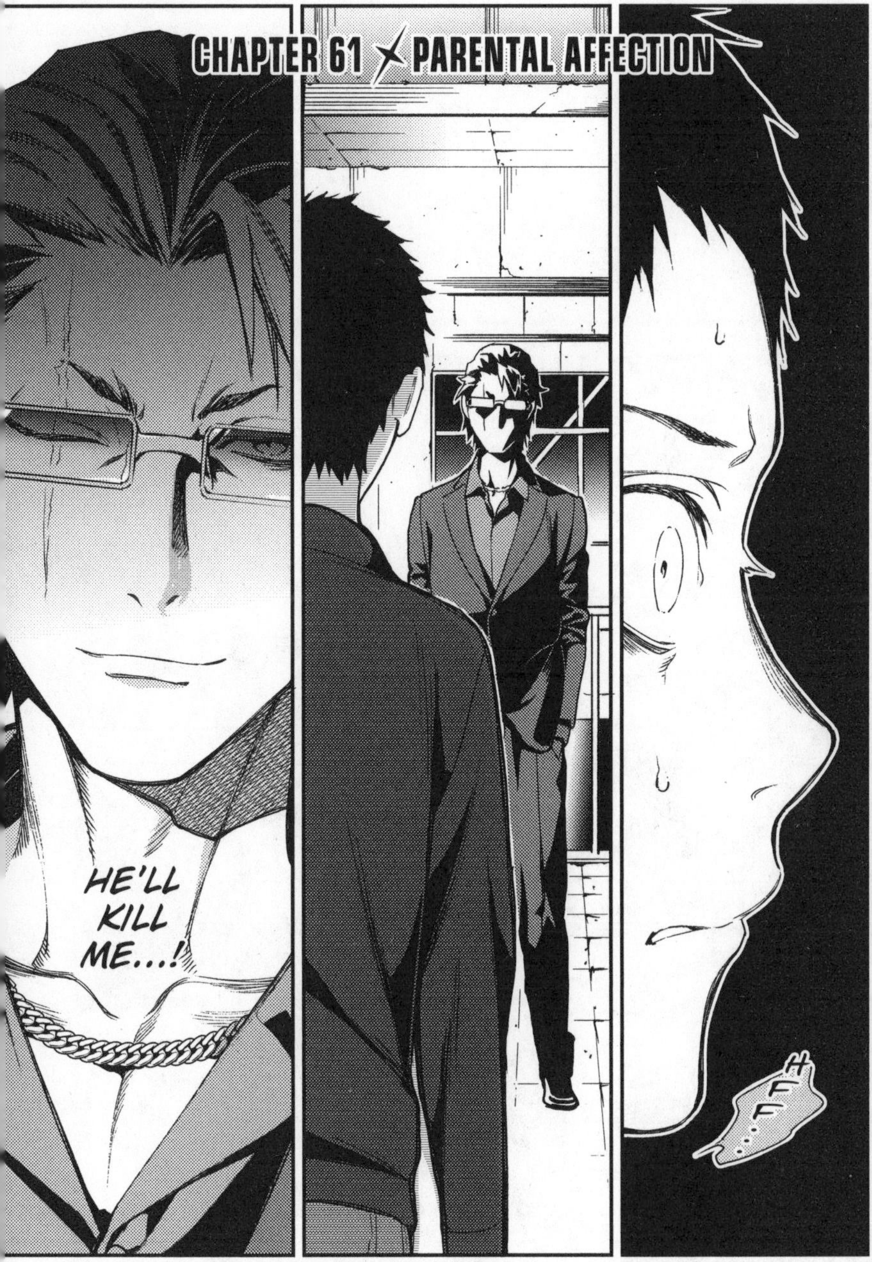
CHAPTER 61 PARENTAL AFFECTION
HFF...
HE'LL KILL ME...!

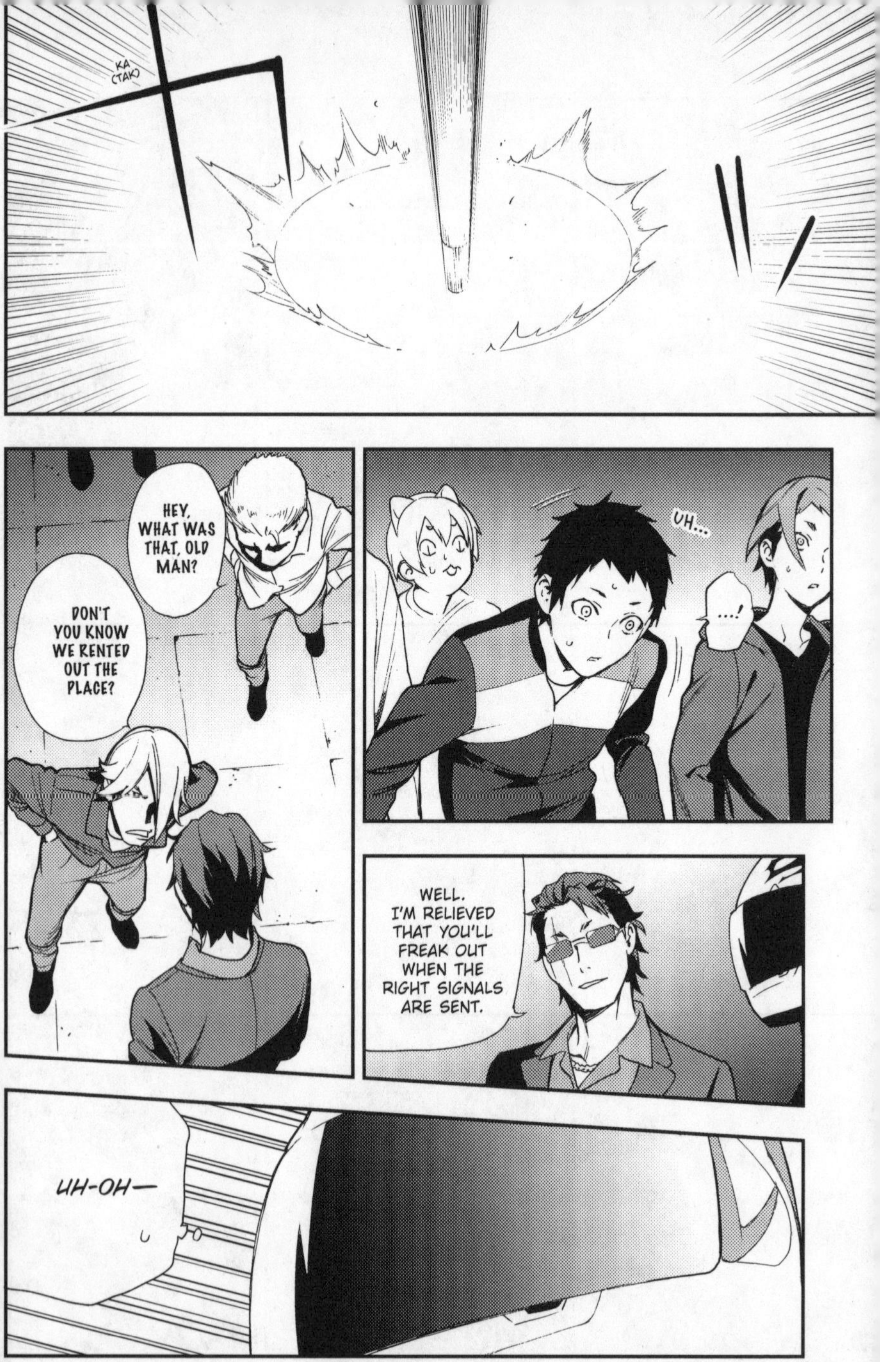
KA (TAK)
UH...
....!
WELL. I'M RELIEVED THAT YOU'LL FREAK OUT WHEN THE RIGHT SIGNALS ARE SENT.
HEY, WHAT WAS THAT, OLD MAN?
DON'T YOU KNOW WE RENTED OUT THE PLACE?
UH-OH—

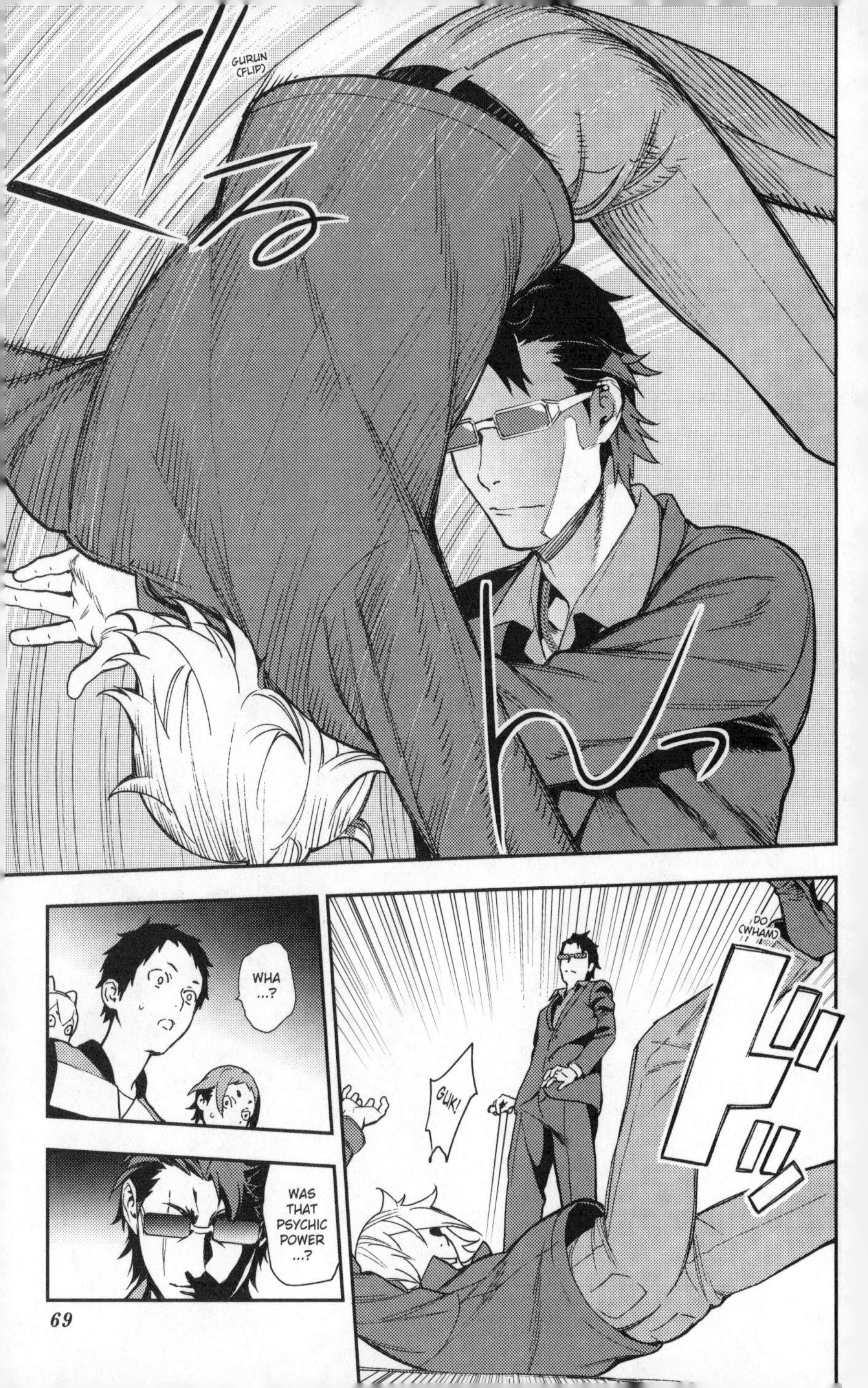
GURUN (FLIP)
DO (WHAM)
GUK!
WHA ...?
WAS THAT PSYCHIC POWER ...?

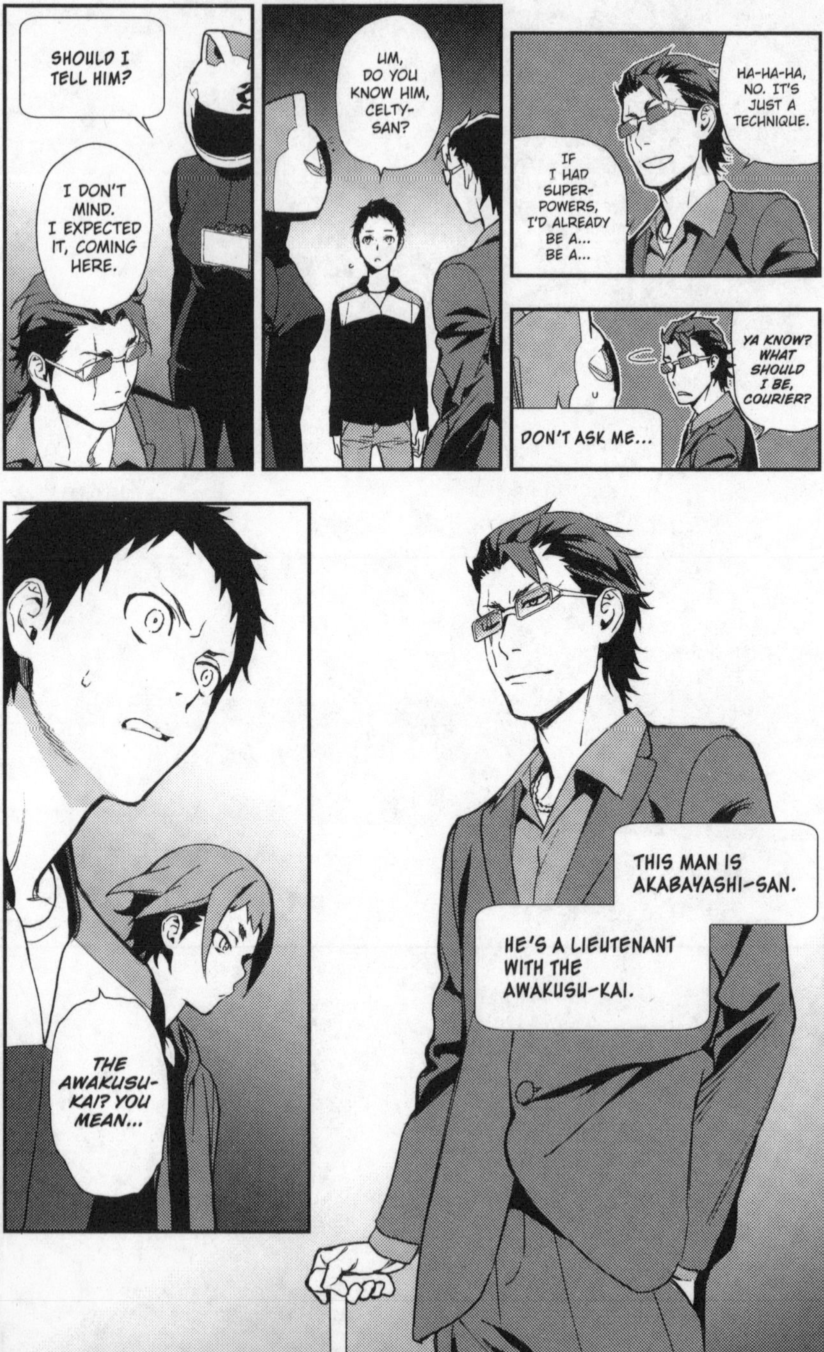
HA-HA-HA, NO. IT'S JUST A TECHNIQUE.
IF I HAD SUPER-POWERS, I'D ALREADY BE A... BE A...
YA KNOW? WHAT SHOULD I BE, COURIER?
DON'T ASK ME...
UM, DO YOU KNOW HIM, CELTY-SAN?
SHOULD I TELL HIM?
I DON'T MIND. I EXPECTED IT, COMING HERE.
THIS MAN IS AKABAYASHI-SAN.
HE'S A LIEUTENANT WITH THE AWAKUSU-KAI.
THE AWAKUSU-KAI? YOU MEAN...

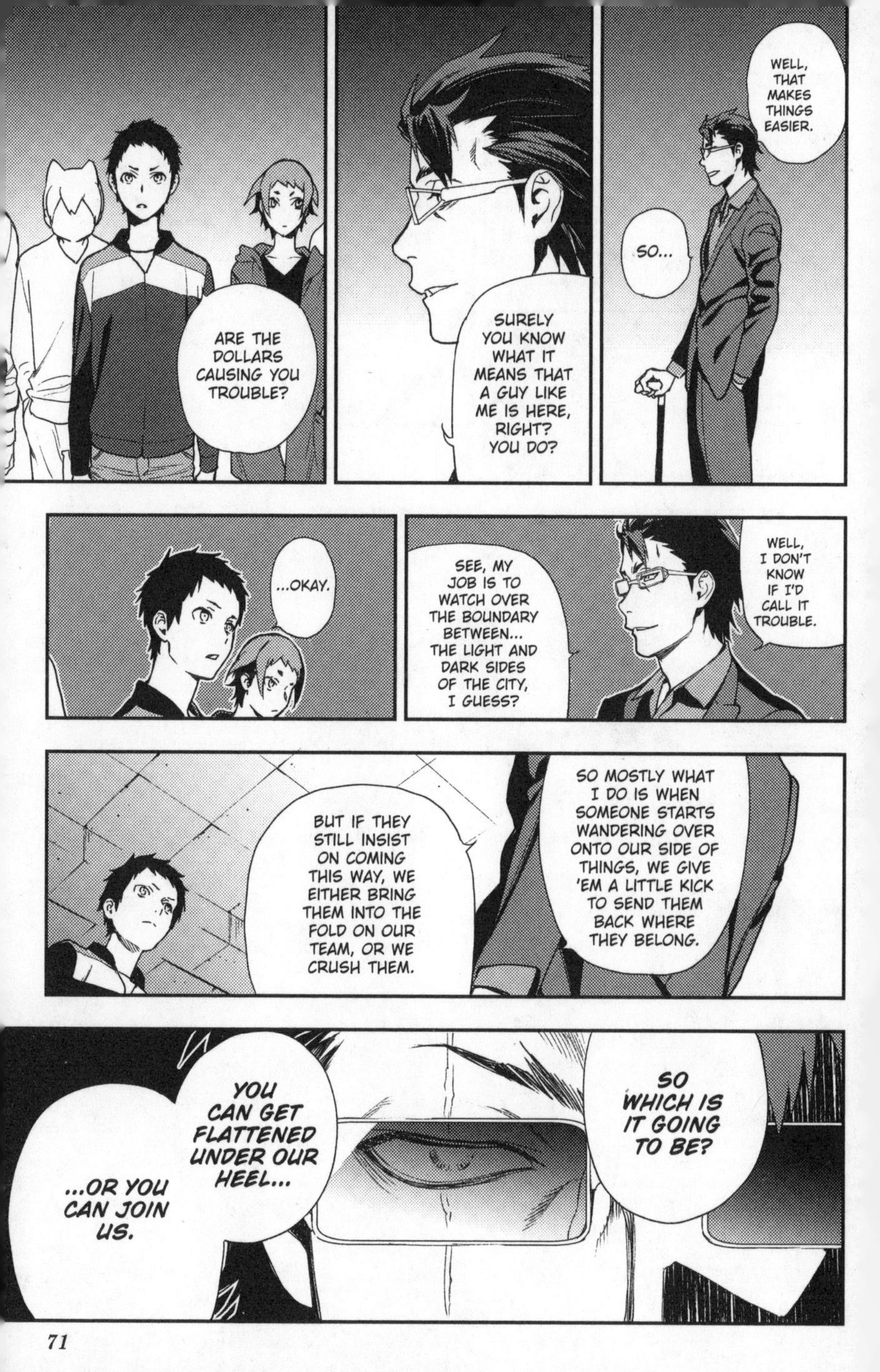
WELL, THAT MAKES THINGS EASIER.
SO...
SURELY YOU KNOW WHAT IT MEANS THAT A GUY LIKE ME IS HERE, RIGHT? YOU DO?
ARE THE DOLLARS CAUSING YOU TROUBLE?
WELL, I DON'T KNOW IF I'D CALL IT TROUBLE.
SEE, MY JOB IS TO WATCH OVER THE BOUNDARY BETWEEN... THE LIGHT AND DARK SIDES OF THE CITY, I GUESS?
...OKAY.
SO MOSTLY WHAT I DO IS WHEN SOMEONE STARTS WANDERING OVER ONTO OUR SIDE OF THINGS, WE GIVE 'EM A LITTLE KICK TO SEND THEM BACK WHERE THEY BELONG.
BUT IF THEY STILL INSIST ON COMING THIS WAY, WE EITHER BRING THEM INTO THE FOLD ON OUR TEAM, OR WE CRUSH THEM.
SO WHICH IS IT GOING TO BE?
YOU CAN GET FLATTENED UNDER OUR HEEL...
...OR YOU CAN JOIN US.

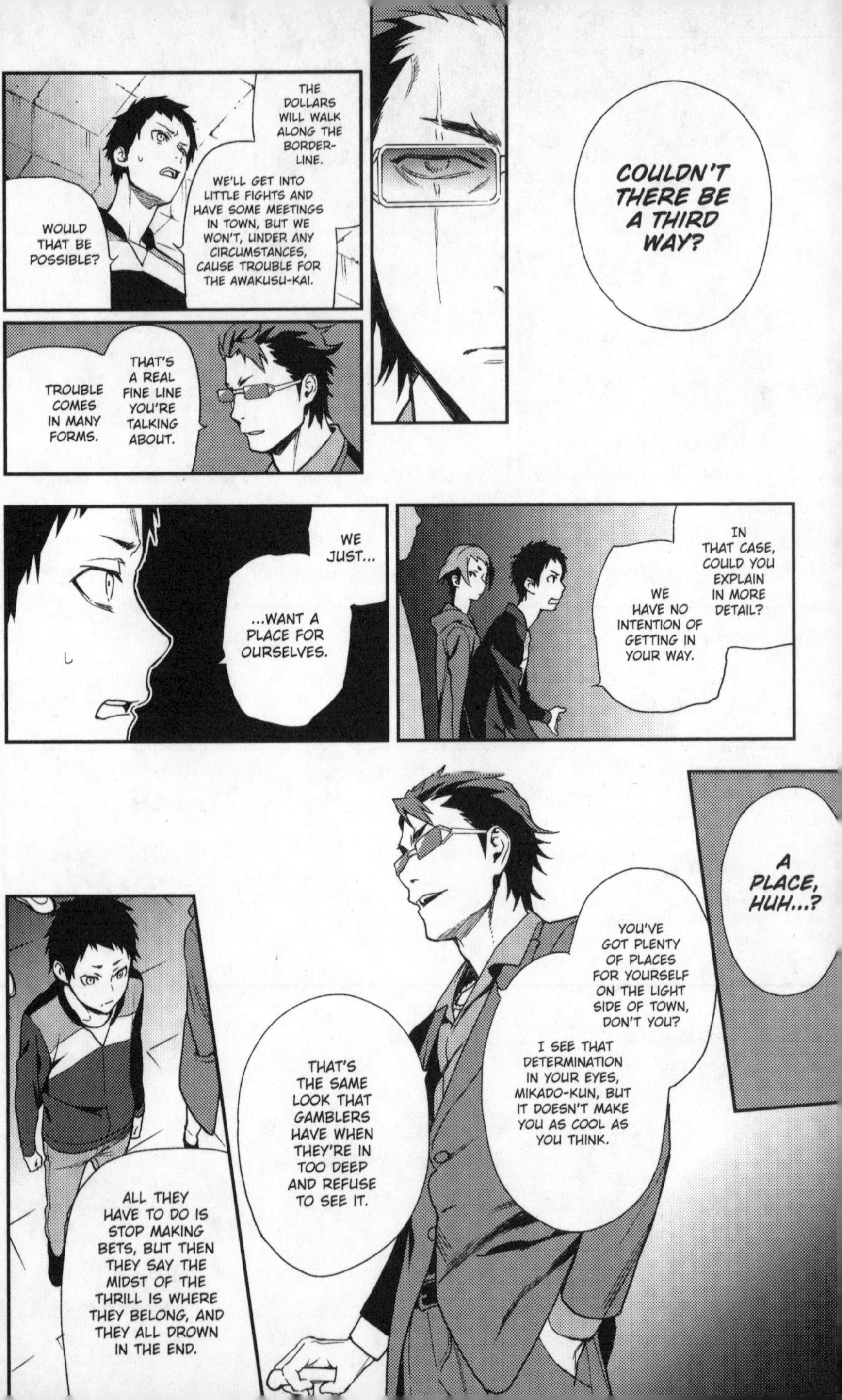
COULDN'T THERE BE A THIRD WAY?
THE DOLLARS WILL WALK ALONG THE BORDER-LINE.
WE'LL GET INTO LITTLE FIGHTS AND HAVE SOME MEETINGS IN TOWN, BUT WE WON'T, UNDER ANY CIRCUMSTANCES, CAUSE TROUBLE FOR THE AWAKUSU-KAI.
WOULD THAT BE POSSIBLE?
THAT'S A REAL FINE LINE YOU'RE TALKING ABOUT.
TROUBLE COMES IN MANY FORMS.
IN THAT CASE, COULD YOU EXPLAIN IN MORE DETAIL?
WE HAVE NO INTENTION OF GETTING IN YOUR WAY.
WE JUST...
...WANT A PLACE FOR OURSELVES.
A PLACE, HUH...?
YOU'VE GOT PLENTY OF PLACES FOR YOURSELF ON THE LIGHT SIDE OF TOWN, DON'T YOU?
I SEE THAT DETERMINATION IN YOUR EYES, MIKADO-KUN, BUT IT DOESN'T MAKE YOU AS COOL AS YOU THINK.
THAT'S THE SAME LOOK THAT GAMBLERS HAVE WHEN THEY'RE IN TOO DEEP AND REFUSE TO SEE IT.
ALL THEY HAVE TO DO IS STOP MAKING BETS, BUT THEN THEY SAY THE MIDST OF THE THRILL IS WHERE THEY BELONG, AND THEY ALL DROWN IN THE END.

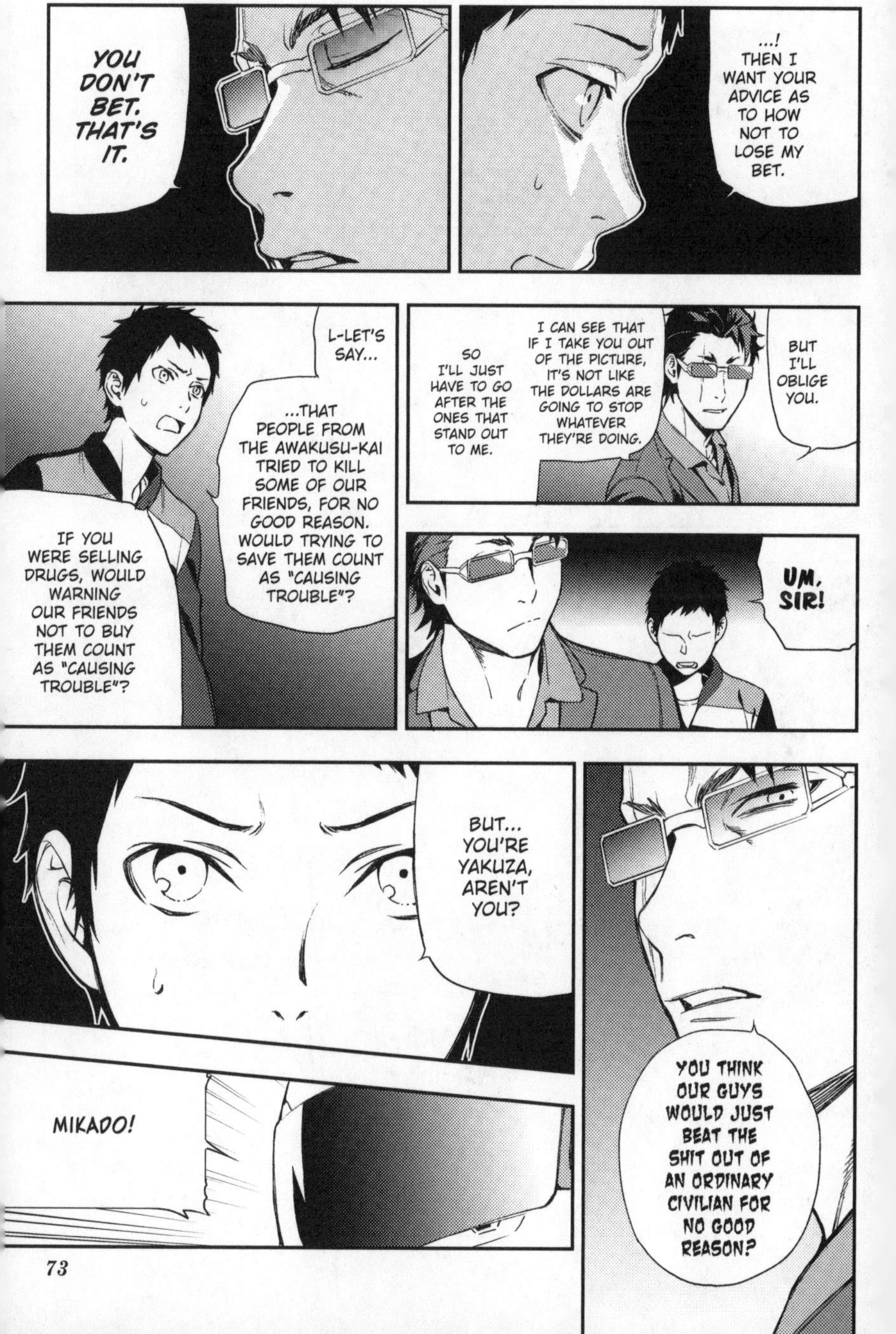
...! THEN I WANT YOUR ADVICE AS TO HOW NOT TO LOSE MY BET.
YOU DON'T BET. THAT'S IT.
BUT I'LL OBLIGE YOU.
I CAN SEE THAT IF I TAKE YOU OUT OF THE PICTURE, IT'S NOT LIKE THE DOLLARS ARE GOING TO STOP WHATEVER THEY'RE DOING.
SO I'LL JUST HAVE TO GO AFTER THE ONES THAT STAND OUT TO ME.
UM, SIR!
L-LET'S SAY...
...THAT PEOPLE FROM THE AWAKUSU-KAI TRIED TO KILL SOME OF OUR FRIENDS, FOR NO GOOD REASON. WOULD TRYING TO SAVE THEM COUNT AS "CAUSING TROUBLE"?
IF YOU WERE SELLING DRUGS, WOULD WARNING OUR FRIENDS NOT TO BUY THEM COUNT AS "CAUSING TROUBLE"?
YOU THINK OUR GUYS WOULD JUST BEAT THE SHIT OUT OF AN ORDINARY CIVILIAN FOR NO GOOD REASON?
BUT... YOU'RE YAKUZA, AREN'T YOU?
MIKADO!

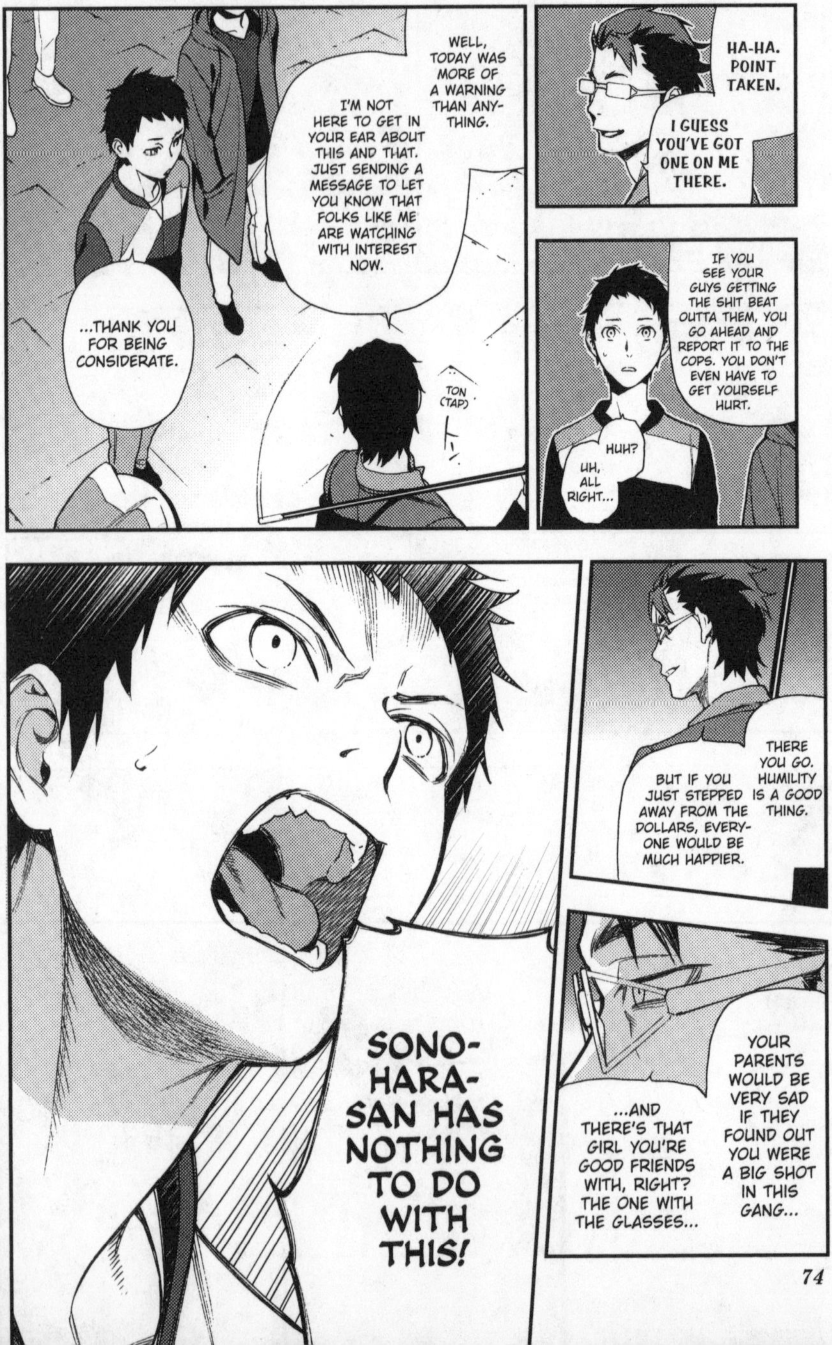

HA-HA. POINT TAKEN.
I GUESS YOU'VE GOT ONE ON ME THERE.
IF YOU SEE YOUR GUYS GETTING THE SHIT BEAT OUTTA THEM, YOU GO AHEAD AND REPORT IT TO THE COPS. YOU DON'T EVEN HAVE TO GET YOURSELF HURT.
HUH?
UH, ALL RIGHT...
WELL, TODAY WAS MORE OF A WARNING THAN ANYTHING.
I'M NOT HERE TO GET IN YOUR EAR ABOUT THIS AND THAT. JUST SENDING A MESSAGE TO LET YOU KNOW THAT FOLKS LIKE ME ARE WATCHING WITH INTEREST NOW.
TON (TAP)
...THANK YOU FOR BEING CONSIDERATE.
THERE YOU GO. HUMILITY IS A GOOD THING.
BUT IF YOU JUST STEPPED AWAY FROM THE DOLLARS, EVERYONE WOULD BE MUCH HAPPIER.
YOUR PARENTS WOULD BE VERY SAD IF THEY FOUND OUT YOU WERE A BIG SHOT IN THIS GANG...
...AND THERE'S THAT GIRL YOU'RE GOOD FRIENDS WITH, RIGHT? THE ONE WITH THE GLASSES...
SONO-HARA-SAN HAS NOTHING TO DO WITH THIS!

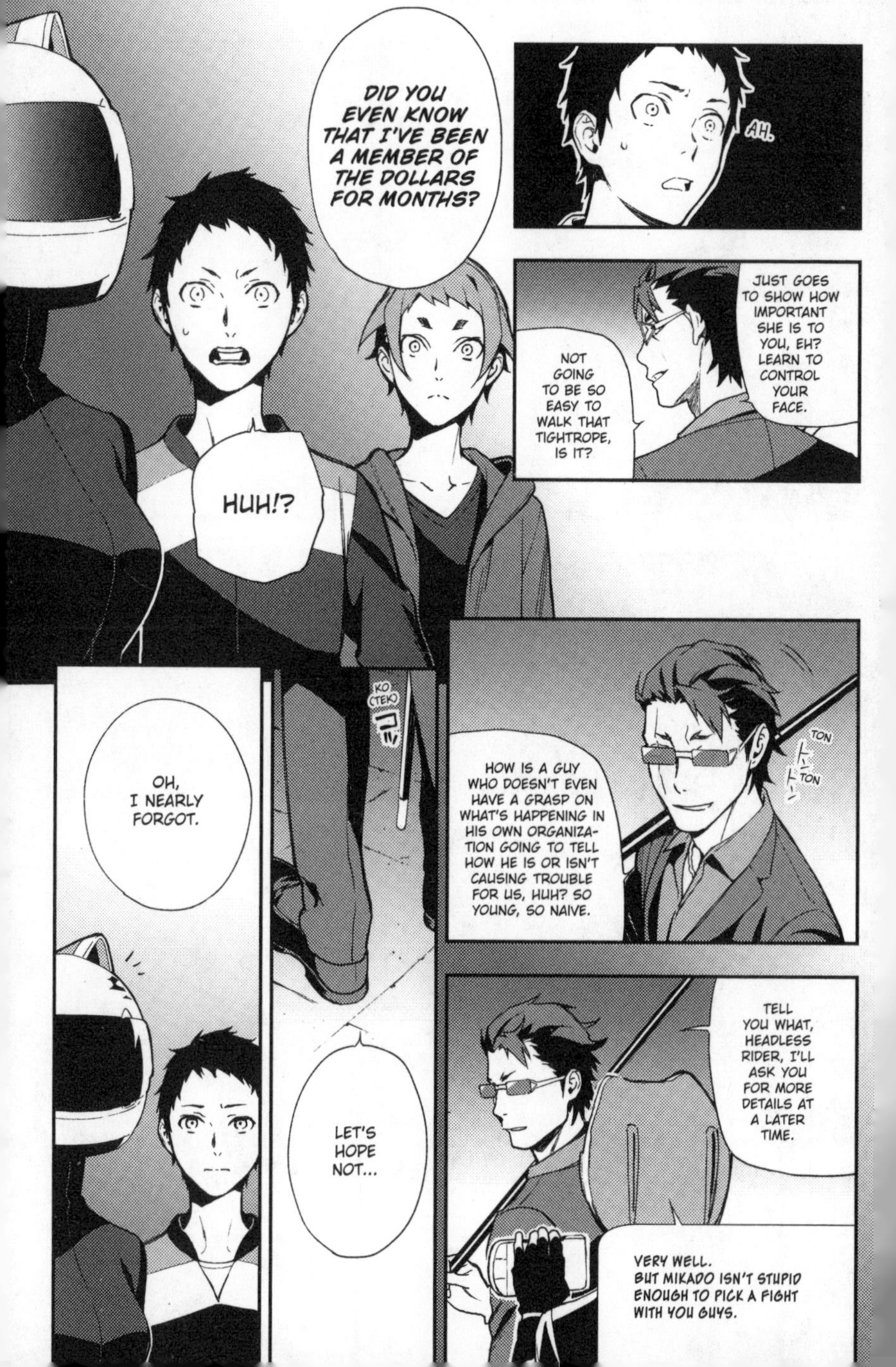
AH.
JUST GOES TO SHOW HOW IMPORTANT SHE IS TO YOU, EH? LEARN TO CONTROL YOUR FACE.
NOT GOING TO BE SO EASY TO WALK THAT TIGHTROPE, IS IT?
DID YOU EVEN KNOW THAT I'VE BEEN A MEMBER OF THE DOLLARS FOR MONTHS?
HUH!?
HOW IS A GUY WHO DOESN'T EVEN HAVE A GRASP ON WHAT'S HAPPENING IN HIS OWN ORGANIZA-TION GOING TO TELL HOW HE IS OR ISN'T CAUSING TROUBLE FOR US, HUH? SO YOUNG, SO NAIVE.
TON TON
TELL YOU WHAT, HEADLESS RIDER, I'LL ASK YOU FOR MORE DETAILS AT A LATER TIME.
VERY WELL. BUT MIKADO ISN'T STUPID ENOUGH TO PICK A FIGHT WITH YOU GUYS.
LET'S HOPE NOT...
KO TEK
OH, I NEARLY FORGOT.

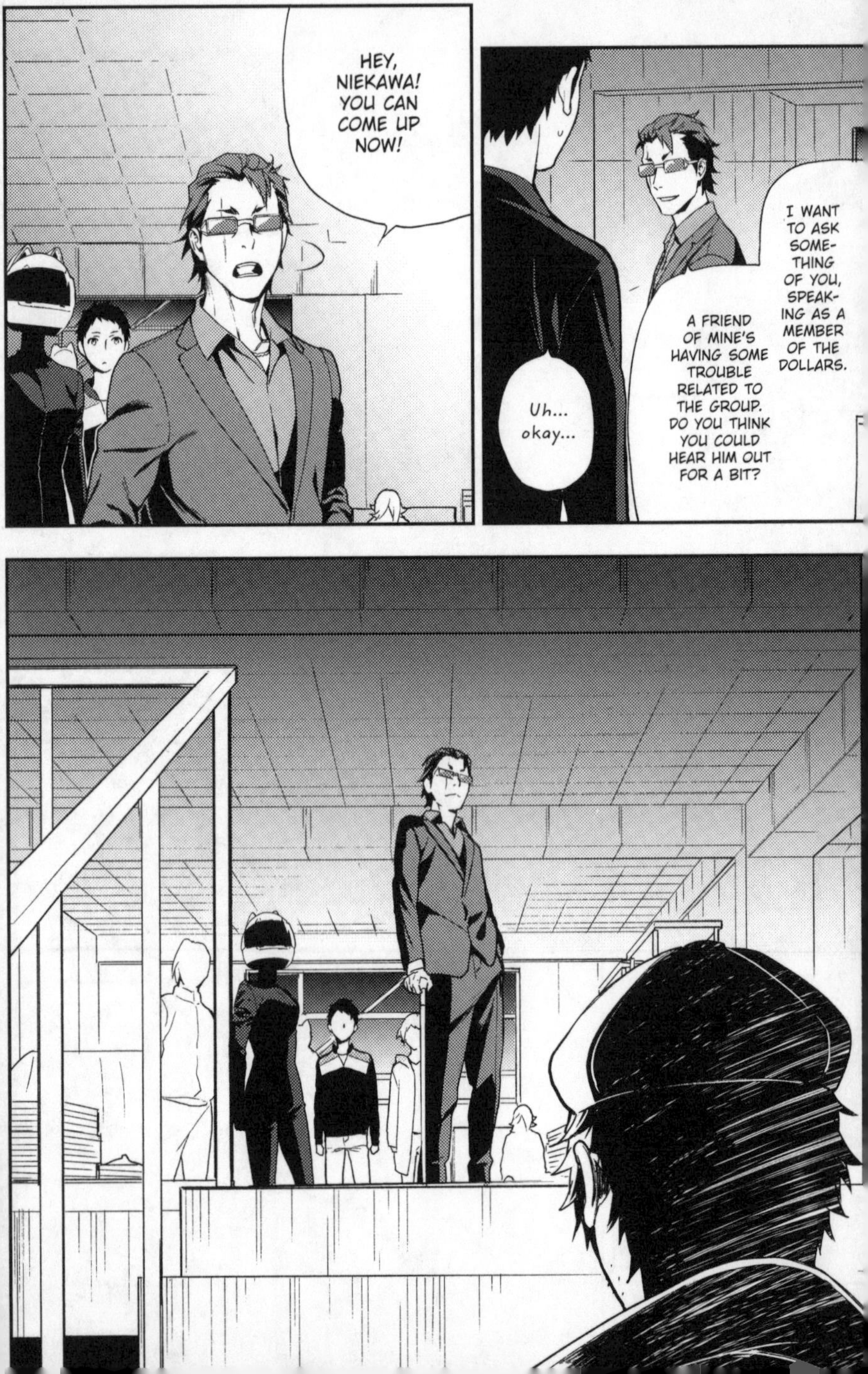
I WANT TO ASK SOME-THING OF YOU, SPEAK-ING AS A MEMBER OF THE DOLLARS.
A FRIEND OF MINE'S HAVING SOME TROUBLE RELATED TO THE GROUP. DO YOU THINK YOU COULD HEAR HIM OUT FOR A BIT?
Uh... okay...
HEY, NIEKAWA! YOU CAN COME UP NOW!

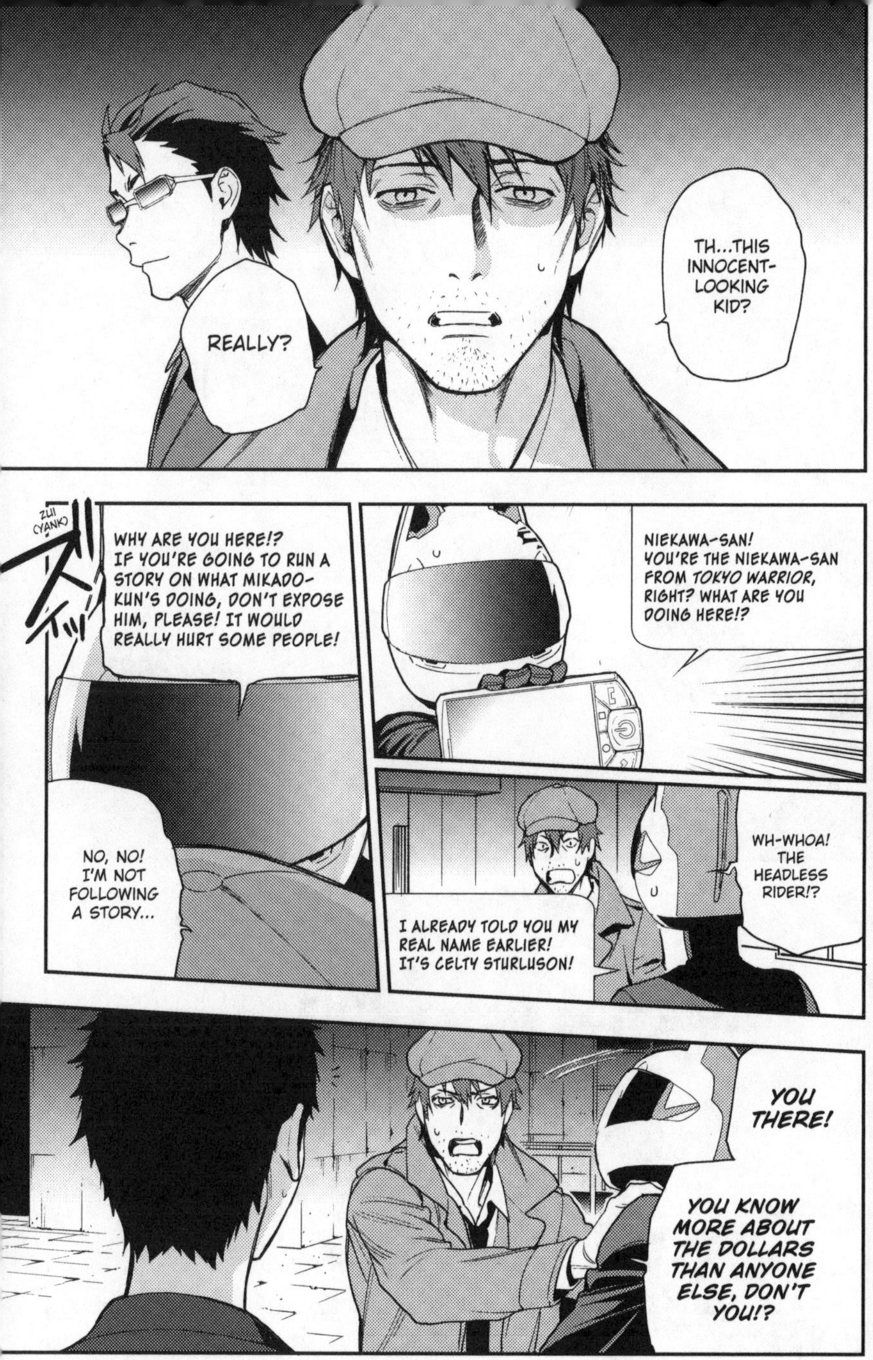
TH...THIS INNOCENT-LOOKING KID?
REALLY?
NIEKAWA-SAN! YOU'RE THE NIEKAWA-SAN FROM *TOKYO WARRIOR*, RIGHT? WHAT ARE YOU DOING HERE!?
WH-WHOA! THE HEADLESS RIDER!?
I ALREADY TOLD YOU MY REAL NAME EARLIER! IT'S CELTY STURLUSON!
ZUI (YANK)
WHY ARE YOU HERE!? IF YOU'RE GOING TO RUN A STORY ON WHAT MIKADO-KUN'S DOING, DON'T EXPOSE HIM, PLEASE! IT WOULD REALLY HURT SOME PEOPLE!
NO, NO! I'M NOT FOLLOWING A STORY...
YOU THERE!
YOU KNOW MORE ABOUT THE DOLLARS THAN ANYONE ELSE, DON'T YOU!?

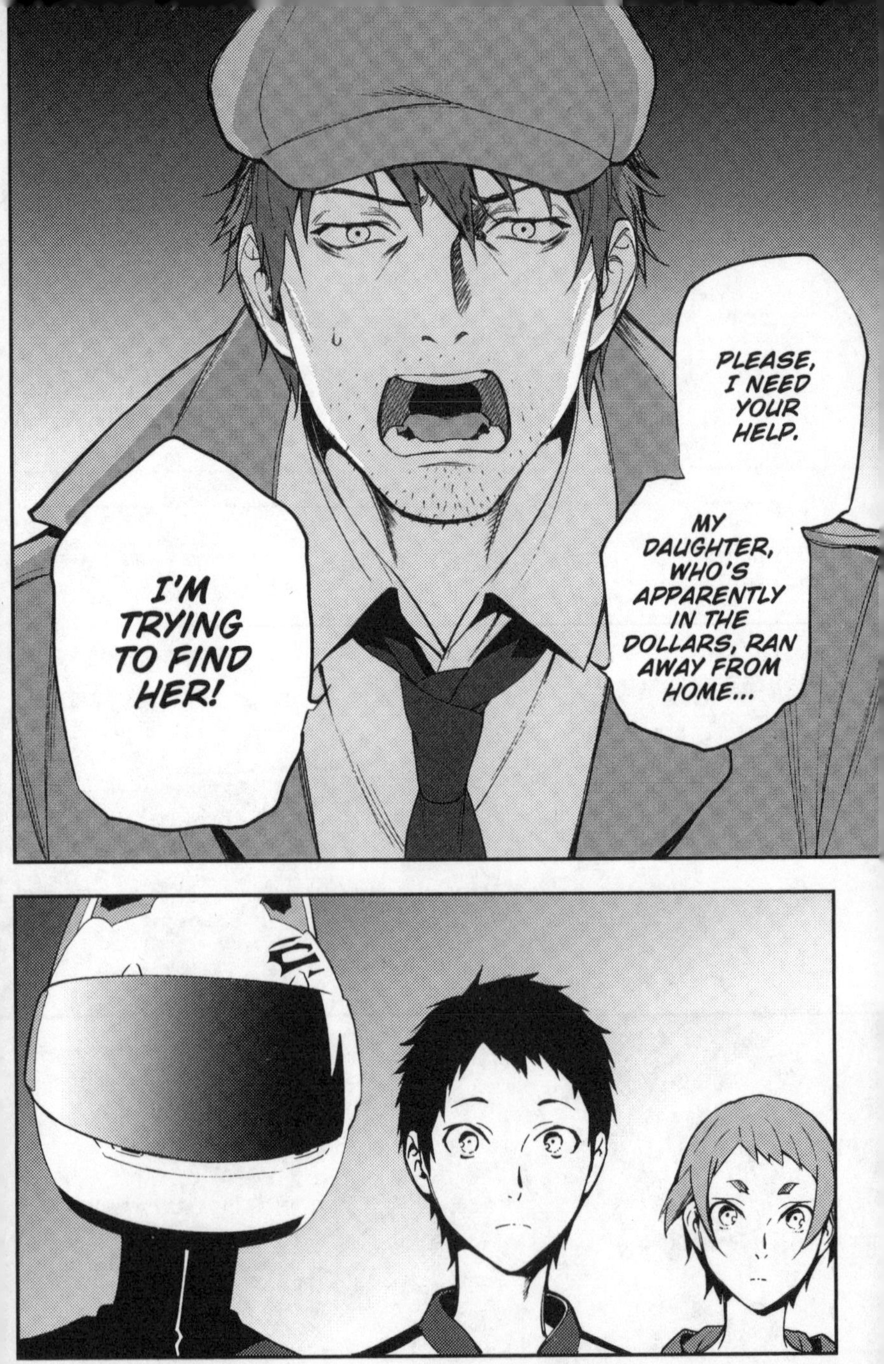
PLEASE, I NEED YOUR HELP.
MY DAUGHTER, WHO'S APPARENTLY IN THE DOLLARS, RAN AWAY FROM HOME...
I'M TRYING TO FIND HER!

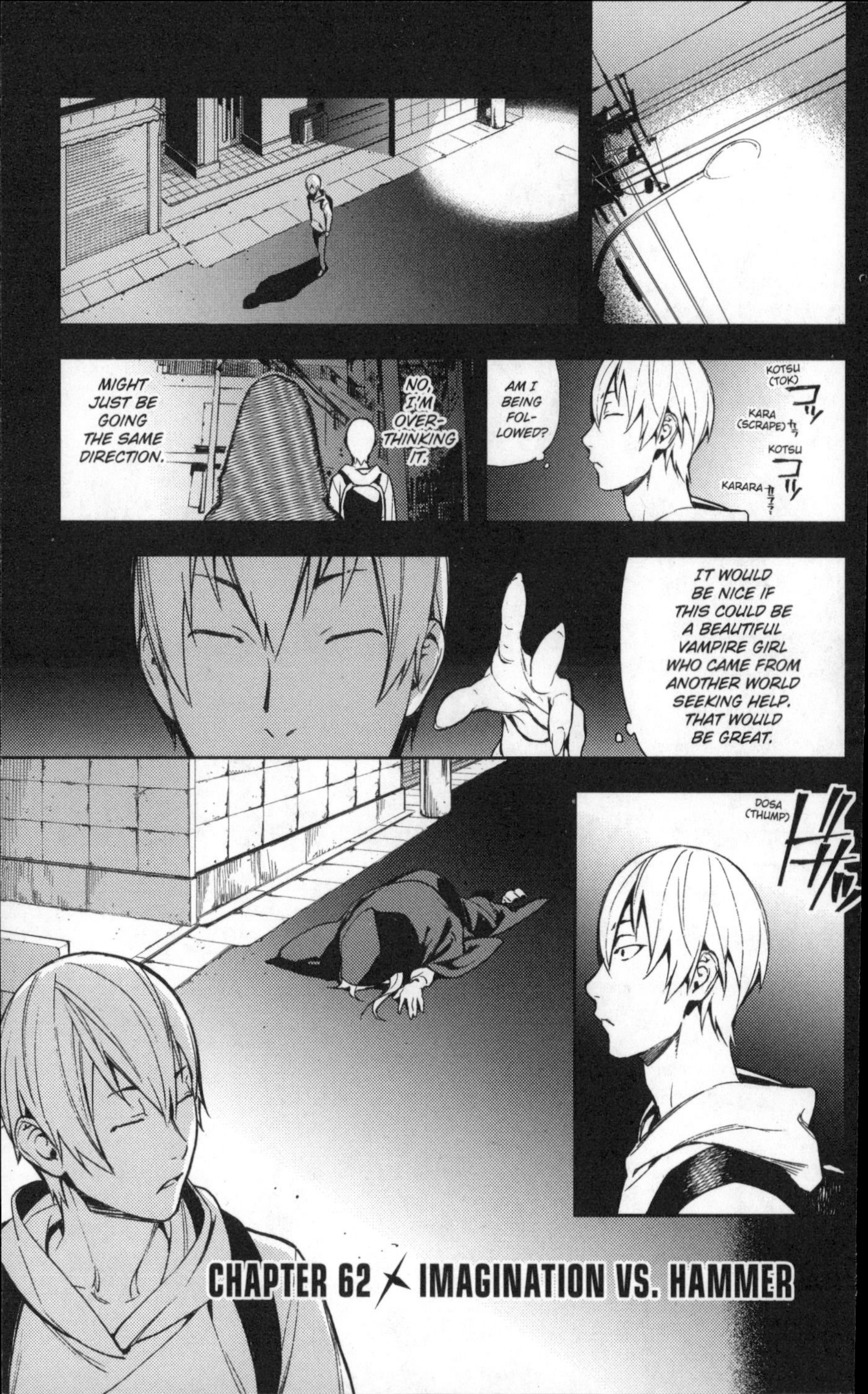
KOTSU (TOK)
KARA (SCRAPE)
KOTSU
KARARA
AM I BEING FOL-LOWED?
NO, I'M OVER-THINKING IT.
MIGHT JUST BE GOING THE SAME DIRECTION.
IT WOULD BE NICE IF THIS COULD BE A BEAUTIFUL VAMPIRE GIRL WHO CAME FROM ANOTHER WORLD SEEKING HELP. THAT WOULD BE GREAT.
DOSA (THUMP)
CHAPTER 62 IMAGINATION VS. HAMMER

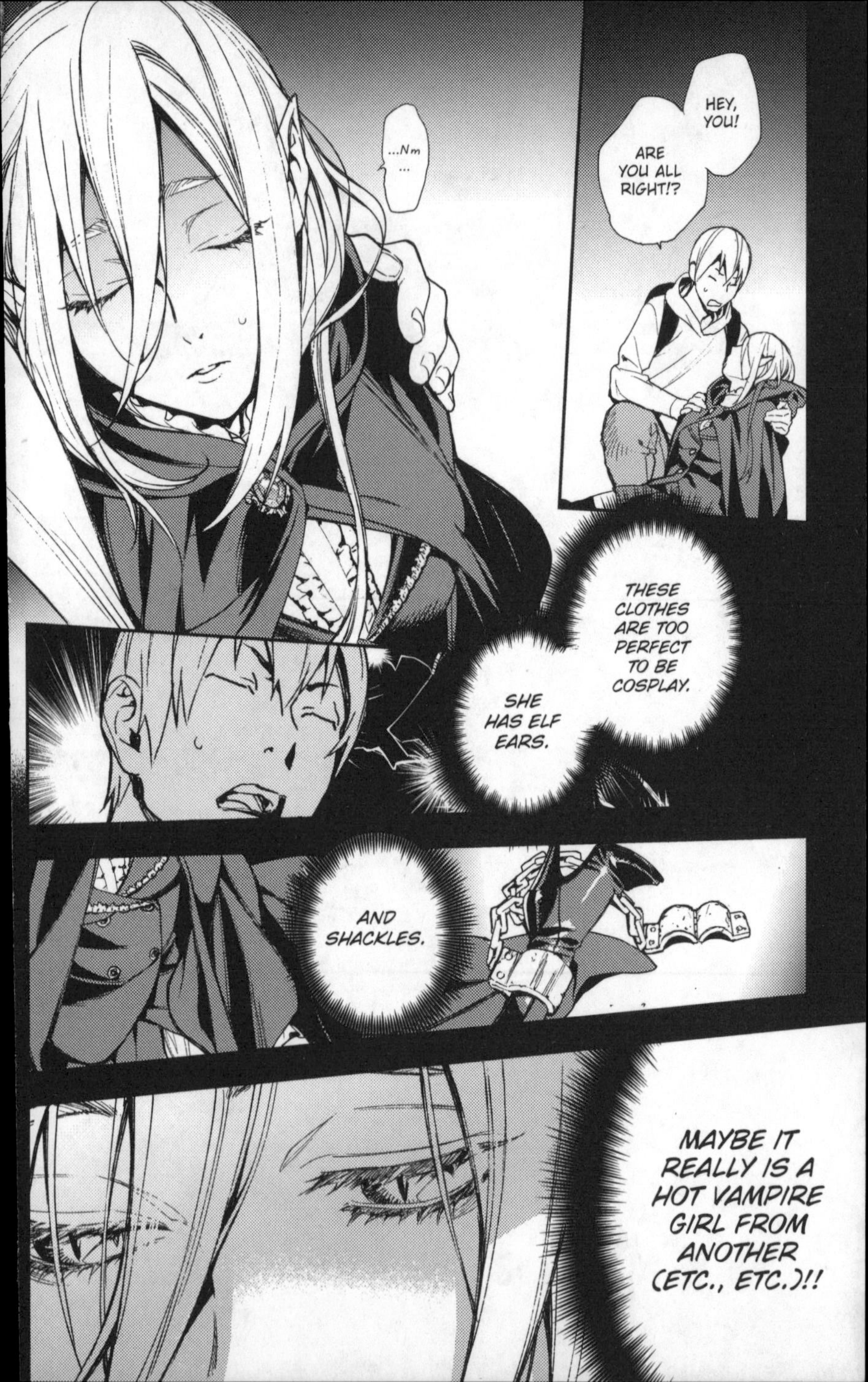
HEY, YOU!
ARE YOU ALL RIGHT!?
...Nm ...
THESE CLOTHES ARE TOO PERFECT TO BE COSPLAY.
SHE HAS ELF EARS.
AND SHACKLES.
MAYBE IT REALLY IS A HOT VAMPIRE GIRL FROM ANOTHER (ETC., ETC.)!!

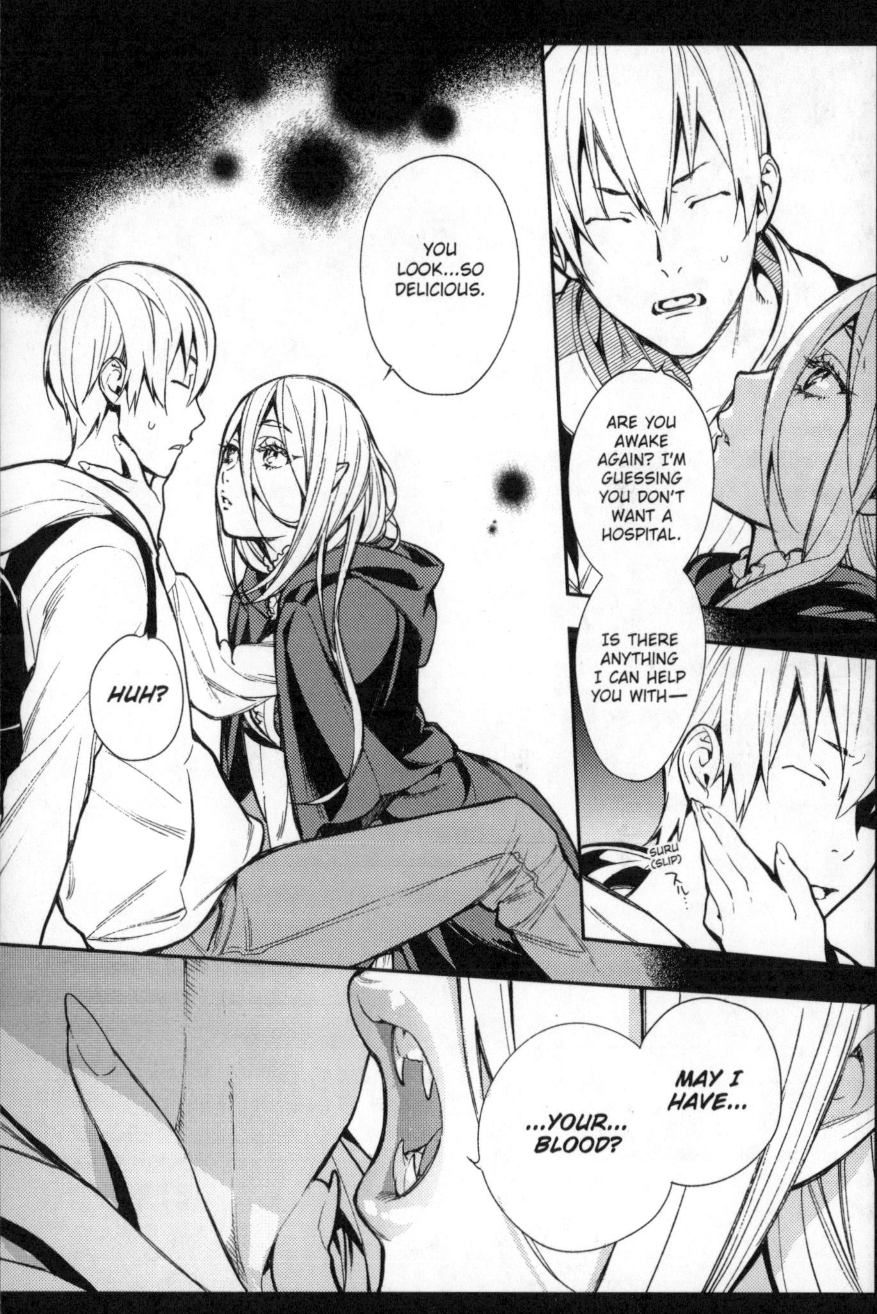
ARE YOU AWAKE AGAIN? I'M GUESSING YOU DON'T WANT A HOSPITAL.
IS THERE ANYTHING I CAN HELP YOU WITH—
SURU (SLIP)
スル…
YOU LOOK...SO DELICIOUS.
HUH?
MAY I HAVE...
...YOUR... BLOOD?

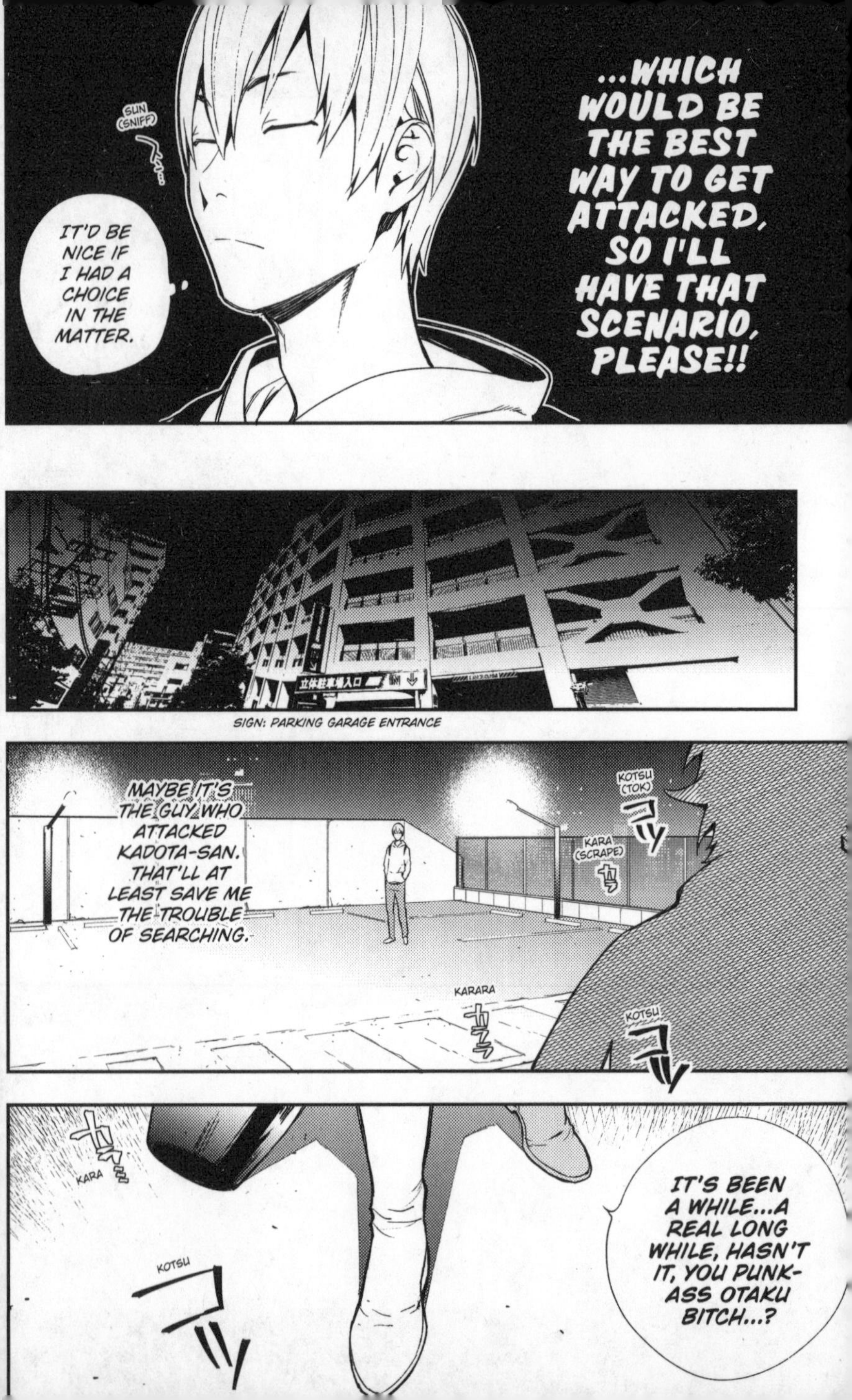
...WHICH WOULD BE THE BEST WAY TO GET ATTACKED, SO I'LL HAVE THAT SCENARIO, PLEASE!!
SUN (SNIFF)
IT'D BE NICE IF I HAD A CHOICE IN THE MATTER.
立体駐車場入口
SIGN: PARKING GARAGE ENTRANCE
KOTSU (TOK)
KARA (SCRAPE)
MAYBE IT'S THE GUY WHO ATTACKED KADOTA-SAN. THAT'LL AT LEAST SAVE ME THE TROUBLE OF SEARCHING.
KARARA
KOTSU
IT'S BEEN A WHILE...A REAL LONG WHILE, HASN'T IT, YOU PUNK-ASS OTAKU BITCH...?
KOTSU
KARA

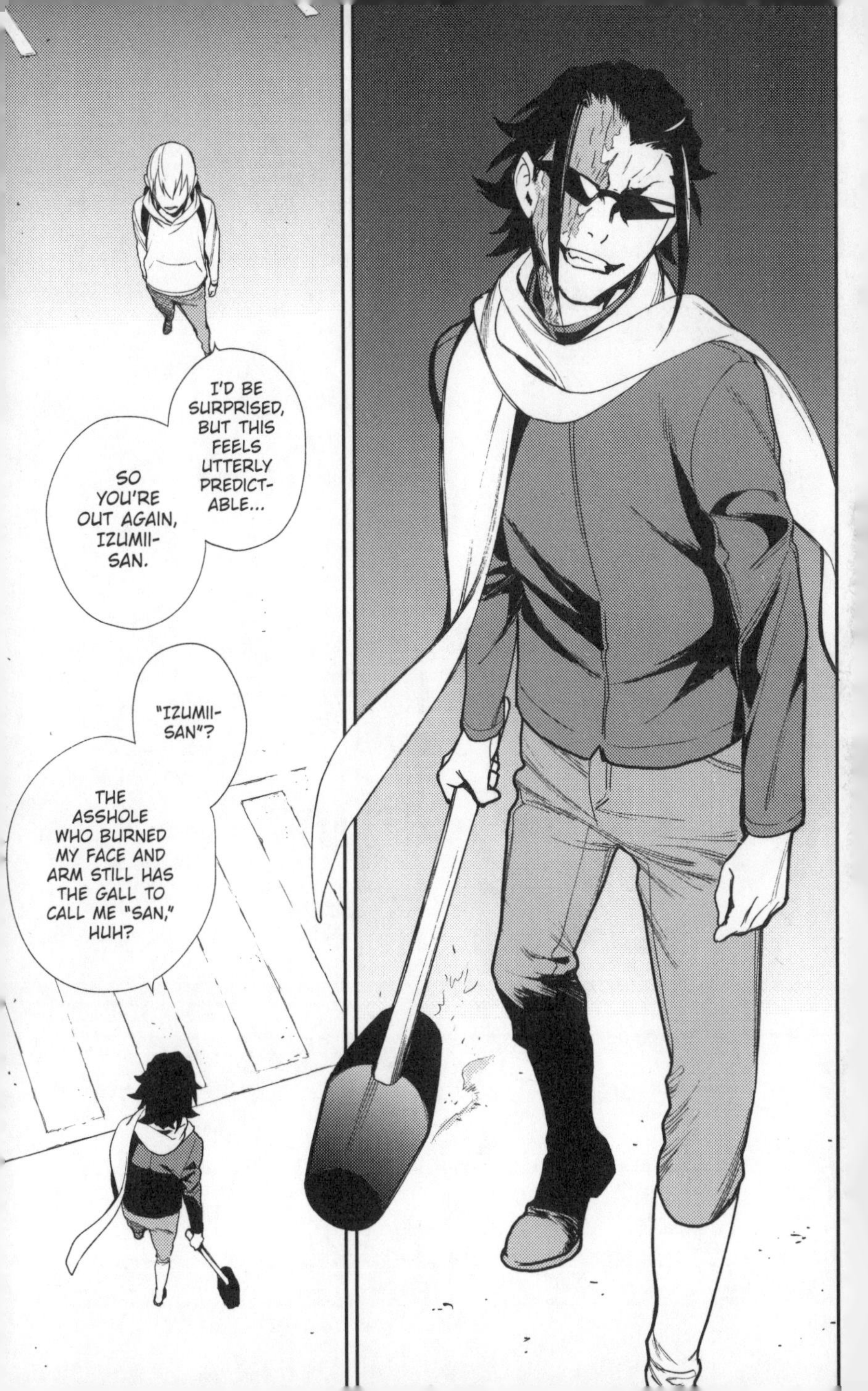
I'D BE SURPRISED, BUT THIS FEELS UTTERLY PREDICT-ABLE...
SO YOU'RE OUT AGAIN, IZUMII-SAN.
"IZUMII-SAN"?
THE ASSHOLE WHO BURNED MY FACE AND ARM STILL HAS THE GALL TO CALL ME "SAN," HUH?

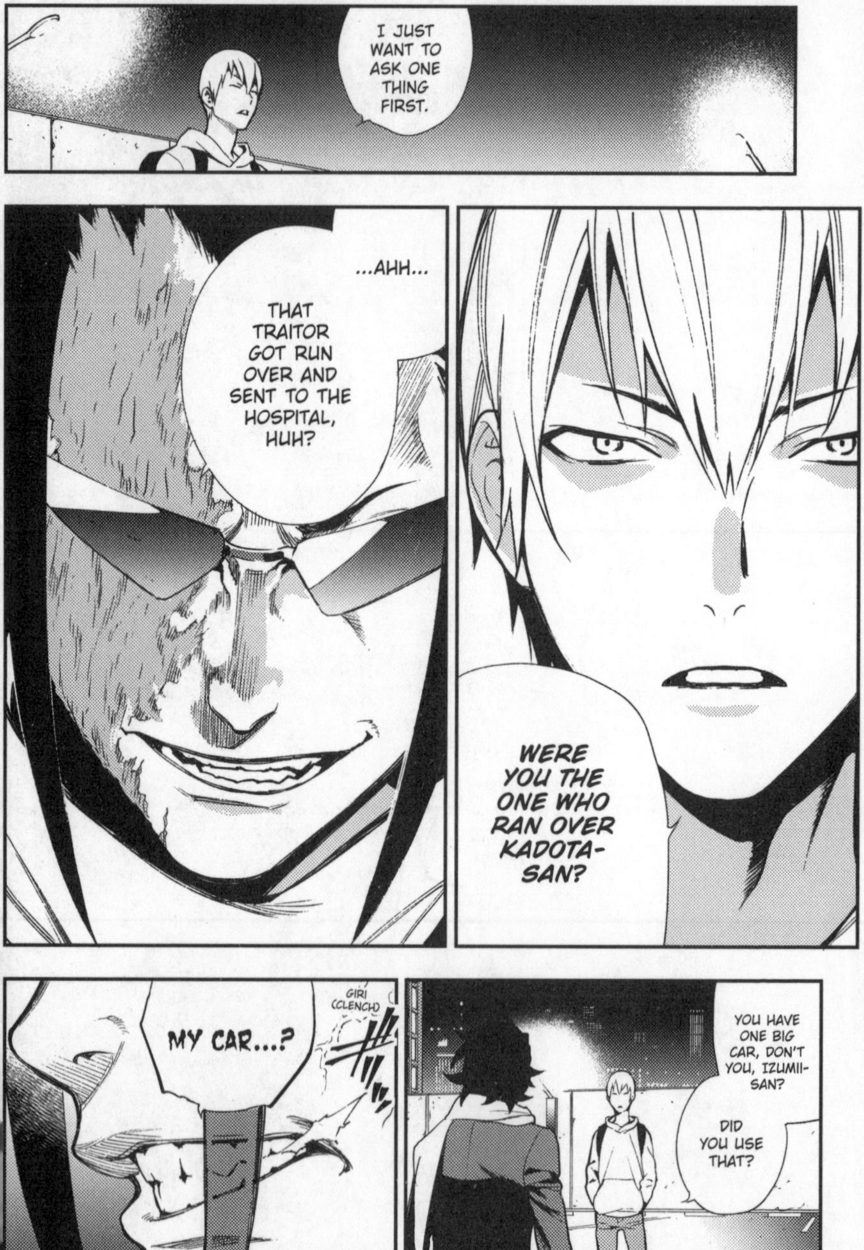
I JUST WANT TO ASK ONE THING FIRST.
WERE YOU THE ONE WHO RAN OVER KADOTA-SAN?
...AHH...
THAT TRAITOR GOT RUN OVER AND SENT TO THE HOSPITAL, HUH?
YOU HAVE ONE BIG CAR, DON'T YOU, IZUMII-SAN?
DID YOU USE THAT?
GIRI (CLENCH)
MY CAR...?

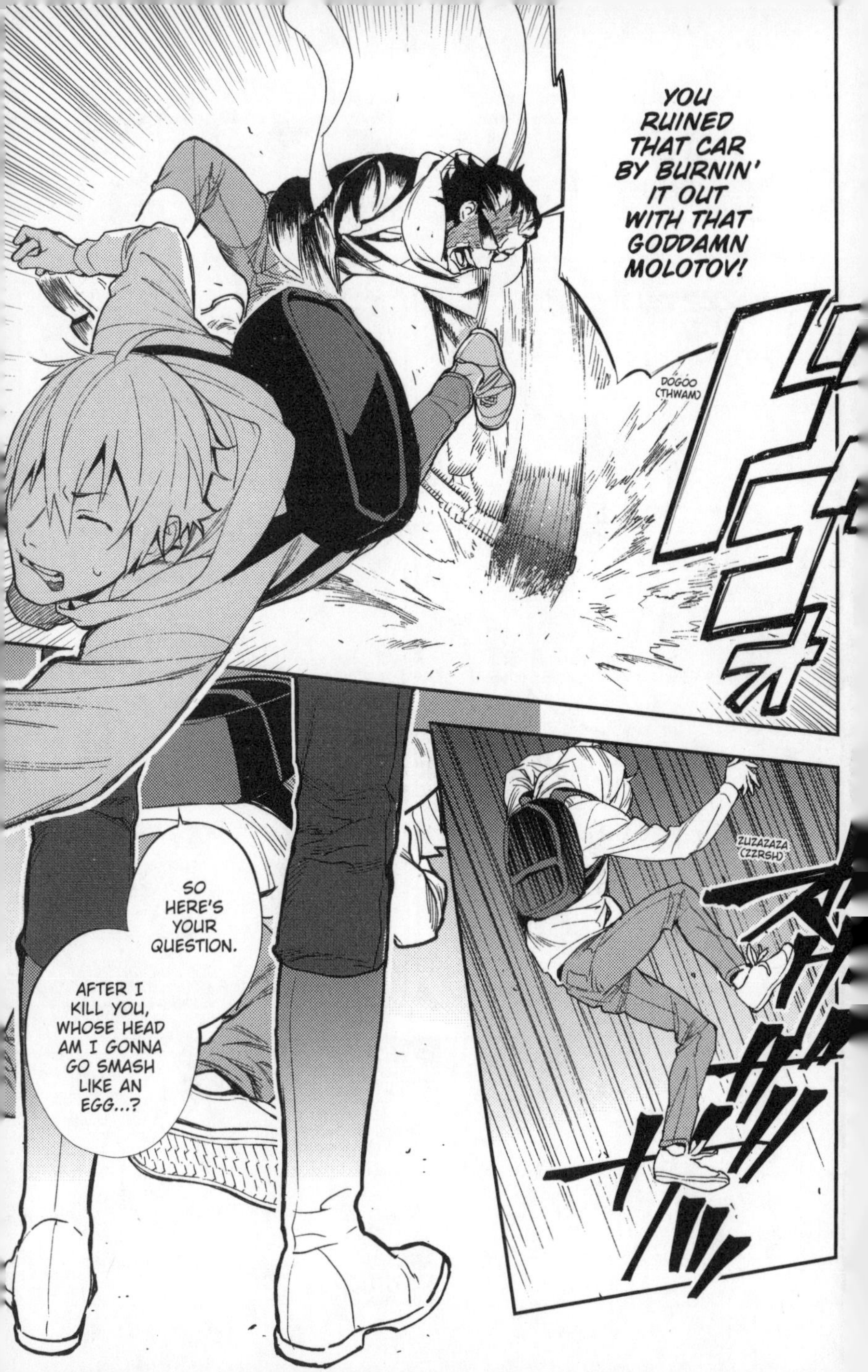
YOU RUINED THAT CAR BY BURNIN' IT OUT WITH THAT GODDAMN MOLOTOV!
DOGOO (THWAM)
ZUZAZAZA (ZZRSH)
SO HERE'S YOUR QUESTION.
AFTER I KILL YOU, WHOSE HEAD AM I GONNA GO SMASH LIKE AN EGG...?

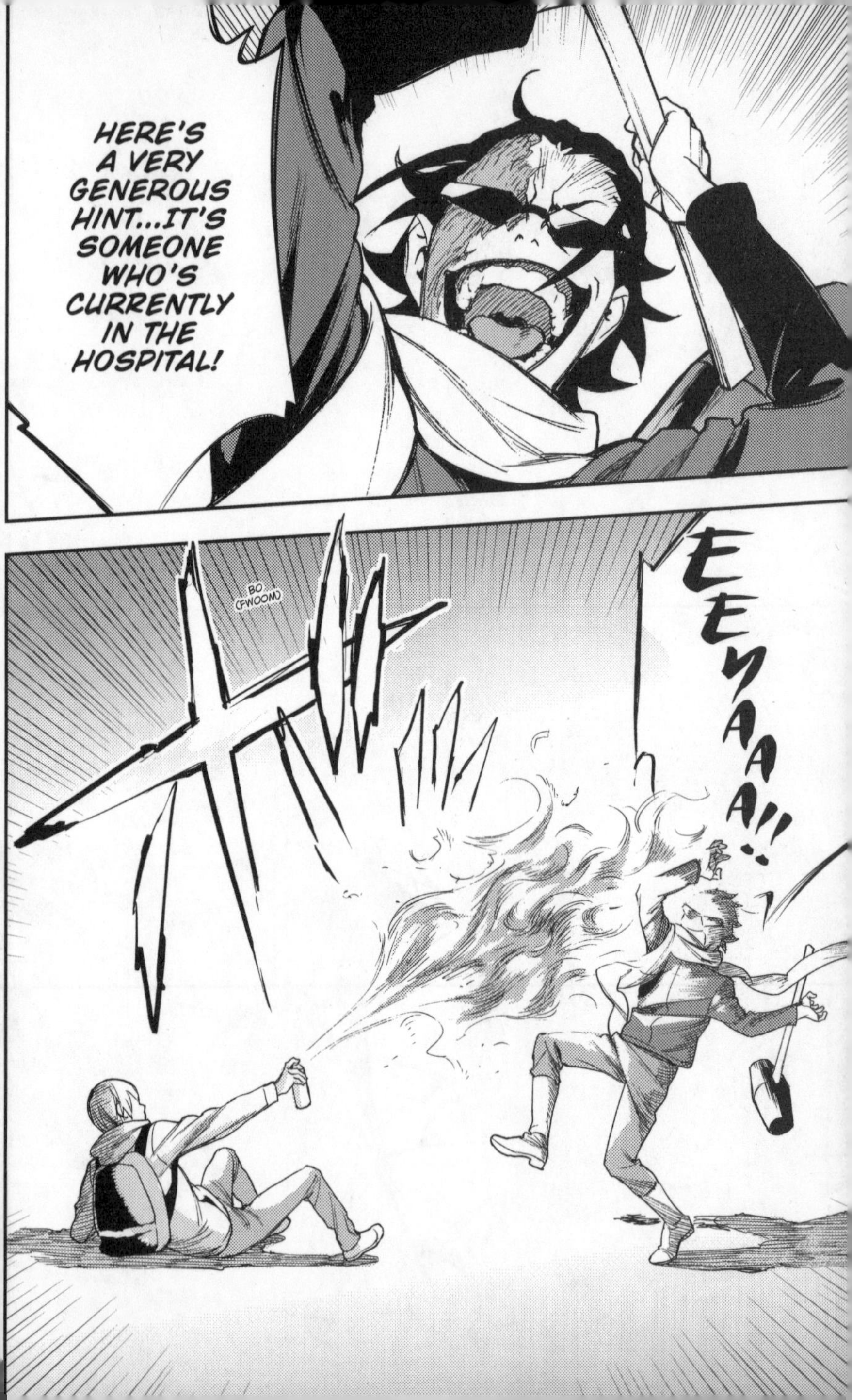
HERE'S A VERY GENEROUS HINT...IT'S SOMEONE WHO'S CURRENTLY IN THE HOSPITAL!
EEYAAAA!!
BO (FWOOM)

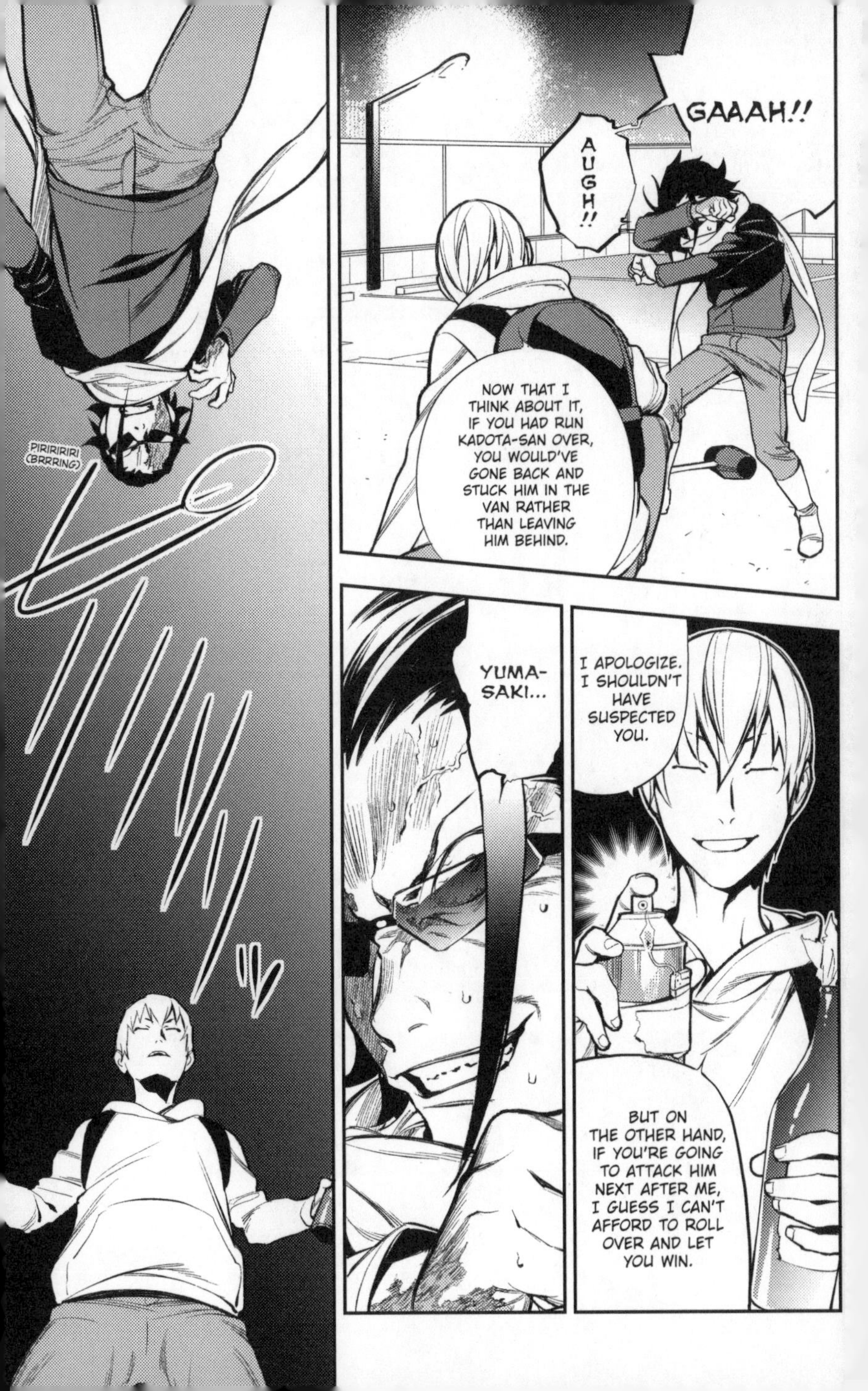
GAAAH!!
AUGH!!
NOW THAT I THINK ABOUT IT, IF YOU HAD RUN KADOTA-SAN OVER, YOU WOULD'VE GONE BACK AND STUCK HIM IN THE VAN RATHER THAN LEAVING HIM BEHIND.
I APOLOGIZE. I SHOULDN'T HAVE SUSPECTED YOU.
BUT ON THE OTHER HAND, IF YOU'RE GOING TO ATTACK HIM NEXT AFTER ME, I GUESS I CAN'T AFFORD TO ROLL OVER AND LET YOU WIN.
YUMA-SAKI...
PIRIRIRIRI (BRRRING)

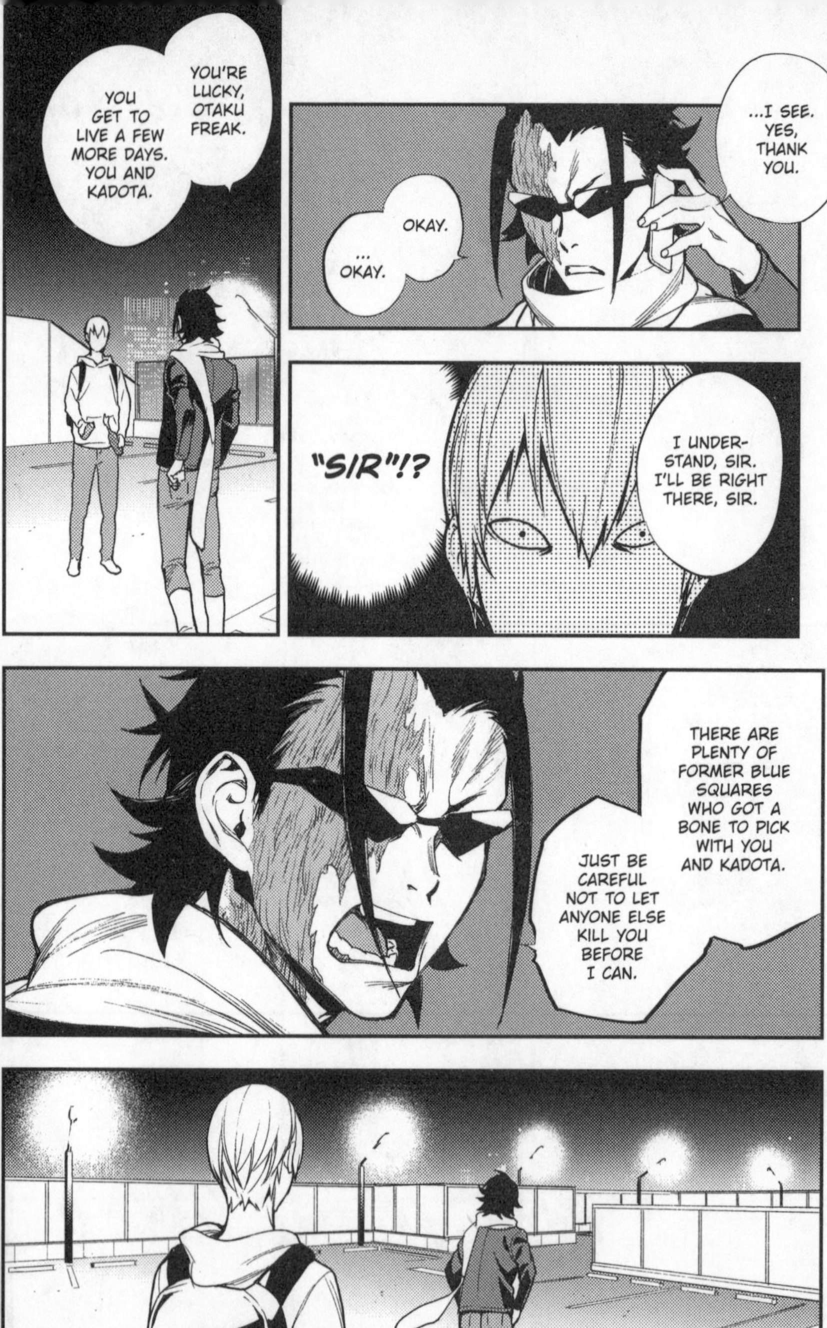
...I SEE. YES, THANK YOU.
OKAY.
... OKAY.
I UNDER-STAND, SIR. I'LL BE RIGHT THERE, SIR.
"SIR"!?
YOU'RE LUCKY, OTAKU FREAK.
YOU GET TO LIVE A FEW MORE DAYS. YOU AND KADOTA.
THERE ARE PLENTY OF FORMER BLUE SQUARES WHO GOT A BONE TO PICK WITH YOU AND KADOTA.
JUST BE CAREFUL NOT TO LET ANYONE ELSE KILL YOU BEFORE I CAN.

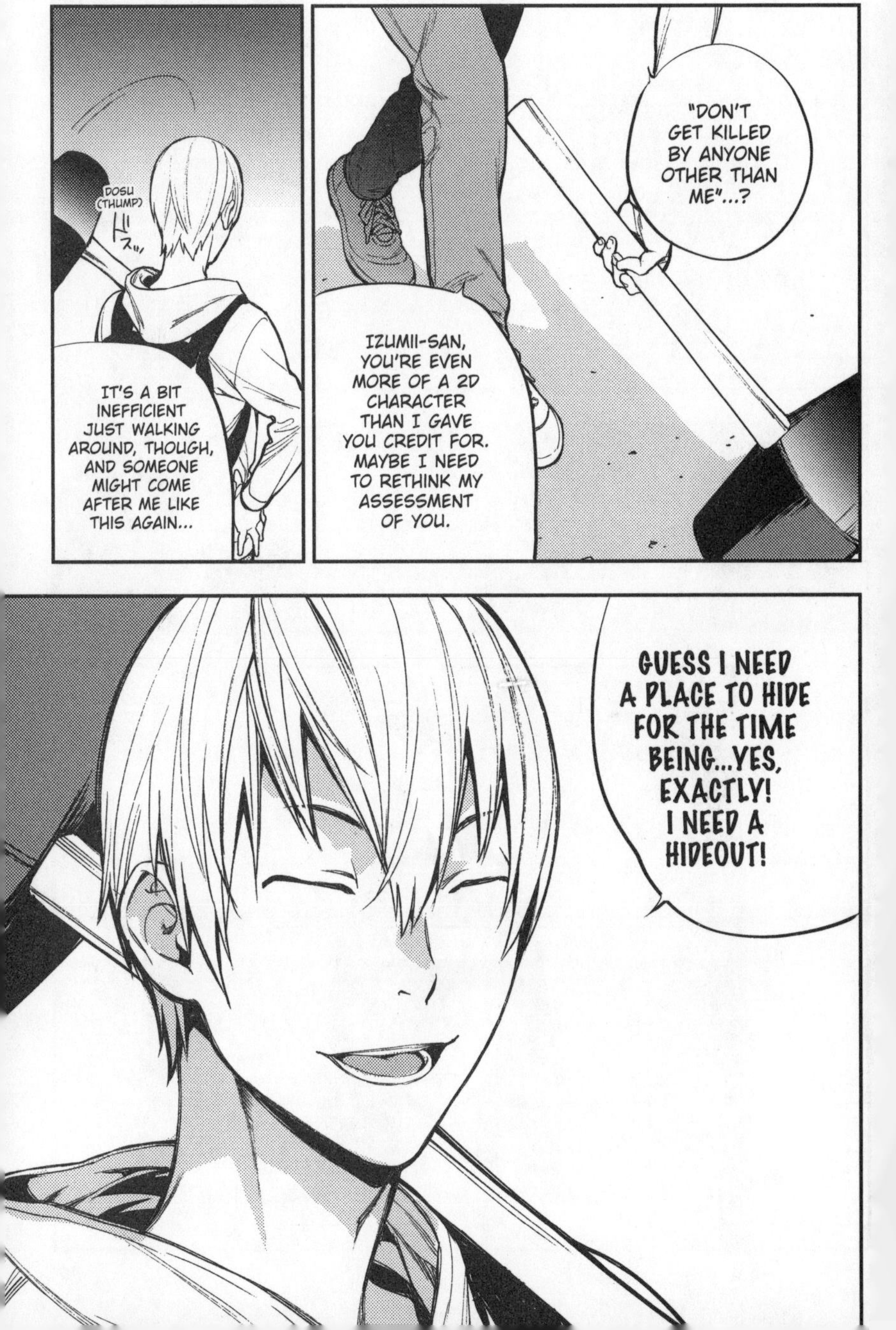
"DON'T GET KILLED BY ANYONE OTHER THAN ME"...?
IZUMII-SAN, YOU'RE EVEN MORE OF A 2D CHARACTER THAN I GAVE YOU CREDIT FOR. MAYBE I NEED TO RETHINK MY ASSESSMENT OF YOU.
DOSU (THUMP)
ドスッ
IT'S A BIT INEFFICIENT JUST WALKING AROUND, THOUGH, AND SOMEONE MIGHT COME AFTER ME LIKE THIS AGAIN...
GUESS I NEED A PLACE TO HIDE FOR THE TIME BEING...YES, EXACTLY! I NEED A HIDEOUT!

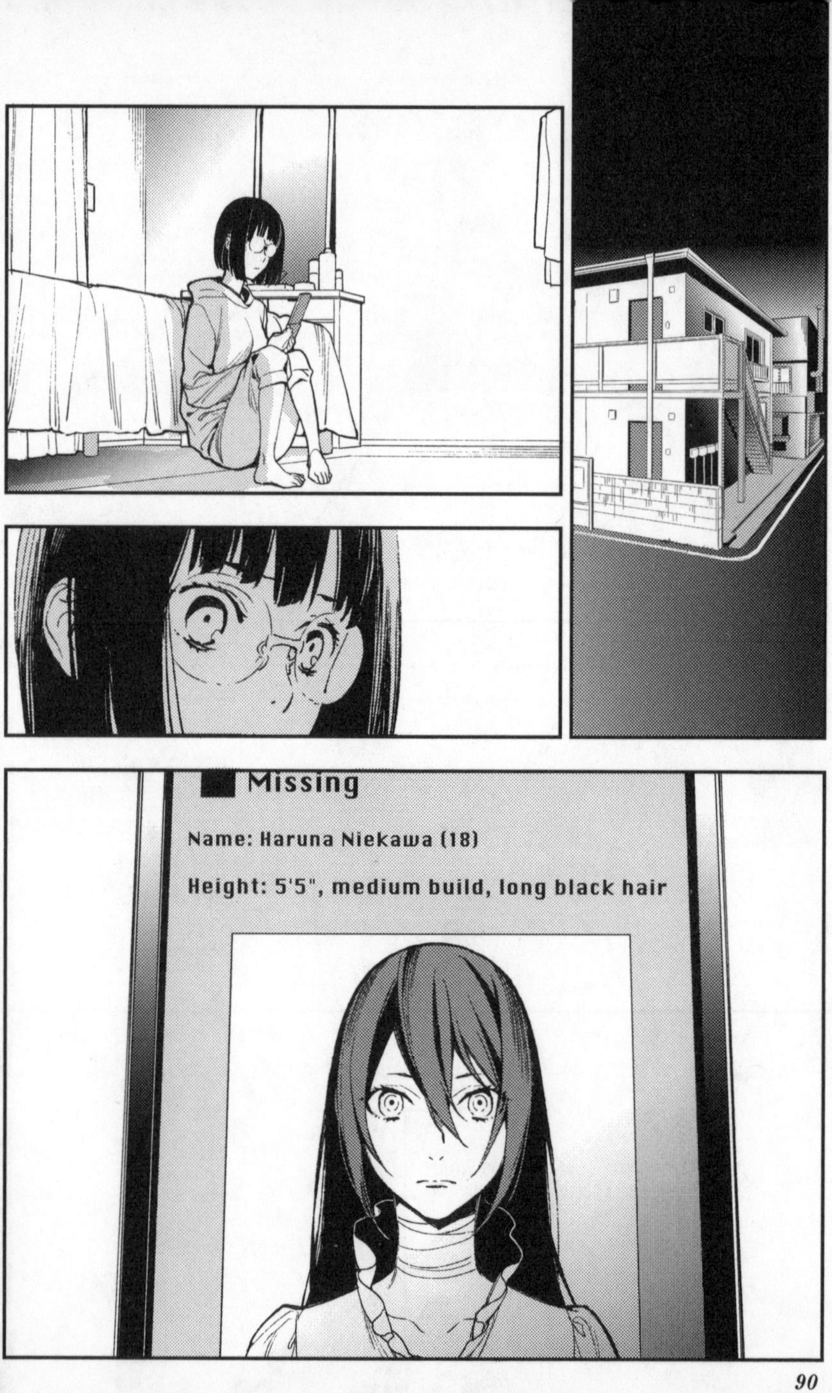
Missing
Name: Haruna Niekawa (18)
Height: 5'5", medium build, long black hair

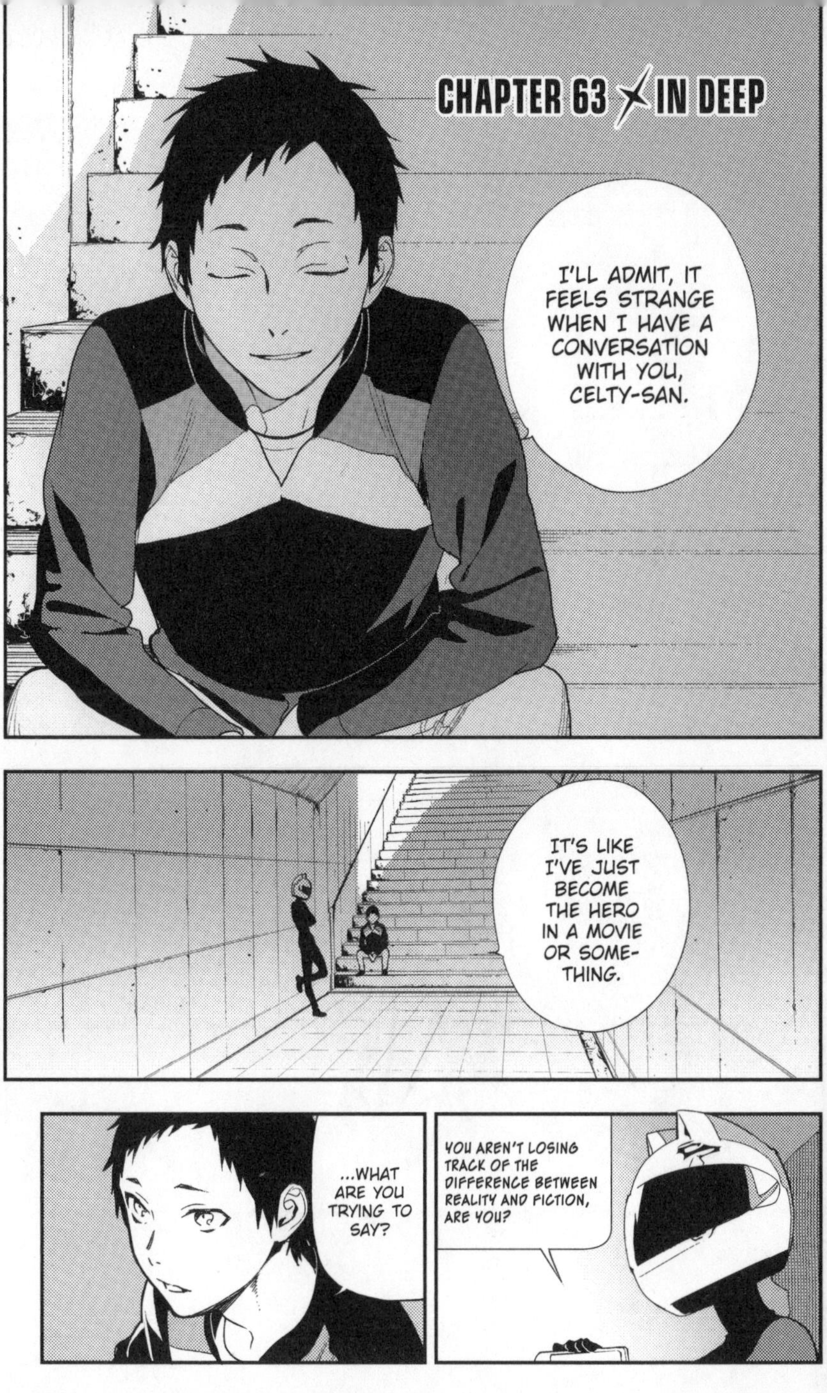
CHAPTER 63 IN DEEP
I'LL ADMIT, IT FEELS STRANGE WHEN I HAVE A CONVERSATION WITH YOU, CELTY-SAN.
IT'S LIKE I'VE JUST BECOME THE HERO IN A MOVIE OR SOME-THING.
YOU AREN'T LOSING TRACK OF THE DIFFERENCE BETWEEN REALITY AND FICTION, ARE YOU?
...WHAT ARE YOU TRYING TO SAY?

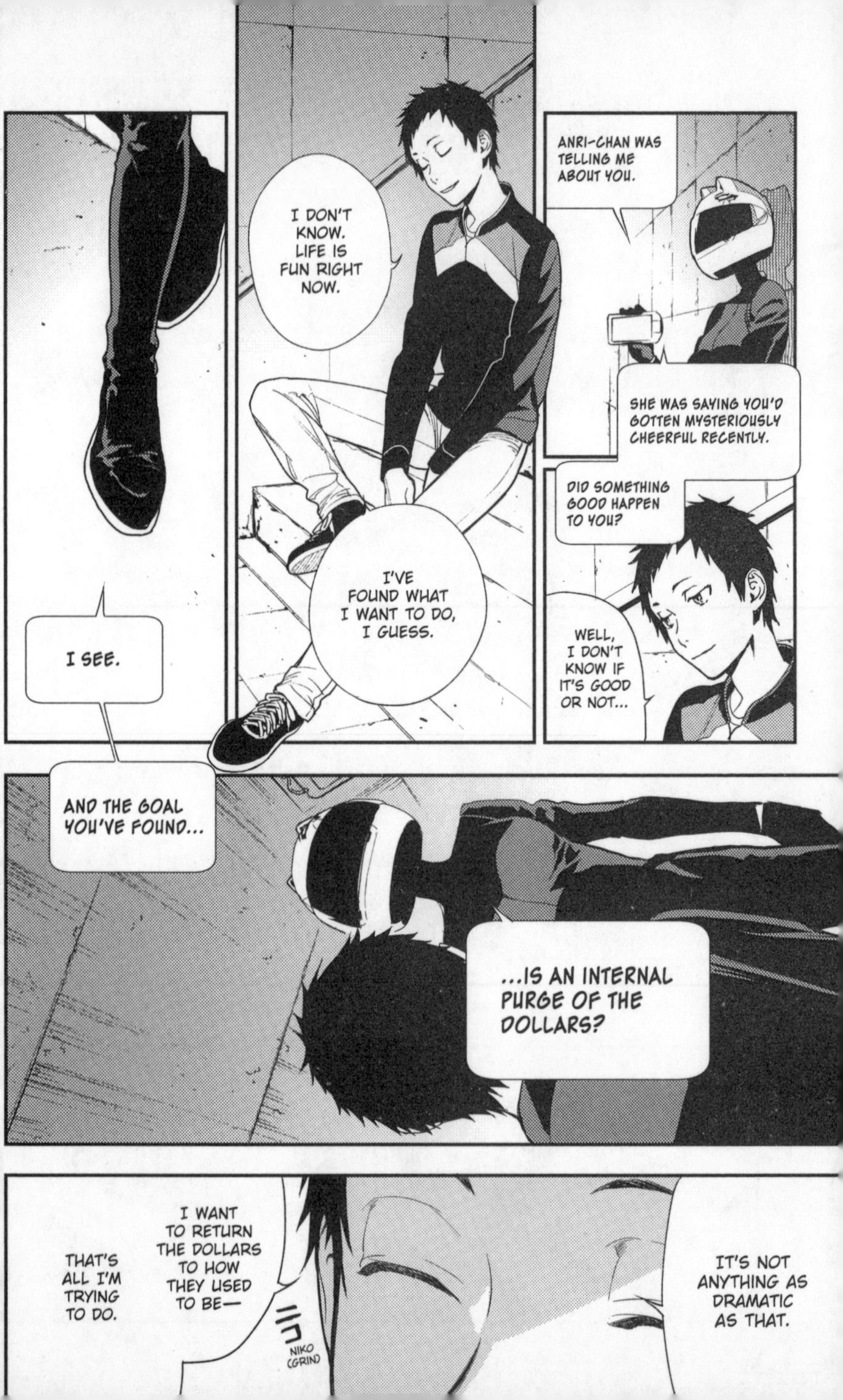
ANRI-CHAN WAS TELLING ME ABOUT YOU.
SHE WAS SAYING YOU'D GOTTEN MYSTERIOUSLY CHEERFUL RECENTLY.
DID SOMETHING GOOD HAPPEN TO YOU?
WELL, I DON'T KNOW IF IT'S GOOD OR NOT...
I DON'T KNOW. LIFE IS FUN RIGHT NOW.
I'VE FOUND WHAT I WANT TO DO, I GUESS.
I SEE.
AND THE GOAL YOU'VE FOUND...
...IS AN INTERNAL PURGE OF THE DOLLARS?
IT'S NOT ANYTHING AS DRAMATIC AS THAT.
ニコ
NIKO (GRIN)
I WANT TO RETURN THE DOLLARS TO HOW THEY USED TO BE—
THAT'S ALL I'M TRYING TO DO.

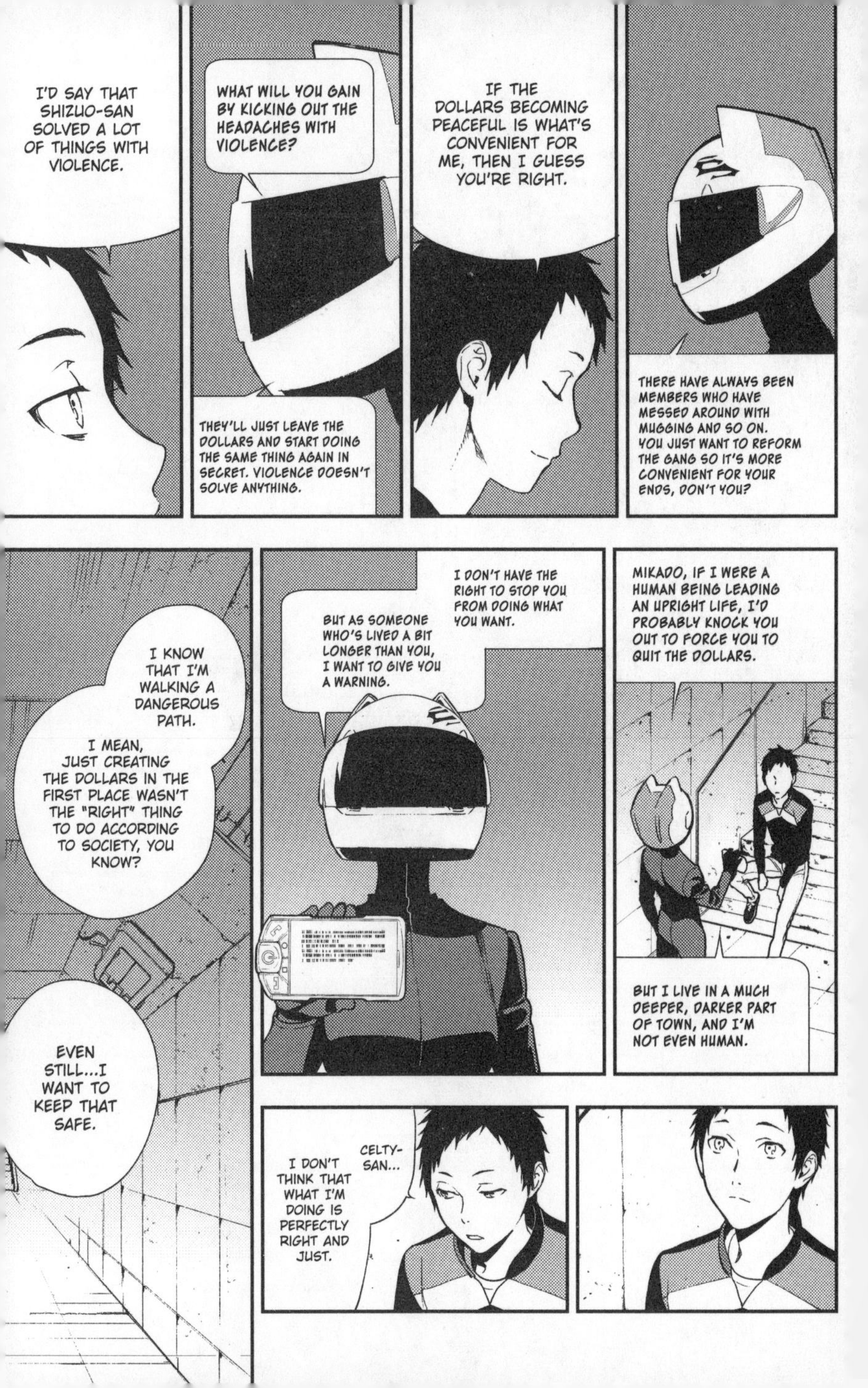
THERE HAVE ALWAYS BEEN MEMBERS WHO HAVE MESSED AROUND WITH MUGGING AND SO ON. YOU JUST WANT TO REFORM THE GANG SO IT'S MORE CONVENIENT FOR YOUR ENDS, DON'T YOU?
IF THE DOLLARS BECOMING PEACEFUL IS WHAT'S CONVENIENT FOR ME, THEN I GUESS YOU'RE RIGHT.
WHAT WILL YOU GAIN BY KICKING OUT THE HEADACHES WITH VIOLENCE?
THEY'LL JUST LEAVE THE DOLLARS AND START DOING THE SAME THING AGAIN IN SECRET. VIOLENCE DOESN'T SOLVE ANYTHING.
I'D SAY THAT SHIZUO-SAN SOLVED A LOT OF THINGS WITH VIOLENCE.
MIKADO, IF I WERE A HUMAN BEING LEADING AN UPRIGHT LIFE, I'D PROBABLY KNOCK YOU OUT TO FORCE YOU TO QUIT THE DOLLARS.
BUT I LIVE IN A MUCH DEEPER, DARKER PART OF TOWN, AND I'M NOT EVEN HUMAN.
I DON'T HAVE THE RIGHT TO STOP YOU FROM DOING WHAT YOU WANT.
BUT AS SOMEONE WHO'S LIVED A BIT LONGER THAN YOU, I WANT TO GIVE YOU A WARNING.
CELTY-SAN...
I DON'T THINK THAT WHAT I'M DOING IS PERFECTLY RIGHT AND JUST.
I KNOW THAT I'M WALKING A DANGEROUS PATH.
I MEAN, JUST CREATING THE DOLLARS IN THE FIRST PLACE WASN'T THE "RIGHT" THING TO DO ACCORDING TO SOCIETY, YOU KNOW?
EVEN STILL...I WANT TO KEEP THAT SAFE.

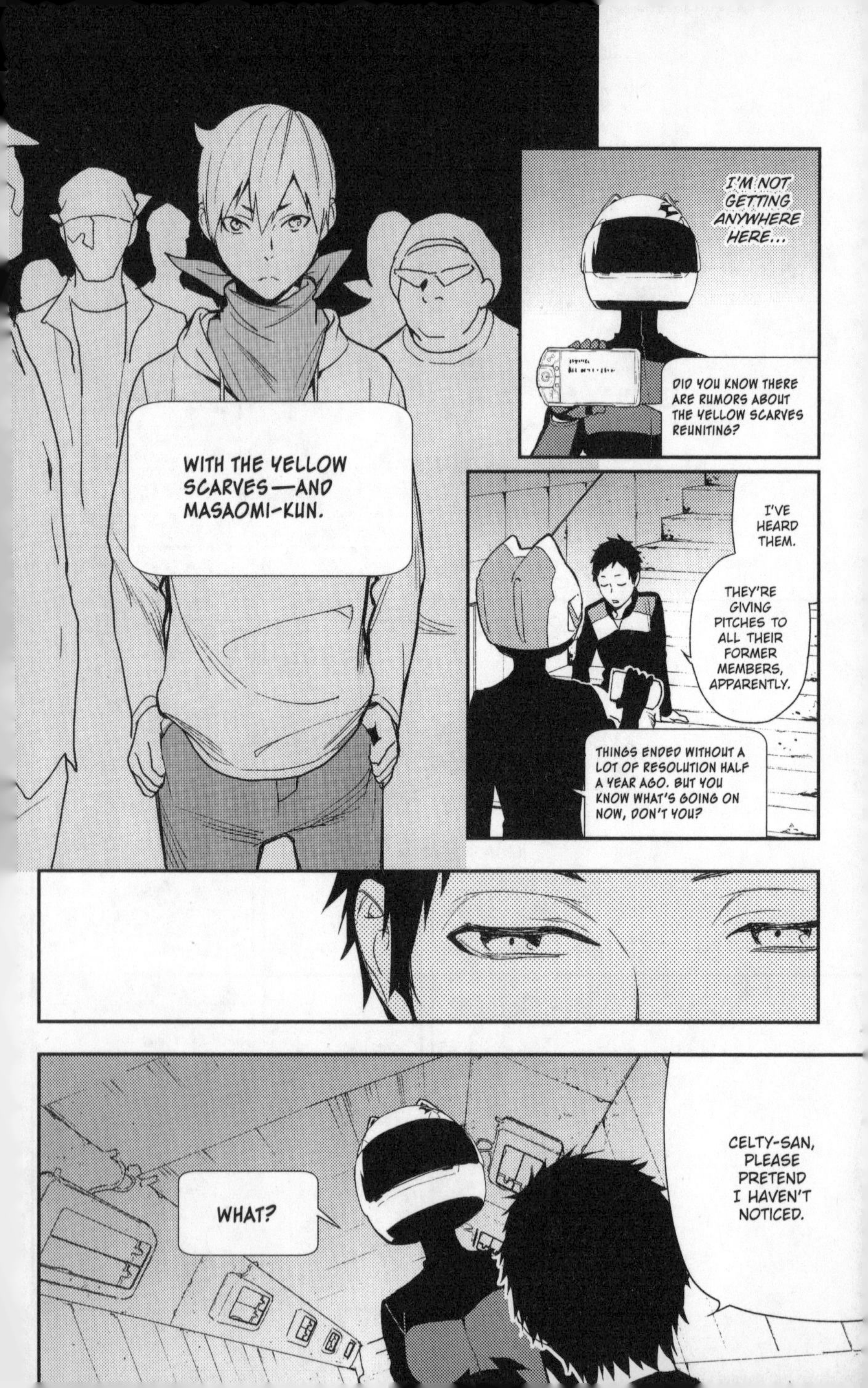
I'M NOT GETTING ANYWHERE HERE...
DID YOU KNOW THERE ARE RUMORS ABOUT THE YELLOW SCARVES REUNITING?
I'VE HEARD THEM.
THEY'RE GIVING PITCHES TO ALL THEIR FORMER MEMBERS, APPARENTLY.
THINGS ENDED WITHOUT A LOT OF RESOLUTION HALF A YEAR AGO. BUT YOU KNOW WHAT'S GOING ON NOW, DON'T YOU?
WITH THE YELLOW SCARVES—AND MASAOMI-KUN.
CELTY-SAN, PLEASE PRETEND I HAVEN'T NOTICED.
WHAT?

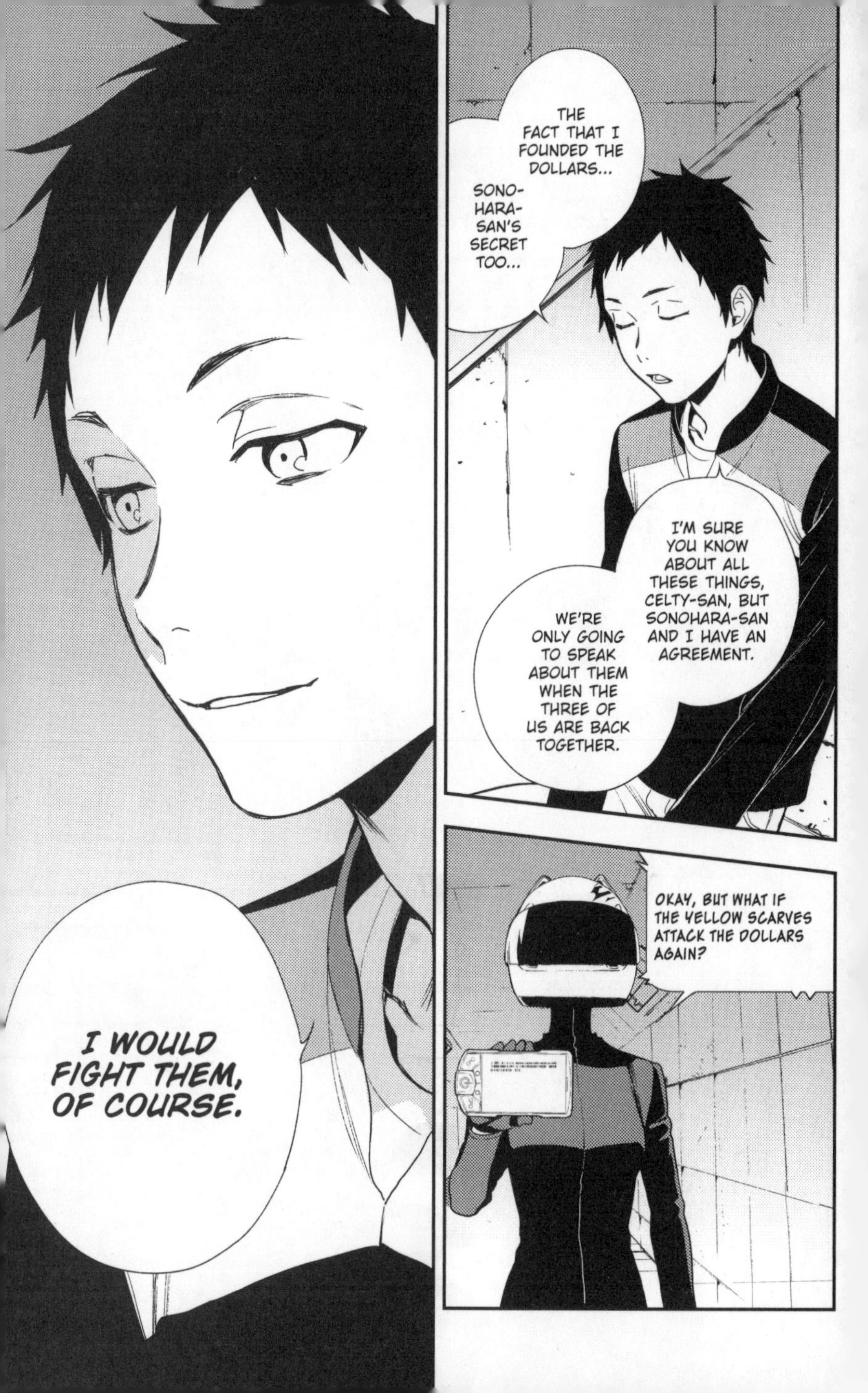
THE FACT THAT I FOUNDED THE DOLLARS... SONOHARA-SAN'S SECRET TOO...
I'M SURE YOU KNOW ABOUT ALL THESE THINGS, CELTY-SAN, BUT SONOHARA-SAN AND I HAVE AN AGREEMENT.
WE'RE ONLY GOING TO SPEAK ABOUT THEM WHEN THE THREE OF US ARE BACK TOGETHER.
OKAY, BUT WHAT IF THE YELLOW SCARVES ATTACK THE DOLLARS AGAIN?
I WOULD FIGHT THEM, OF COURSE.

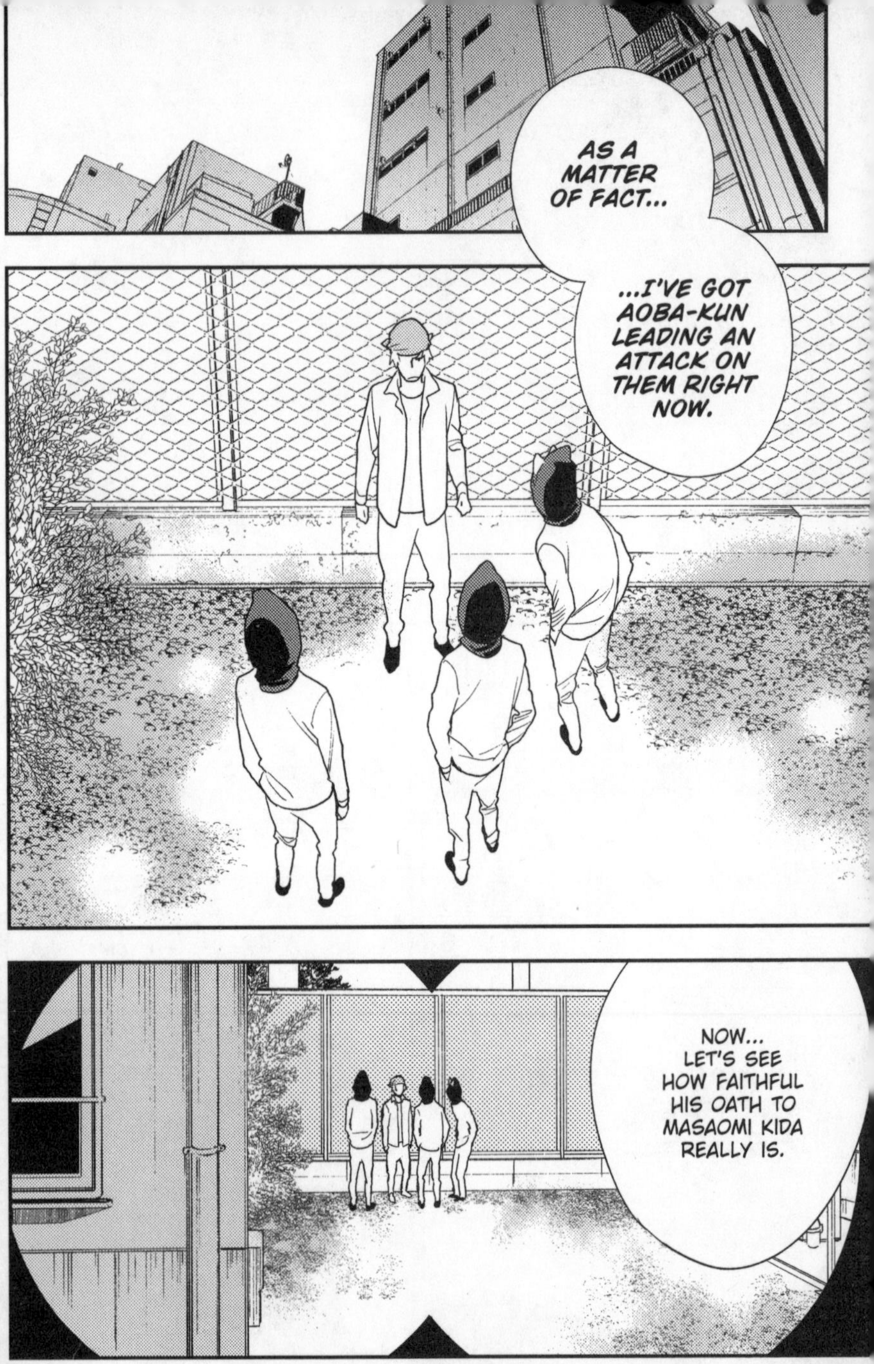
AS A MATTER OF FACT...
...I'VE GOT AOBA-KUN LEADING AN ATTACK ON THEM RIGHT NOW.
NOW... LET'S SEE HOW FAITHFUL HIS OATH TO MASAOMI KIDA REALLY IS.

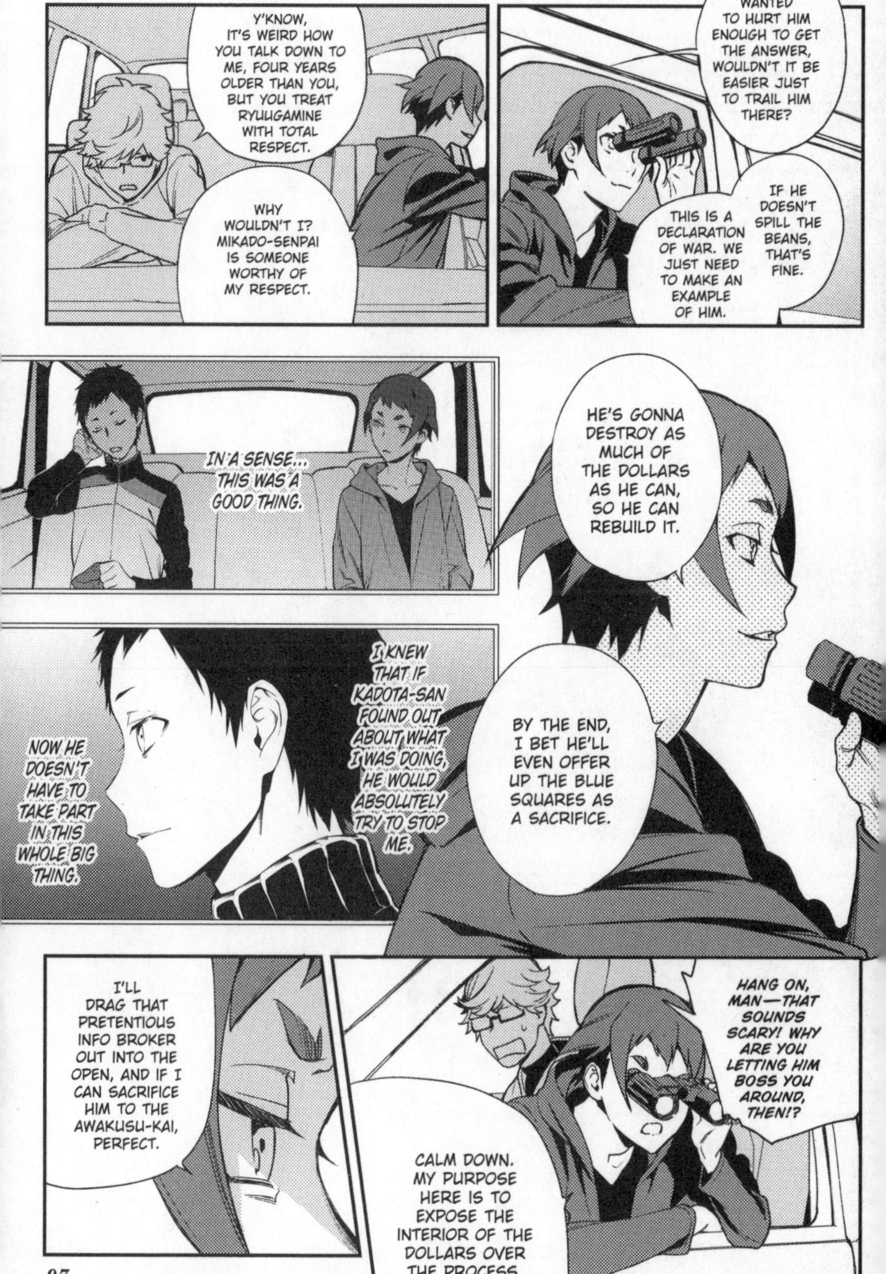
IF YOU WANTED TO HURT HIM ENOUGH TO GET THE ANSWER, WOULDN'T IT BE EASIER JUST TO TRAIL HIM THERE?
IF HE DOESN'T SPILL THE BEANS, THAT'S FINE.
THIS IS A DECLARATION OF WAR. WE JUST NEED TO MAKE AN EXAMPLE OF HIM.
Y'KNOW, IT'S WEIRD HOW YOU TALK DOWN TO ME, FOUR YEARS OLDER THAN YOU, BUT YOU TREAT RYUUGAMINE WITH TOTAL RESPECT.
WHY WOULDN'T I? MIKADO-SENPAI IS SOMEONE WORTHY OF MY RESPECT.
HE'S GONNA DESTROY AS MUCH OF THE DOLLARS AS HE CAN, SO HE CAN REBUILD IT.
BY THE END, I BET HE'LL EVEN OFFER UP THE BLUE SQUARES AS A SACRIFICE.
IN A SENSE... THIS WAS A GOOD THING.
I KNEW THAT IF KADOTA-SAN FOUND OUT ABOUT WHAT I WAS DOING, HE WOULD ABSOLUTELY TRY TO STOP ME.
NOW HE DOESN'T HAVE TO TAKE PART IN THIS WHOLE BIG THING.
HANG ON, MAN—THAT SOUNDS SCARY! WHY ARE YOU LETTING HIM BOSS YOU AROUND, THEN!?
CALM DOWN. MY PURPOSE HERE IS TO EXPOSE THE INTERIOR OF THE DOLLARS OVER THE PROCESS.
I'LL DRAG THAT PRETENTIOUS INFO BROKER OUT INTO THE OPEN, AND IF I CAN SACRIFICE HIM TO THE AWAKUSU-KAI, PERFECT.

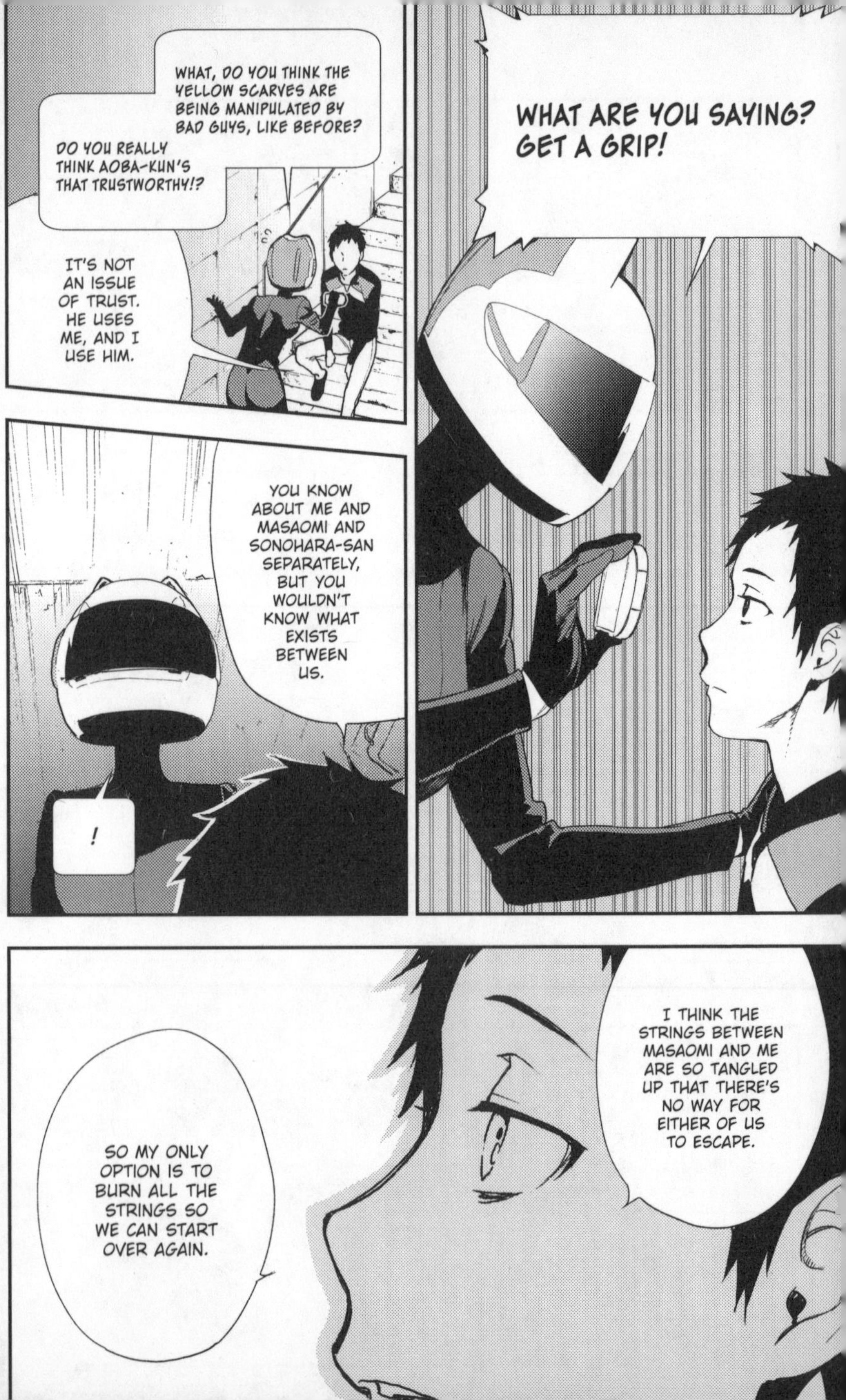
WHAT ARE YOU SAYING? GET A GRIP!
WHAT, DO YOU THINK THE YELLOW SCARVES ARE BEING MANIPULATED BY BAD GUYS, LIKE BEFORE?
DO YOU REALLY THINK AOBA-KUN'S THAT TRUSTWORTHY!?
IT'S NOT AN ISSUE OF TRUST. HE USES ME, AND I USE HIM.
YOU KNOW ABOUT ME AND MASAOMI AND SONOHARA-SAN SEPARATELY, BUT YOU WOULDN'T KNOW WHAT EXISTS BETWEEN US.
!
I THINK THE STRINGS BETWEEN MASAOMI AND ME ARE SO TANGLED UP THAT THERE'S NO WAY FOR EITHER OF US TO ESCAPE.
SO MY ONLY OPTION IS TO BURN ALL THE STRINGS SO WE CAN START OVER AGAIN.

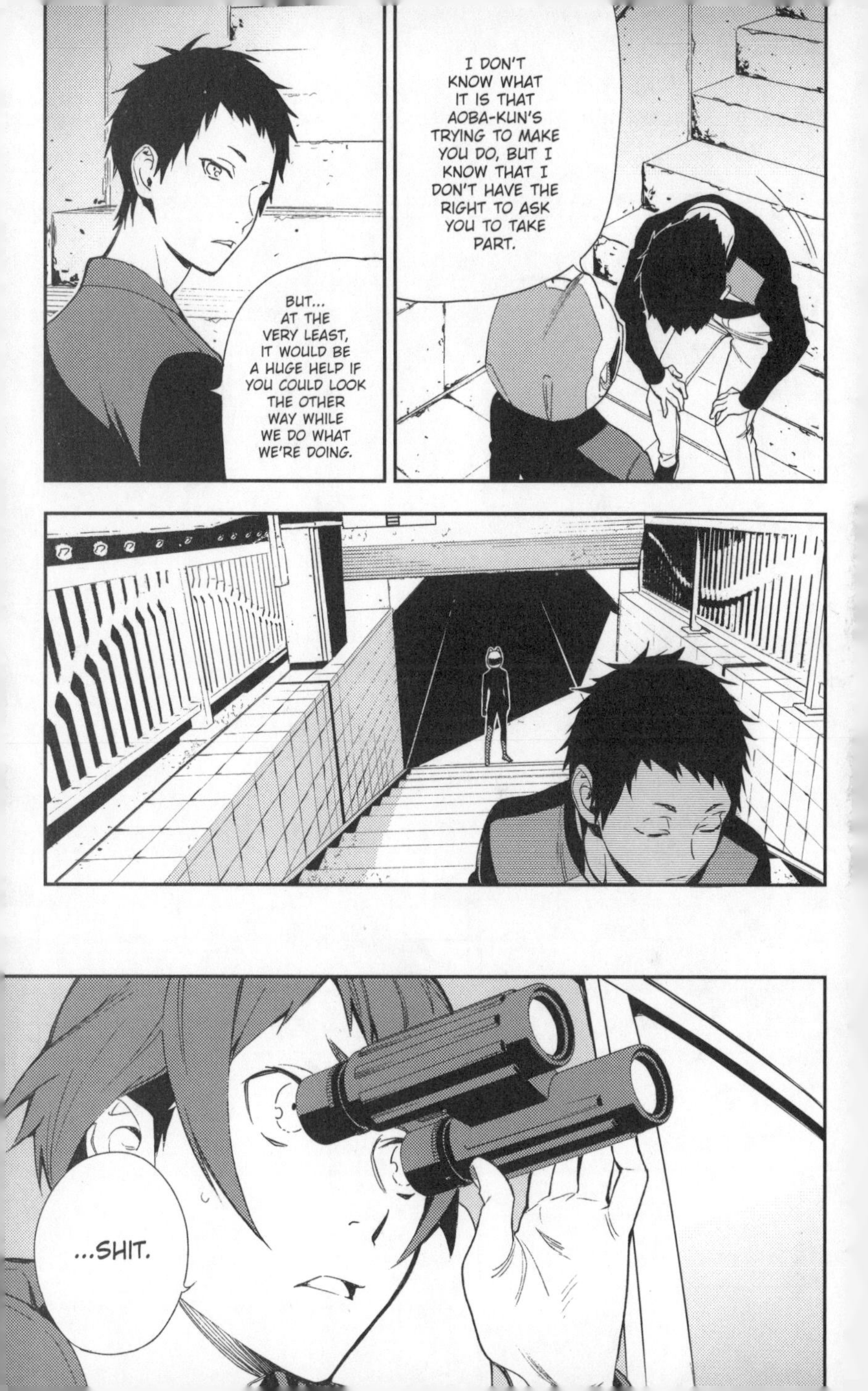
I DON'T KNOW WHAT IT IS THAT AOBA-KUN'S TRYING TO MAKE YOU DO, BUT I KNOW THAT I DON'T HAVE THE RIGHT TO ASK YOU TO TAKE PART.
BUT... AT THE VERY LEAST, IT WOULD BE A HUGE HELP IF YOU COULD LOOK THE OTHER WAY WHILE WE DO WHAT WE'RE DOING.
...SHIT.

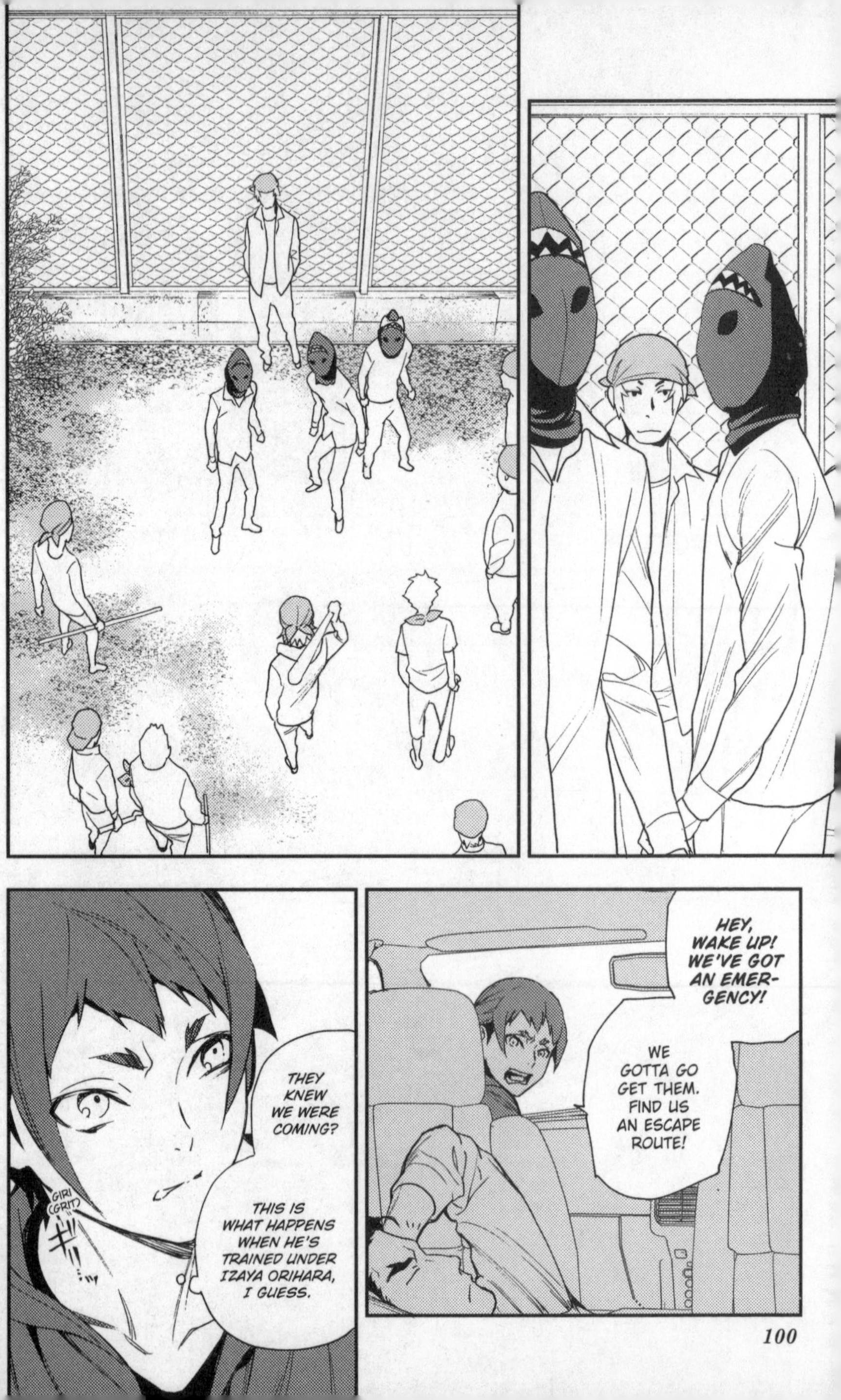
HEY, WAKE UP! WE'VE GOT AN EMERGENCY!
WE GOTTA GO GET THEM. FIND US AN ESCAPE ROUTE!
THEY KNEW WE WERE COMING?
THIS IS WHAT HAPPENS WHEN HE'S TRAINED UNDER IZAYA ORIHARA, I GUESS.
GIRI (GRIT)

SIGN: KARAOKE & PARTIES PASERA

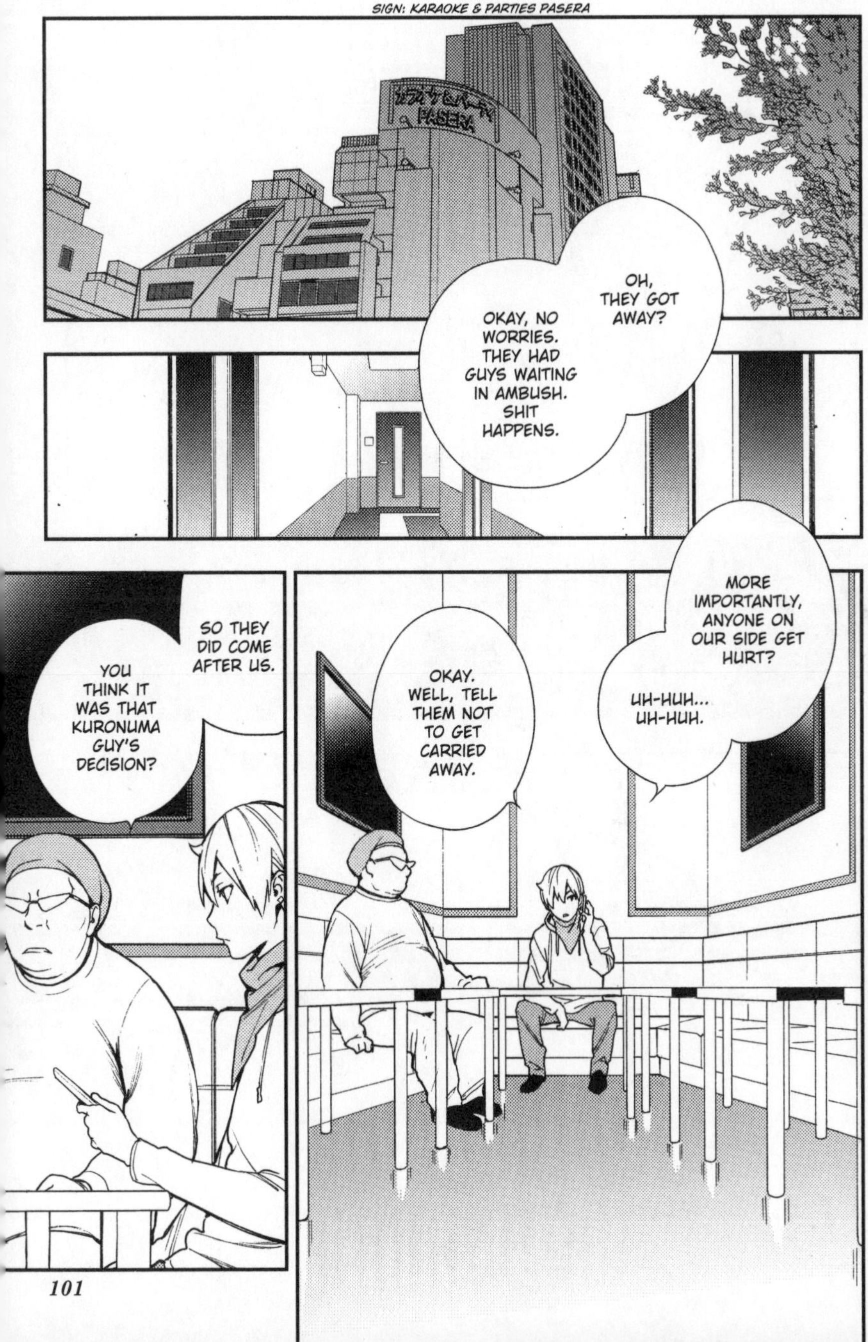
OH, THEY GOT AWAY?
OKAY, NO WORRIES. THEY HAD GUYS WAITING IN AMBUSH. SHIT HAPPENS.
MORE IMPORTANTLY, ANYONE ON OUR SIDE GET HURT?
UH-HUH... UH-HUH.
OKAY. WELL, TELL THEM NOT TO GET CARRIED AWAY.
SO THEY DID COME AFTER US.
YOU THINK IT WAS THAT KURONUMA GUY'S DECISION?

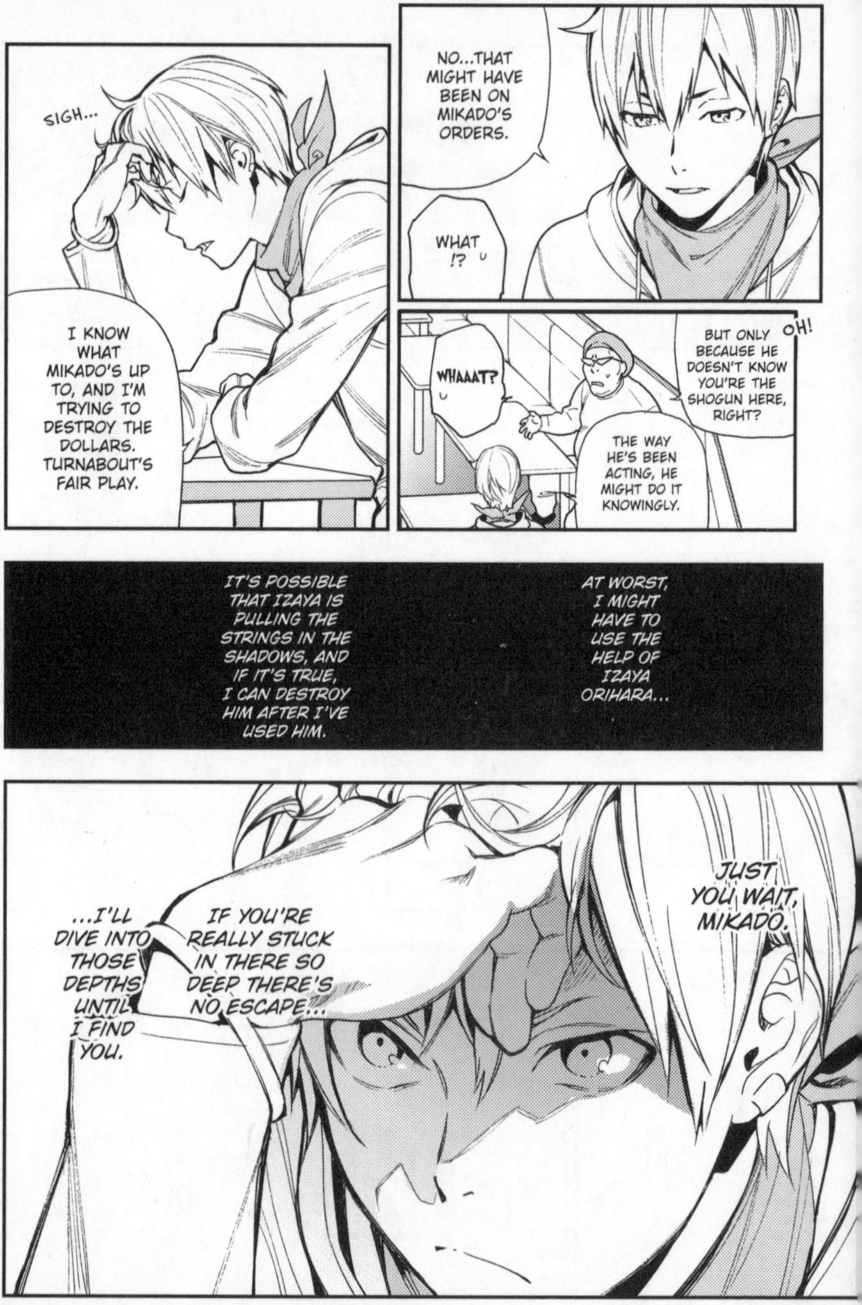
NO...THAT MIGHT HAVE BEEN ON MIKADO'S ORDERS.
WHAT!?
OH!
BUT ONLY BECAUSE HE DOESN'T KNOW YOU'RE THE SHOGUN HERE, RIGHT?
WHAAAT?
THE WAY HE'S BEEN ACTING, HE MIGHT DO IT KNOWINGLY.
SIGH...
I KNOW WHAT MIKADO'S UP TO, AND I'M TRYING TO DESTROY THE DOLLARS. TURNABOUT'S FAIR PLAY.
AT WORST, I MIGHT HAVE TO USE THE HELP OF IZAYA ORIHARA...
IT'S POSSIBLE THAT IZAYA IS PULLING THE STRINGS IN THE SHADOWS, AND IF IT'S TRUE, I CAN DESTROY HIM AFTER I'VE USED HIM.
JUST YOU WAIT, MIKADO.
IF YOU'RE REALLY STUCK IN THERE SO DEEP THERE'S NO ESCAPE...
...I'LL DIVE INTO THOSE DEPTHS UNTIL I FIND YOU.

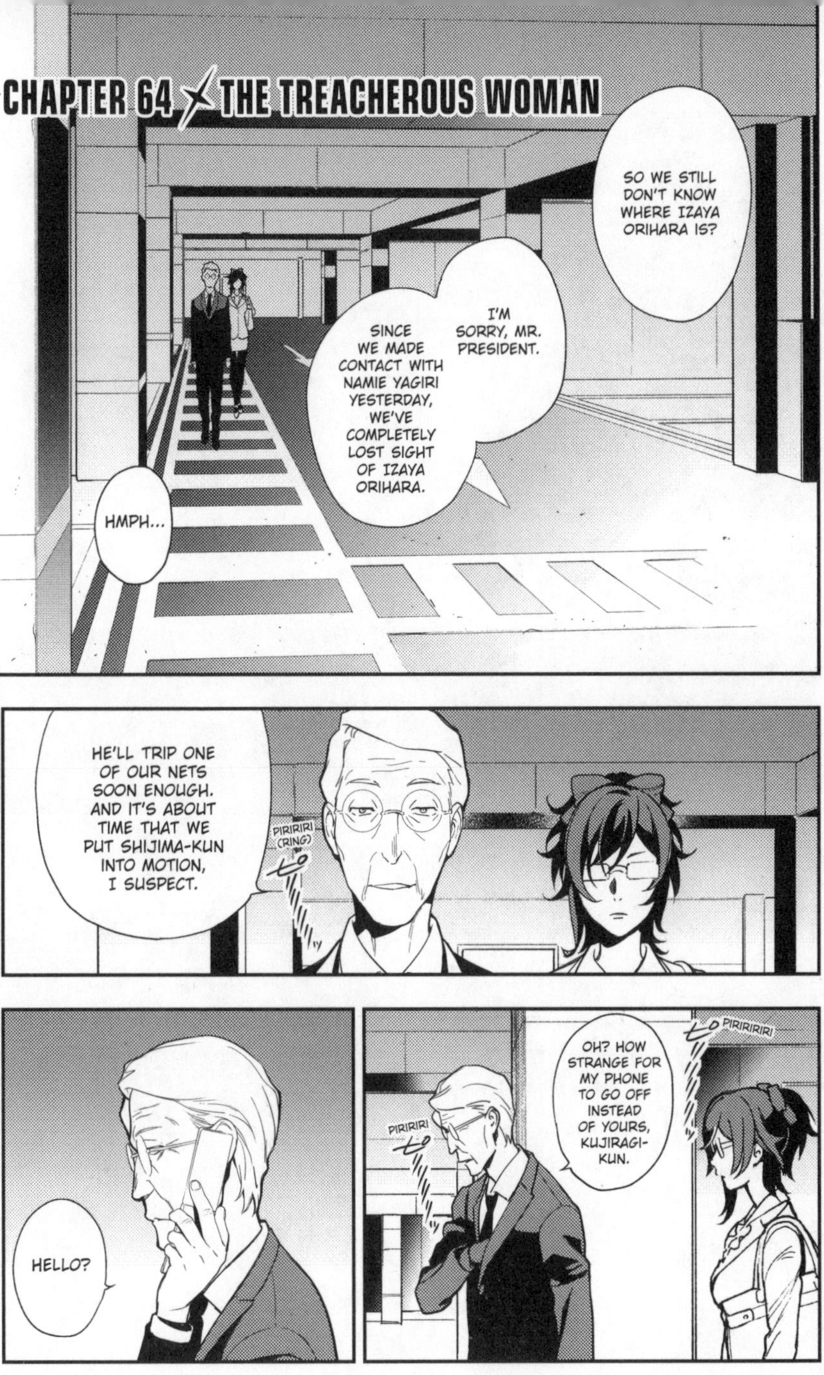
CHAPTER 64 × THE TREACHEROUS WOMAN
SO WE STILL DON'T KNOW WHERE IZAYA ORIHARA IS?
I'M SORRY, MR. PRESIDENT.
SINCE WE MADE CONTACT WITH NAMIE YAGIRI YESTERDAY, WE'VE COMPLETELY LOST SIGHT OF IZAYA ORIHARA.
HMPH...
PIRIRIRI (RING)
HE'LL TRIP ONE OF OUR NETS SOON ENOUGH. AND IT'S ABOUT TIME THAT WE PUT SHIJIMA-KUN INTO MOTION, I SUSPECT.
PIRIRIRIRI
OH? HOW STRANGE FOR MY PHONE TO GO OFF INSTEAD OF YOURS, KUJIRAGI-KUN.
PIRIRIRI
HELLO?

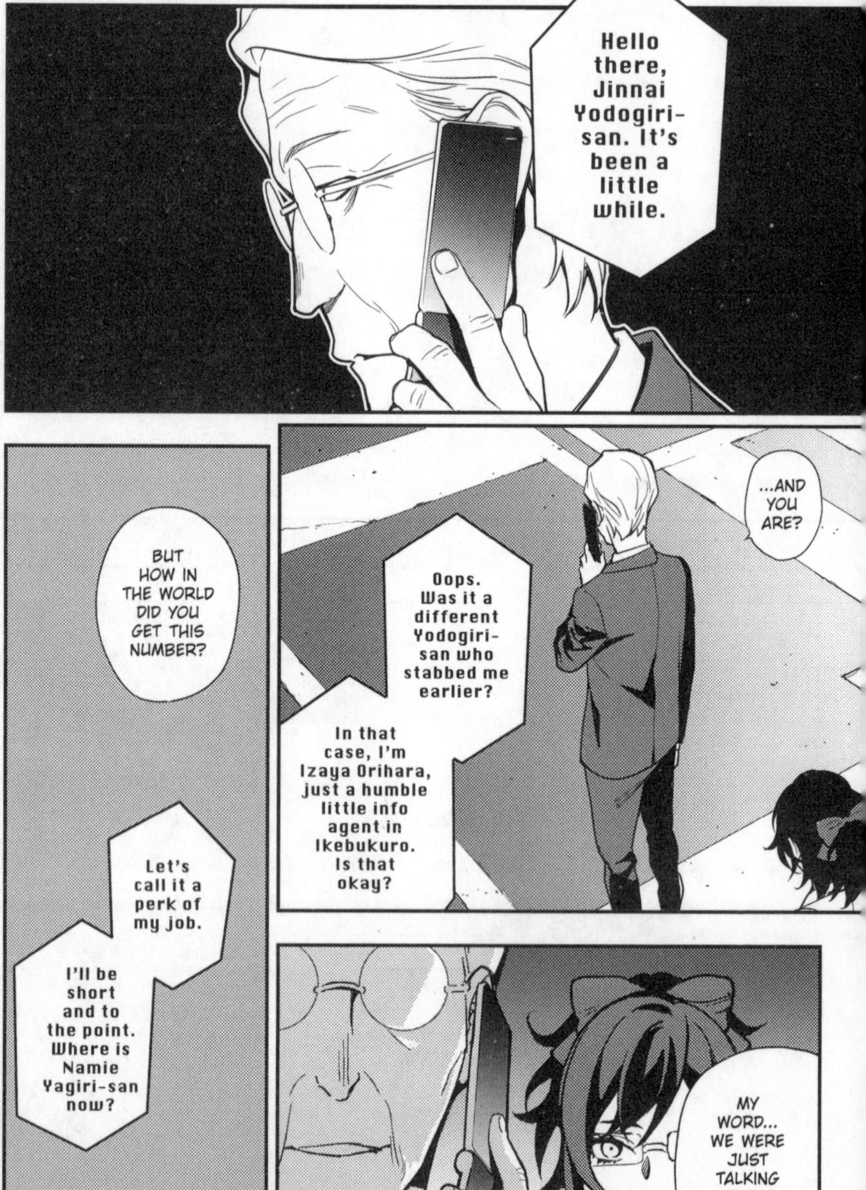
Hello there, Jinnai Yodogiri-san. It's been a little while.
...AND YOU ARE?
Oops. Was it a different Yodogiri-san who stabbed me earlier?
In that case, I'm Izaya Orihara, just a humble little info agent in Ikebukuro. Is that okay?
MY WORD... WE WERE JUST TALKING ABOUT YOU.
BUT HOW IN THE WORLD DID YOU GET THIS NUMBER?
Let's call it a perk of my job.
I'll be short and to the point. Where is Namie Yagiri-san now?

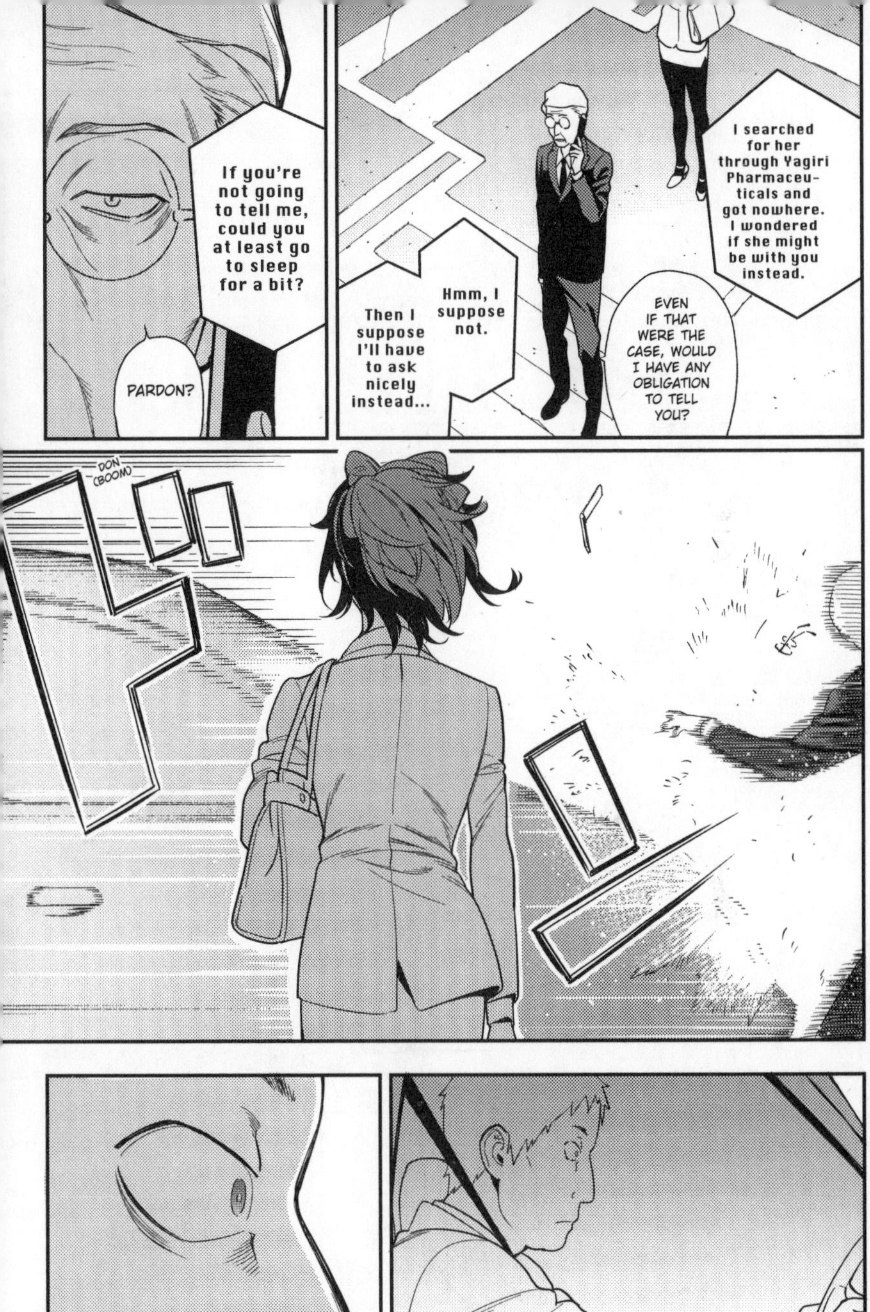
I searched for her through Yagiri Pharmaceuticals and got nowhere. I wondered if she might be with you instead.
EVEN IF THAT WERE THE CASE, WOULD I HAVE ANY OBLIGATION TO TELL YOU?
Hmm, I suppose not.
Then I suppose I'll have to ask nicely instead...
If you're not going to tell me, could you at least go to sleep for a bit?
PARDON?
DON (BOOM)

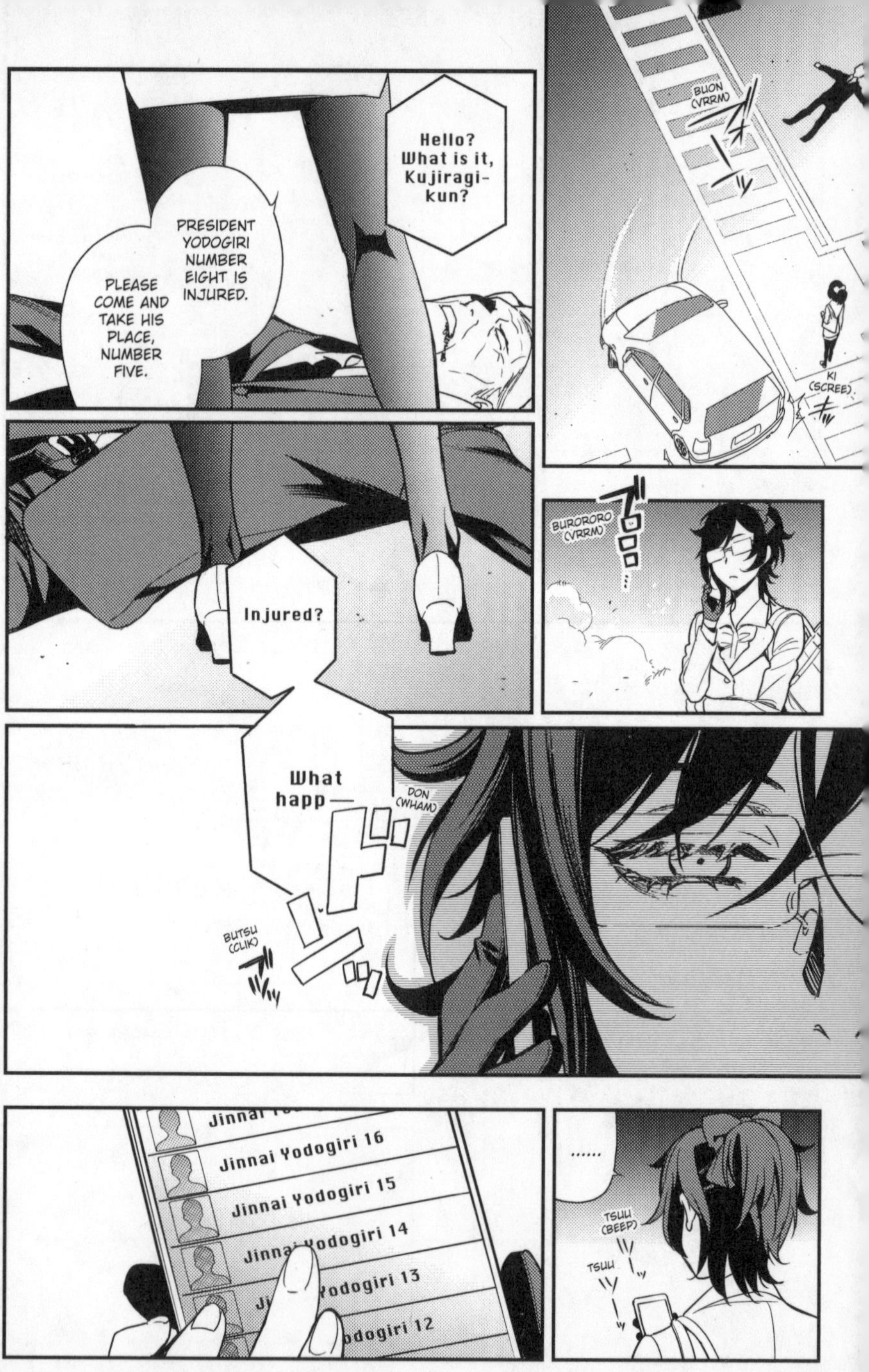
BUON (VRRM)
KI (SCREE)
Hello? What is it, Kujiragi-kun?
PRESIDENT YODOGIRI NUMBER EIGHT IS INJURED.
PLEASE COME AND TAKE HIS PLACE, NUMBER FIVE.
BURORORO (VRRM)
Injured?
What happ—
DON (WHAM)
BUTSU (CLIK)
......
TSUU (BEEP)
TSUU
Jinnai Yodogiri 16
Jinnai Yodogiri 15
Jinnai Yodogiri 14
Yodogiri 13
odogiri 12

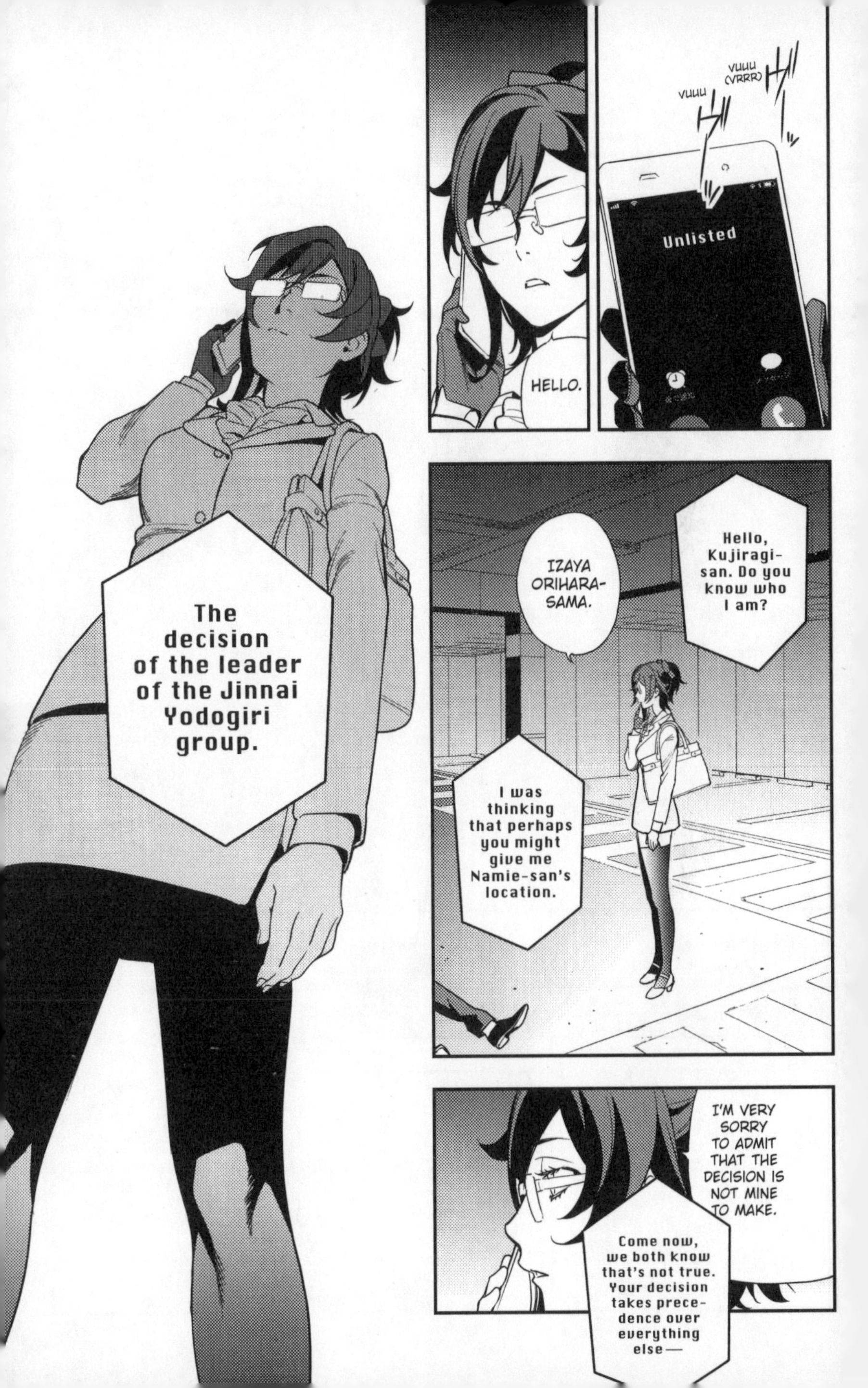
VUUU (VRRR)
VUUU
Unlisted
HELLO.
Hello, Kujiragi-san. Do you know who I am?
IZAYA ORIHARA-SAMA.
I was thinking that perhaps you might give me Namie-san's location.
I'M VERY SORRY TO ADMIT THAT THE DECISION IS NOT MINE TO MAKE.
Come now, we both know that's not true. Your decision takes precedence over everything else—
The decision of the leader of the Jinnai Yodogiri group.

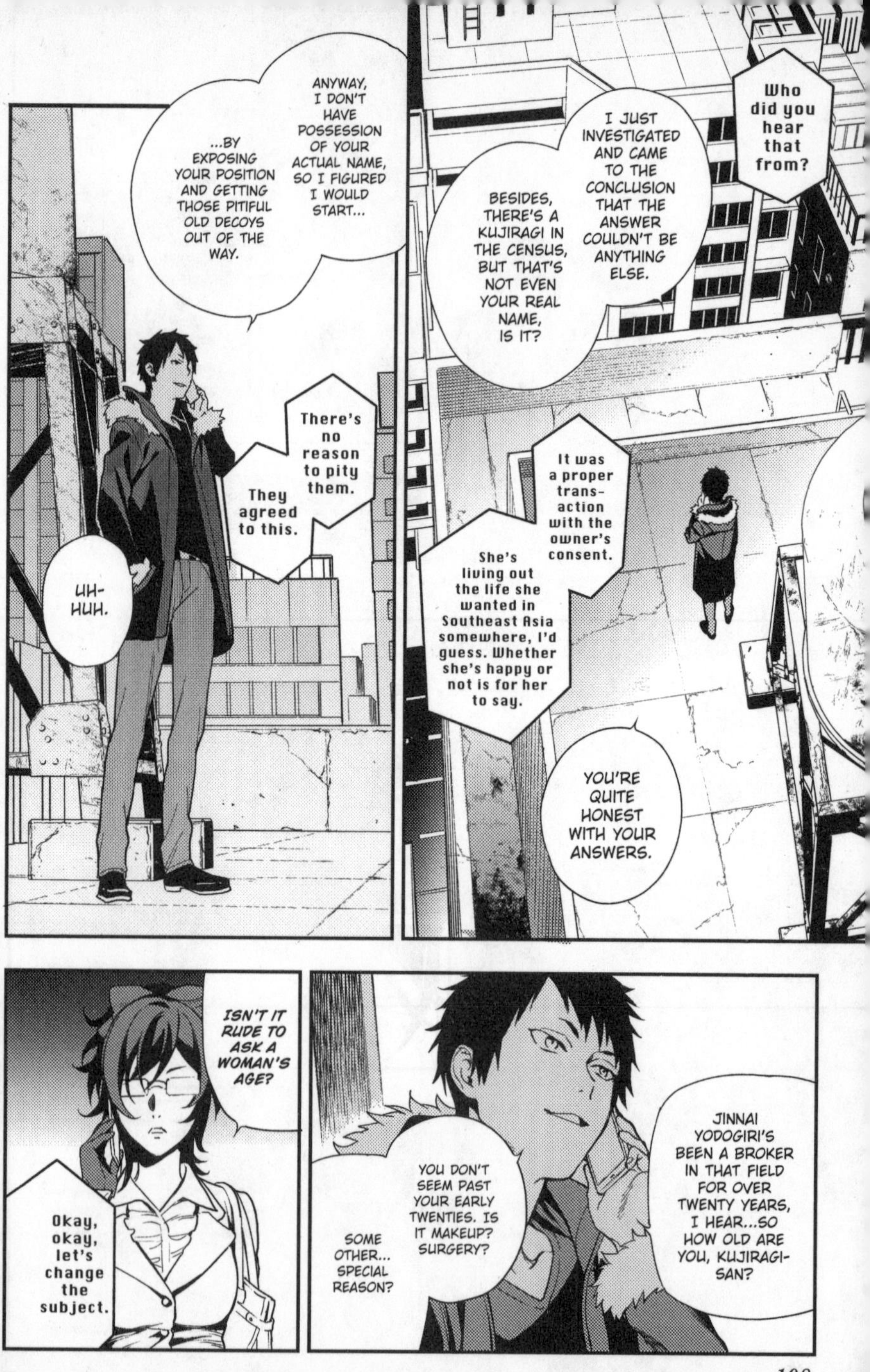
Who did you hear that from?
I JUST INVESTIGATED AND CAME TO THE CONCLUSION THAT THE ANSWER COULDN'T BE ANYTHING ELSE.
BESIDES, THERE'S A KUJIRAGI IN THE CENSUS, BUT THAT'S NOT EVEN YOUR REAL NAME, IS IT?
It was a proper transaction with the owner's consent.
She's living out the life she wanted in Southeast Asia somewhere, I'd guess. Whether she's happy or not is for her to say.
YOU'RE QUITE HONEST WITH YOUR ANSWERS.
ANYWAY, I DON'T HAVE POSSESSION OF YOUR ACTUAL NAME, SO I FIGURED I WOULD START...
...BY EXPOSING YOUR POSITION AND GETTING THOSE PITIFUL OLD DECOYS OUT OF THE WAY.
There's no reason to pity them.
They agreed to this.
UH-HUH.
JINNAI YODOGIRI'S BEEN A BROKER IN THAT FIELD FOR OVER TWENTY YEARS, I HEAR...SO HOW OLD ARE YOU, KUJIRAGI-SAN?
YOU DON'T SEEM PAST YOUR EARLY TWENTIES. IS IT MAKEUP? SURGERY?
SOME OTHER... SPECIAL REASON?
ISN'T IT RUDE TO ASK A WOMAN'S AGE?
Okay, okay, let's change the subject.

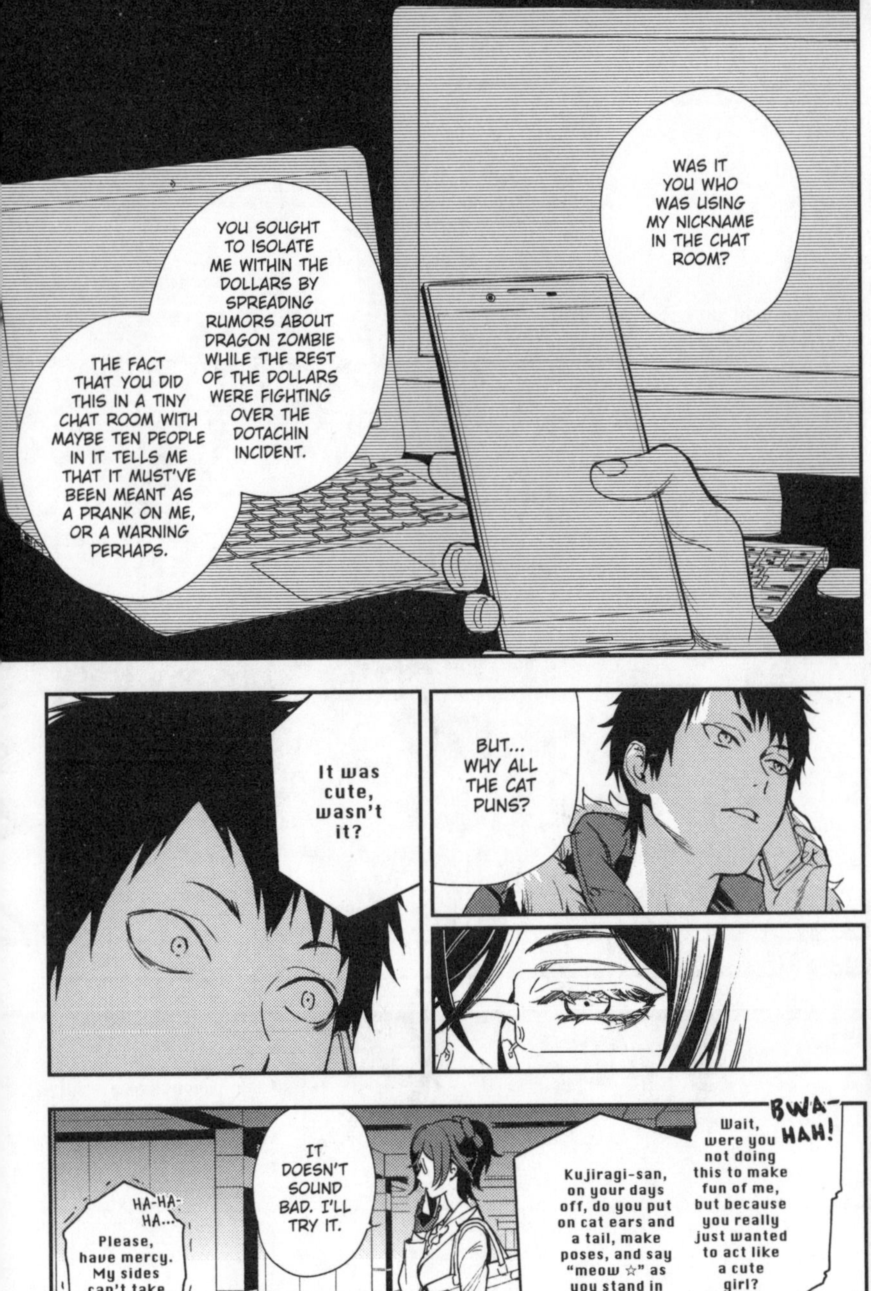
WAS IT YOU WHO WAS USING MY NICKNAME IN THE CHAT ROOM?
YOU SOUGHT TO ISOLATE ME WITHIN THE DOLLARS BY SPREADING RUMORS ABOUT DRAGON ZOMBIE WHILE THE REST OF THE DOLLARS WERE FIGHTING OVER THE DOTACHIN INCIDENT.
THE FACT THAT YOU DID THIS IN A TINY CHAT ROOM WITH MAYBE TEN PEOPLE IN IT TELLS ME THAT IT MUST'VE BEEN MEANT AS A PRANK ON ME, OR A WARNING PERHAPS.
BUT... WHY ALL THE CAT PUNS?
It was cute, wasn't it?
BWA-HAH!
Wait, were you not doing this to make fun of me, but because you really just wanted to act like a cute girl?
Kujiragi-san, on your days off, do you put on cat ears and a tail, make poses, and say "meow ☆" as you stand in front of the meow-ror?
IT DOESN'T SOUND BAD. I'LL TRY IT.
HA-HA-HA...
Please, have mercy. My sides can't take this.

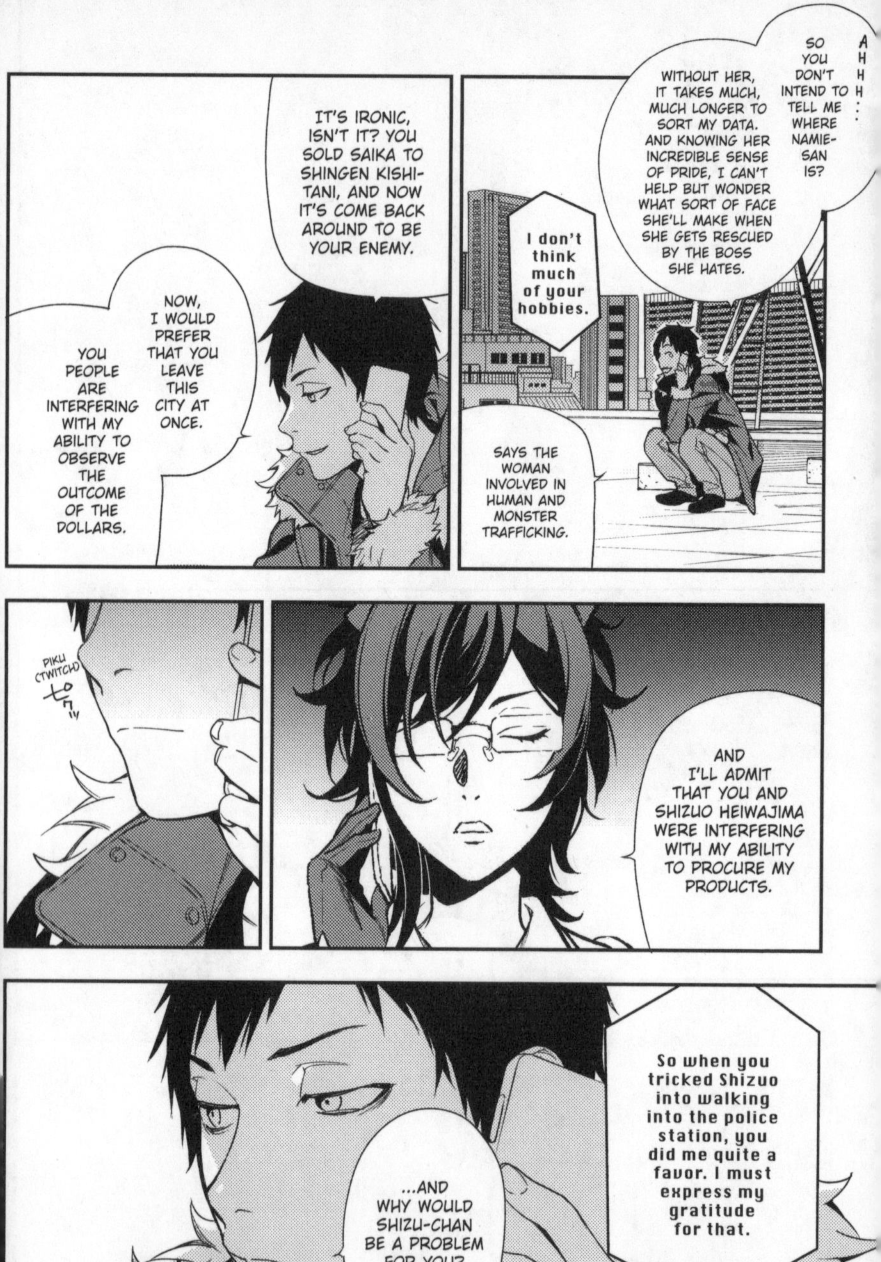
AHHH...
SO YOU DON'T INTEND TO TELL ME WHERE NAMIE-SAN IS?
WITHOUT HER, IT TAKES MUCH, MUCH LONGER TO SORT MY DATA. AND KNOWING HER INCREDIBLE SENSE OF PRIDE, I CAN'T HELP BUT WONDER WHAT SORT OF FACE SHE'LL MAKE WHEN SHE GETS RESCUED BY THE BOSS SHE HATES.
I don't think much of your hobbies.
SAYS THE WOMAN INVOLVED IN HUMAN AND MONSTER TRAFFICKING.
IT'S IRONIC, ISN'T IT? YOU SOLD SAIKA TO SHINGEN KISHITANI, AND NOW IT'S COME BACK AROUND TO BE YOUR ENEMY.
NOW, I WOULD PREFER THAT YOU LEAVE THIS CITY AT ONCE.
YOU PEOPLE ARE INTERFERING WITH MY ABILITY TO OBSERVE THE OUTCOME OF THE DOLLARS.
AND I'LL ADMIT THAT YOU AND SHIZUO HEIWAJIMA WERE INTERFERING WITH MY ABILITY TO PROCURE MY PRODUCTS.
PIKU (TWITCH)
ピクッ
So when you tricked Shizuo into walking into the police station, you did me quite a favor. I must express my gratitude for that.
...AND WHY WOULD SHIZU-CHAN BE A PROBLEM FOR YOU?

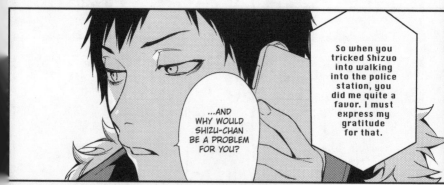

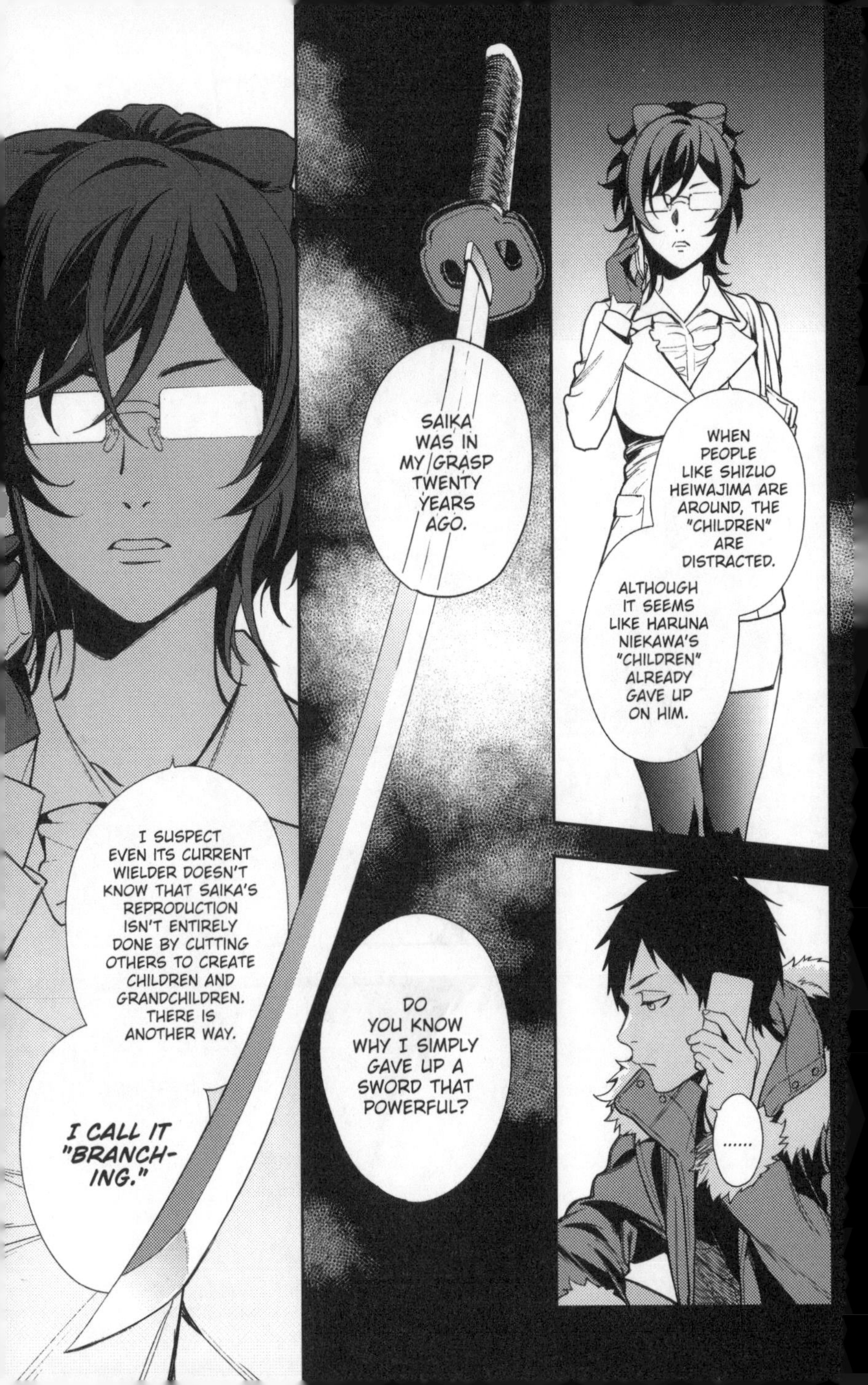
WHEN PEOPLE LIKE SHIZUO HEIWAJIMA ARE AROUND, THE "CHILDREN" ARE DISTRACTED.
ALTHOUGH IT SEEMS LIKE HARUNA NIEKAWA'S "CHILDREN" ALREADY GAVE UP ON HIM.
......
SAIKA WAS IN MY GRASP TWENTY YEARS AGO.
DO YOU KNOW WHY I SIMPLY GAVE UP A SWORD THAT POWERFUL?
I SUSPECT EVEN ITS CURRENT WIELDER DOESN'T KNOW THAT SAIKA'S REPRODUCTION ISN'T ENTIRELY DONE BY CUTTING OTHERS TO CREATE CHILDREN AND GRANDCHILDREN. THERE IS ANOTHER WAY.
I CALL IT "BRANCHING."

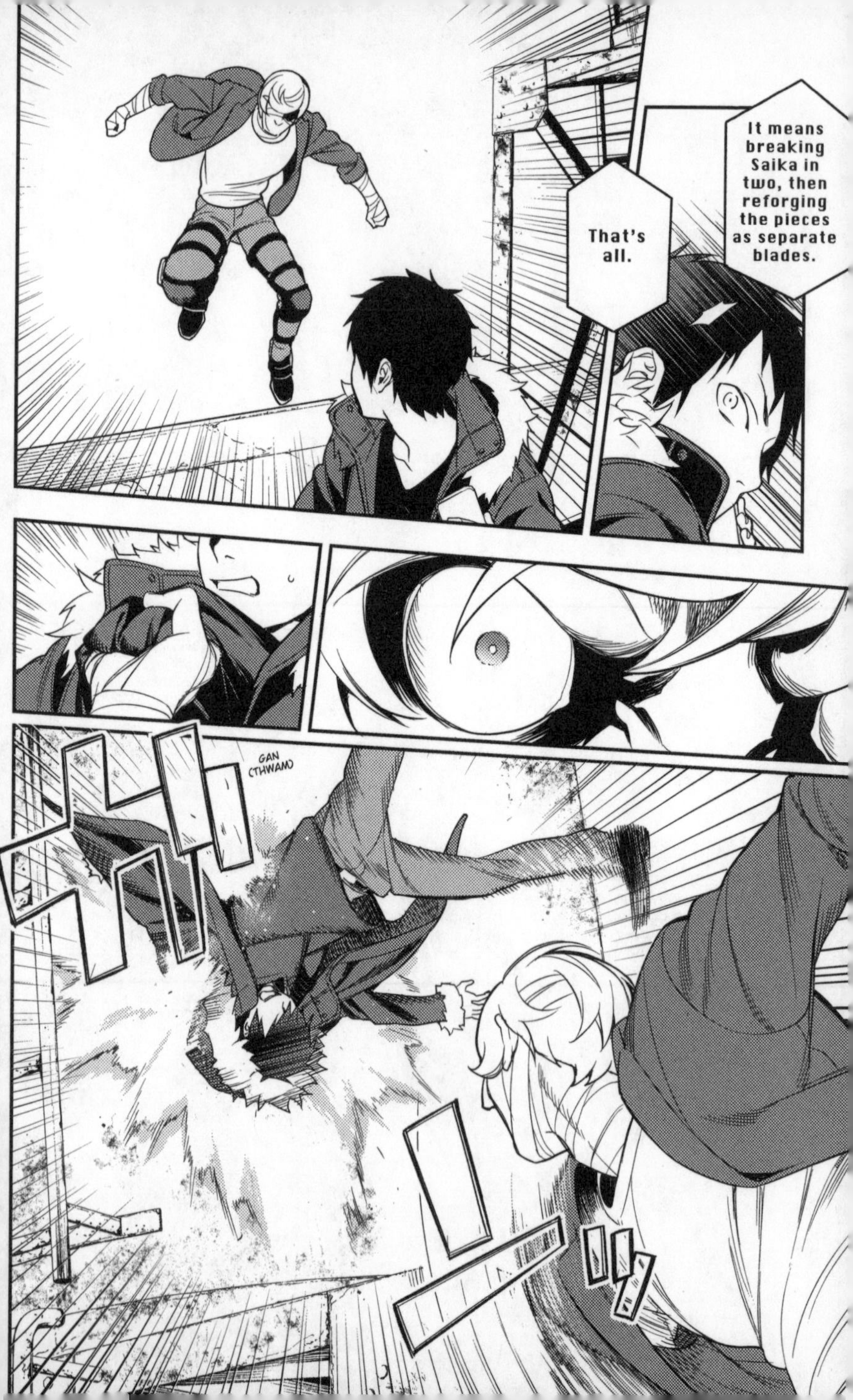
It means breaking Saika in two, then reforging the pieces as separate blades.
That's all.
GAN (THWAM)

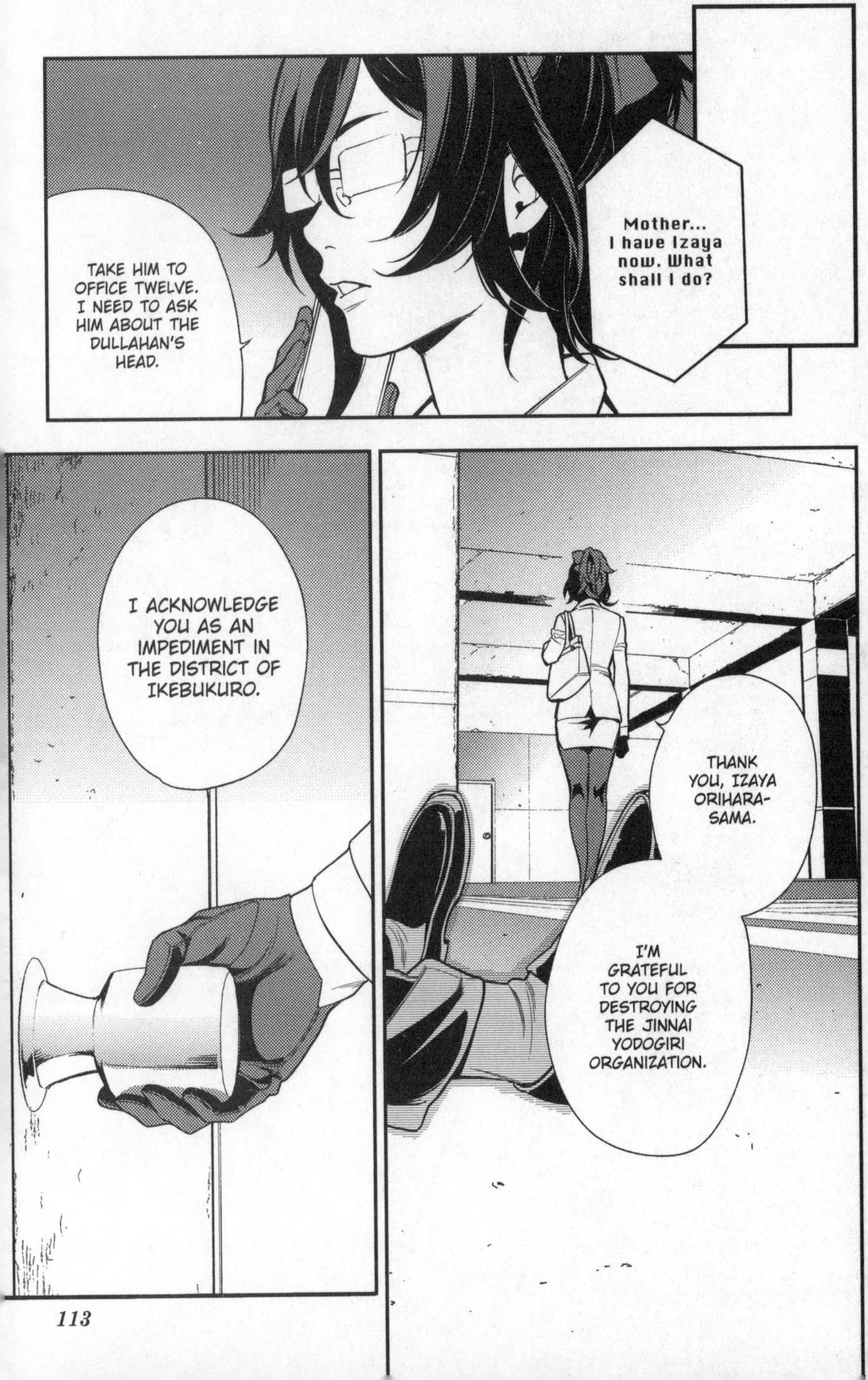
Mother... I have Izaya now. What shall I do?
TAKE HIM TO OFFICE TWELVE. I NEED TO ASK HIM ABOUT THE DULLAHAN'S HEAD.
THANK YOU, IZAYA ORIHARA-SAMA.
I'M GRATEFUL TO YOU FOR DESTROYING THE JINNAI YODOGIRI ORGANIZATION.
I ACKNOWLEDGE YOU AS AN IMPEDIMENT IN THE DISTRICT OF IKEBUKURO.

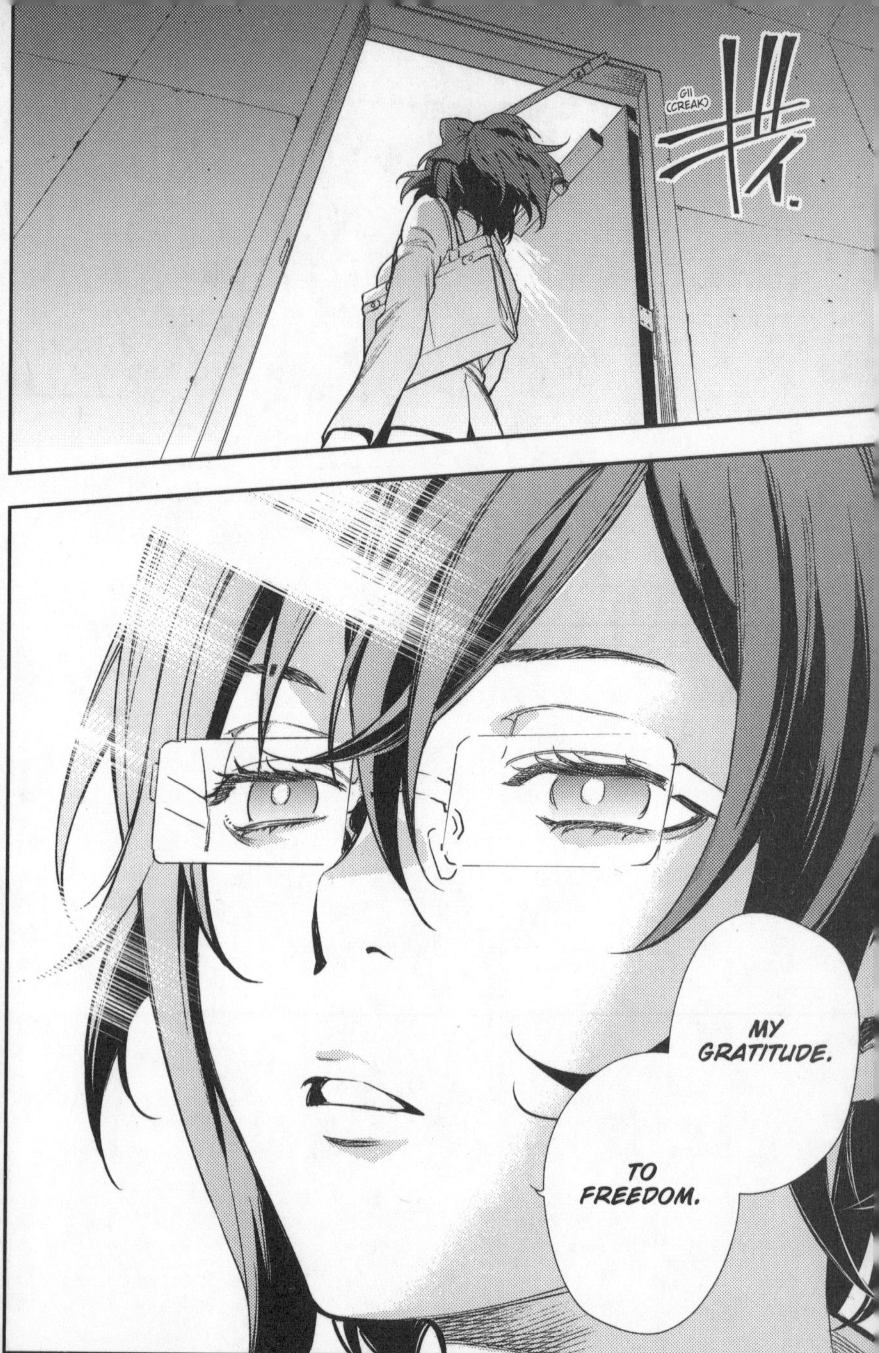
ギィ
GII (CREAK)
MY GRATITUDE.
TO FREEDOM.

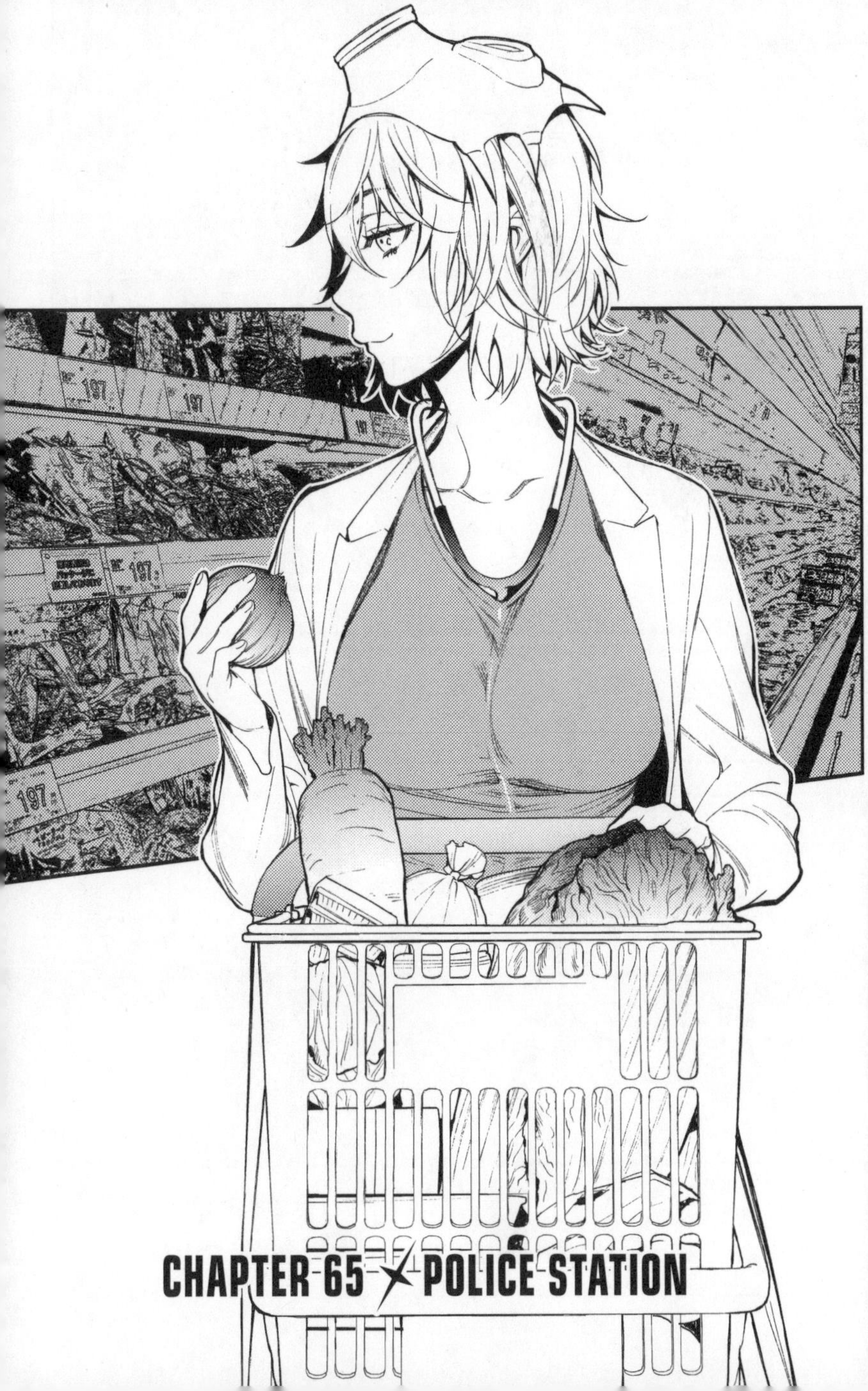
CHAPTER 65 POLICE STATION

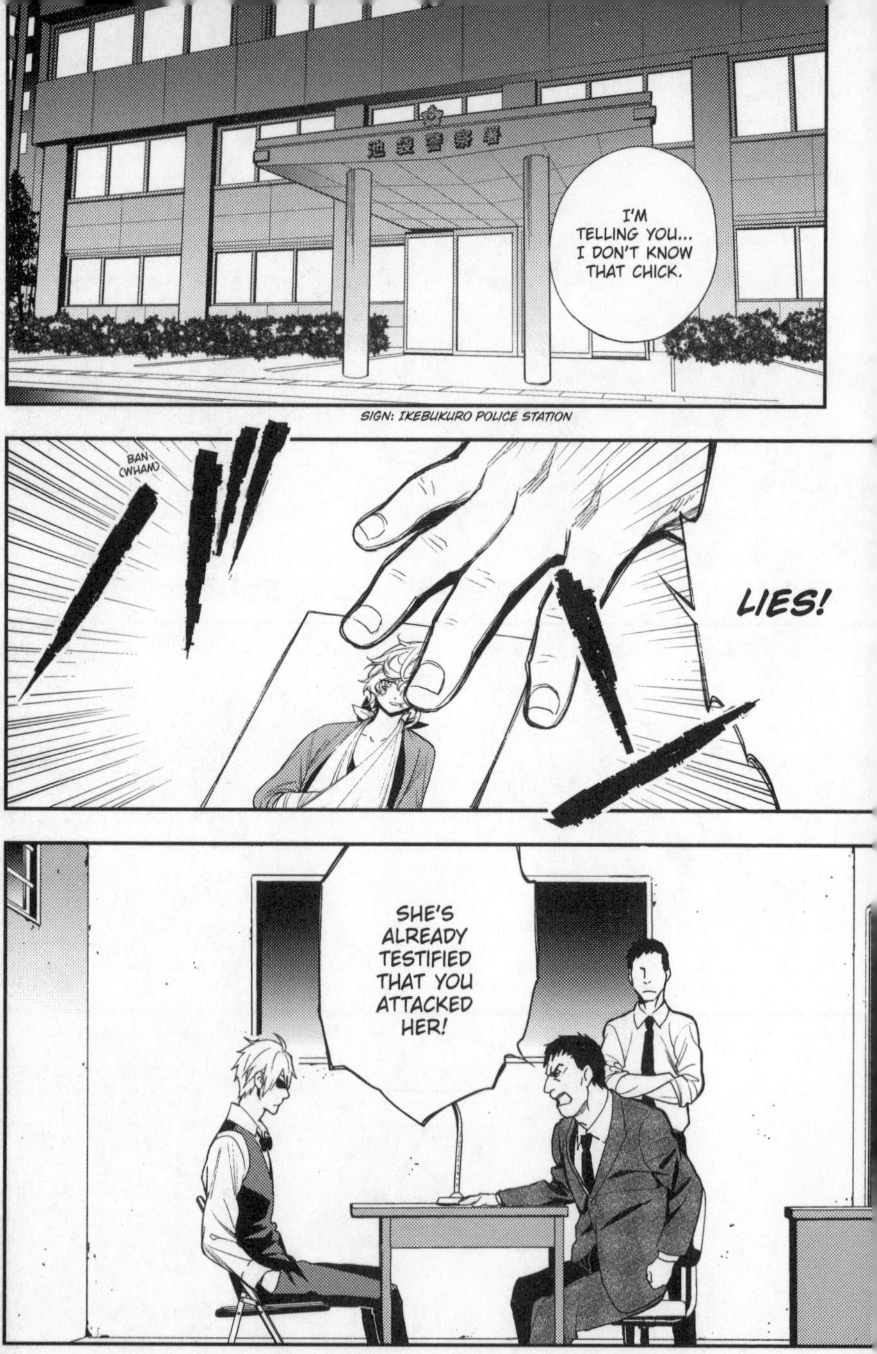
I'M TELLING YOU... I DON'T KNOW THAT CHICK.
SIGN: IKEBUKURO POLICE STATION
BAN (WHAM)
LIES!
SHE'S ALREADY TESTIFIED THAT YOU ATTACKED HER!

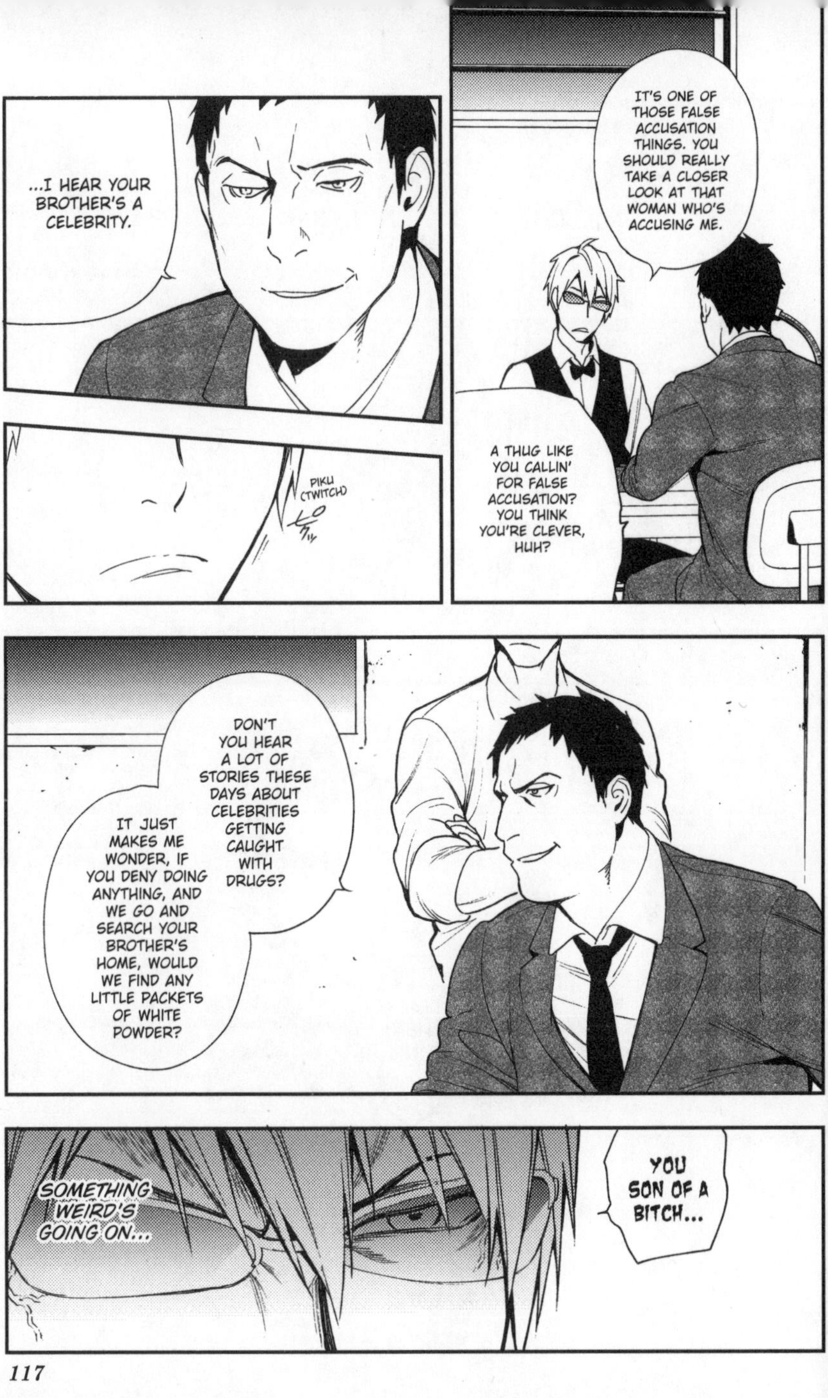
IT'S ONE OF THOSE FALSE ACCUSATION THINGS. YOU SHOULD REALLY TAKE A CLOSER LOOK AT THAT WOMAN WHO'S ACCUSING ME.
A THUG LIKE YOU CALLIN' FOR FALSE ACCUSATION? YOU THINK YOU'RE CLEVER, HUH?
...I HEAR YOUR BROTHER'S A CELEBRITY.
PIKU (TWITCH)
DON'T YOU HEAR A LOT OF STORIES THESE DAYS ABOUT CELEBRITIES GETTING CAUGHT WITH DRUGS?
IT JUST MAKES ME WONDER, IF YOU DENY DOING ANYTHING, AND WE GO AND SEARCH YOUR BROTHER'S HOME, WOULD WE FIND ANY LITTLE PACKETS OF WHITE POWDER?
YOU SON OF A BITCH...
SOMETHING WEIRD'S GOING ON...

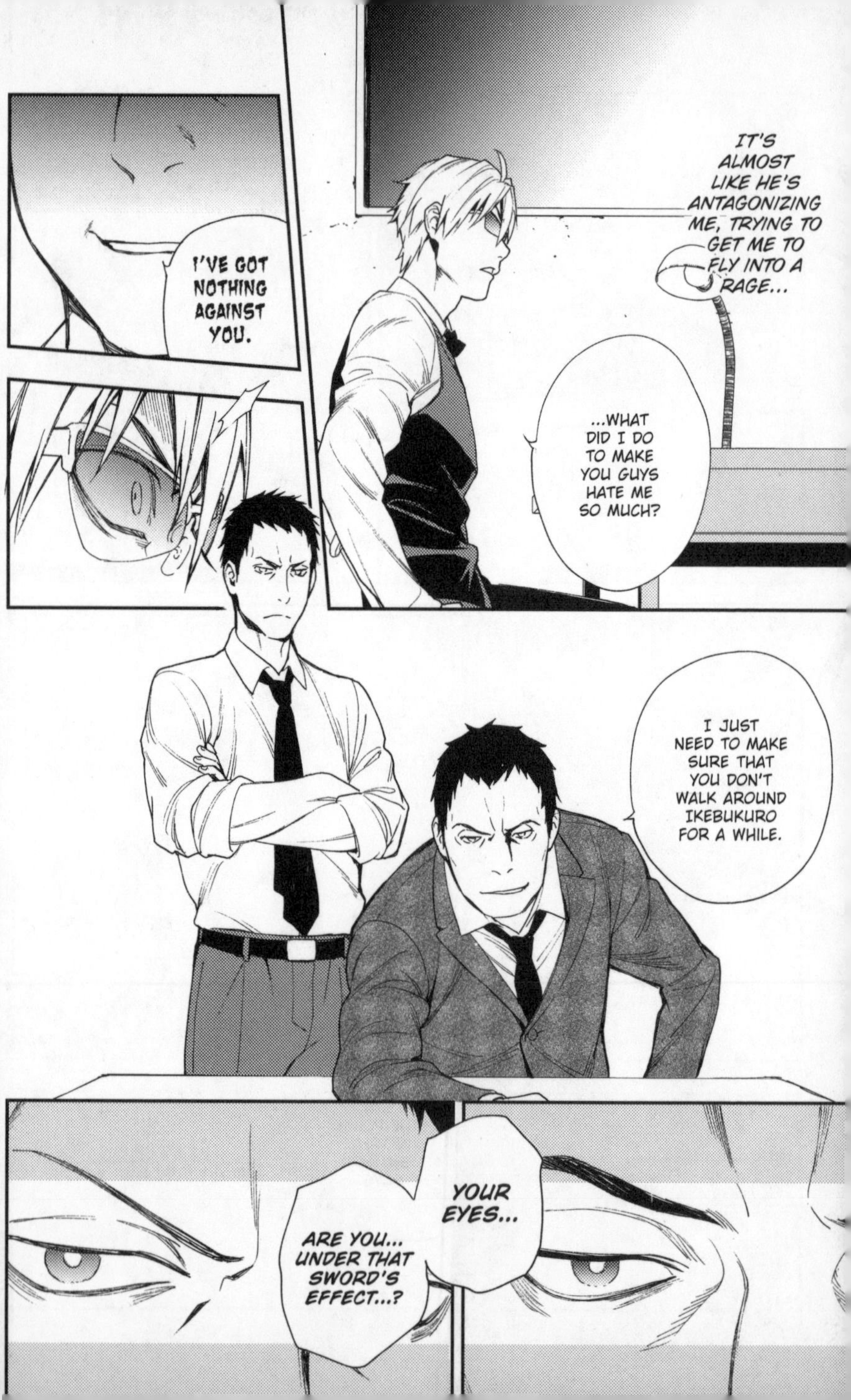
IT'S ALMOST LIKE HE'S ANTAGONIZING ME, TRYING TO GET ME TO FLY INTO A RAGE...
...WHAT DID I DO TO MAKE YOU GUYS HATE ME SO MUCH?
I'VE GOT NOTHING AGAINST YOU.
I JUST NEED TO MAKE SURE THAT YOU DON'T WALK AROUND IKEBUKURO FOR A WHILE.
YOUR EYES...
ARE YOU... UNDER THAT SWORD'S EFFECT...?

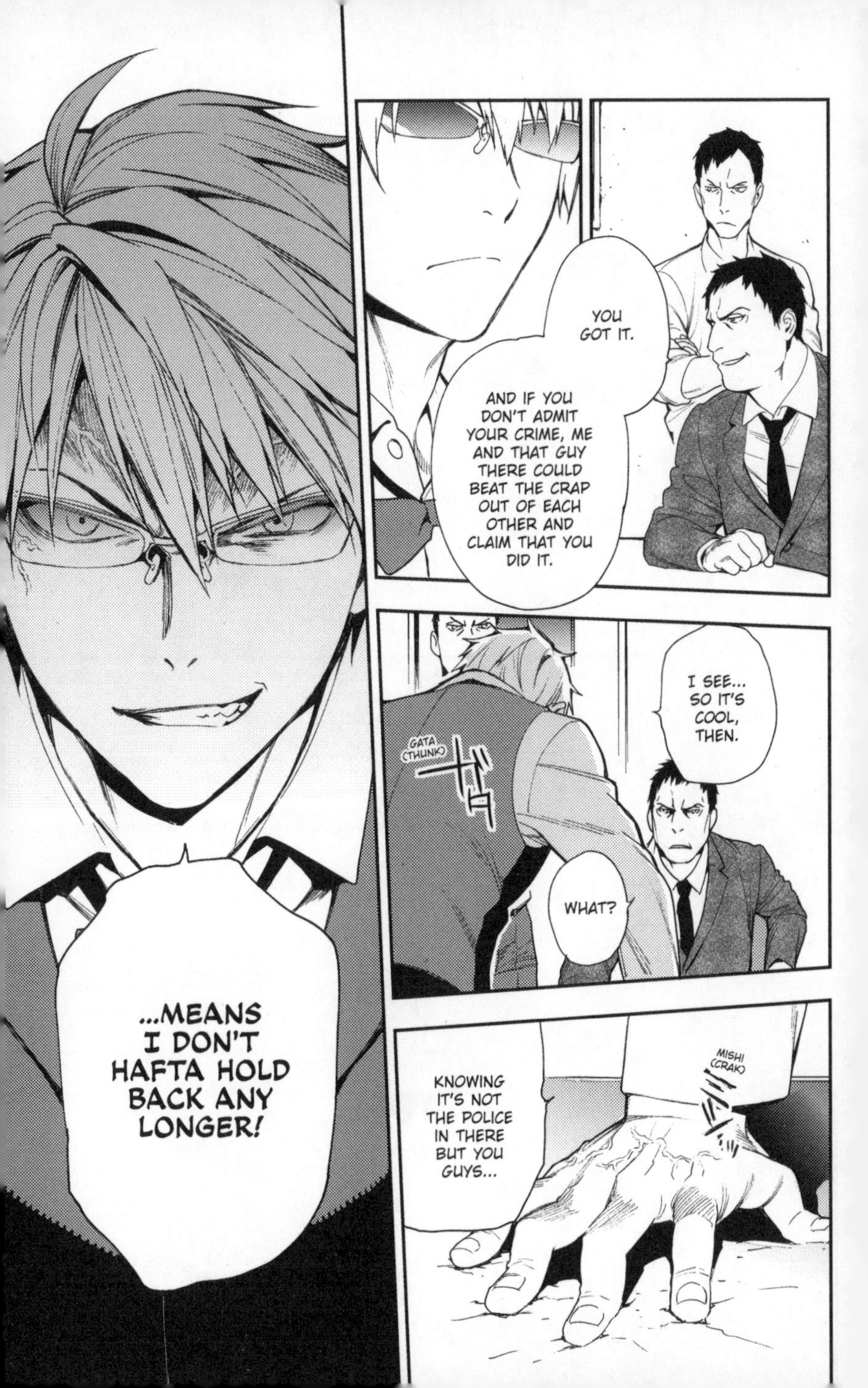
YOU GOT IT.
AND IF YOU DON'T ADMIT YOUR CRIME, ME AND THAT GUY THERE COULD BEAT THE CRAP OUT OF EACH OTHER AND CLAIM THAT YOU DID IT.
I SEE... SO IT'S COOL, THEN.
GATA (THUNK)
WHAT?
MISHI (CRAK)
KNOWING IT'S NOT THE POLICE IN THERE BUT YOU GUYS...
...MEANS I DON'T HAFTA HOLD BACK ANY LONGER!

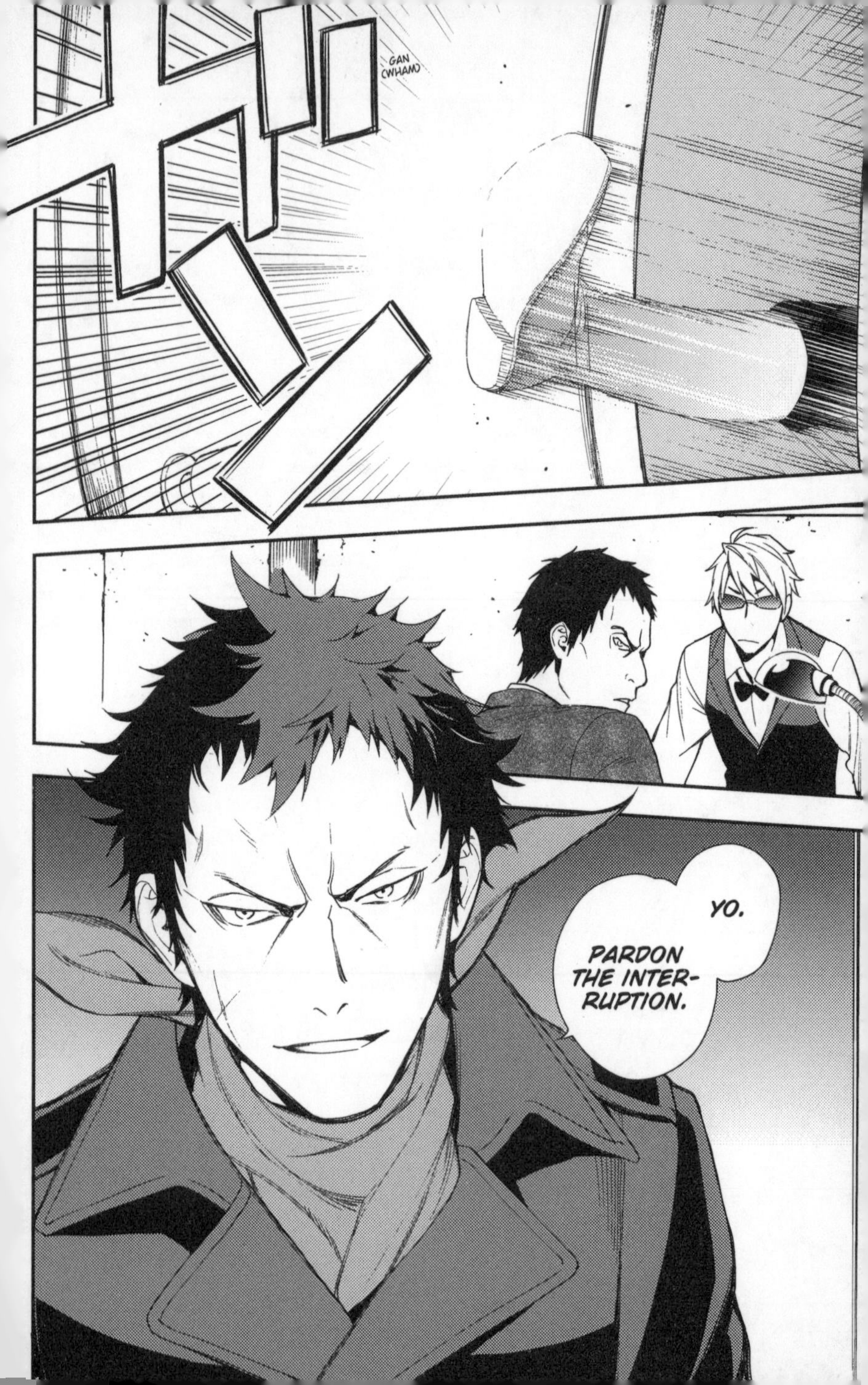
GAN (WHAM)
YO.
PARDON THE INTER-RUPTION.

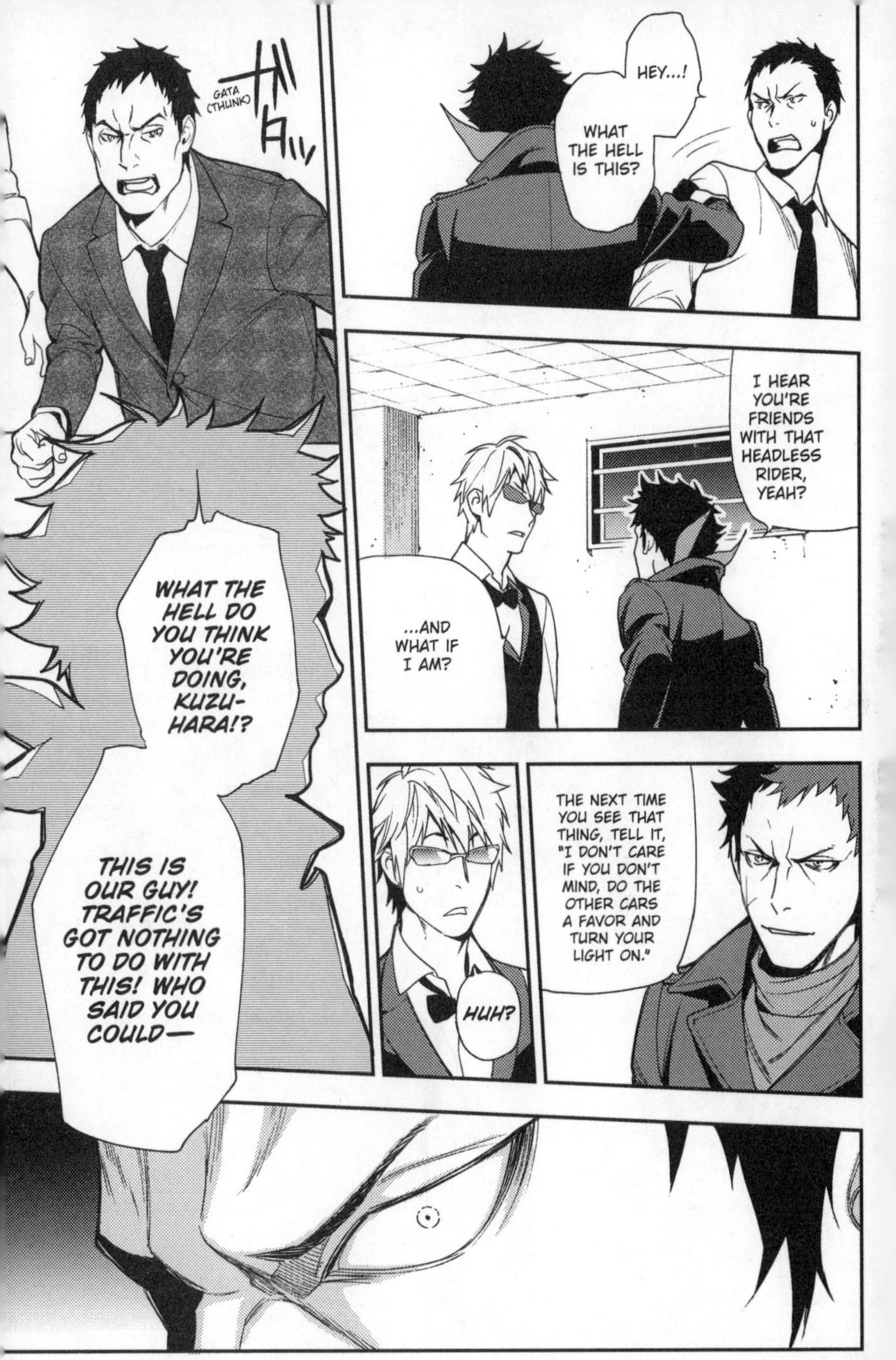
HEY...!
WHAT THE HELL IS THIS?
I HEAR YOU'RE FRIENDS WITH THAT HEADLESS RIDER, YEAH?
...AND WHAT IF I AM?
THE NEXT TIME YOU SEE THAT THING, TELL IT, "I DON'T CARE IF YOU DON'T MIND, DO THE OTHER CARS A FAVOR AND TURN YOUR LIGHT ON."
HUH?
GATA (THUNK)
WHAT THE HELL DO YOU THINK YOU'RE DOING, KUZU-HARA!?
THIS IS OUR GUY! TRAFFIC'S GOT NOTHING TO DO WITH THIS! WHO SAID YOU COULD—

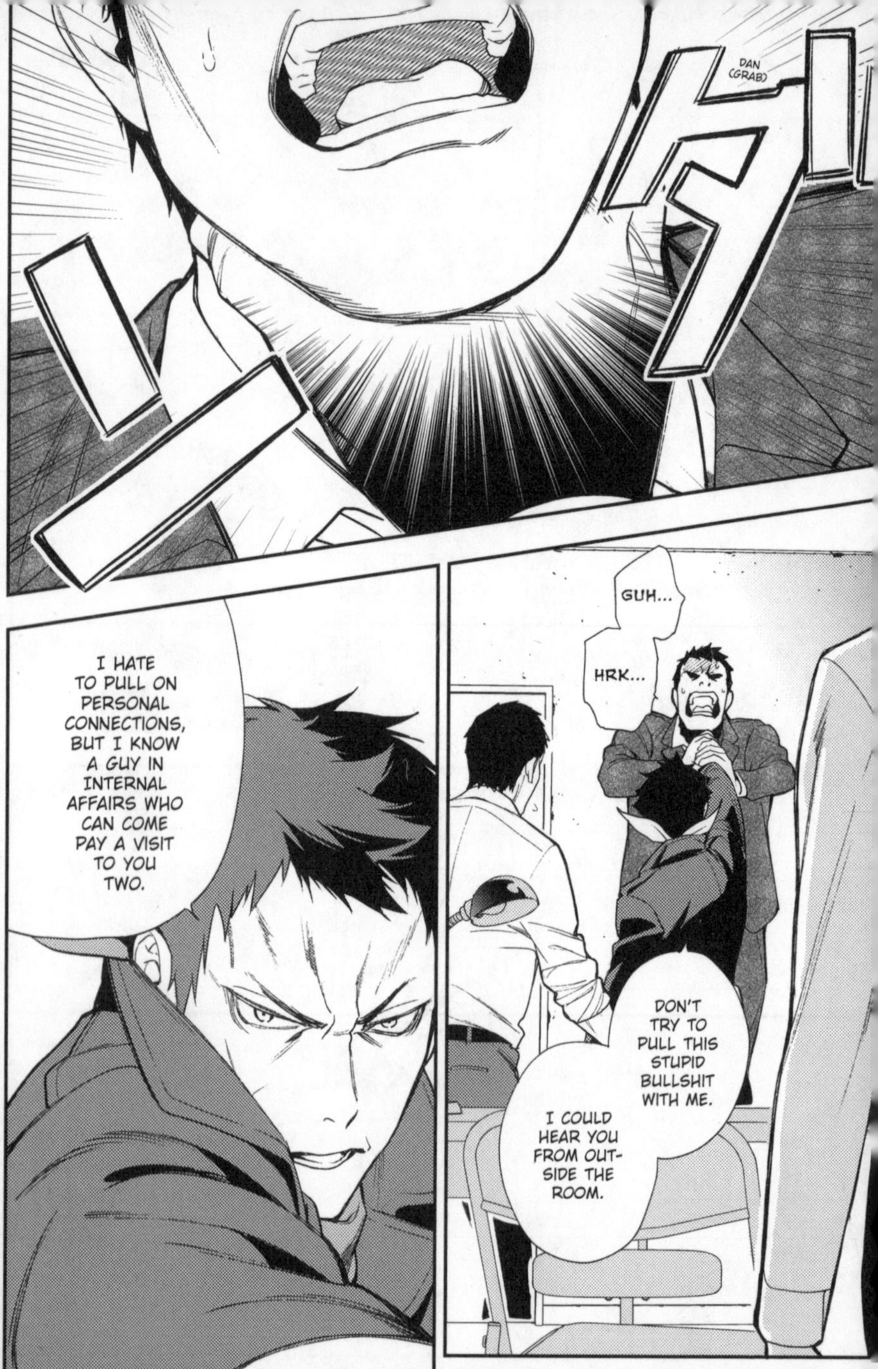
DAN
(GRAB)
GUH...
HRK...
DON'T TRY TO PULL THIS STUPID BULLSHIT WITH ME.
I COULD HEAR YOU FROM OUT-SIDE THE ROOM.
I HATE TO PULL ON PERSONAL CONNECTIONS, BUT I KNOW A GUY IN INTERNAL AFFAIRS WHO CAN COME PAY A VISIT TO YOU TWO.

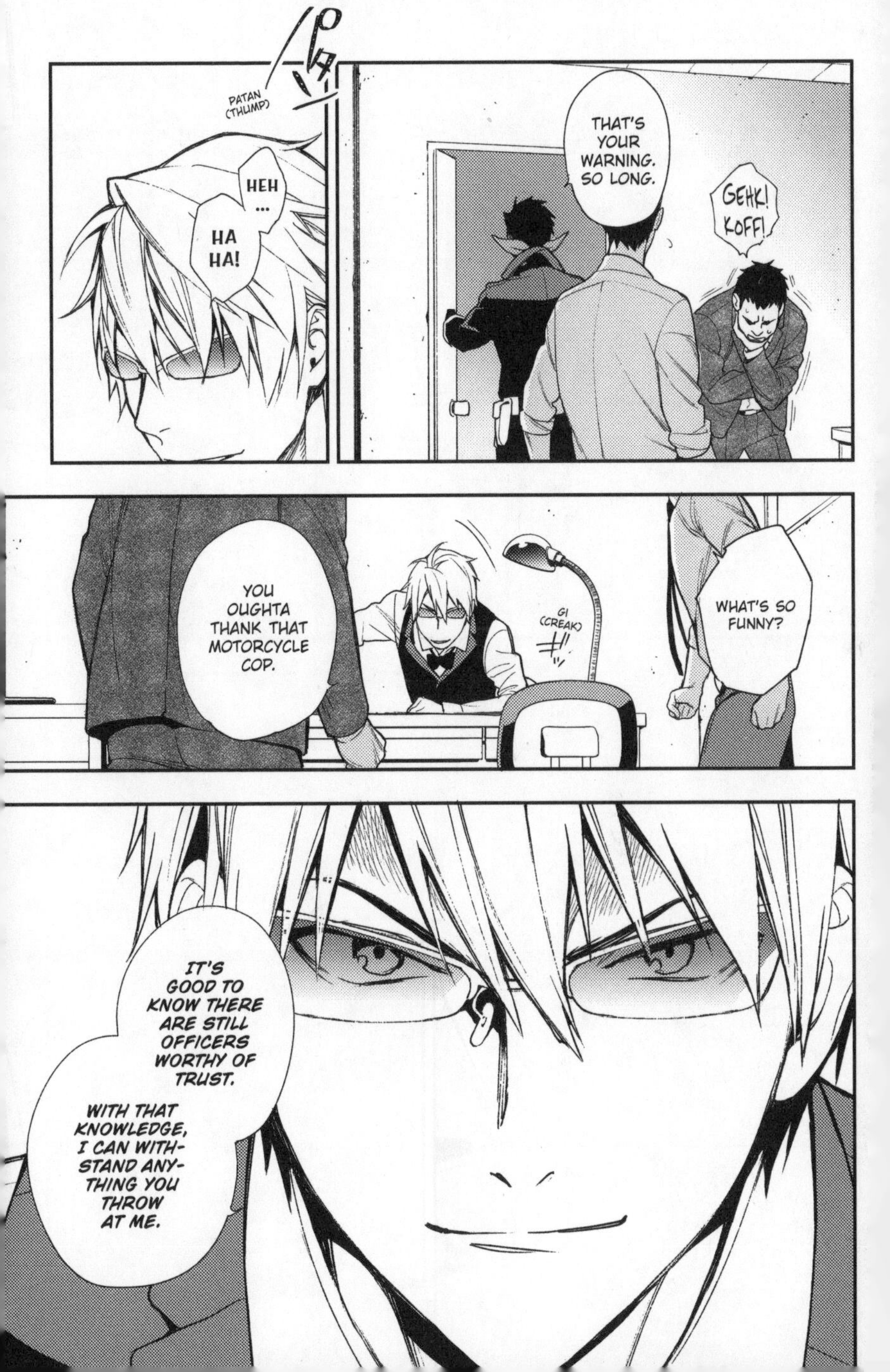
THAT'S YOUR WARNING. SO LONG.
GEHK! KOFF!
PATAN (THUMP)
HEH ... HA HA!
WHAT'S SO FUNNY?
GI (CREAK)
YOU OUGHTA THANK THAT MOTORCYCLE COP.
IT'S GOOD TO KNOW THERE ARE STILL OFFICERS WORTHY OF TRUST.
WITH THAT KNOWLEDGE, I CAN WITH-STAND ANY-THING YOU THROW AT ME.

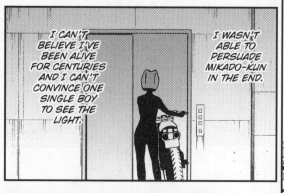

I WASN'T ABLE TO PERSUADE MIKADO-KUN IN THE END.
I CAN'T BELIEVE I'VE BEEN ALIVE FOR CENTURIES AND I CAN'T CONVINCE ONE SINGLE BOY TO SEE THE LIGHT.
I'M EX-HAUSTED...
I'M HAVING ENOUGH OF A TIME TAKING CARE OF MYSELF...
OH MY, CELTY-SAN.
ARE YOU RETURNING TO HOME?
AH. HELLO, EMILIA-SAN.
WHY SO MUCH STUFF?
TODAY IS PARTYDAY OF THE WEEK FOR EVERYONE!
?

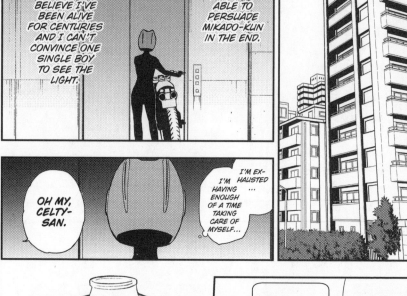

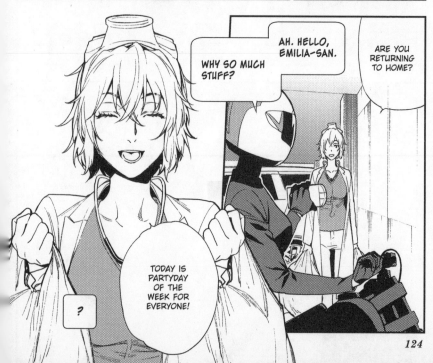

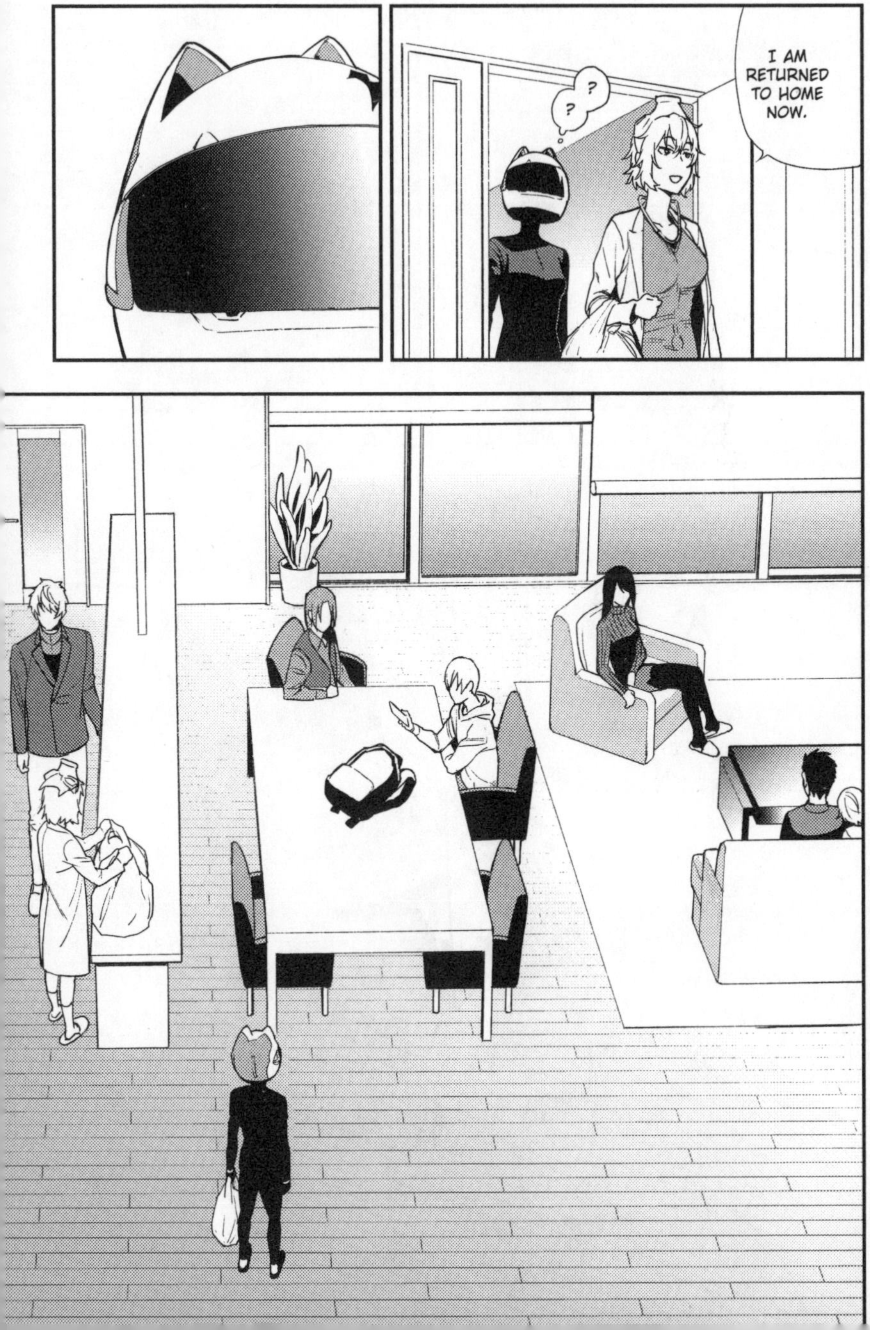

I AM RETURNED TO HOME NOW.
? ?
?

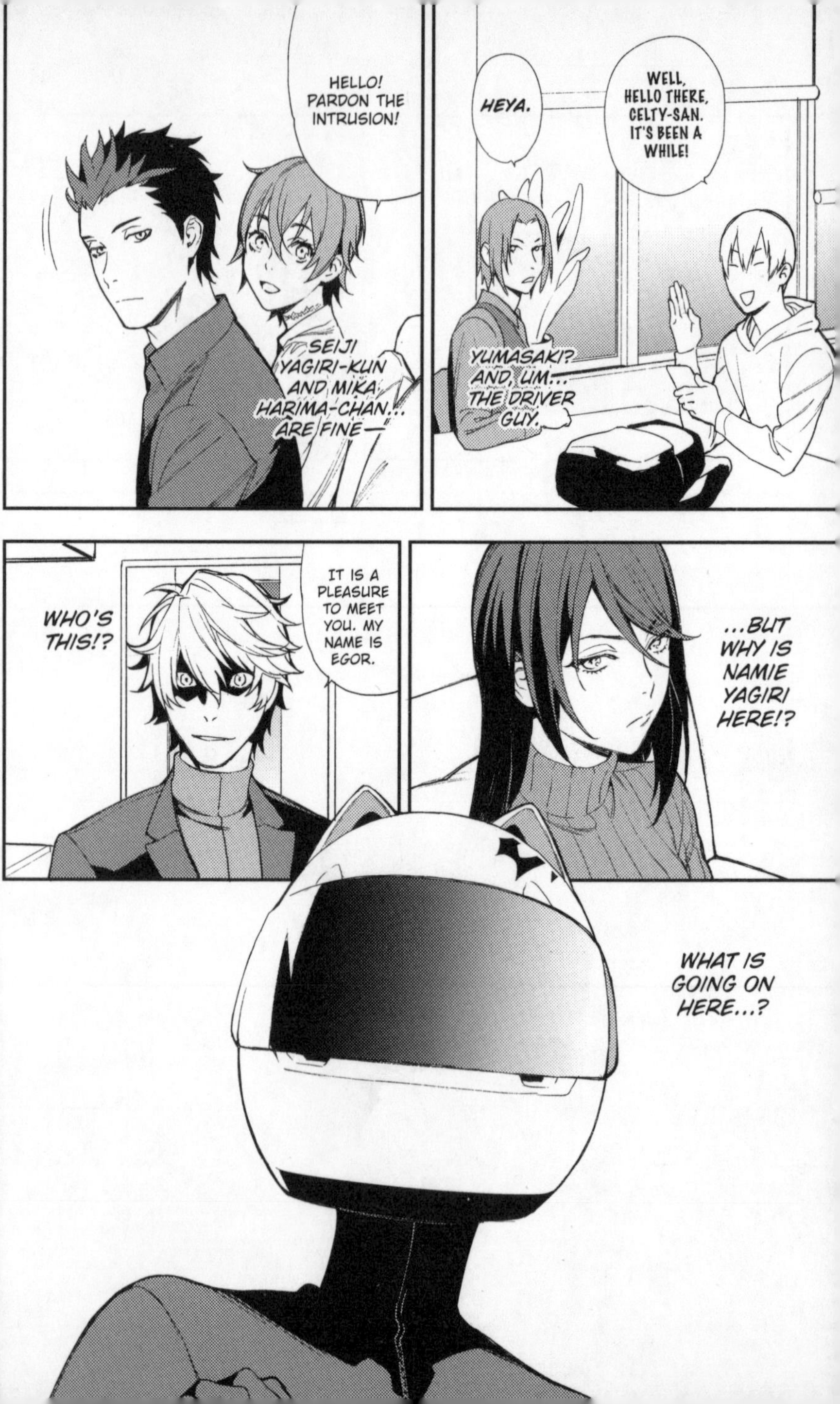
WELL, HELLO THERE, CELTY-SAN. IT'S BEEN A WHILE!
HEYA.
YUMASAKI!? AND, UM... THE DRIVER GUY.
HELLO! PARDON THE INTRUSION!
SEIJI YAGIRI-KUN AND MIKA HARIMA-CHAN... ARE FINE—
...BUT WHY IS NAMIE YAGIRI HERE!?
IT IS A PLEASURE TO MEET YOU. MY NAME IS EGOR.
WHO'S THIS!?
WHAT IS GOING ON HERE...?

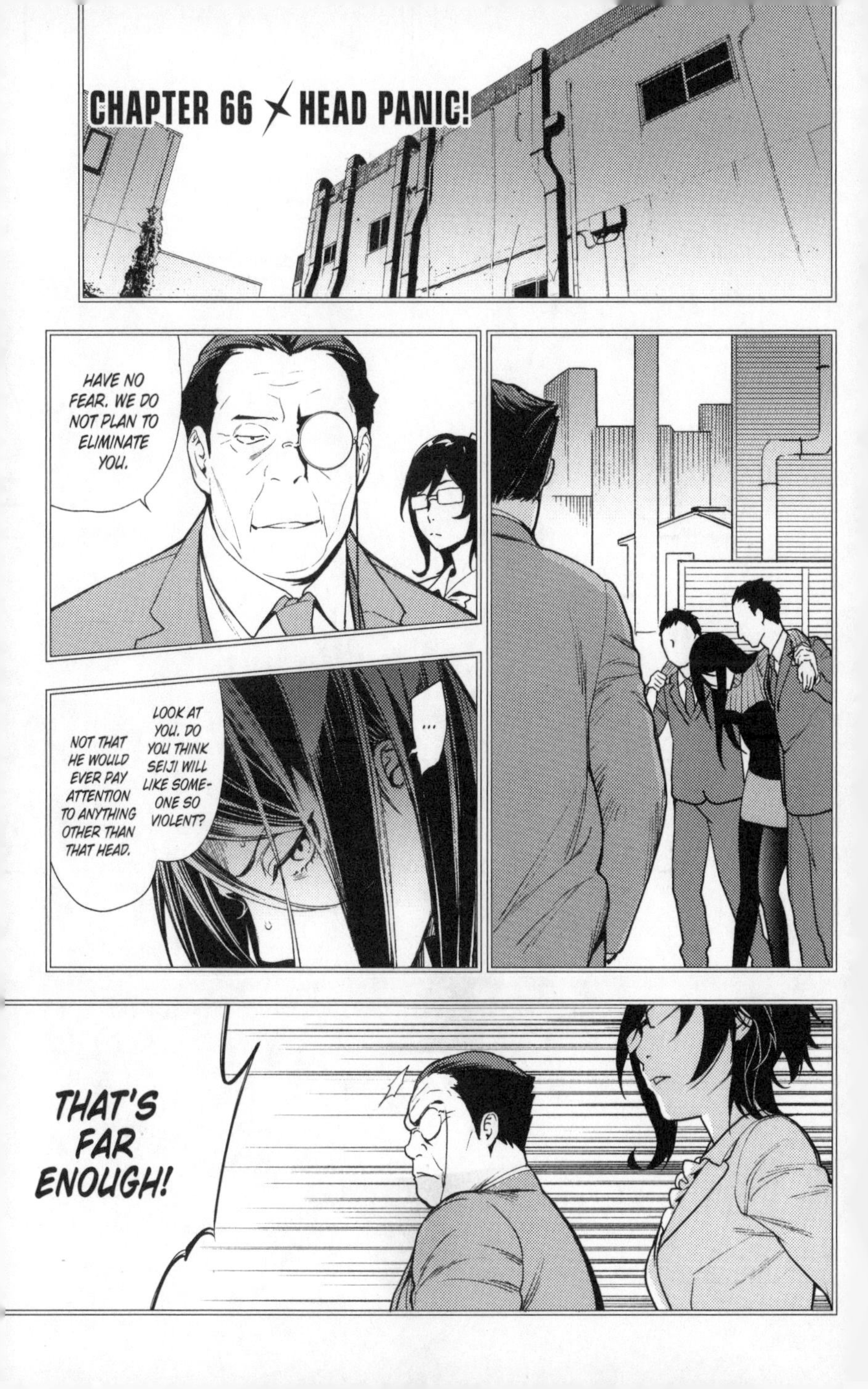
CHAPTER 66 ✗ HEAD PANIC!
HAVE NO FEAR. WE DO NOT PLAN TO ELIMINATE YOU.
...
LOOK AT YOU. DO YOU THINK SEIJI WILL LIKE SOME-ONE SO VIOLENT?
NOT THAT HE WOULD EVER PAY ATTENTION TO ANYTHING OTHER THAN THAT HEAD.
THAT'S FAR ENOUGH!

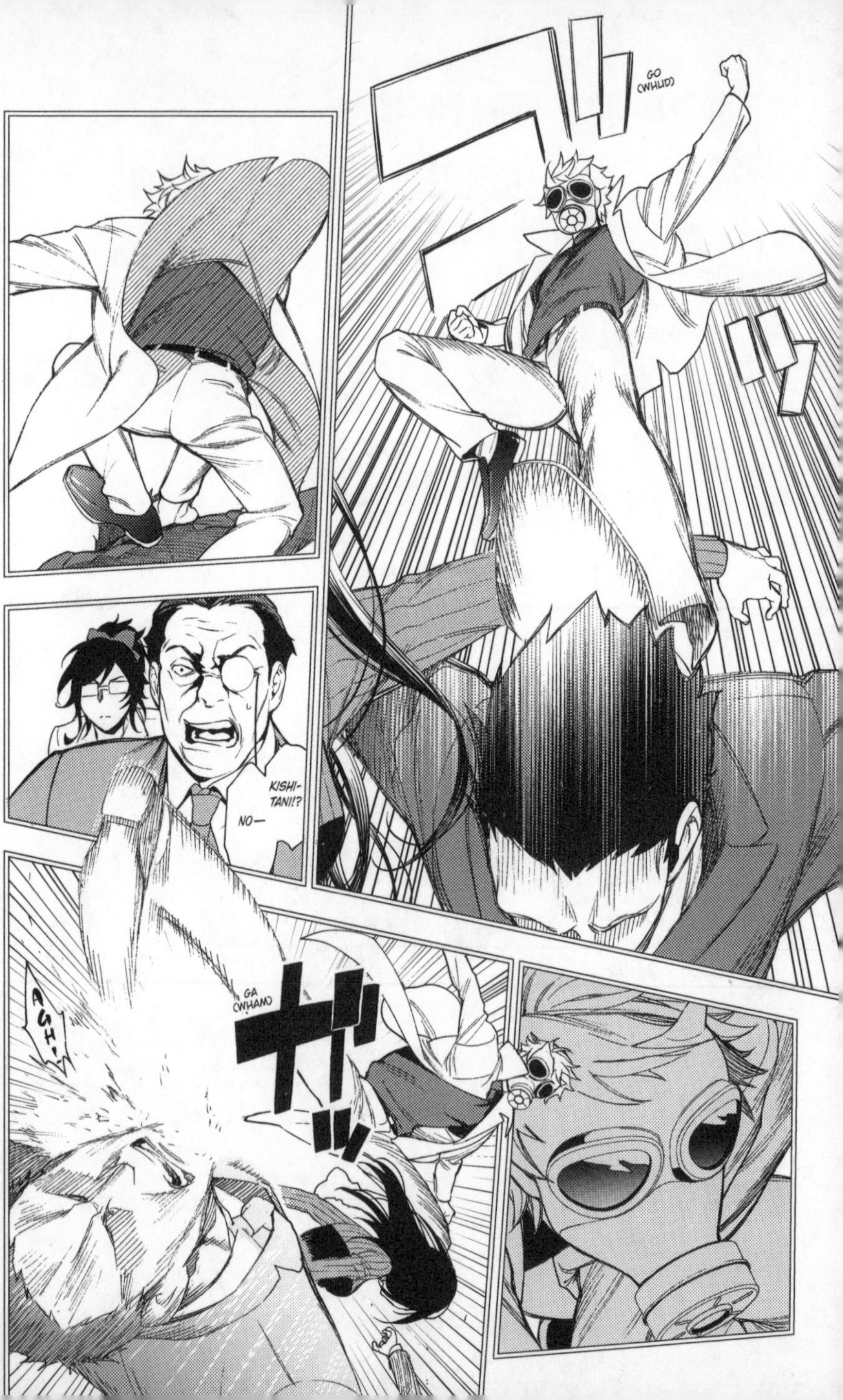
GO (WHUD)
KISHI-TANI!?
NO—
GA (WHAM)
AGH!

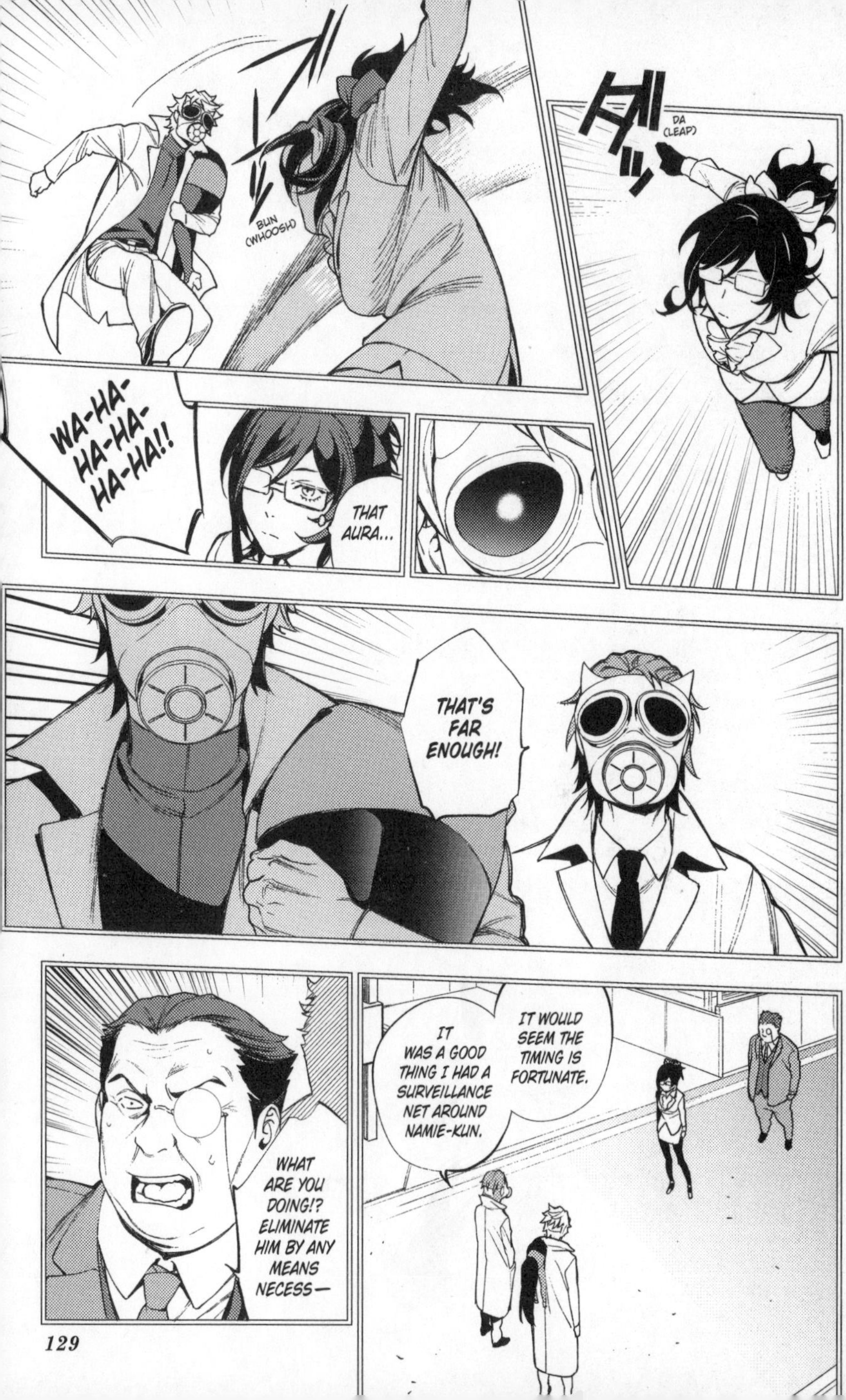

DA (LEAP)
BUN (WHOOSH)
THAT AURA...
WA-HA-HA-HA-HA-HA!!
THAT'S FAR ENOUGH!
IT WOULD SEEM THE TIMING IS FORTUNATE.
IT WAS A GOOD THING I HAD A SURVEILLANCE NET AROUND NAMIE-KUN.
WHAT ARE YOU DOING!? ELIMINATE HIM BY ANY MEANS NECESS—

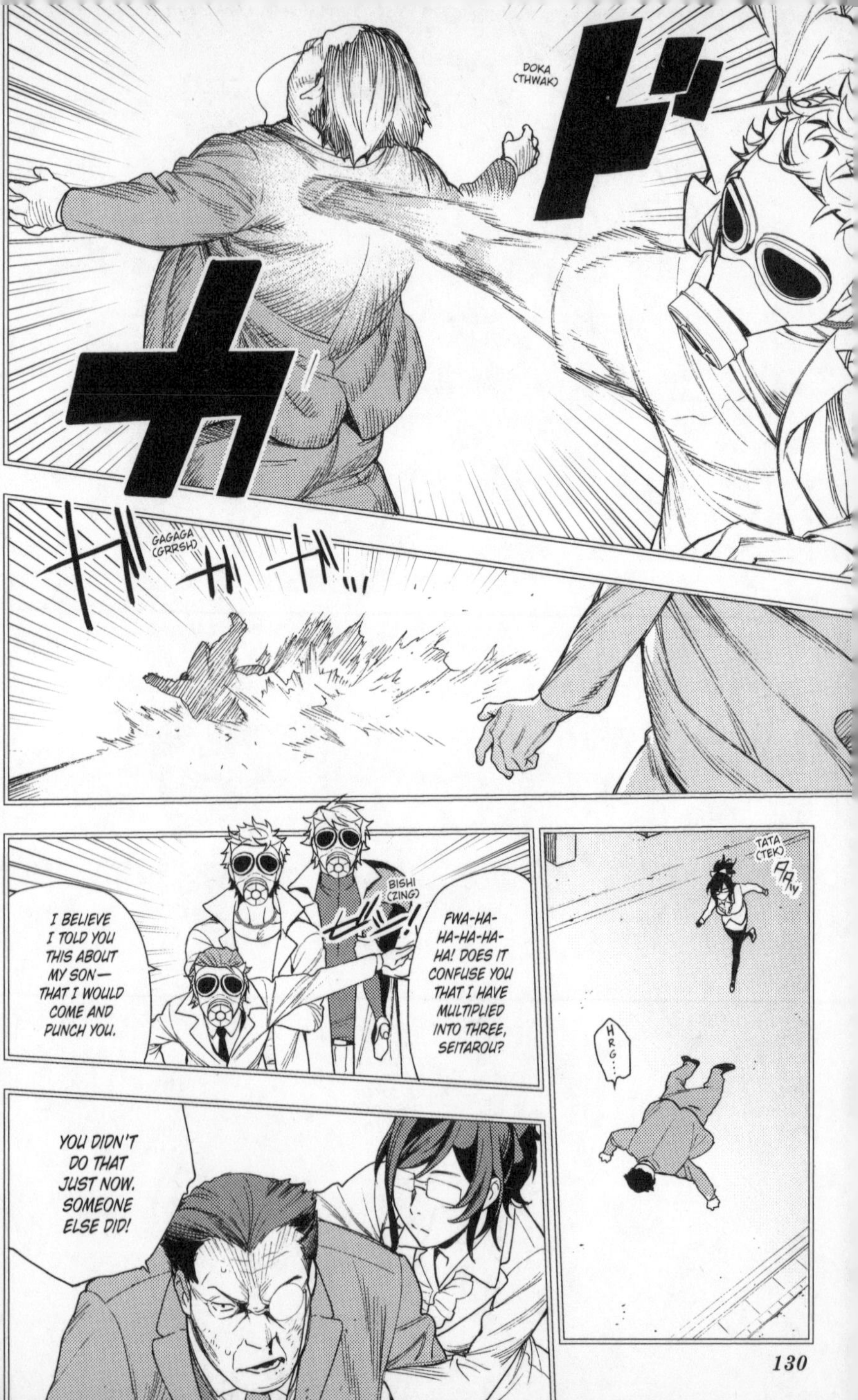
DOKA (THWAK)
GAGAGA (GRRSH)
TATA (TEK)
HRG...
FWA-HA-HA-HA-HA-HA! DOES IT CONFUSE YOU THAT I HAVE MULTIPLIED INTO THREE, SEITAROU?
BISHI (ZING)
I BELIEVE I TOLD YOU THIS ABOUT MY SON—THAT I WOULD COME AND PUNCH YOU.
YOU DIDN'T DO THAT JUST NOW. SOMEONE ELSE DID!

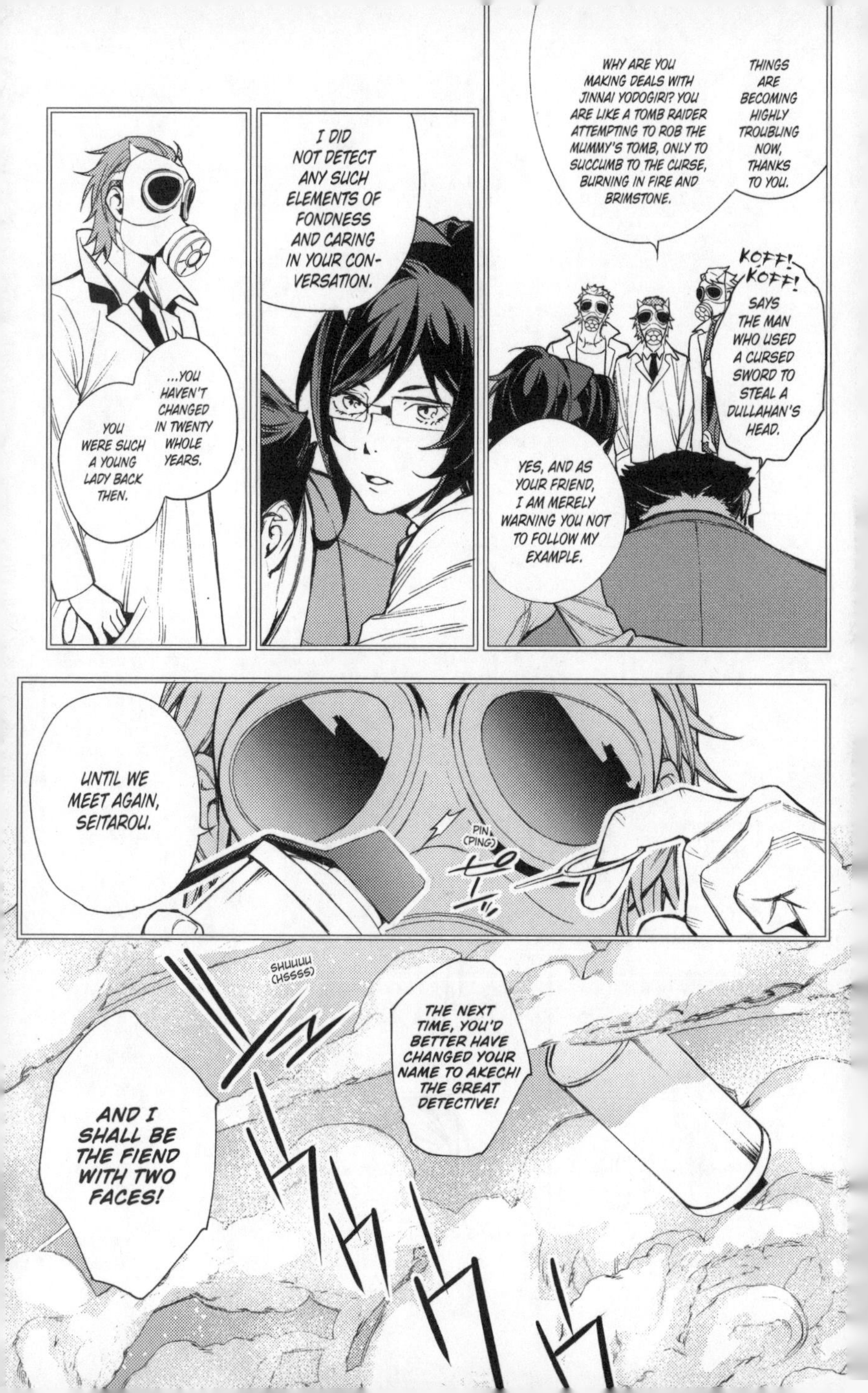
THINGS ARE BECOMING HIGHLY TROUBLING NOW, THANKS TO YOU.
WHY ARE YOU MAKING DEALS WITH JINNAI YODOGIRI? YOU ARE LIKE A TOMB RAIDER ATTEMPTING TO ROB THE MUMMY'S TOMB, ONLY TO SUCCUMB TO THE CURSE, BURNING IN FIRE AND BRIMSTONE.
KOFF! KOFF!
SAYS THE MAN WHO USED A CURSED SWORD TO STEAL A DULLAHAN'S HEAD.
YES, AND AS YOUR FRIEND, I AM MERELY WARNING YOU NOT TO FOLLOW MY EXAMPLE.
I DID NOT DETECT ANY SUCH ELEMENTS OF FONDNESS AND CARING IN YOUR CON-VERSATION.
...YOU HAVEN'T CHANGED IN TWENTY WHOLE YEARS.
YOU WERE SUCH A YOUNG LADY BACK THEN.
PING (PING)
UNTIL WE MEET AGAIN, SEITAROU.
SHUUUU (HSSSS)
THE NEXT TIME, YOU'D BETTER HAVE CHANGED YOUR NAME TO AKECHI THE GREAT DETECTIVE!
AND I SHALL BE THE FIEND WITH TWO FACES!

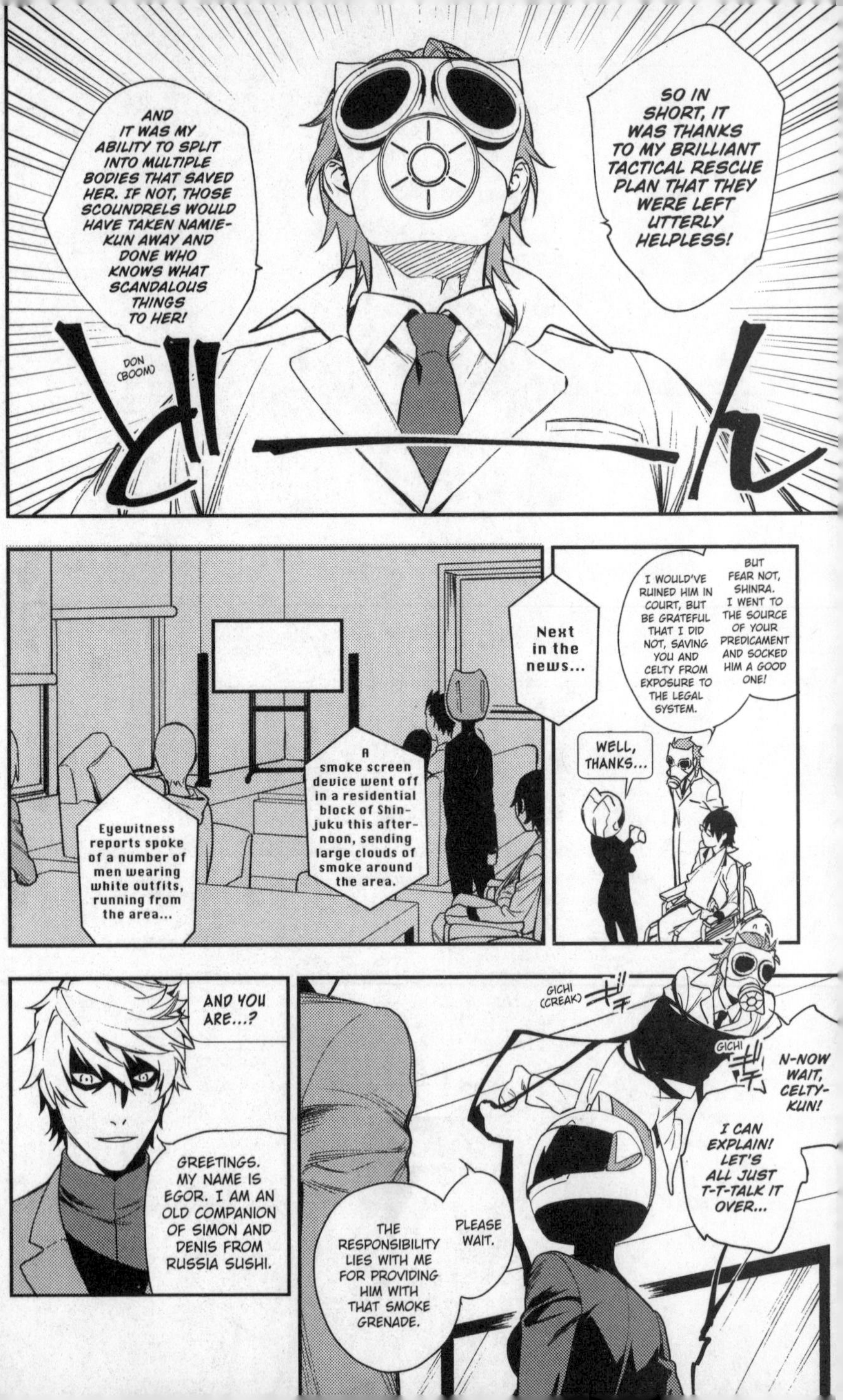
SO IN SHORT, IT WAS THANKS TO MY BRILLIANT TACTICAL RESCUE PLAN THAT THEY WERE LEFT UTTERLY HELPLESS!
AND IT WAS MY ABILITY TO SPLIT INTO MULTIPLE BODIES THAT SAVED HER. IF NOT, THOSE SCOUNDRELS WOULD HAVE TAKEN NAMIE-KUN AWAY AND DONE WHO KNOWS WHAT SCANDALOUS THINGS TO HER!
DON (BOOM)
BUT FEAR NOT, SHINRA. I WENT TO THE SOURCE OF YOUR PREDICAMENT AND SOCKED HIM A GOOD ONE!
I WOULD'VE RUINED HIM IN COURT, BUT BE GRATEFUL THAT I DID NOT, SAVING YOU AND CELTY FROM EXPOSURE TO THE LEGAL SYSTEM.
WELL, THANKS...
Next in the news...
A smoke screen device went off in a residential block of Shinjuku this afternoon, sending large clouds of smoke around the area.
Eyewitness reports spoke of a number of men wearing white outfits, running from the area...
GICHI (CREAK)
GICHI
N-NOW WAIT, CELTY-KUN!
I CAN EXPLAIN! LET'S ALL JUST T-T-TALK IT OVER...
PLEASE WAIT.
THE RESPONSIBILITY LIES WITH ME FOR PROVIDING HIM WITH THAT SMOKE GRENADE.
AND YOU ARE...?
GREETINGS. MY NAME IS EGOR. I AM AN OLD COMPANION OF SIMON AND DENIS FROM RUSSIA SUSHI.

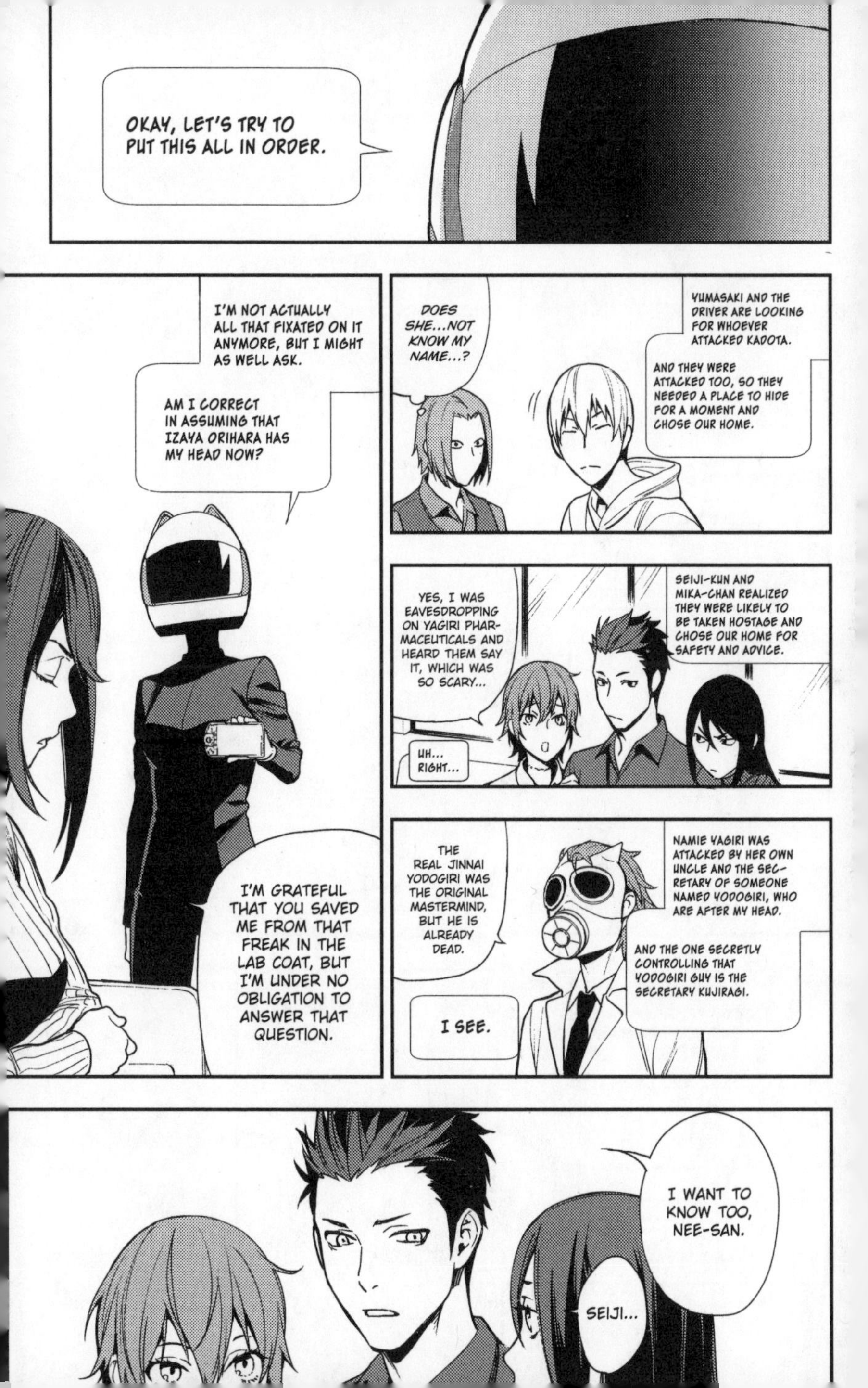
OKAY, LET'S TRY TO PUT THIS ALL IN ORDER.
YUMASAKI AND THE DRIVER ARE LOOKING FOR WHOEVER ATTACKED KADOTA.
AND THEY WERE ATTACKED TOO, SO THEY NEEDED A PLACE TO HIDE FOR A MOMENT AND CHOSE OUR HOME.
DOES SHE...NOT KNOW MY NAME...?
SEIJI-KUN AND MIKA-CHAN REALIZED THEY WERE LIKELY TO BE TAKEN HOSTAGE AND CHOSE OUR HOME FOR SAFETY AND ADVICE.
YES, I WAS EAVESDROPPING ON YAGIRI PHARMACEUTICALS AND HEARD THEM SAY IT, WHICH WAS SO SCARY...
UH... RIGHT...
NAMIE YAGIRI WAS ATTACKED BY HER OWN UNCLE AND THE SECRETARY OF SOMEONE NAMED YODOGIRI, WHO ARE AFTER MY HEAD.
AND THE ONE SECRETLY CONTROLLING THAT YODOGIRI GUY IS THE SECRETARY KUJIRAGI.
THE REAL JINNAI YODOGIRI WAS THE ORIGINAL MASTERMIND, BUT HE IS ALREADY DEAD.
I SEE.
I'M NOT ACTUALLY ALL THAT FIXATED ON IT ANYMORE, BUT I MIGHT AS WELL ASK.
AM I CORRECT IN ASSUMING THAT IZAYA ORIHARA HAS MY HEAD NOW?
I'M GRATEFUL THAT YOU SAVED ME FROM THAT FREAK IN THE LAB COAT, BUT I'M UNDER NO OBLIGATION TO ANSWER THAT QUESTION.
I WANT TO KNOW TOO, NEE-SAN.
SEIJI...

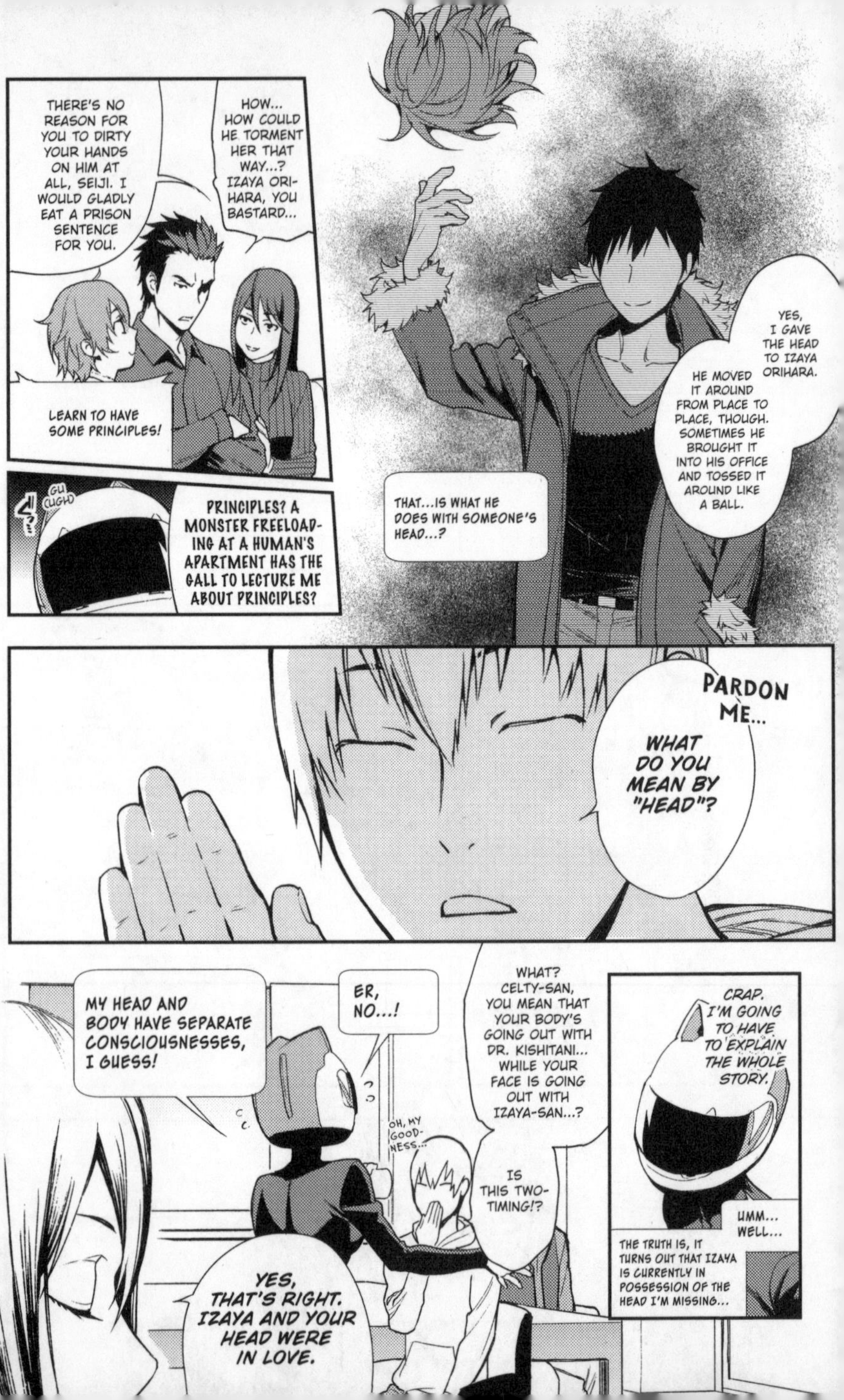
YES, I GAVE THE HEAD TO IZAYA ORIHARA.
HE MOVED IT AROUND FROM PLACE TO PLACE, THOUGH. SOMETIMES HE BROUGHT IT INTO HIS OFFICE AND TOSSED IT AROUND LIKE A BALL.
THAT...IS WHAT HE DOES WITH SOMEONE'S HEAD...?
HOW... HOW COULD HE TORMENT HER THAT WAY...? IZAYA ORIHARA, YOU BASTARD...
THERE'S NO REASON FOR YOU TO DIRTY YOUR HANDS ON HIM AT ALL, SEIJI. I WOULD GLADLY EAT A PRISON SENTENCE FOR YOU.
LEARN TO HAVE SOME PRINCIPLES!
GU UGH
PRINCIPLES? A MONSTER FREELOADING AT A HUMAN'S APARTMENT HAS THE GALL TO LECTURE ME ABOUT PRINCIPLES?
PARDON ME...
WHAT DO YOU MEAN BY "HEAD"?
CRAP. I'M GOING TO HAVE TO EXPLAIN THE WHOLE STORY.
UMM... WELL...
THE TRUTH IS, IT TURNS OUT THAT IZAYA IS CURRENTLY IN POSSESSION OF THE HEAD I'M MISSING...
WHAT? CELTY-SAN, YOU MEAN THAT YOUR BODY'S GOING OUT WITH DR. KISHITANI... WHILE YOUR FACE IS GOING OUT WITH IZAYA-SAN...?
IS THIS TWO-TIMING!?
OH, MY GOODNESS...
ER, NO...!
MY HEAD AND BODY HAVE SEPARATE CONSCIOUSNESSES, I GUESS!
YES, THAT'S RIGHT. IZAYA AND YOUR HEAD WERE IN LOVE.

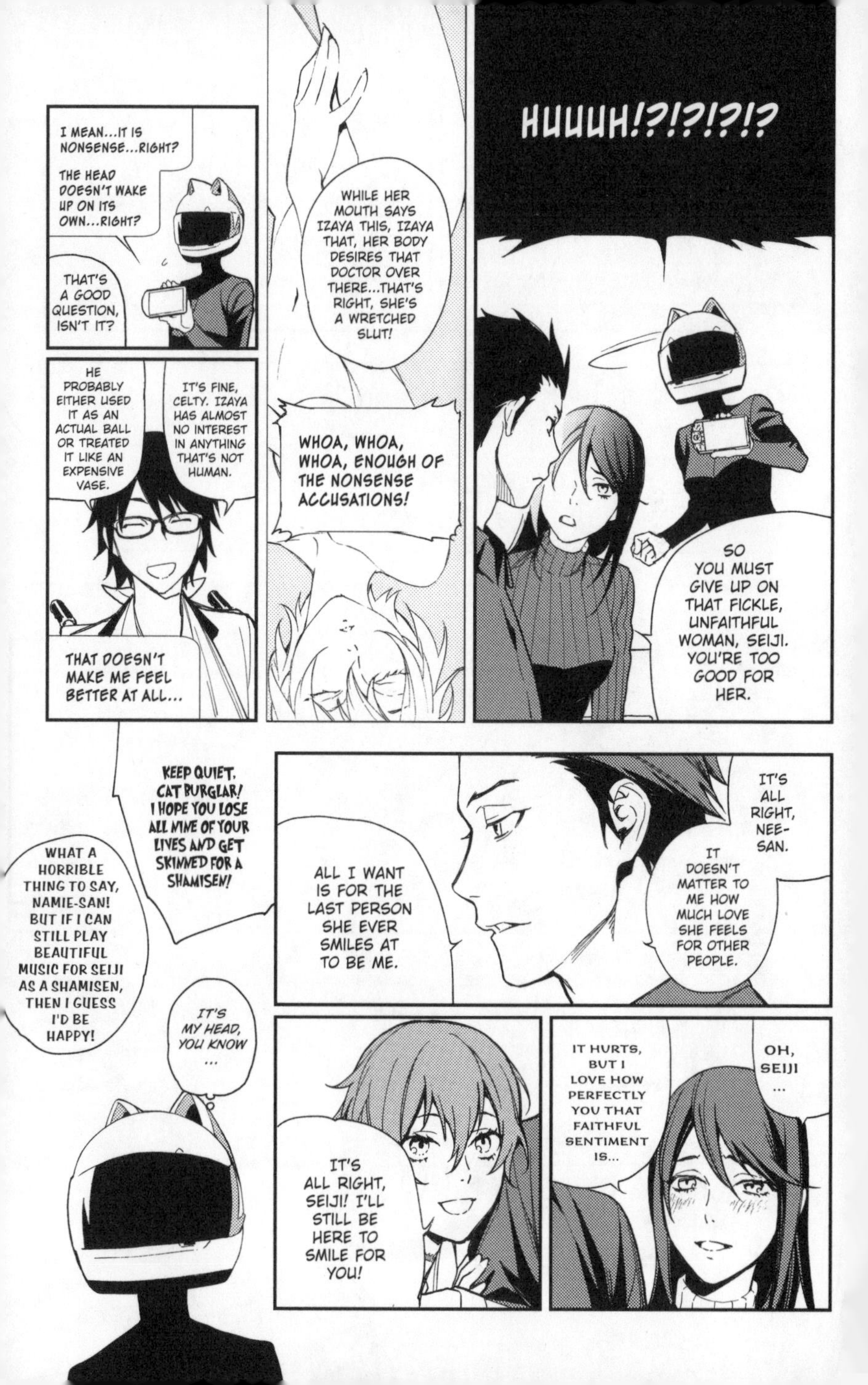
HUUUH!?!?!?!?
SO YOU MUST GIVE UP ON THAT FICKLE, UNFAITHFUL WOMAN, SEIJI. YOU'RE TOO GOOD FOR HER.
WHILE HER MOUTH SAYS IZAYA THIS, IZAYA THAT, HER BODY DESIRES THAT DOCTOR OVER THERE...THAT'S RIGHT, SHE'S A WRETCHED SLUT!
WHOA, WHOA, WHOA, ENOUGH OF THE NONSENSE ACCUSATIONS!
I MEAN...IT IS NONSENSE...RIGHT?
THE HEAD DOESN'T WAKE UP ON ITS OWN...RIGHT?
THAT'S A GOOD QUESTION, ISN'T IT?
IT'S FINE, CELTY. IZAYA HAS ALMOST NO INTEREST IN ANYTHING THAT'S NOT HUMAN.
HE PROBABLY EITHER USED IT AS AN ACTUAL BALL OR TREATED IT LIKE AN EXPENSIVE VASE.
THAT DOESN'T MAKE ME FEEL BETTER AT ALL...
IT'S ALL RIGHT, NEE-SAN.
IT DOESN'T MATTER TO ME HOW MUCH LOVE SHE FEELS FOR OTHER PEOPLE.
ALL I WANT IS FOR THE LAST PERSON SHE EVER SMILES AT TO BE ME.
OH, SEIJI...
IT HURTS, BUT I LOVE HOW PERFECTLY YOU THAT FAITHFUL SENTIMENT IS...
IT'S ALL RIGHT, SEIJI! I'LL STILL BE HERE TO SMILE FOR YOU!
KEEP QUIET, CAT BURGLAR! I HOPE YOU LOSE ALL NINE OF YOUR LIVES AND GET SKINNED FOR A SHAMISEN!
WHAT A HORRIBLE THING TO SAY, NAMIE-SAN! BUT IF I CAN STILL PLAY BEAUTIFUL MUSIC FOR SEIJI AS A SHAMISEN, THEN I GUESS I'D BE HAPPY!
IT'S MY HEAD, YOU KNOW...

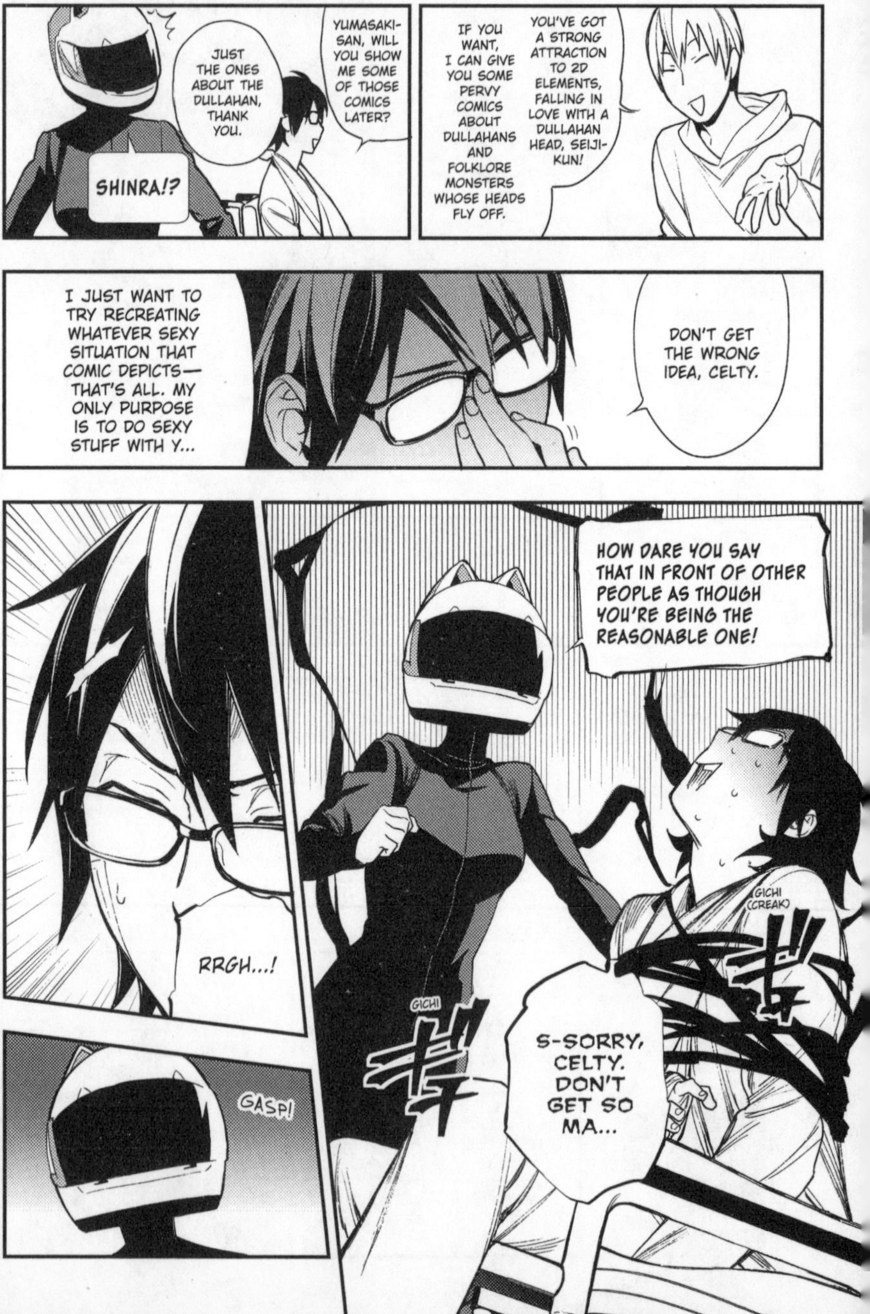
YOU'VE GOT A STRONG ATTRACTION TO 2D ELEMENTS, FALLING IN LOVE WITH A DULLAHAN HEAD, SEIJI-KUN!
IF YOU WANT, I CAN GIVE YOU SOME PERVY COMICS ABOUT DULLAHANS AND FOLKLORE MONSTERS WHOSE HEADS FLY OFF.
YUMASAKI-SAN, WILL YOU SHOW ME SOME OF THOSE COMICS LATER?
JUST THE ONES ABOUT THE DULLAHAN, THANK YOU.
SHINRA!?
DON'T GET THE WRONG IDEA, CELTY.
I JUST WANT TO TRY RECREATING WHATEVER SEXY SITUATION THAT COMIC DEPICTS—THAT'S ALL. MY ONLY PURPOSE IS TO DO SEXY STUFF WITH Y...
HOW DARE YOU SAY THAT IN FRONT OF OTHER PEOPLE AS THOUGH YOU'RE BEING THE REASONABLE ONE!
GICHI (CREAK)
S-SORRY, CELTY. DON'T GET SO MA...
GICHI
RRGH...!
GASP!

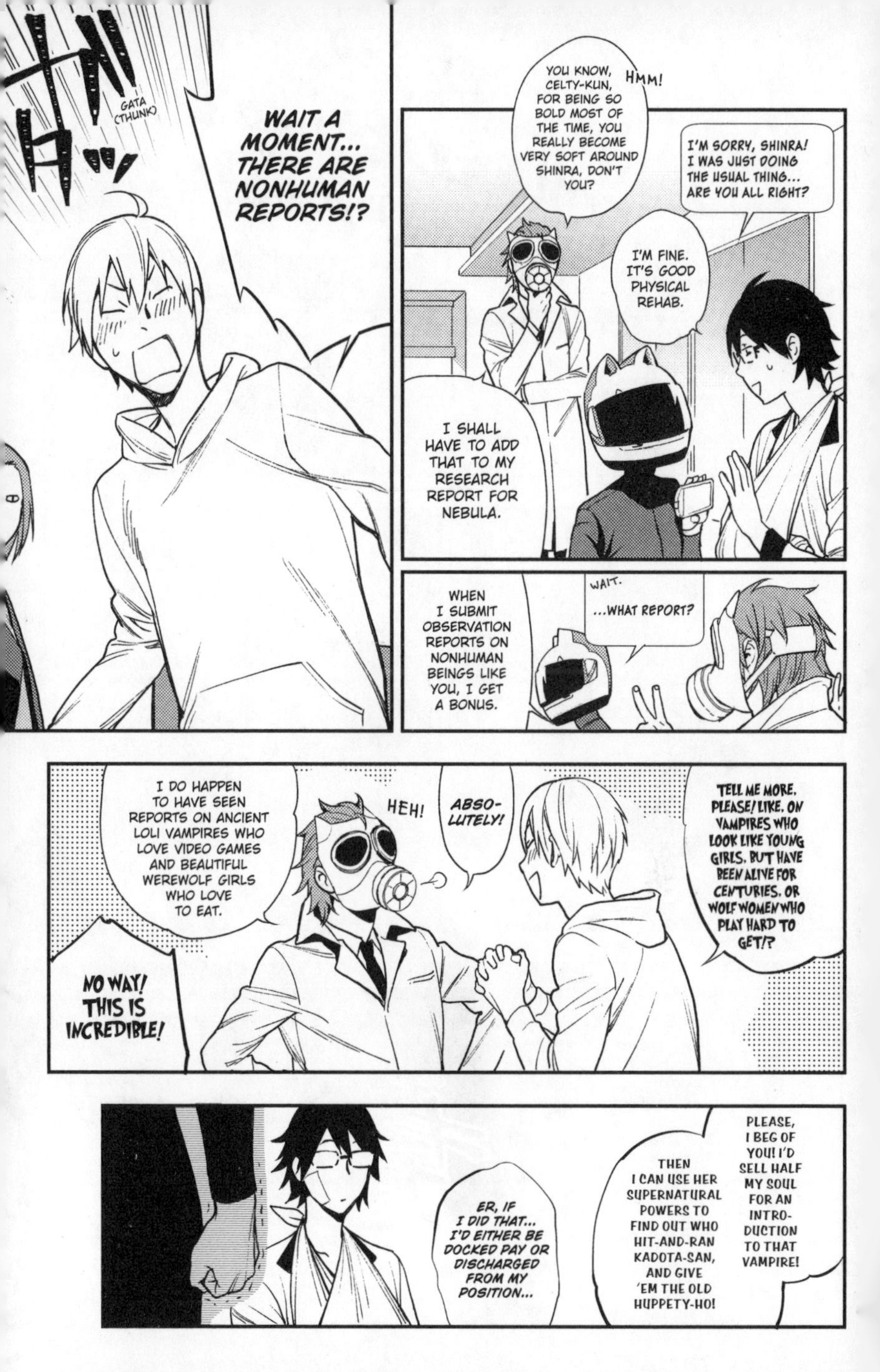

I'M SORRY, SHINRA! I WAS JUST DOING THE USUAL THING... ARE YOU ALL RIGHT?
I'M FINE. IT'S GOOD PHYSICAL REHAB.
HMM!
YOU KNOW, CELTY-KUN, FOR BEING SO BOLD MOST OF THE TIME, YOU REALLY BECOME VERY SOFT AROUND SHINRA, DON'T YOU?
I SHALL HAVE TO ADD THAT TO MY RESEARCH REPORT FOR NEBULA.
WAIT.
...WHAT REPORT?
WHEN I SUBMIT OBSERVATION REPORTS ON NONHUMAN BEINGS LIKE YOU, I GET A BONUS.
GATA (THUNK)
WAIT A MOMENT... THERE ARE NONHUMAN REPORTS!?
TELL ME MORE, PLEASE! LIKE, ON VAMPIRES WHO LOOK LIKE YOUNG GIRLS, BUT HAVE BEEN ALIVE FOR CENTURIES, OR WOLF WOMEN WHO PLAY HARD TO GET!?
ABSO-LUTELY!
HEH!
I DO HAPPEN TO HAVE SEEN REPORTS ON ANCIENT LOLI VAMPIRES WHO LOVE VIDEO GAMES AND BEAUTIFUL WEREWOLF GIRLS WHO LOVE TO EAT.
NO WAY! THIS IS INCREDIBLE!
PLEASE, I BEG OF YOU! I'D SELL HALF MY SOUL FOR AN INTRO-DUCTION TO THAT VAMPIRE!
THEN I CAN USE HER SUPERNATURAL POWERS TO FIND OUT WHO HIT-AND-RAN KADOTA-SAN, AND GIVE 'EM THE OLD HUPPETY-HO!
ER, IF I DID THAT... I'D EITHER BE DOCKED PAY OR DISCHARGED FROM MY POSITION...

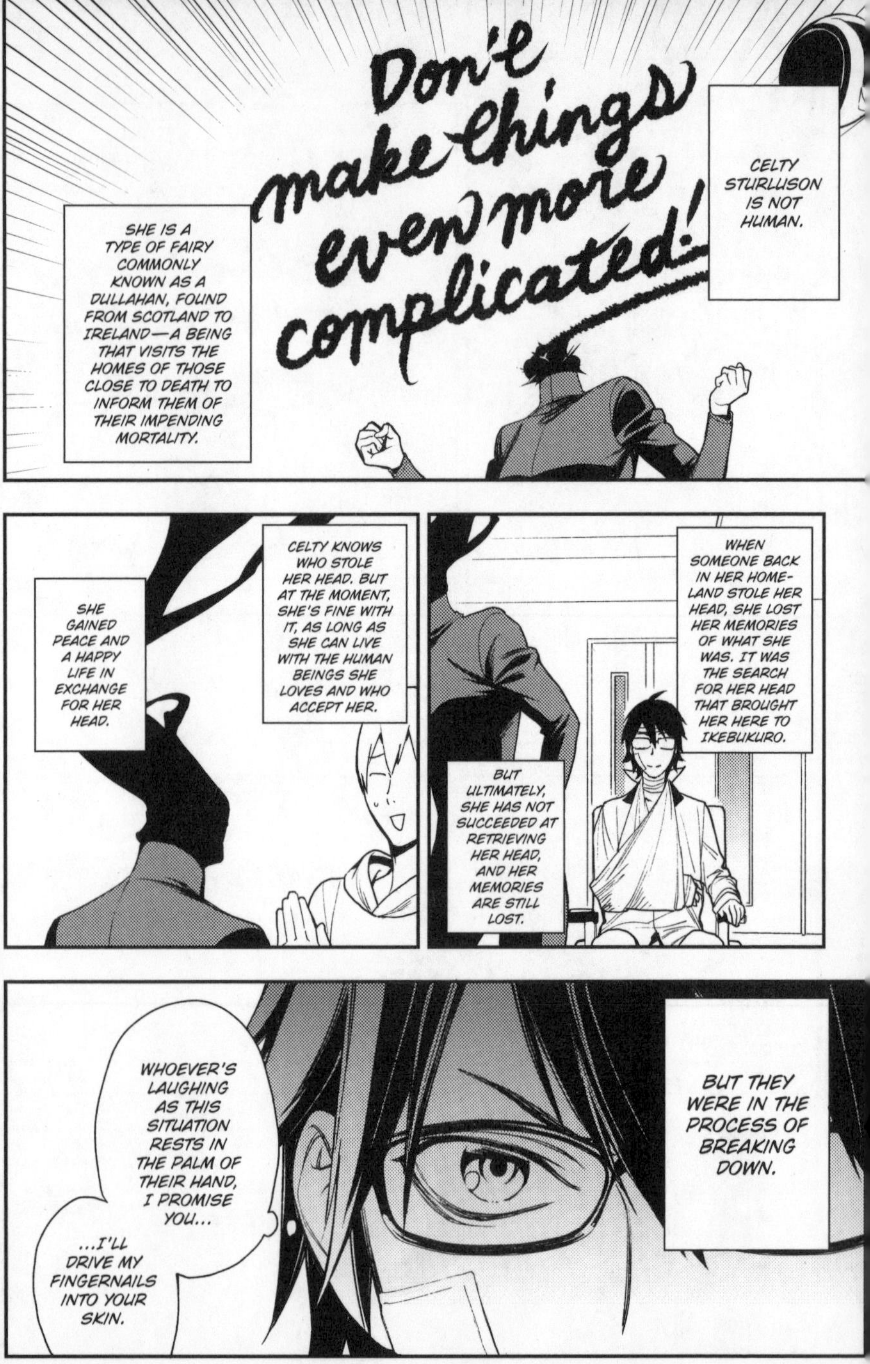
CELTY STURLUSON IS NOT HUMAN.
Don't make things even more complicated!
SHE IS A TYPE OF FAIRY COMMONLY KNOWN AS A DULLAHAN, FOUND FROM SCOTLAND TO IRELAND—A BEING THAT VISITS THE HOMES OF THOSE CLOSE TO DEATH TO INFORM THEM OF THEIR IMPENDING MORTALITY.
WHEN SOMEONE BACK IN HER HOME-LAND STOLE HER HEAD, SHE LOST HER MEMORIES OF WHAT SHE WAS. IT WAS THE SEARCH FOR HER HEAD THAT BROUGHT HER HERE TO IKEBUKURO.
BUT ULTIMATELY, SHE HAS NOT SUCCEEDED AT RETRIEVING HER HEAD, AND HER MEMORIES ARE STILL LOST.
CELTY KNOWS WHO STOLE HER HEAD. BUT AT THE MOMENT, SHE'S FINE WITH IT, AS LONG AS SHE CAN LIVE WITH THE HUMAN BEINGS SHE LOVES AND WHO ACCEPT HER.
SHE GAINED PEACE AND A HAPPY LIFE IN EXCHANGE FOR HER HEAD.
BUT THEY WERE IN THE PROCESS OF BREAKING DOWN.
WHOEVER'S LAUGHING AS THIS SITUATION RESTS IN THE PALM OF THEIR HAND, I PROMISE YOU...
...I'LL DRIVE MY FINGERNAILS INTO YOUR SKIN.

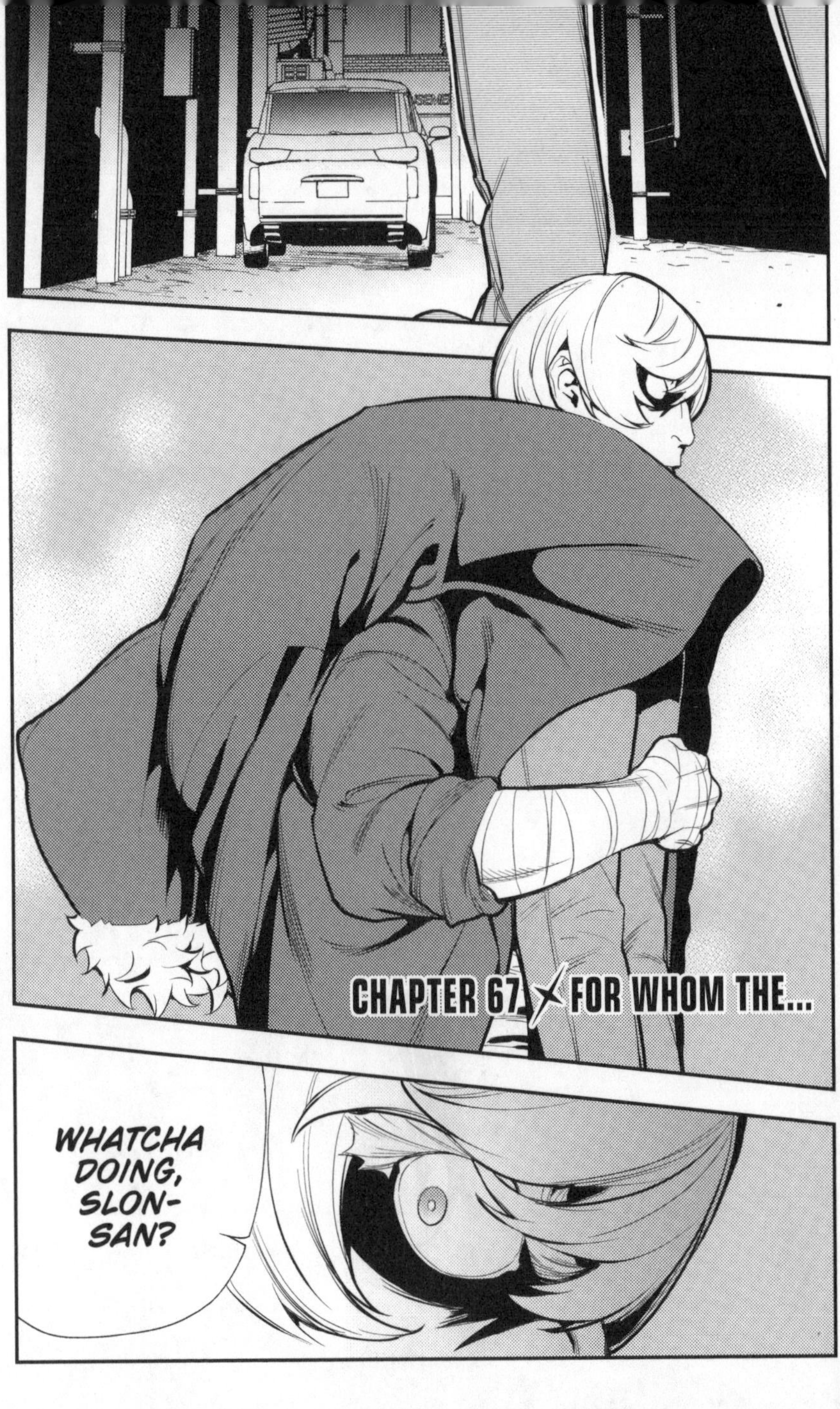
CHAPTER 67 ✗ FOR WHOM THE...
WHATCHA DOING, SLON-SAN?

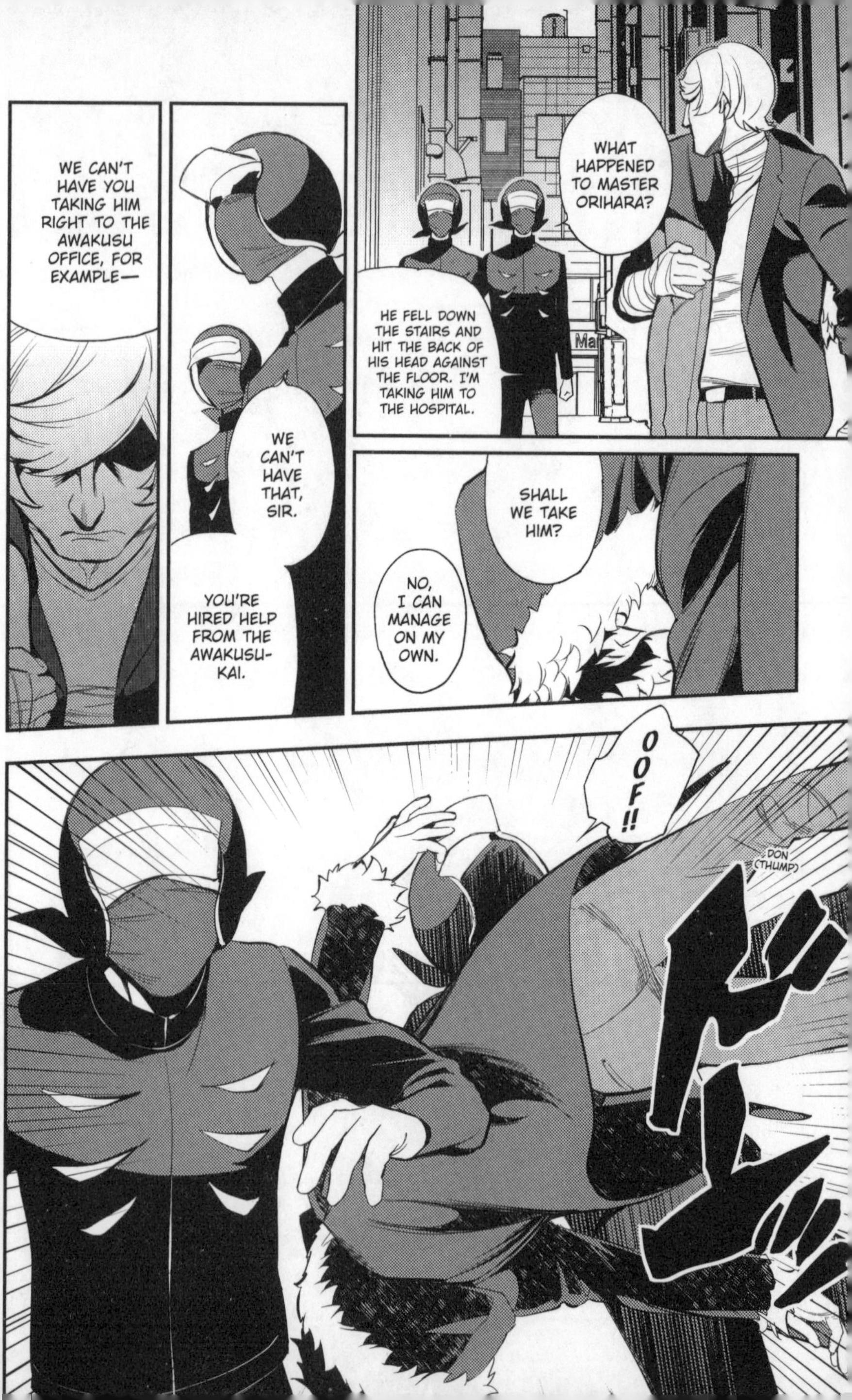
WHAT HAPPENED TO MASTER ORIHARA?
HE FELL DOWN THE STAIRS AND HIT THE BACK OF HIS HEAD AGAINST THE FLOOR. I'M TAKING HIM TO THE HOSPITAL.
SHALL WE TAKE HIM?
NO, I CAN MANAGE ON MY OWN.
WE CAN'T HAVE THAT, SIR.
YOU'RE HIRED HELP FROM THE AWAKUSU-KAI.
WE CAN'T HAVE YOU TAKING HIM RIGHT TO THE AWAKUSU OFFICE, FOR EXAMPLE—
OOF!!
DON (THUMP)

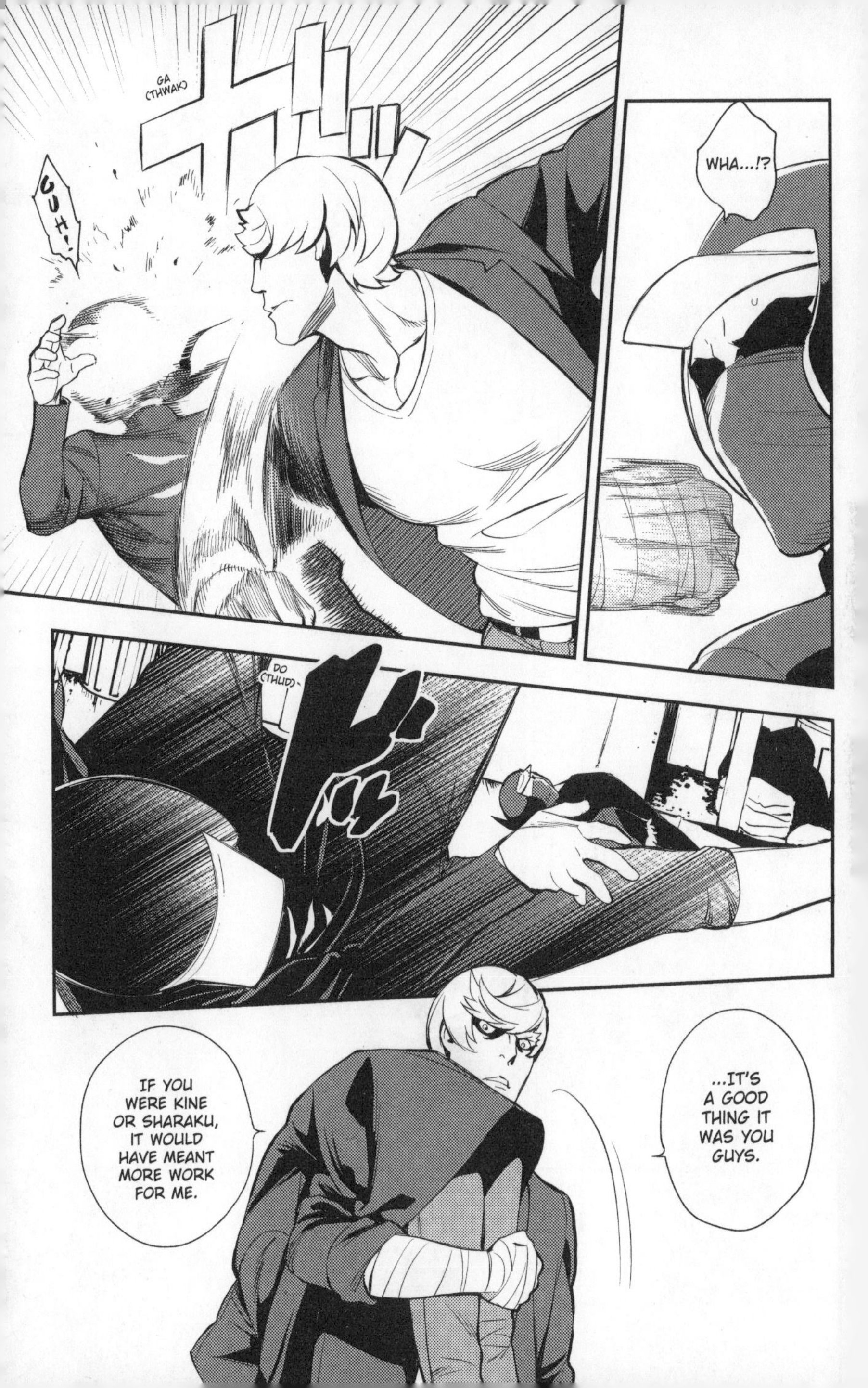
WHA...!?
GA (THWAK)
UUH!
DO (THUD)
...IT'S A GOOD THING IT WAS YOU GUYS.
IF YOU WERE KINE OR SHARAKU, IT WOULD HAVE MEANT MORE WORK FOR ME.

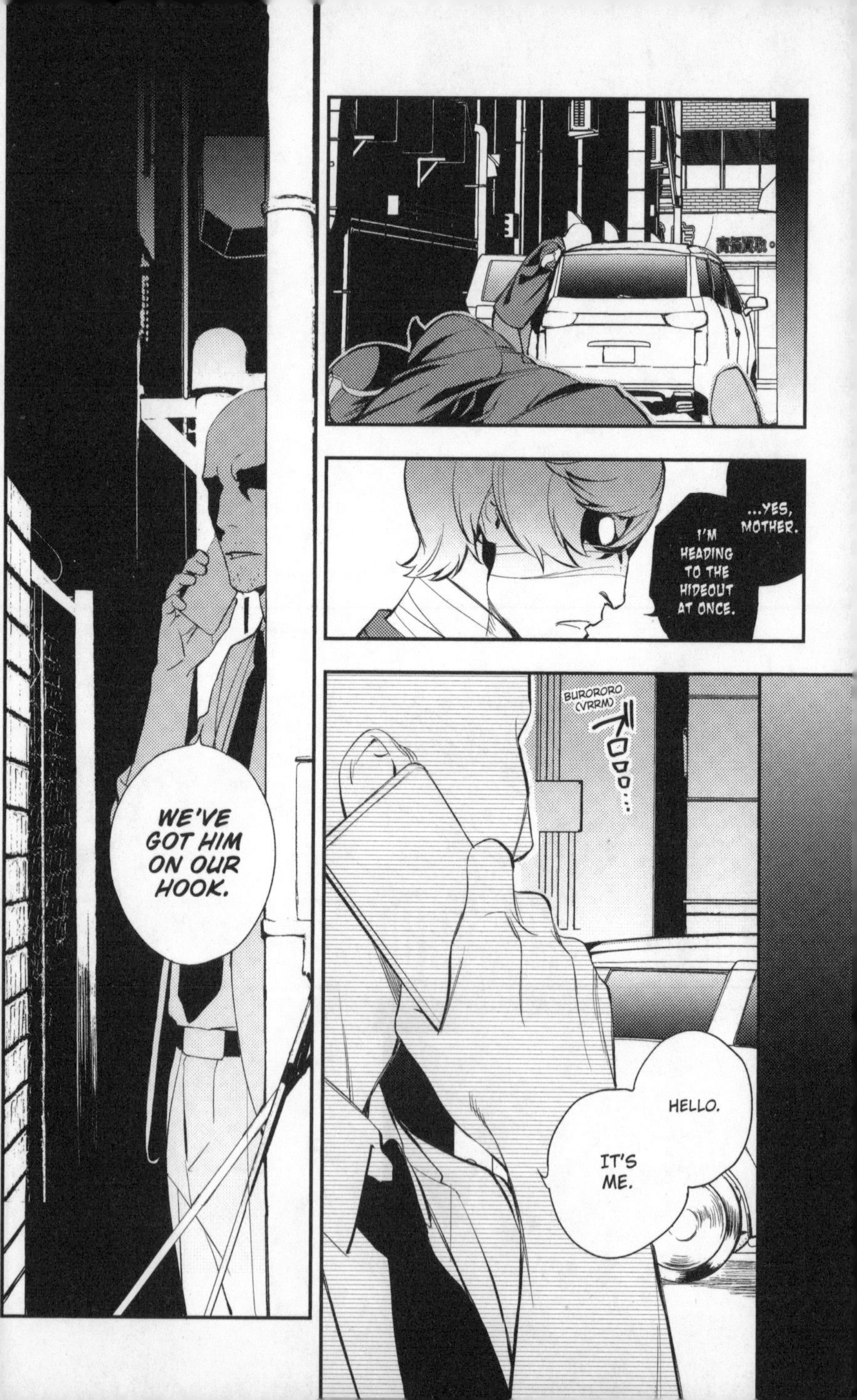
...YES, MOTHER.
I'M HEADING TO THE HIDEOUT AT ONCE.
BURORORO (VRRM)
HELLO. IT'S ME.
WE'VE GOT HIM ON OUR HOOK.

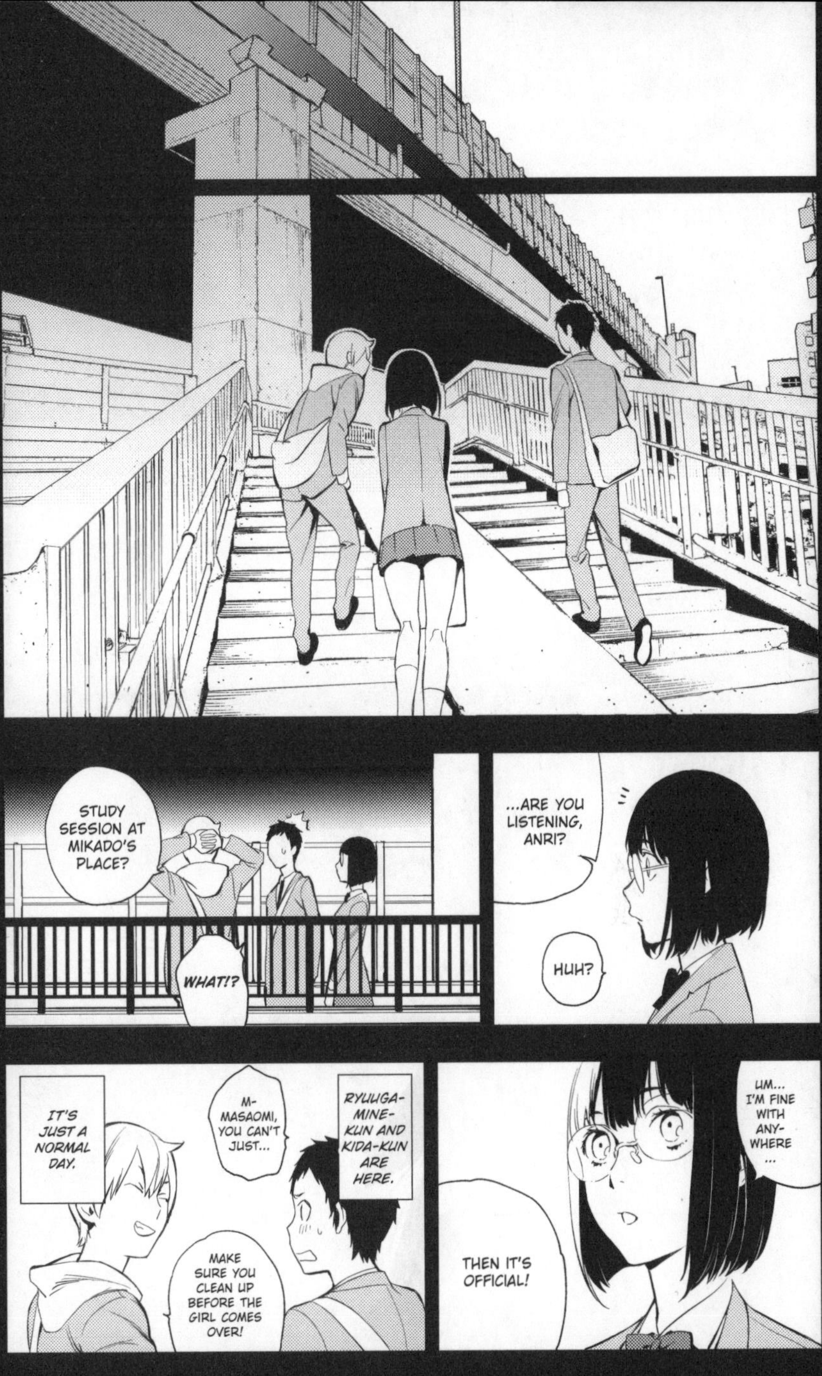
...ARE YOU LISTENING, ANRI?
HUH?
STUDY SESSION AT MIKADO'S PLACE?
WHAT!?
UM... I'M FINE WITH ANY-WHERE...
THEN IT'S OFFICIAL!
RYUUGA-MINE-KUN AND KIDA-KUN ARE HERE.
M-MASAOMI, YOU CAN'T JUST...
IT'S JUST A NORMAL DAY.
MAKE SURE YOU CLEAN UP BEFORE THE GIRL COMES OVER!

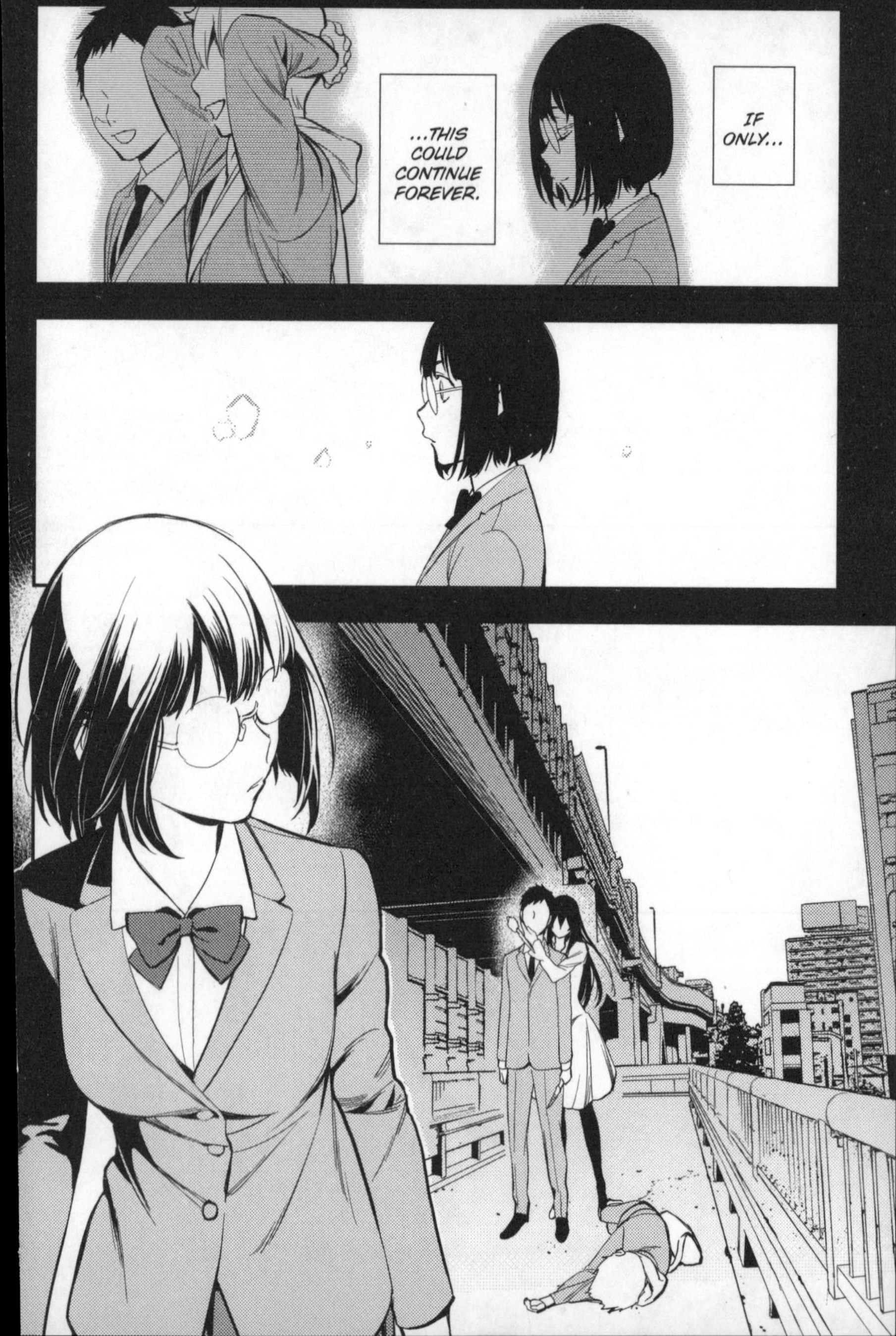
IF ONLY...
...THIS COULD CONTINUE FOREVER.

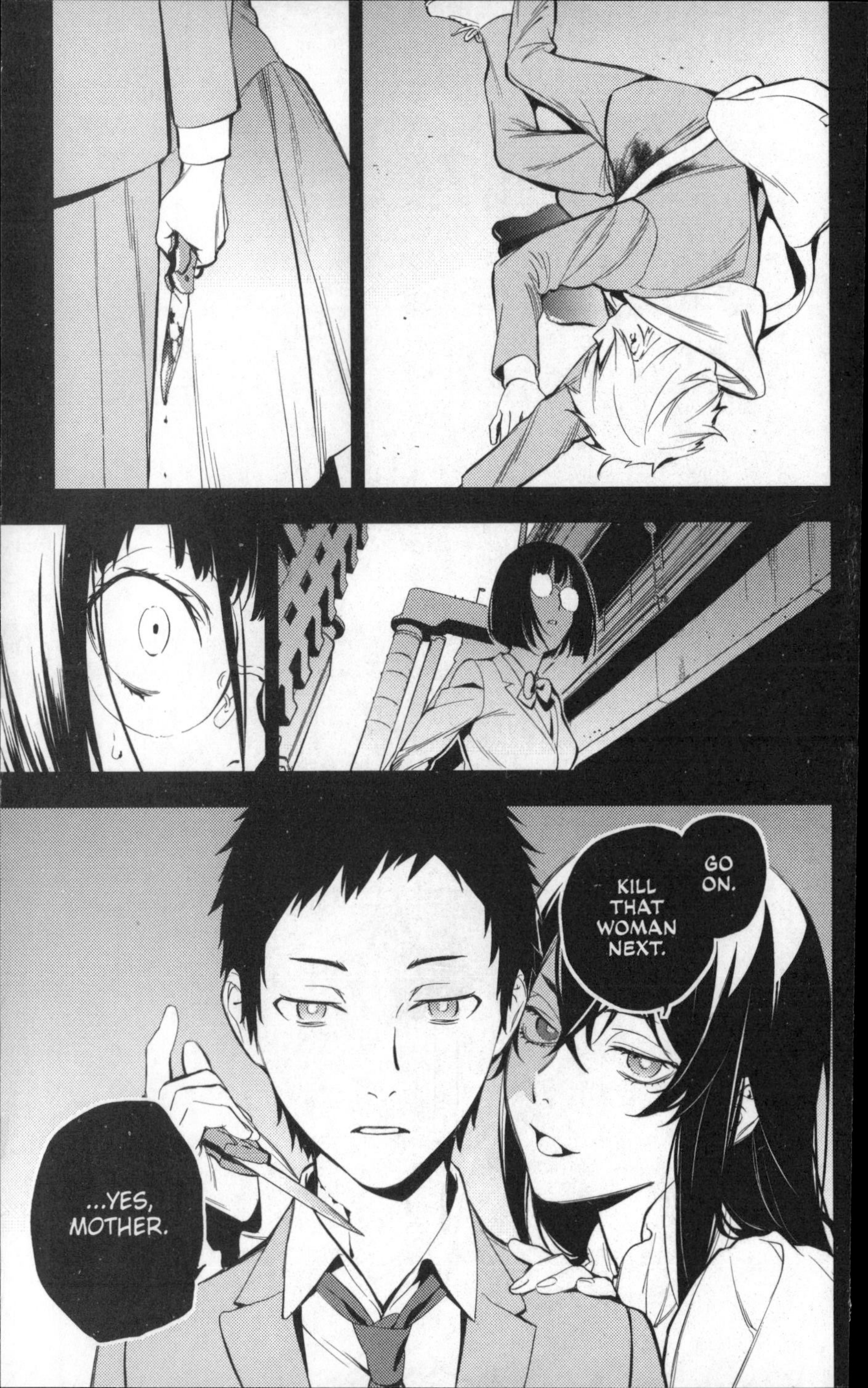
GO ON.
KILL THAT WOMAN NEXT.
...YES, MOTHER.

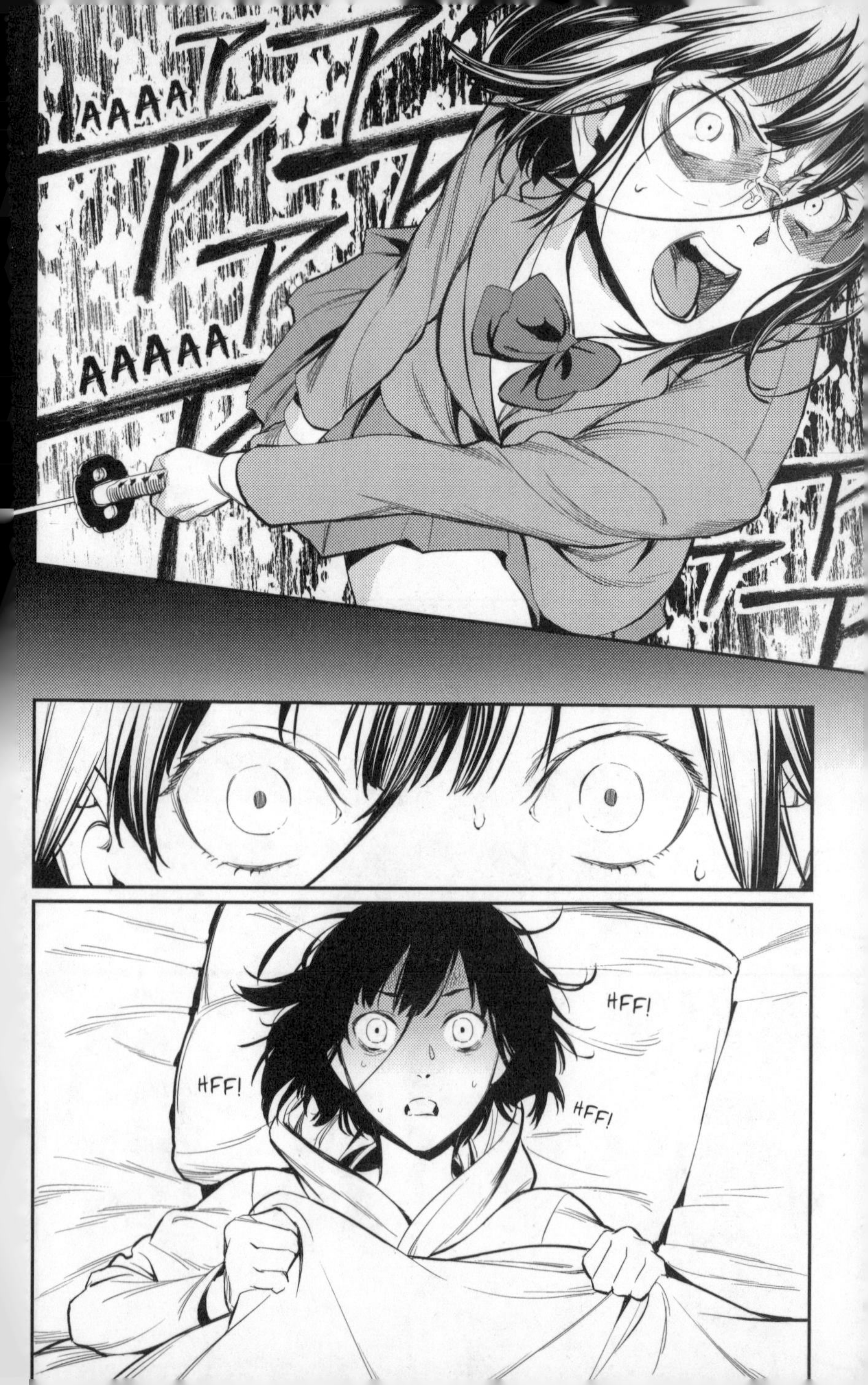
AAAA
AAAAA
HFF!
HFF!
HFF!

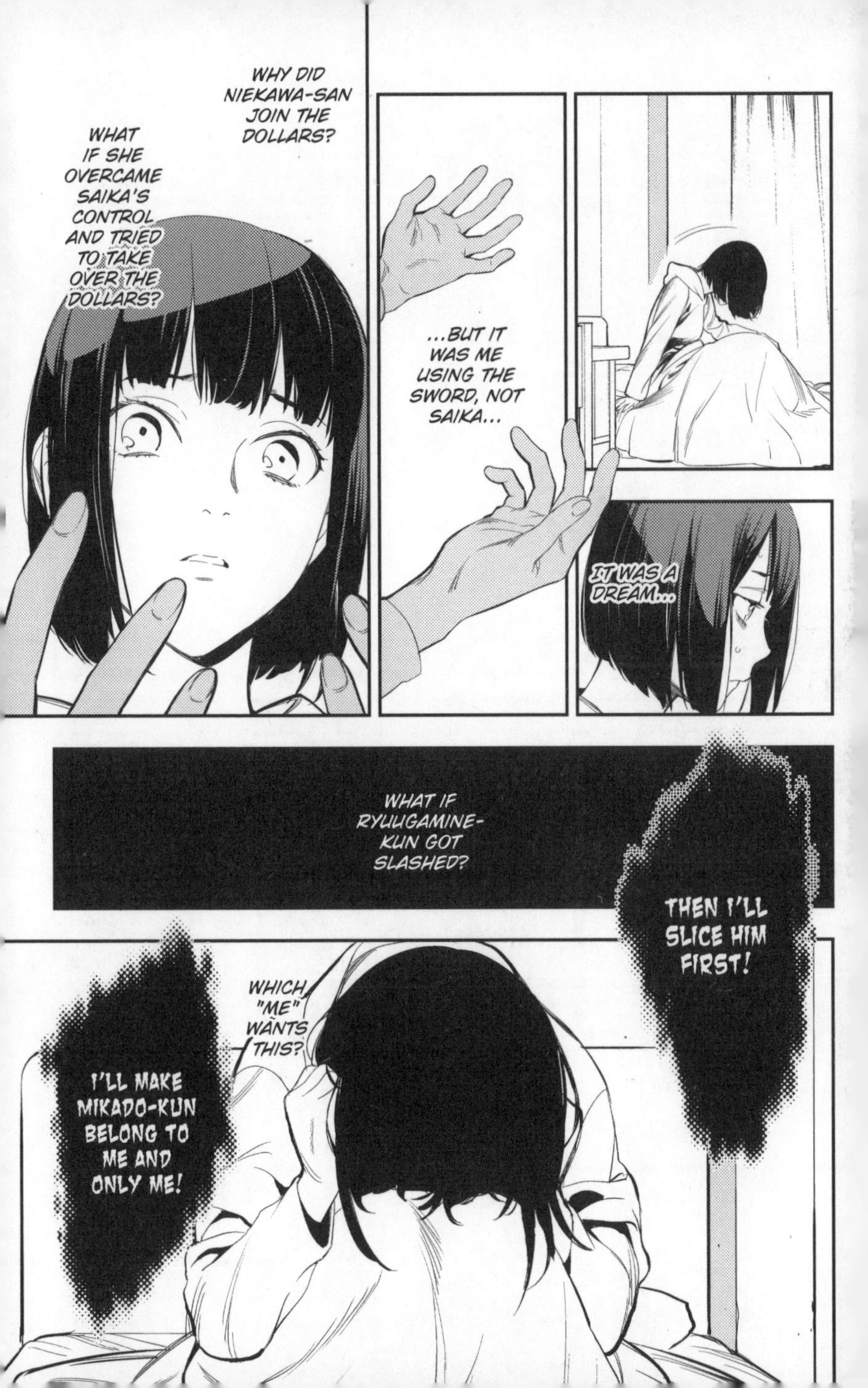
IT WAS A DREAM...
...BUT IT WAS ME USING THE SWORD, NOT SAIKA...
WHY DID NIEKAWA-SAN JOIN THE DOLLARS?
WHAT IF SHE OVERCAME SAIKA'S CONTROL AND TRIED TO TAKE OVER THE DOLLARS?
WHAT IF RYUUGAMINE-KUN GOT SLASHED?
THEN I'LL SLICE HIM FIRST!
WHICH "ME" WANTS THIS?
I'LL MAKE MIKADO-KUN BELONG TO ME AND ONLY ME!

SIGN: RAIRA GENERAL HOSPITAL

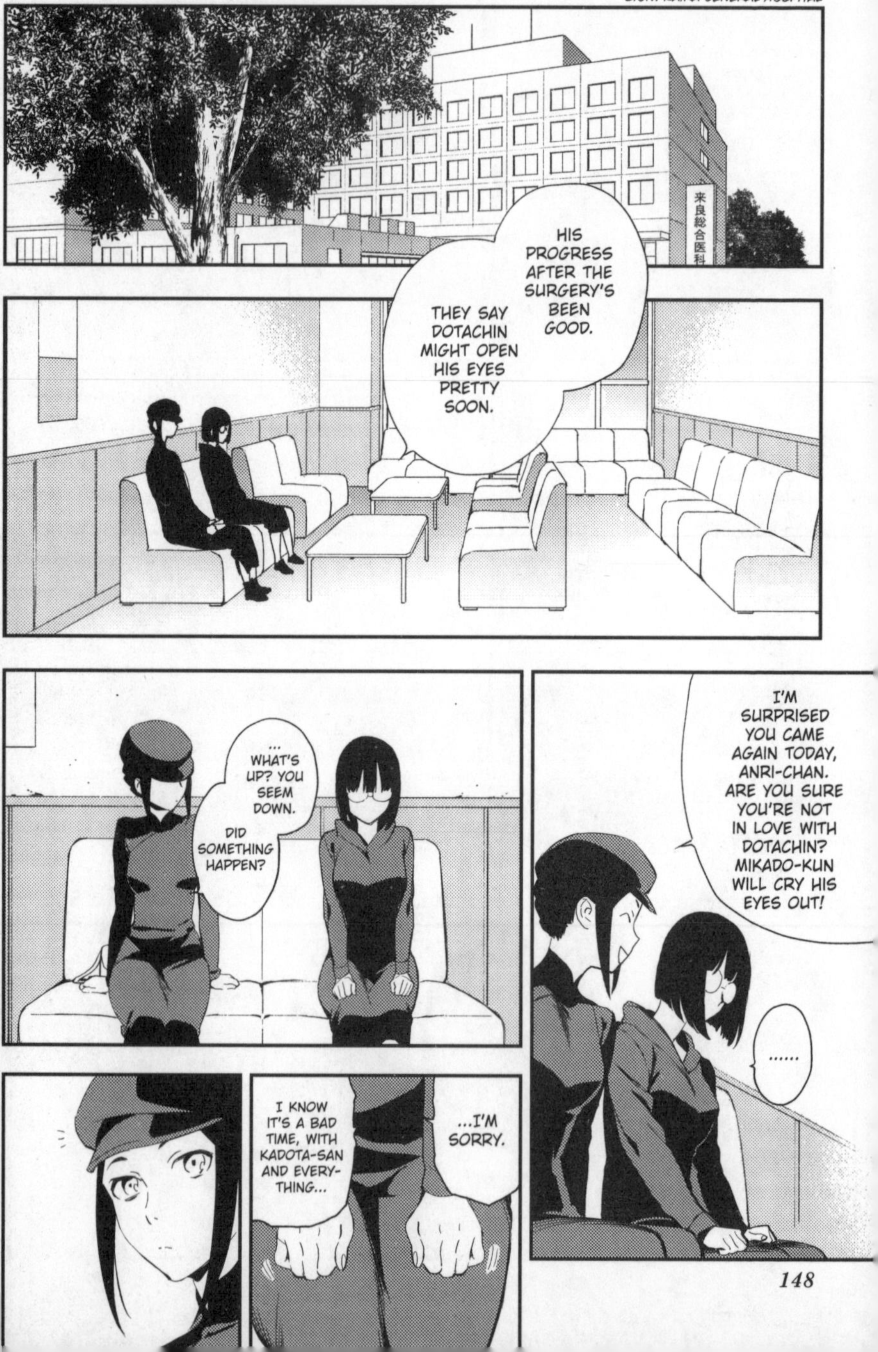
来良総合医科
HIS PROGRESS AFTER THE SURGERY'S BEEN GOOD.
THEY SAY DOTACHIN MIGHT OPEN HIS EYES PRETTY SOON.
I'M SURPRISED YOU CAME AGAIN TODAY, ANRI-CHAN. ARE YOU SURE YOU'RE NOT IN LOVE WITH DOTACHIN? MIKADO-KUN WILL CRY HIS EYES OUT!
......
...WHAT'S UP? YOU SEEM DOWN.
DID SOMETHING HAPPEN?
...I'M SORRY.
I KNOW IT'S A BAD TIME, WITH KADOTA-SAN AND EVERY-THING...

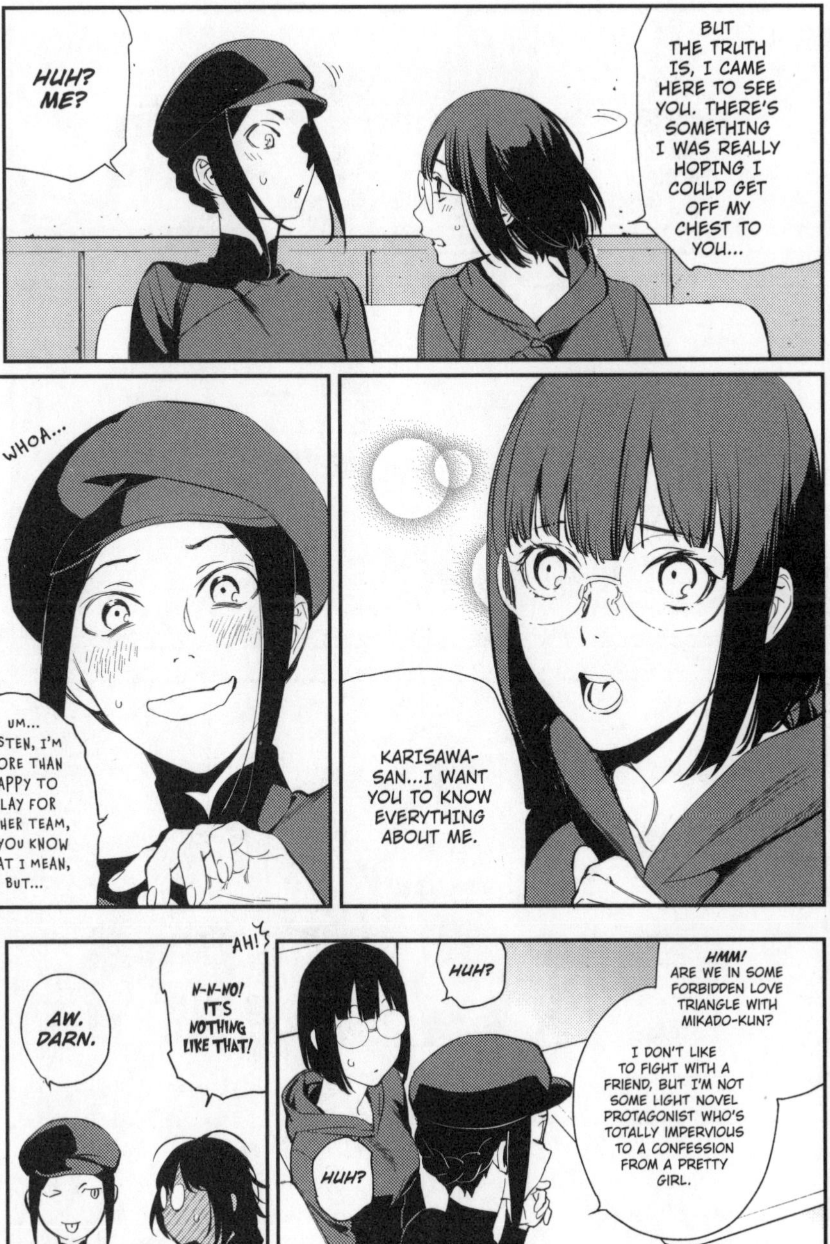
BUT THE TRUTH IS, I CAME HERE TO SEE YOU. THERE'S SOMETHING I WAS REALLY HOPING I COULD GET OFF MY CHEST TO YOU...
HUH? ME?
KARISAWA-SAN...I WANT YOU TO KNOW EVERYTHING ABOUT ME.
WHOA...
UM... LISTEN, I'M MORE THAN HAPPY TO PLAY FOR EITHER TEAM, IF YOU KNOW WHAT I MEAN, BUT...
HMM! ARE WE IN SOME FORBIDDEN LOVE TRIANGLE WITH MIKADO-KUN?
HUH?
I DON'T LIKE TO FIGHT WITH A FRIEND, BUT I'M NOT SOME LIGHT NOVEL PROTAGONIST WHO'S TOTALLY IMPERVIOUS TO A CONFESSION FROM A PRETTY GIRL.
HUH?
AH!
N-N-NO! IT'S NOTHING LIKE THAT!
AW. DARN.

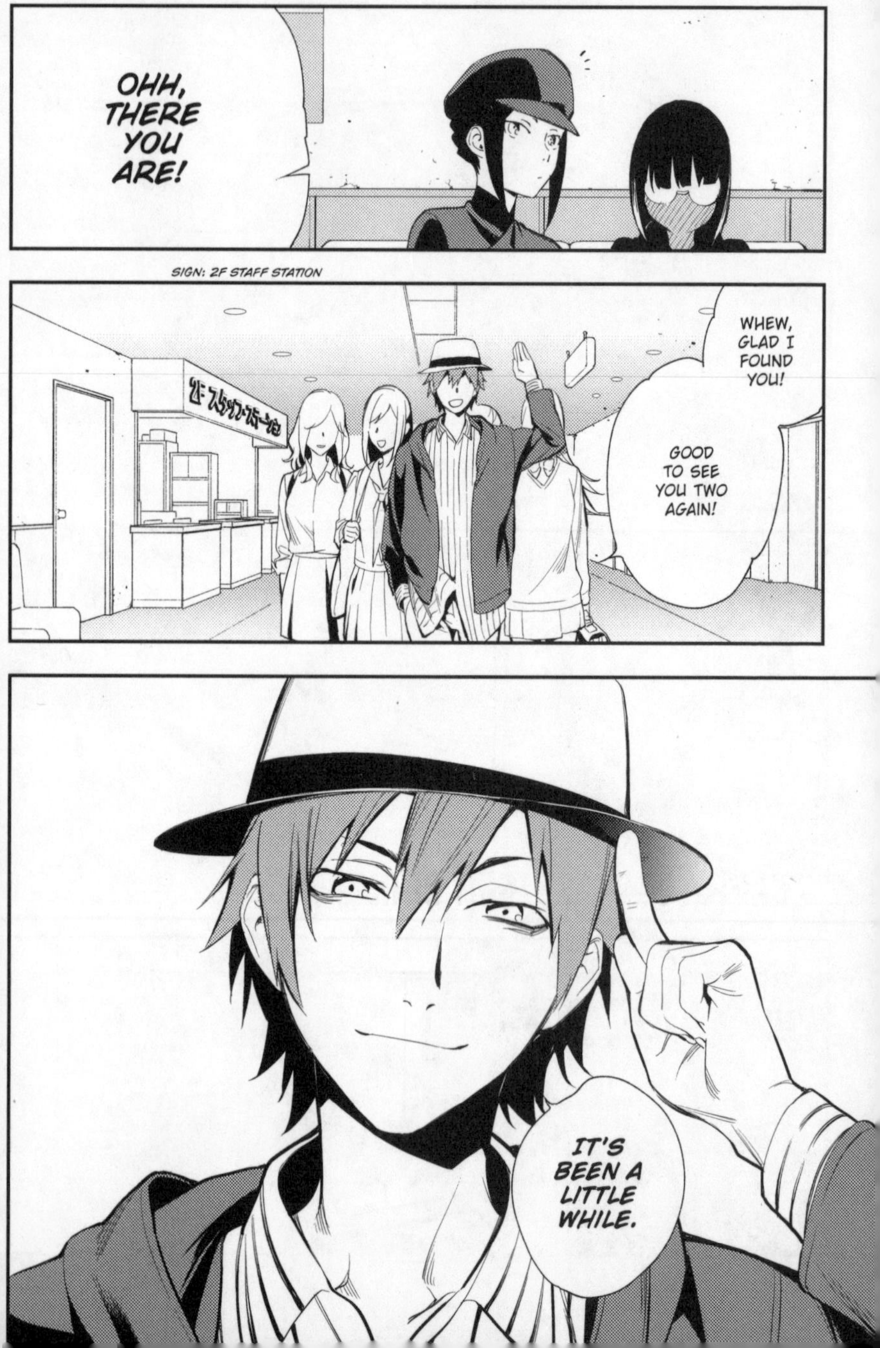
OHH, THERE YOU ARE!
SIGN: 2F STAFF STATION
WHEW, GLAD I FOUND YOU!
GOOD TO SEE YOU TWO AGAIN!
IT'S BEEN A LITTLE WHILE.

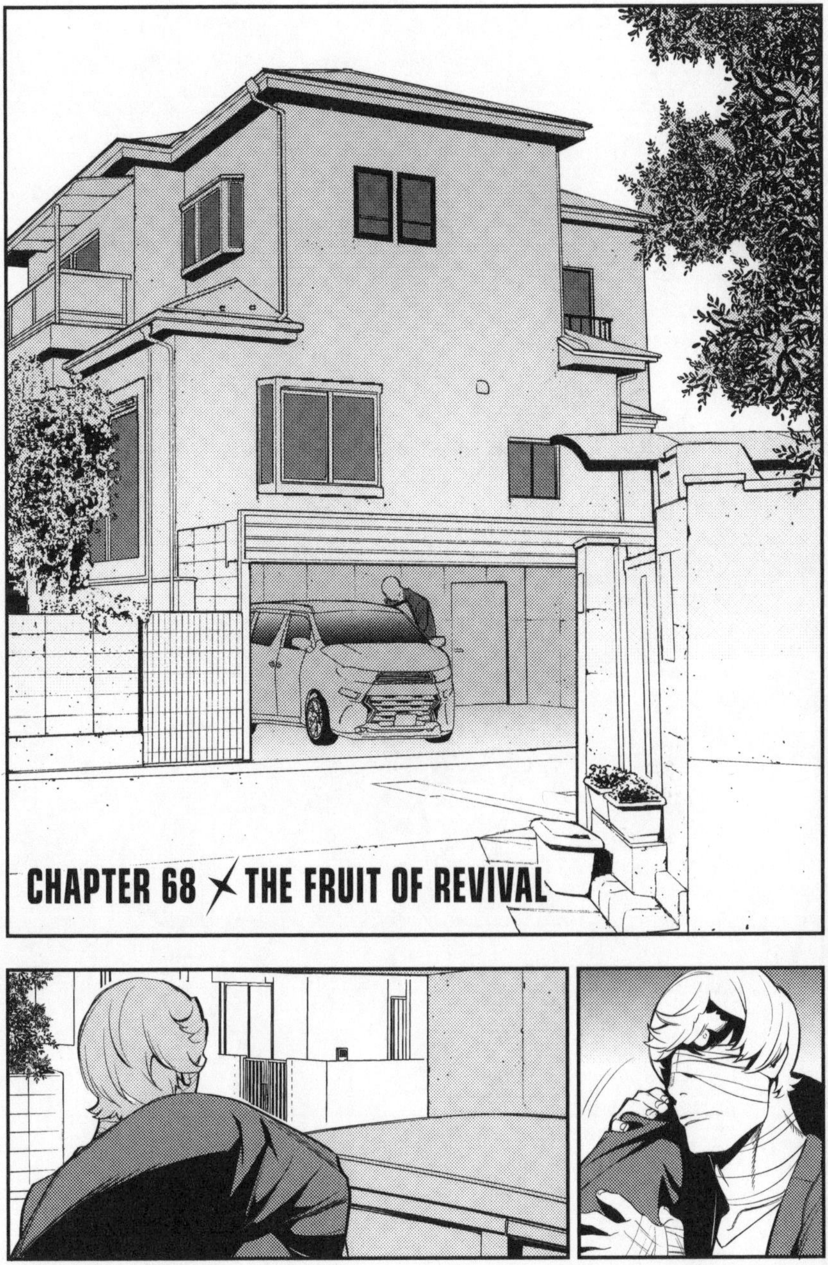
CHAPTER 68 THE FRUIT OF REVIVAL

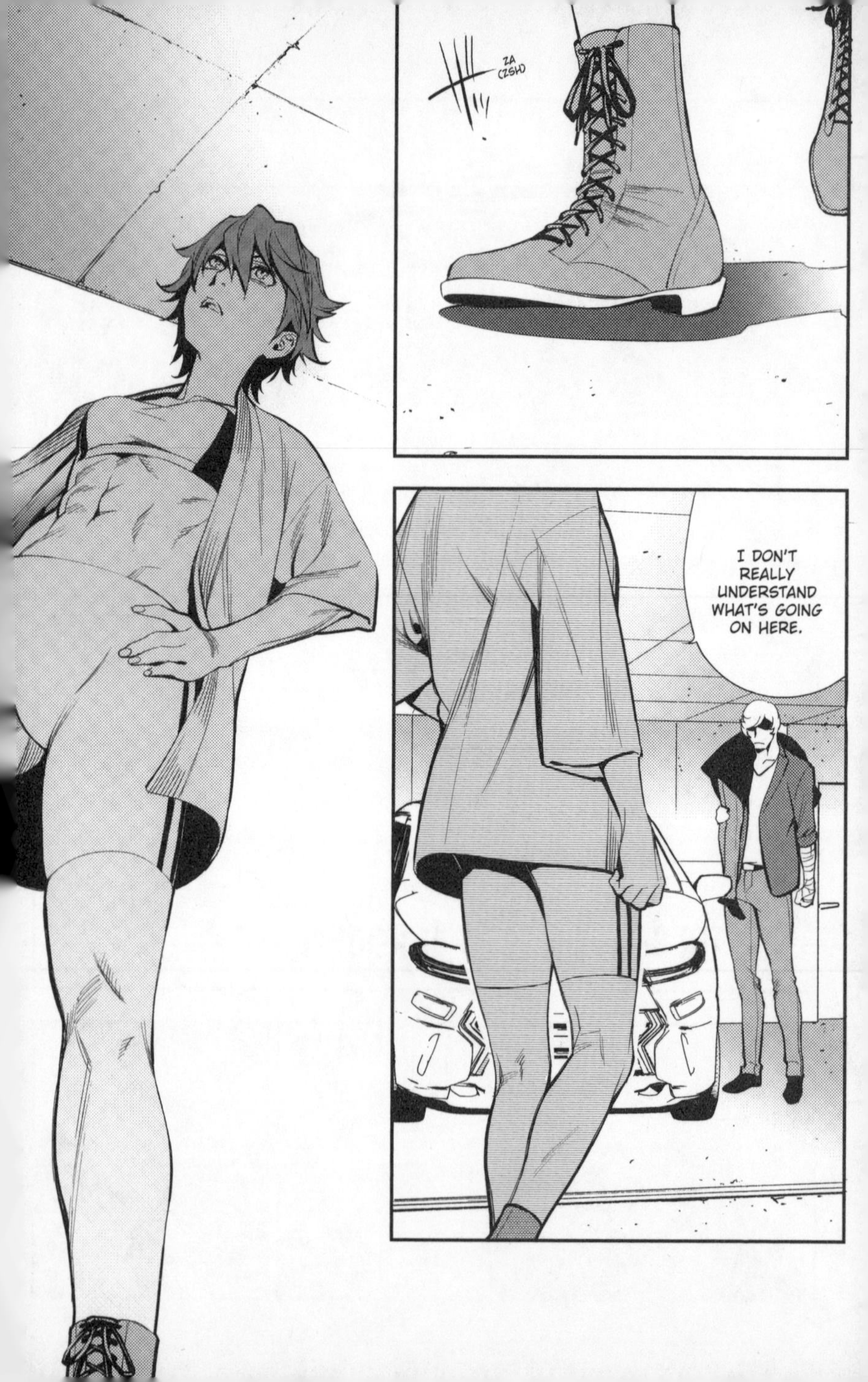
ZA (ZSH)
I DON'T REALLY UNDERSTAND WHAT'S GOING ON HERE.

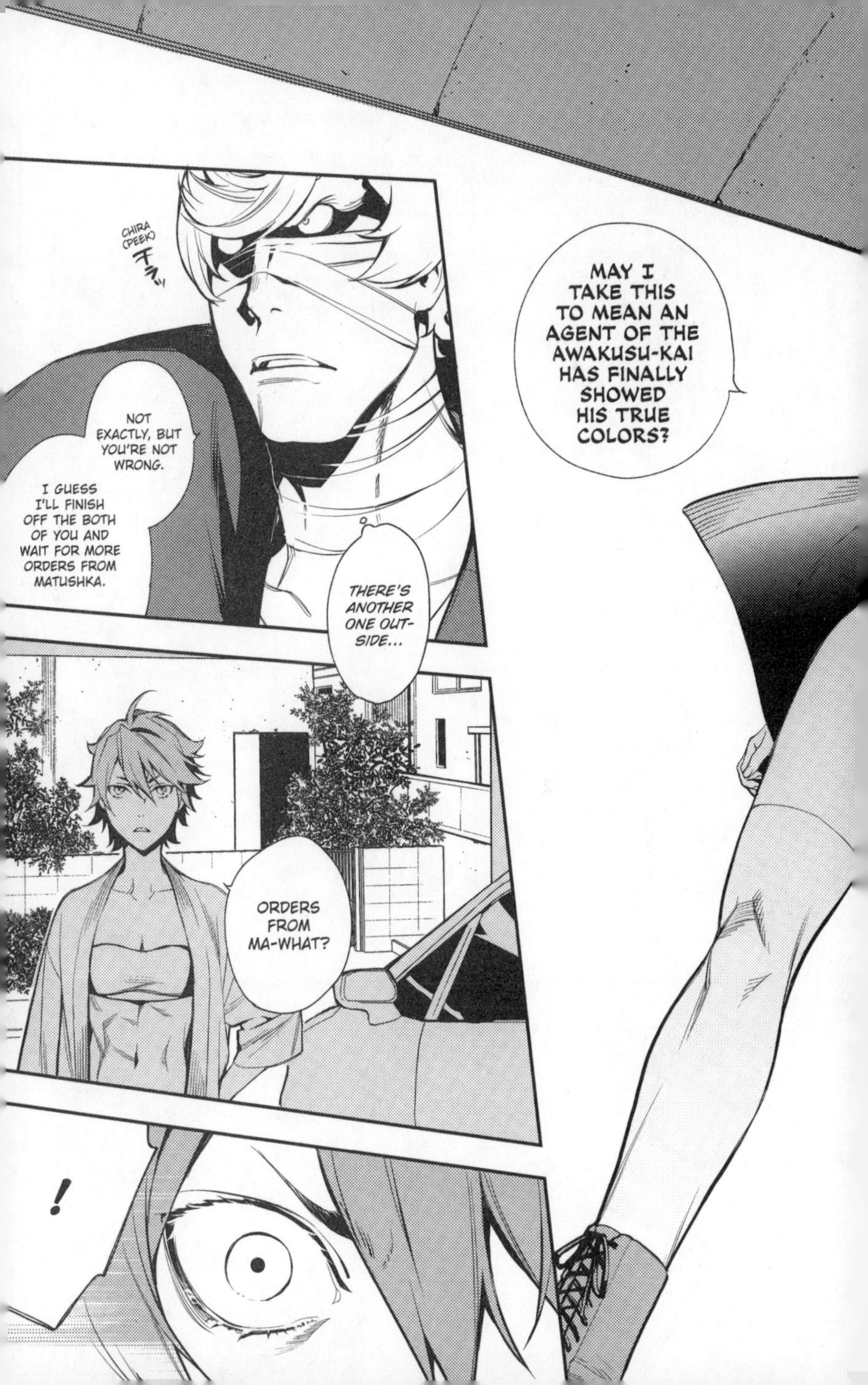
MAY I TAKE THIS TO MEAN AN AGENT OF THE AWAKUSU-KAI HAS FINALLY SHOWED HIS TRUE COLORS?
CHIRA (PEEK)
チラッ
NOT EXACTLY, BUT YOU'RE NOT WRONG.
I GUESS I'LL FINISH OFF THE BOTH OF YOU AND WAIT FOR MORE ORDERS FROM MATUSHKA.
THERE'S ANOTHER ONE OUT-SIDE...
ORDERS FROM MA-WHAT?
!

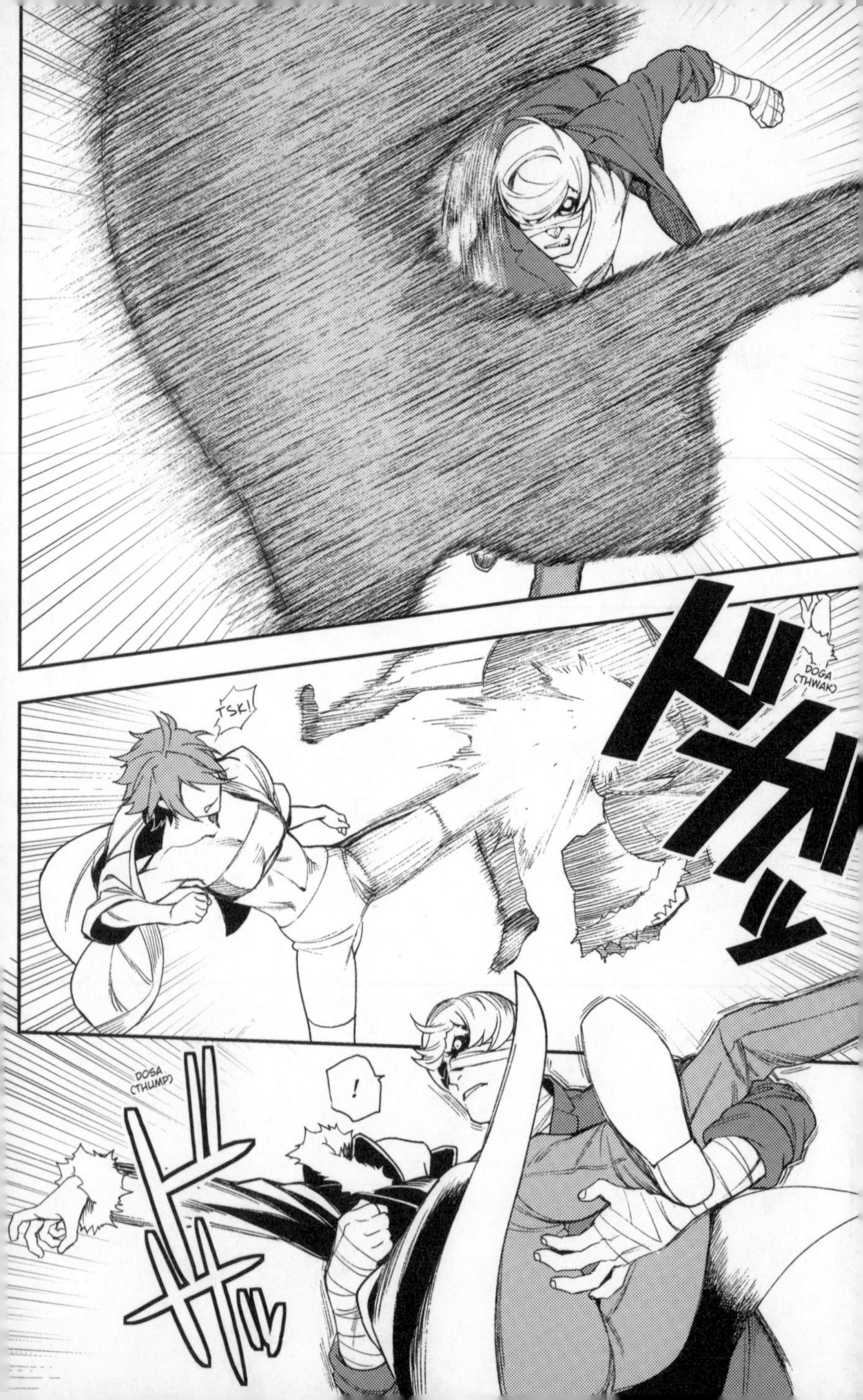
ドガッ
DOGA (THWAK)
TSK!
!
ドサッ
DOSA (THUMP)

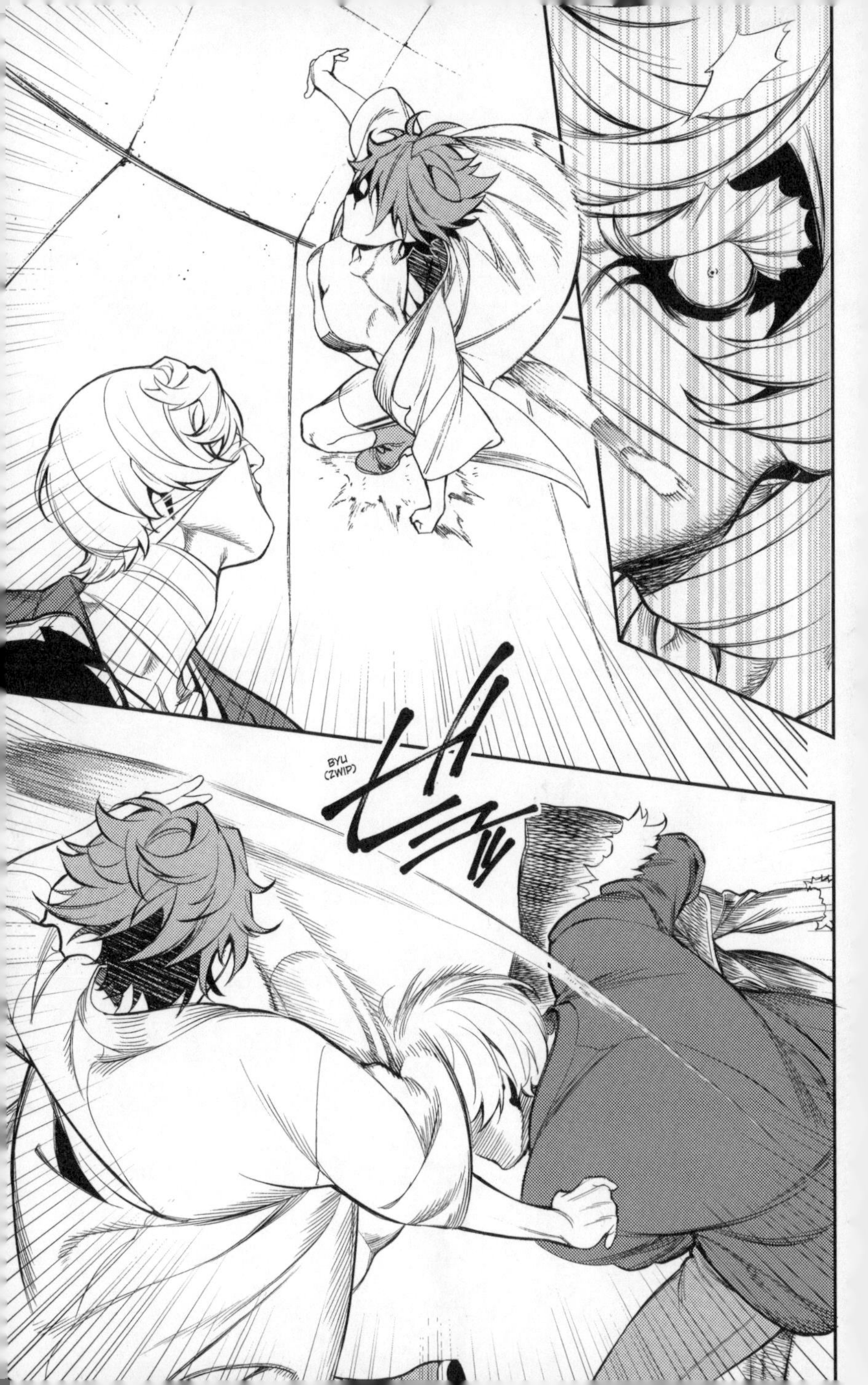
BYU
(ZWIP)

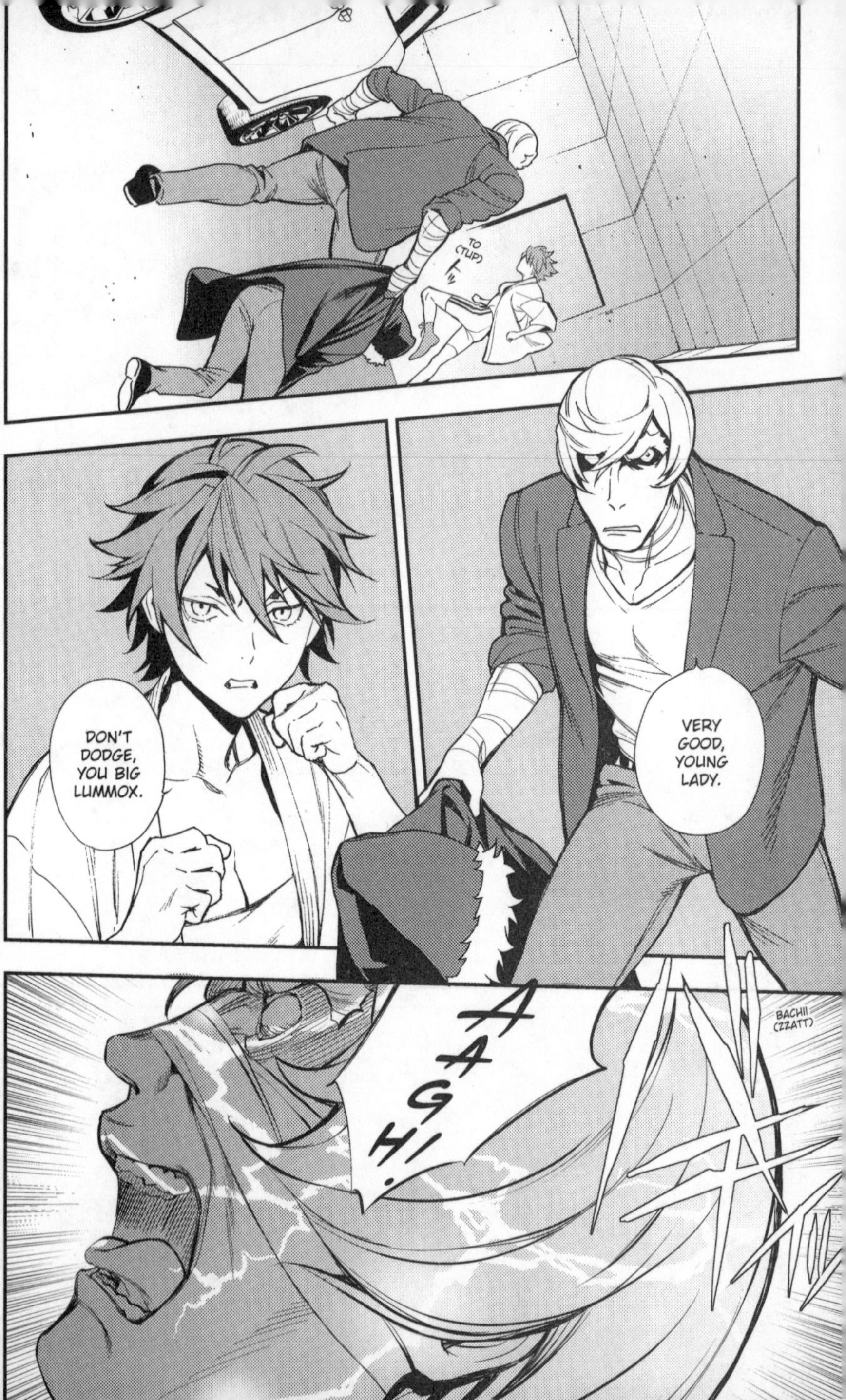
TO (TUP)
VERY GOOD, YOUNG LADY.
DON'T DODGE, YOU BIG LUMMOX.
BACHII (ZZATT)
AAGH!!

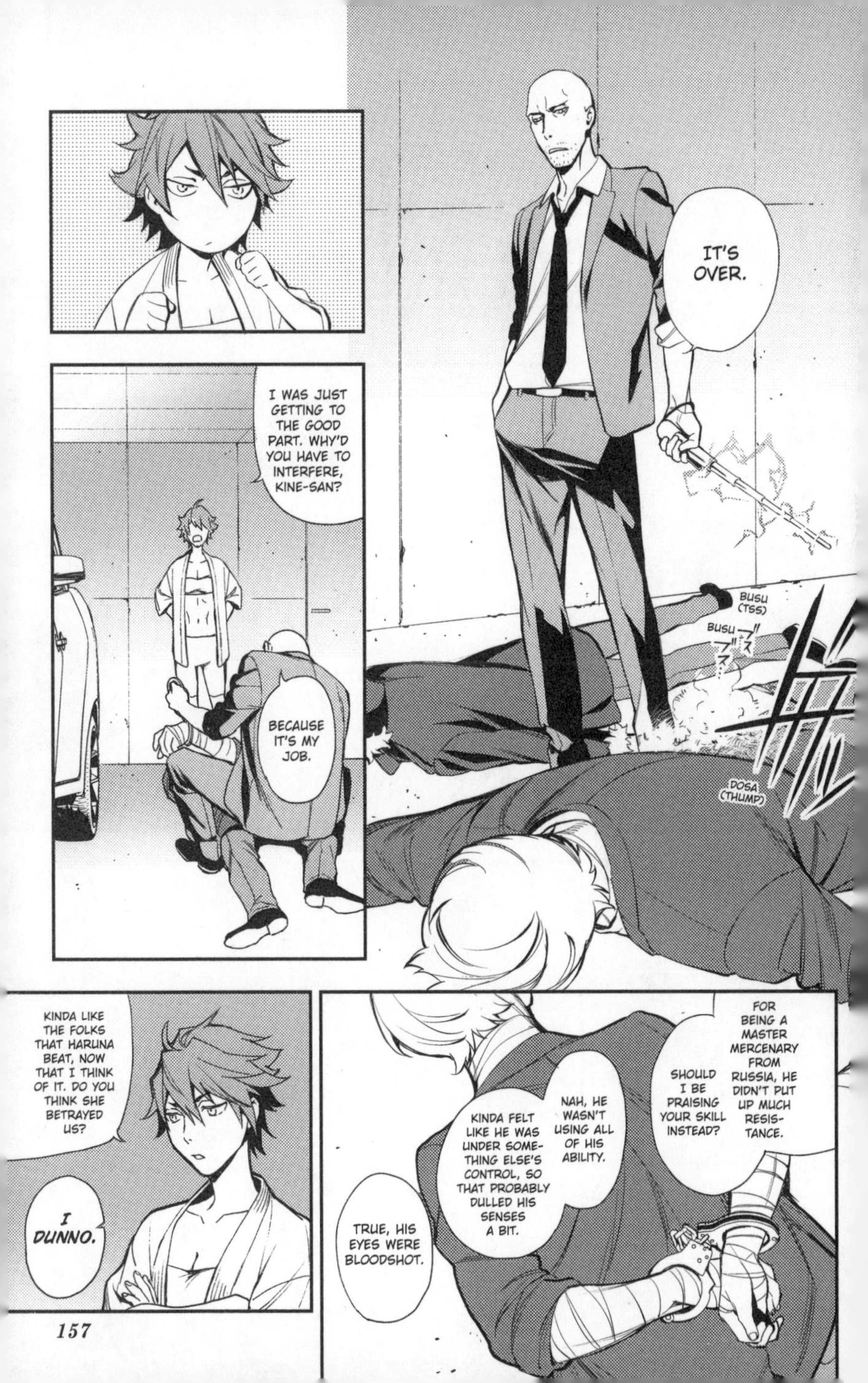

IT'S OVER.
BUSU (TSS)
BUSU
DOSA (THUMP)
I WAS JUST GETTING TO THE GOOD PART. WHY'D YOU HAVE TO INTERFERE, KINE-SAN?
BECAUSE IT'S MY JOB.
FOR BEING A MASTER MERCENARY FROM RUSSIA, HE DIDN'T PUT UP MUCH RESIS-TANCE.
SHOULD I BE PRAISING YOUR SKILL INSTEAD?
NAH, HE WASN'T USING ALL OF HIS ABILITY.
KINDA FELT LIKE HE WAS UNDER SOME-THING ELSE'S CONTROL, SO THAT PROBABLY DULLED HIS SENSES A BIT.
TRUE, HIS EYES WERE BLOODSHOT.
KINDA LIKE THE FOLKS THAT HARUNA BEAT, NOW THAT I THINK OF IT. DO YOU THINK SHE BETRAYED US?
I DUNNO.

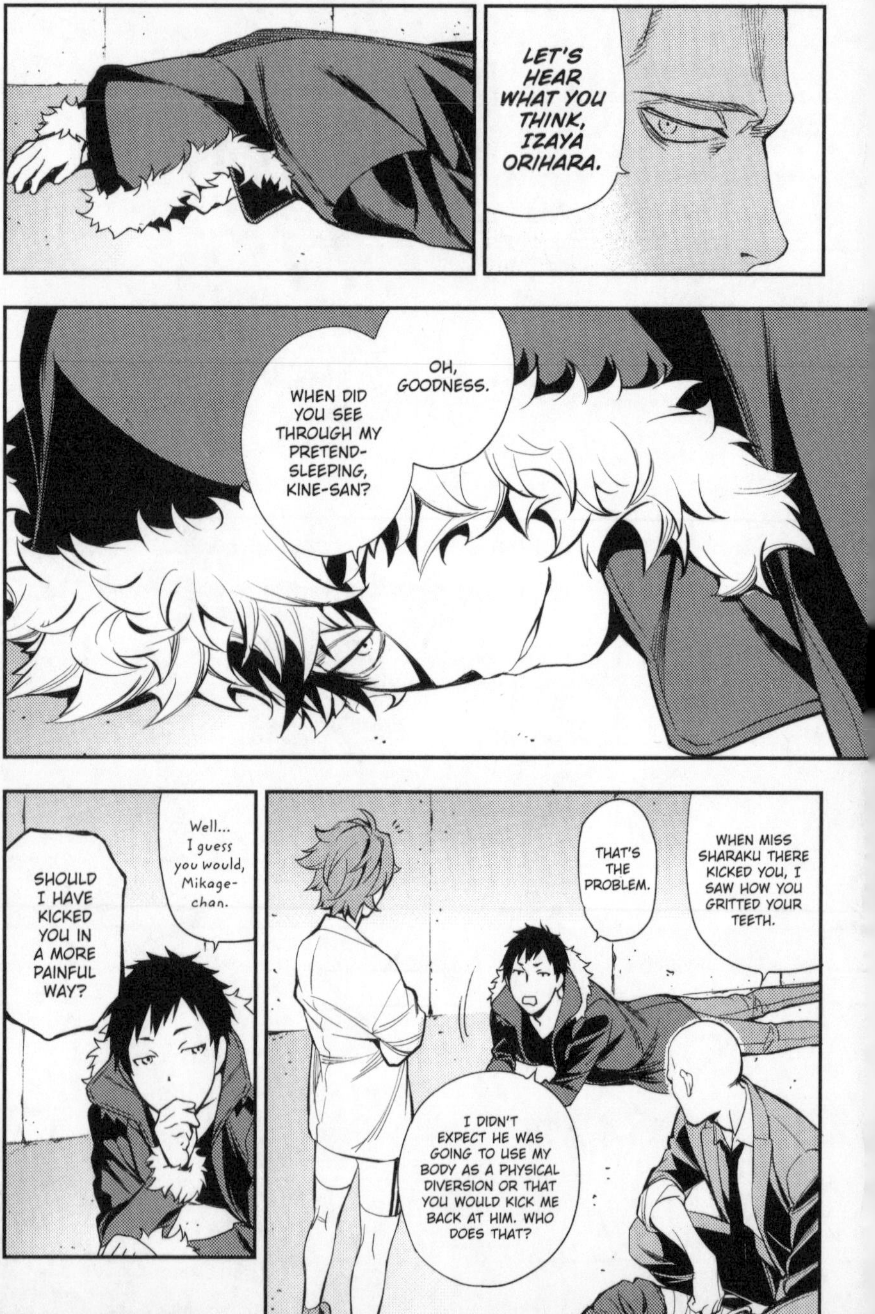
LET'S HEAR WHAT YOU THINK, IZAYA ORIHARA.
OH, GOODNESS.
WHEN DID YOU SEE THROUGH MY PRETEND-SLEEPING, KINE-SAN?
WHEN MISS SHARAKU THERE KICKED YOU, I SAW HOW YOU GRITTED YOUR TEETH.
THAT'S THE PROBLEM.
I DIDN'T EXPECT HE WAS GOING TO USE MY BODY AS A PHYSICAL DIVERSION OR THAT YOU WOULD KICK ME BACK AT HIM. WHO DOES THAT?
SHOULD I HAVE KICKED YOU IN A MORE PAINFUL WAY?
Well... I guess you would, Mikage-chan.

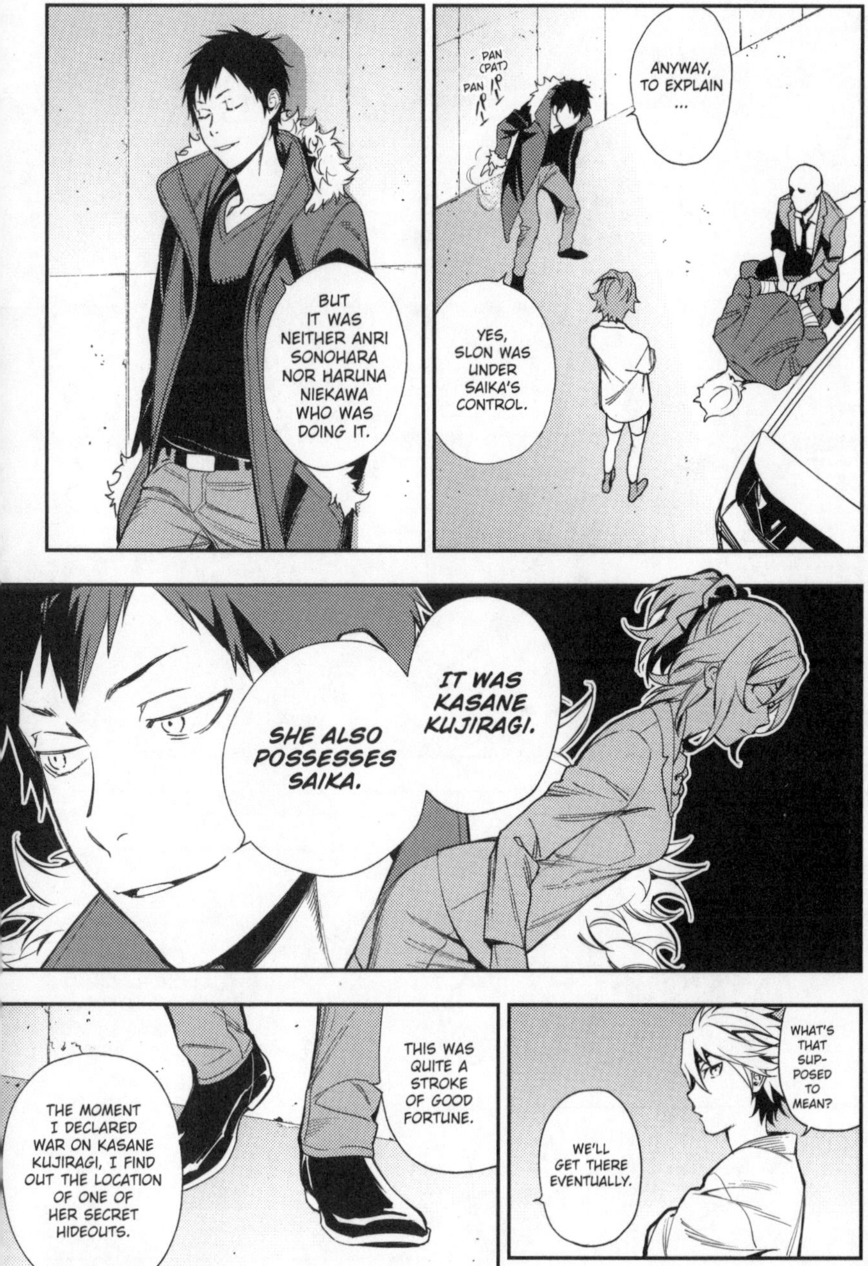
ANYWAY, TO EXPLAIN ...
PAN (PAT) PAN
YES, SLON WAS UNDER SAIKA'S CONTROL.
BUT IT WAS NEITHER ANRI SONOHARA NOR HARUNA NIEKAWA WHO WAS DOING IT.
IT WAS KASANE KUJIRAGI.
SHE ALSO POSSESSES SAIKA.
WHAT'S THAT SUP-POSED TO MEAN?
WE'LL GET THERE EVENTUALLY.
THIS WAS QUITE A STROKE OF GOOD FORTUNE.
THE MOMENT I DECLARED WAR ON KASANE KUJIRAGI, I FIND OUT THE LOCATION OF ONE OF HER SECRET HIDEOUTS.

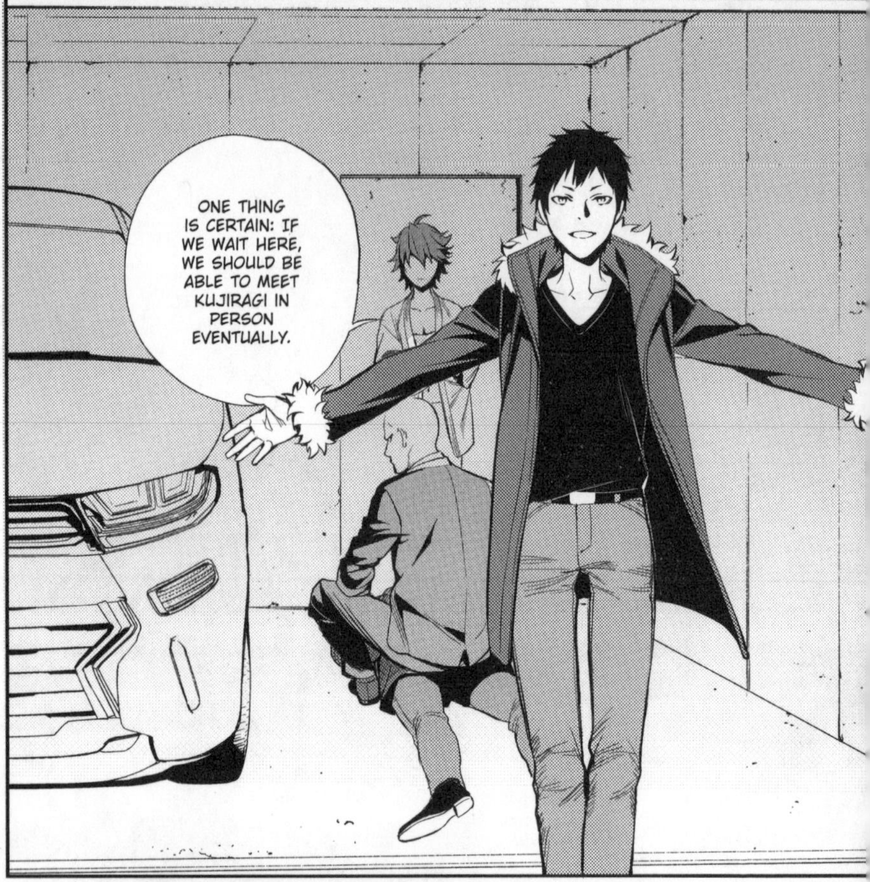
ONE THING IS CERTAIN: IF WE WAIT HERE, WE SHOULD BE ABLE TO MEET KUJIRAGI IN PERSON EVENTUALLY.
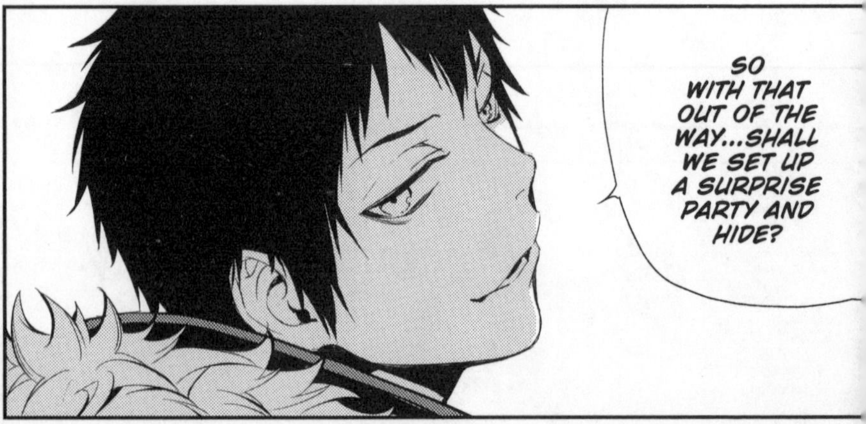
SO WITH THAT OUT OF THE WAY...SHALL WE SET UP A SURPRISE PARTY AND HIDE?

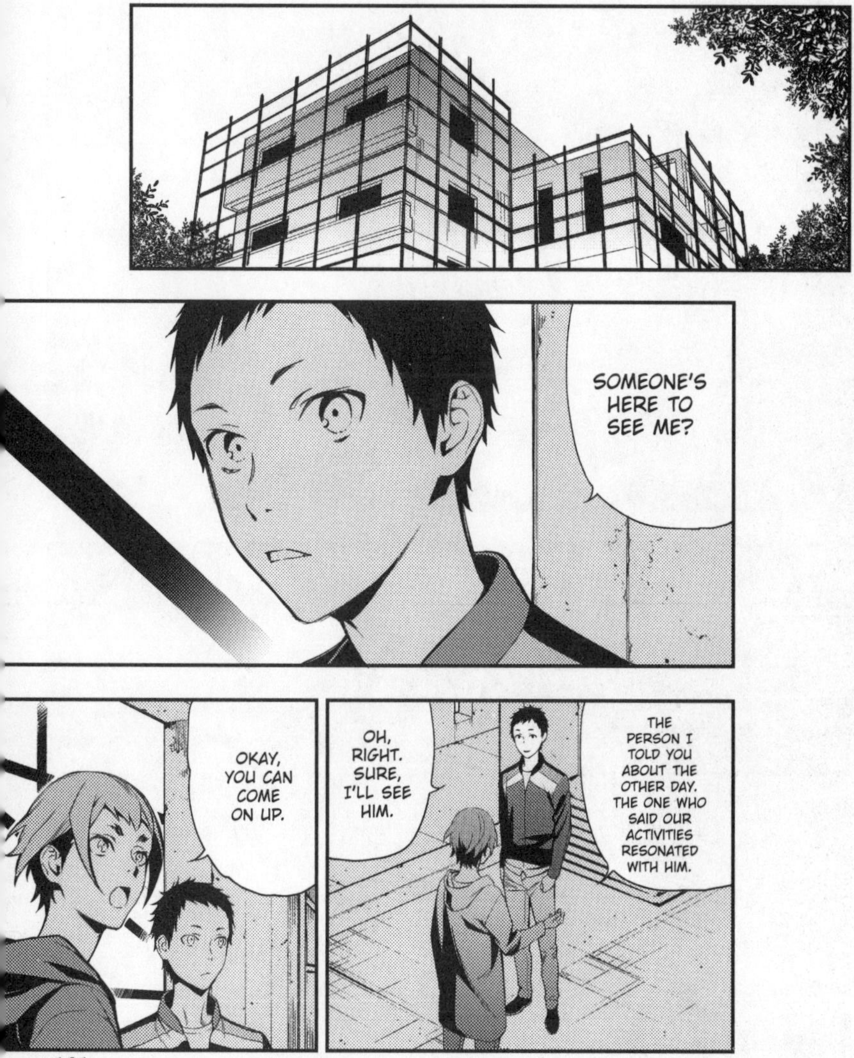
SOMEONE'S HERE TO SEE ME?
THE PERSON I TOLD YOU ABOUT THE OTHER DAY. THE ONE WHO SAID OUR ACTIVITIES RESONATED WITH HIM.
OH, RIGHT. SURE, I'LL SEE HIM.
OKAY, YOU CAN COME ON UP.

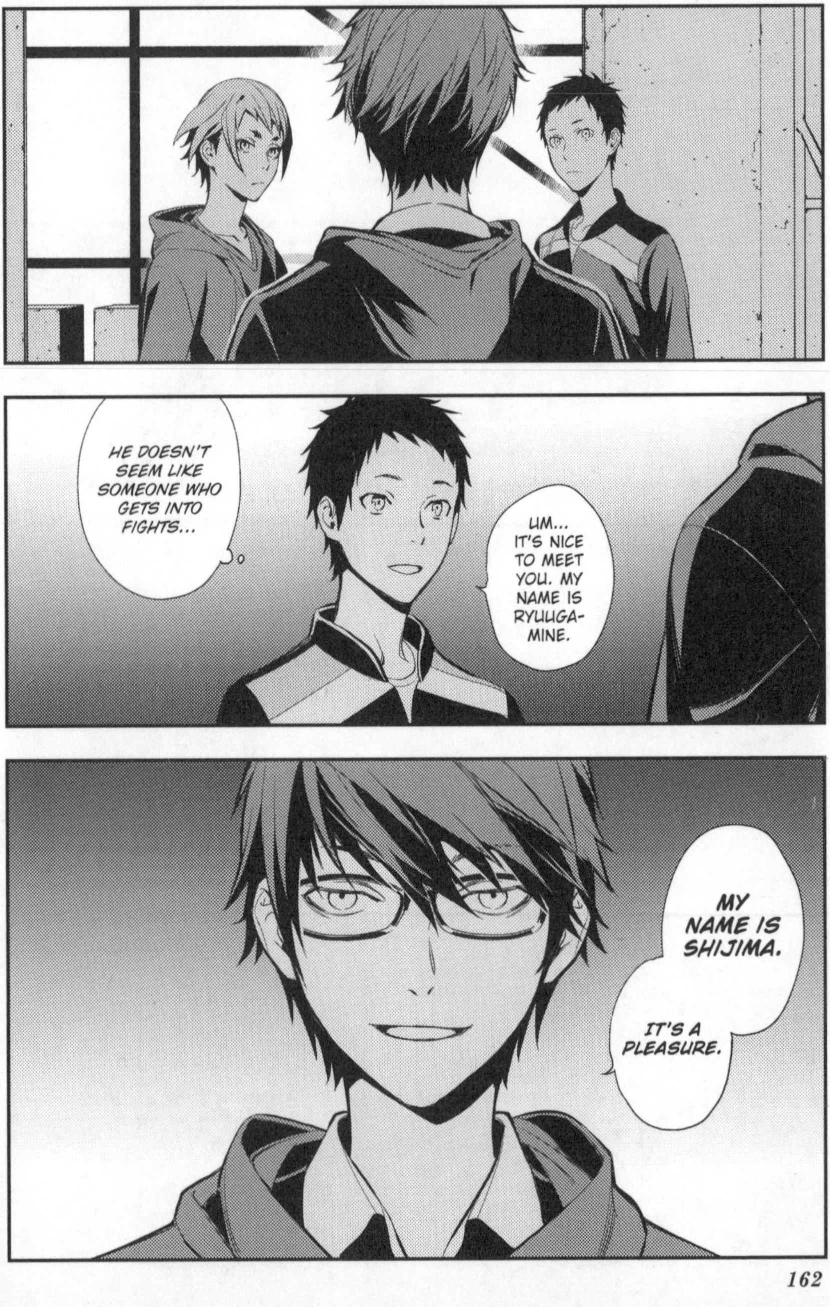
UM... IT'S NICE TO MEET YOU. MY NAME IS RYUUGA-MINE.
HE DOESN'T SEEM LIKE SOMEONE WHO GETS INTO FIGHTS...
MY NAME IS SHIJIMA.
IT'S A PLEASURE.

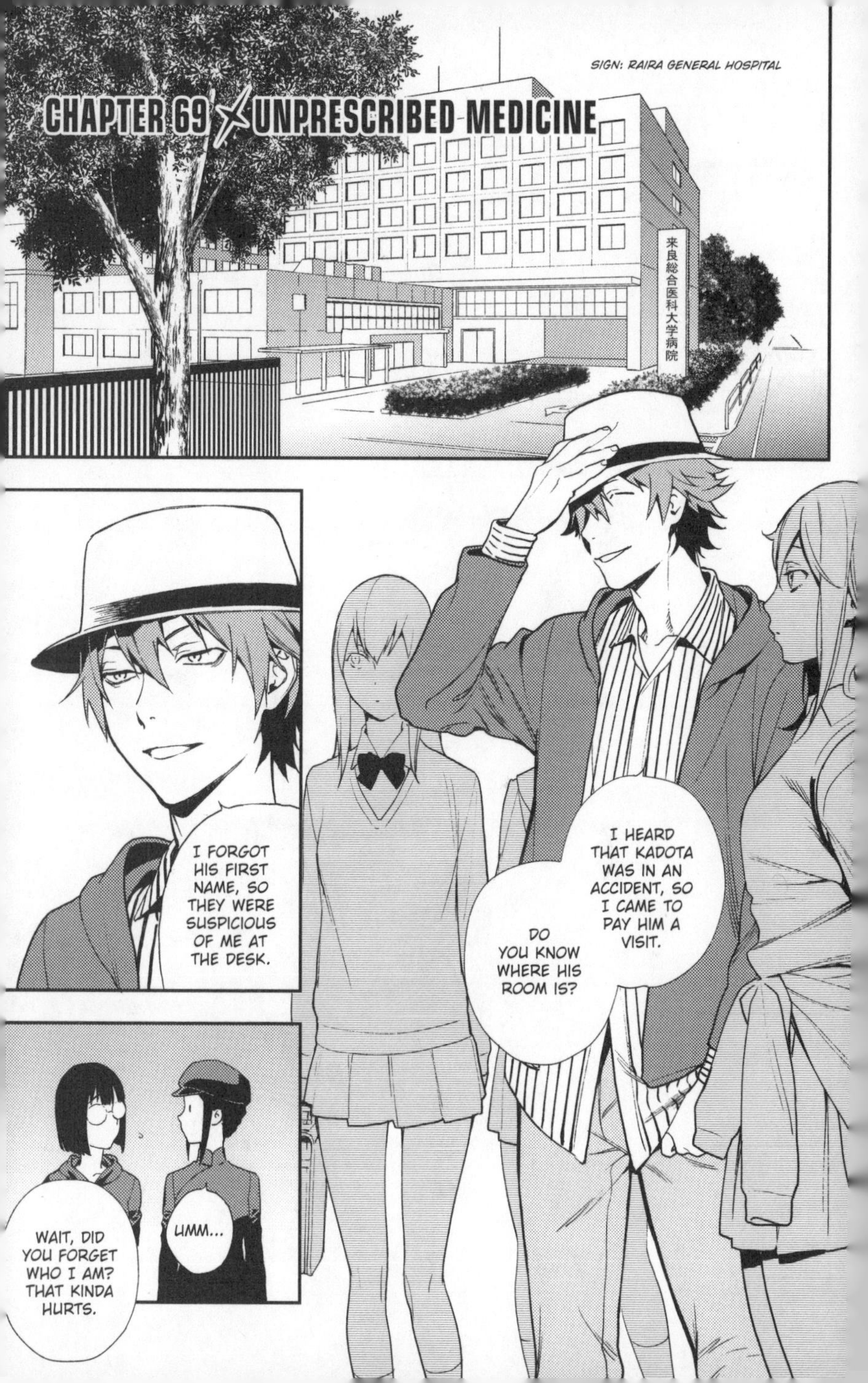
CHAPTER 69 UNPRESCRIBED MEDICINE
SIGN: RAIRA GENERAL HOSPITAL
来良総合医科大学病院
I HEARD THAT KADOTA WAS IN AN ACCIDENT, SO I CAME TO PAY HIM A VISIT.
DO YOU KNOW WHERE HIS ROOM IS?
I FORGOT HIS FIRST NAME, SO THEY WERE SUSPICIOUS OF ME AT THE DESK.
UMM...
WAIT, DID YOU FORGET WHO I AM? THAT KINDA HURTS.

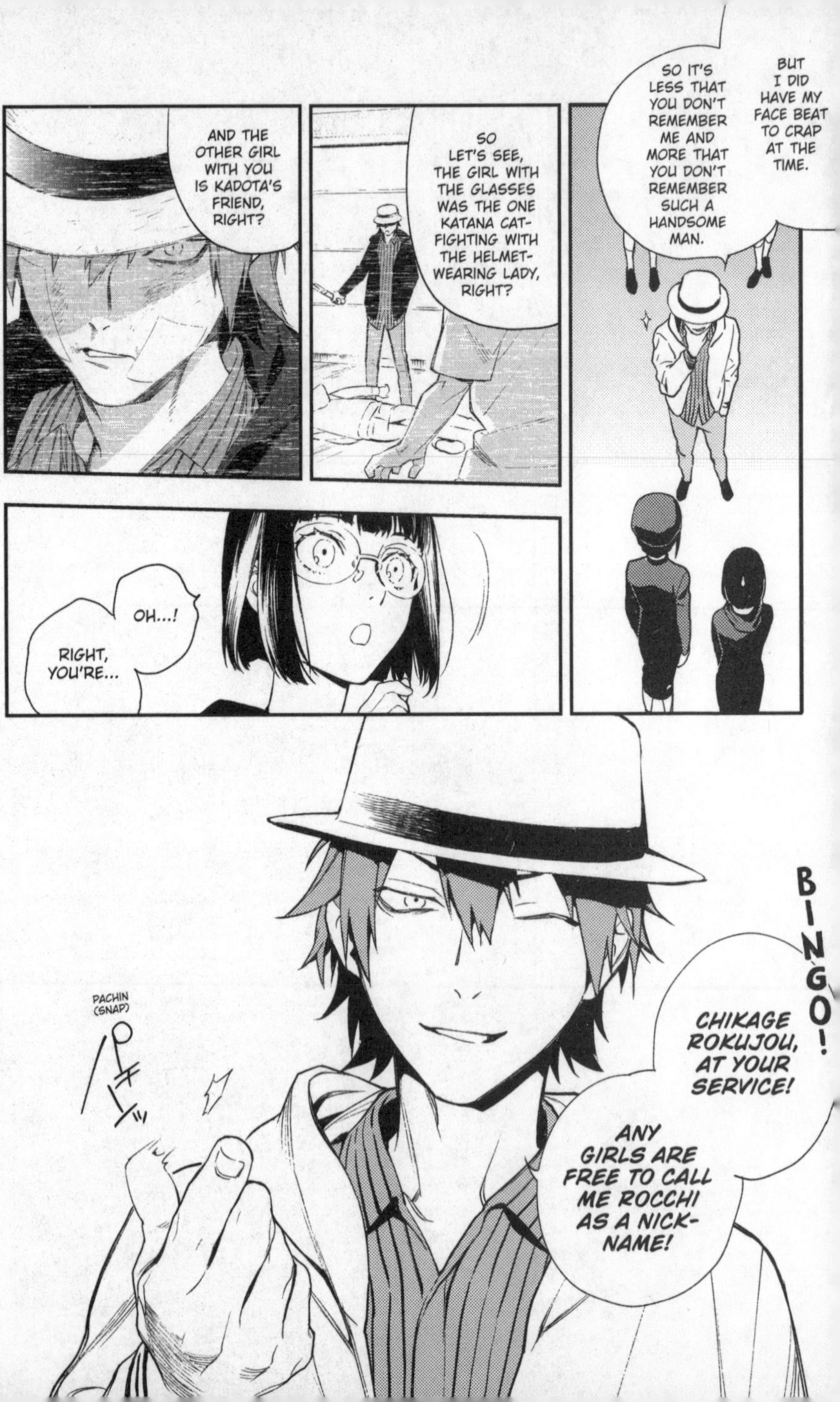
BUT I DID HAVE MY FACE BEAT TO CRAP AT THE TIME.
SO IT'S LESS THAT YOU DON'T REMEMBER ME AND MORE THAT YOU DON'T REMEMBER SUCH A HANDSOME MAN.
SO LET'S SEE, THE GIRL WITH THE GLASSES WAS THE ONE KATANA CAT-FIGHTING WITH THE HELMET-WEARING LADY, RIGHT?
AND THE OTHER GIRL WITH YOU IS KADOTA'S FRIEND, RIGHT?
OH...!
RIGHT, YOU'RE...
BINGO!
CHIKAGE ROKUJOU, AT YOUR SERVICE!
ANY GIRLS ARE FREE TO CALL ME ROCCHI AS A NICK-NAME!
PACHIN (SNAP)

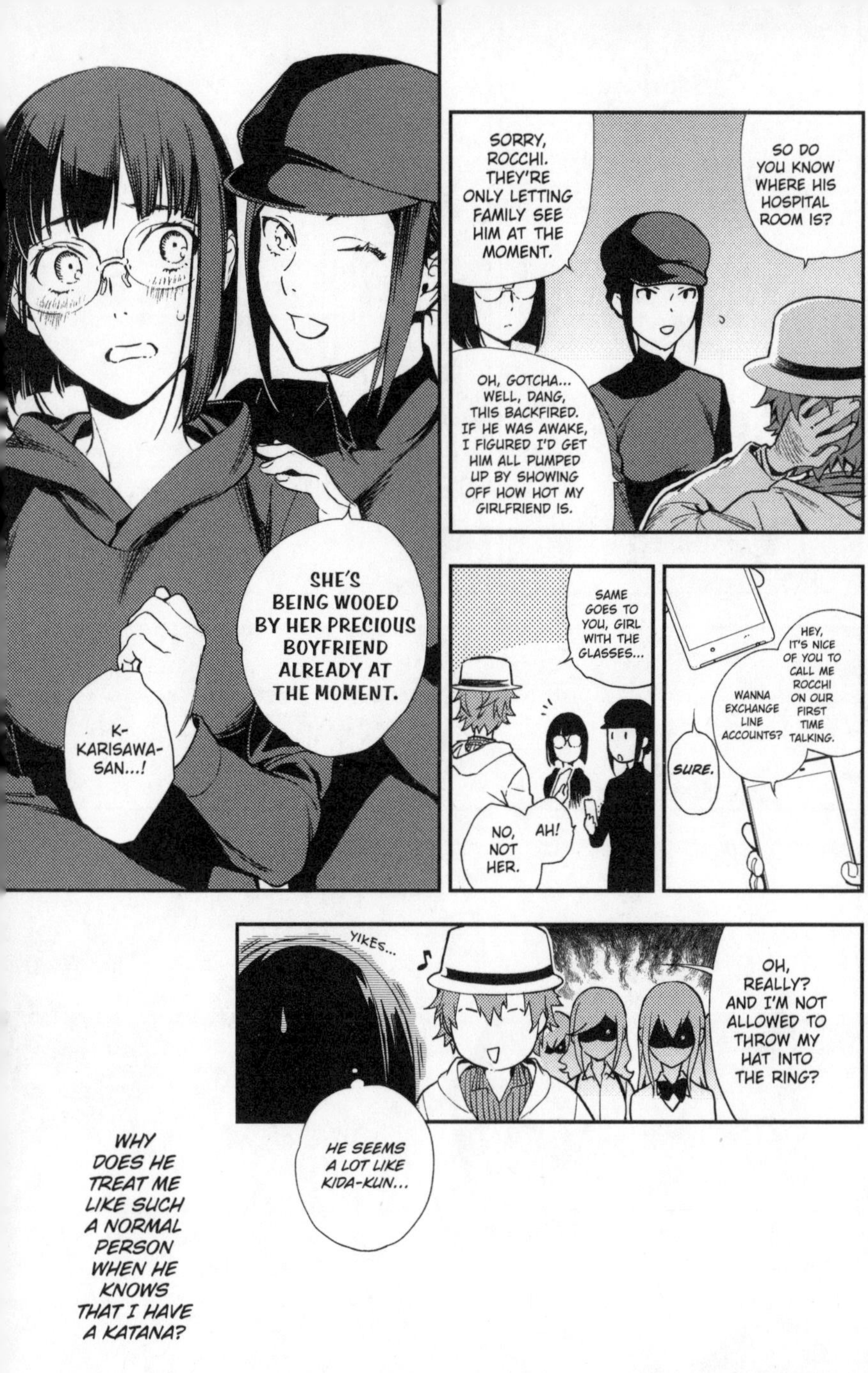
SO DO YOU KNOW WHERE HIS HOSPITAL ROOM IS?
SORRY, ROCCHI. THEY'RE ONLY LETTING FAMILY SEE HIM AT THE MOMENT.
OH, GOTCHA... WELL, DANG, THIS BACKFIRED. IF HE WAS AWAKE, I FIGURED I'D GET HIM ALL PUMPED UP BY SHOWING OFF HOW HOT MY GIRLFRIEND IS.
HEY, IT'S NICE OF YOU TO CALL ME ROCCHI ON OUR FIRST TIME TALKING.
WANNA EXCHANGE LINE ACCOUNTS?
SURE.
SAME GOES TO YOU, GIRL WITH THE GLASSES...
AH!
NO, NOT HER.
SHE'S BEING WOOED BY HER PRECIOUS BOYFRIEND ALREADY AT THE MOMENT.
K-KARISAWA-SAN...!
OH, REALLY? AND I'M NOT ALLOWED TO THROW MY HAT INTO THE RING?
YIKES...
HE SEEMS A LOT LIKE KIDA-KUN...
WHY DOES HE TREAT ME LIKE SUCH A NORMAL PERSON WHEN HE KNOWS THAT I HAVE A KATANA?

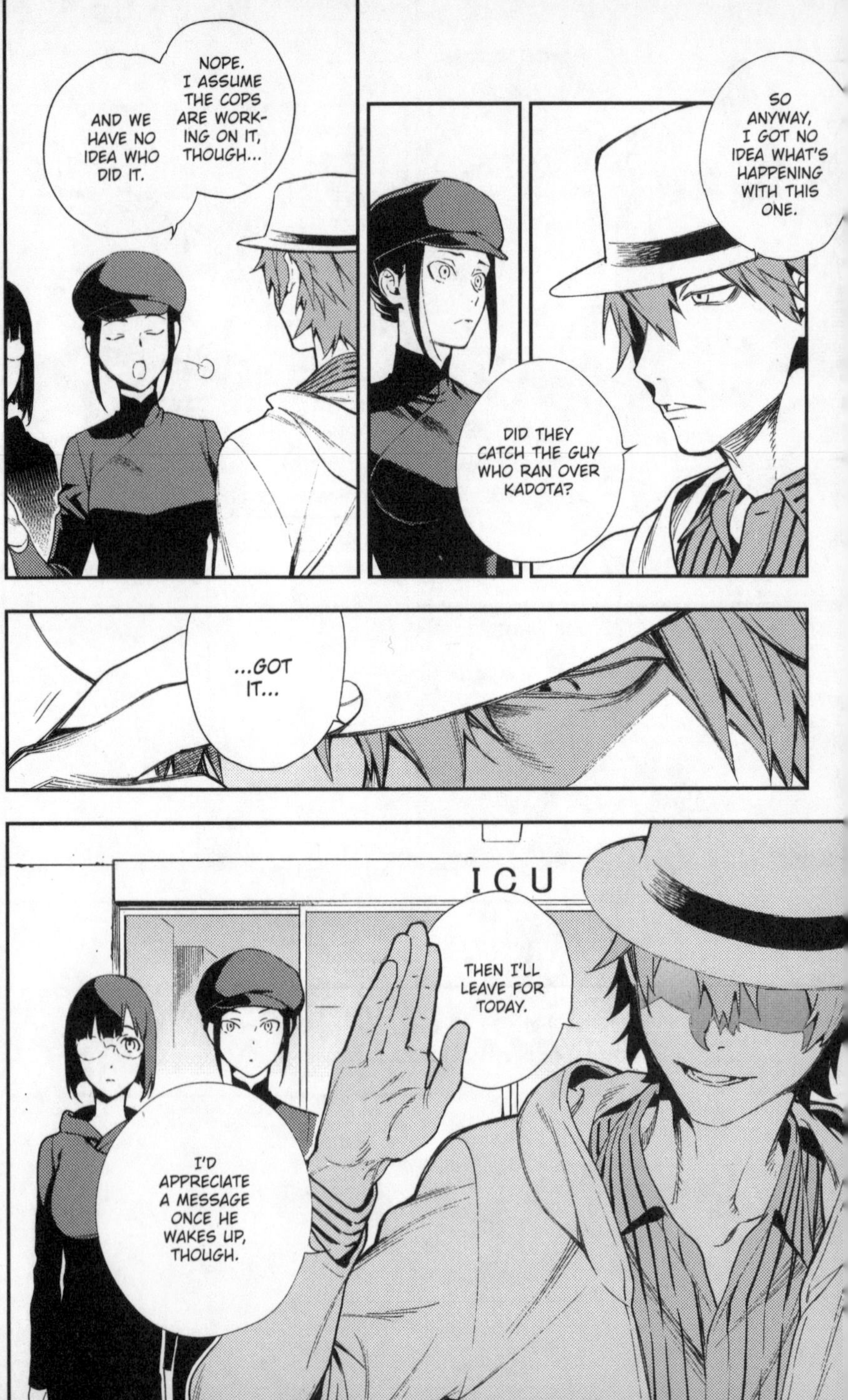
SO ANYWAY, I GOT NO IDEA WHAT'S HAPPENING WITH THIS ONE.
DID THEY CATCH THE GUY WHO RAN OVER KADOTA?
NOPE. I ASSUME THE COPS ARE WORK-ING ON IT, THOUGH...
AND WE HAVE NO IDEA WHO DID IT.
...GOT IT...
ICU
THEN I'LL LEAVE FOR TODAY.
I'D APPRECIATE A MESSAGE ONCE HE WAKES UP, THOUGH.

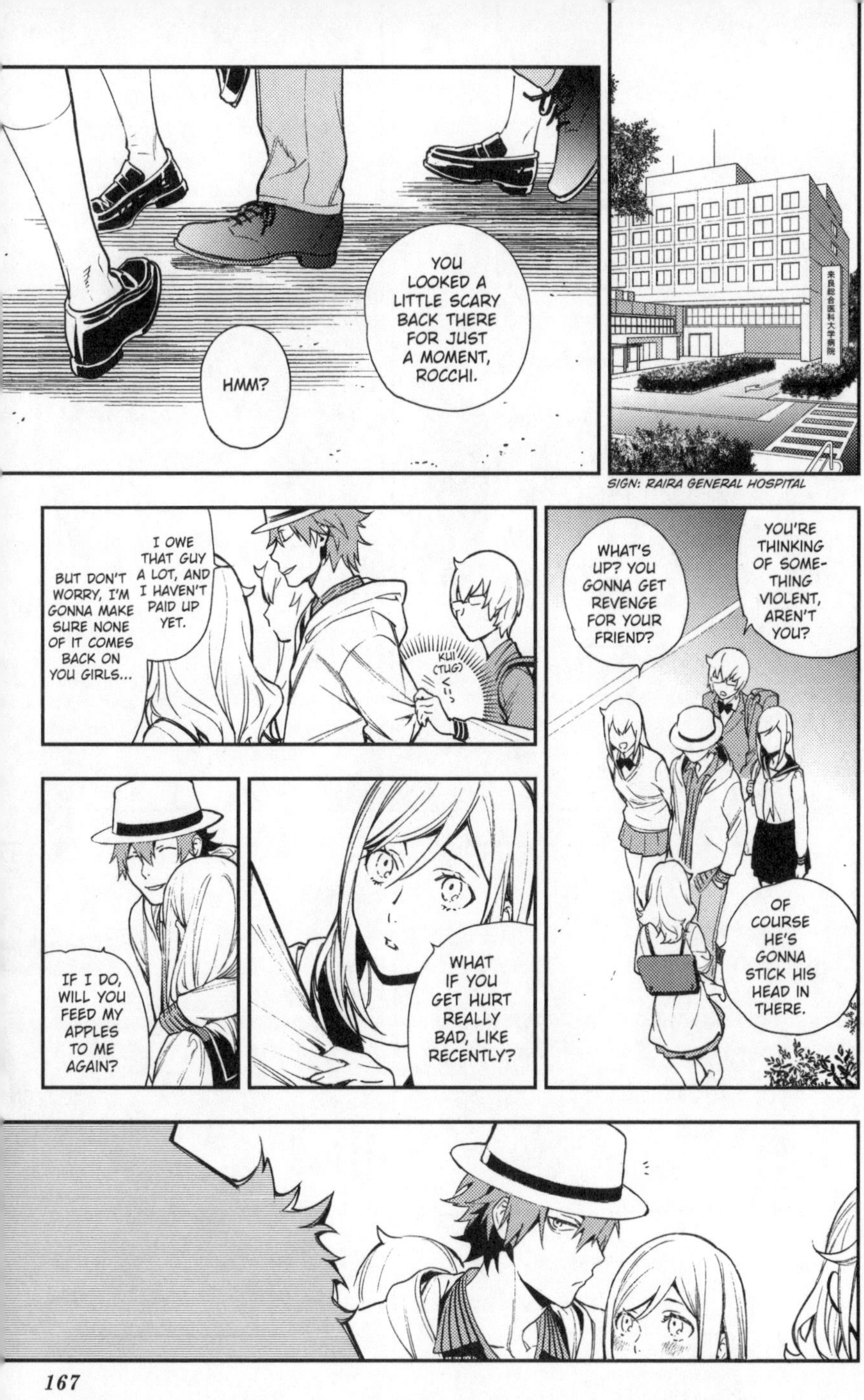
来良総合医科大学病院
SIGN: RAIRA GENERAL HOSPITAL
YOU LOOKED A LITTLE SCARY BACK THERE FOR JUST A MOMENT, ROCCHI.
HMM?
YOU'RE THINKING OF SOME-THING VIOLENT, AREN'T YOU?
WHAT'S UP? YOU GONNA GET REVENGE FOR YOUR FRIEND?
OF COURSE HE'S GONNA STICK HIS HEAD IN THERE.
I OWE THAT GUY A LOT, AND I HAVEN'T PAID UP YET.
BUT DON'T WORRY, I'M GONNA MAKE SURE NONE OF IT COMES BACK ON YOU GIRLS...
KUI (TUG)
WHAT IF YOU GET HURT REALLY BAD, LIKE RECENTLY?
IF I DO, WILL YOU FEED MY APPLES TO ME AGAIN?

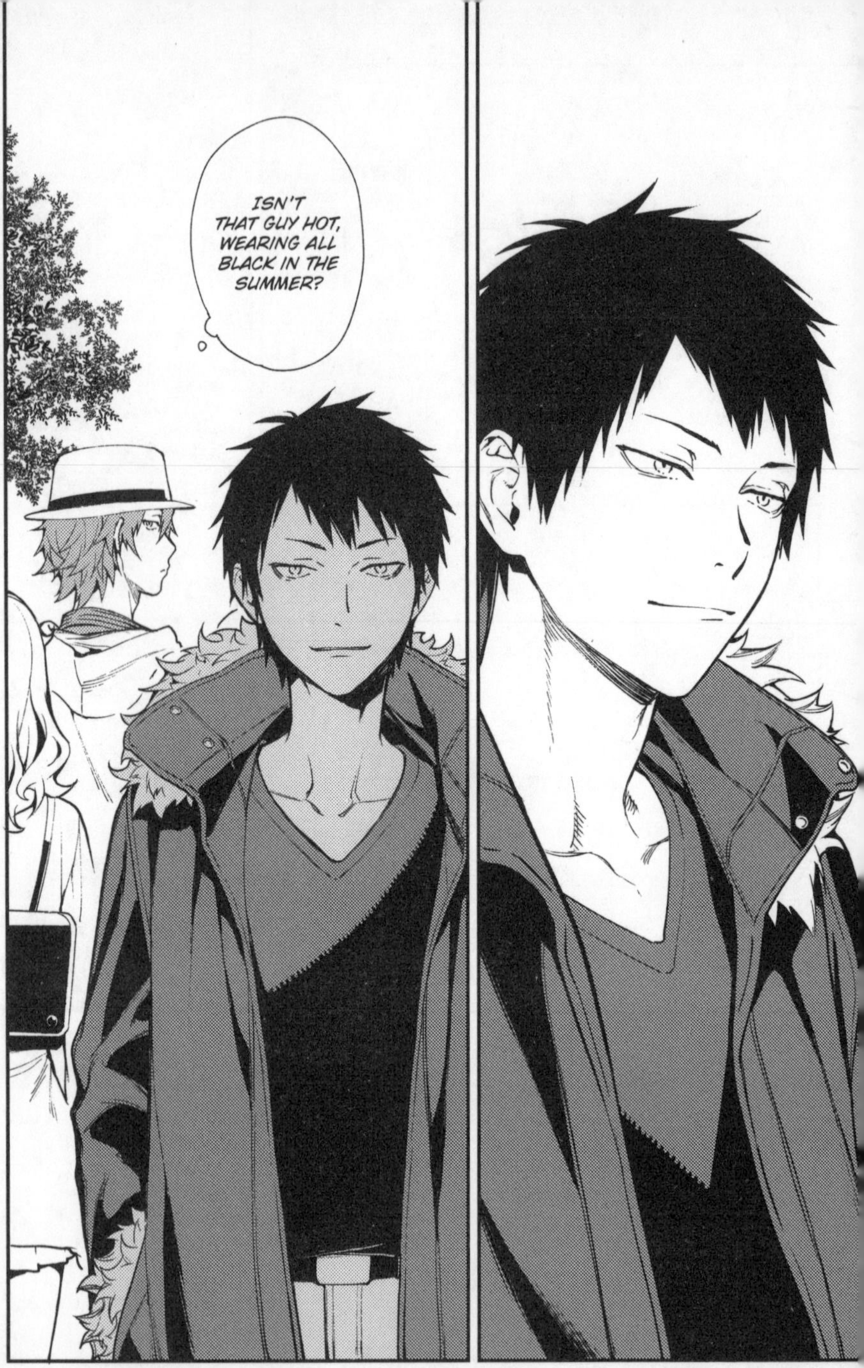
ISN'T THAT GUY HOT, WEARING ALL BLACK IN THE SUMMER?

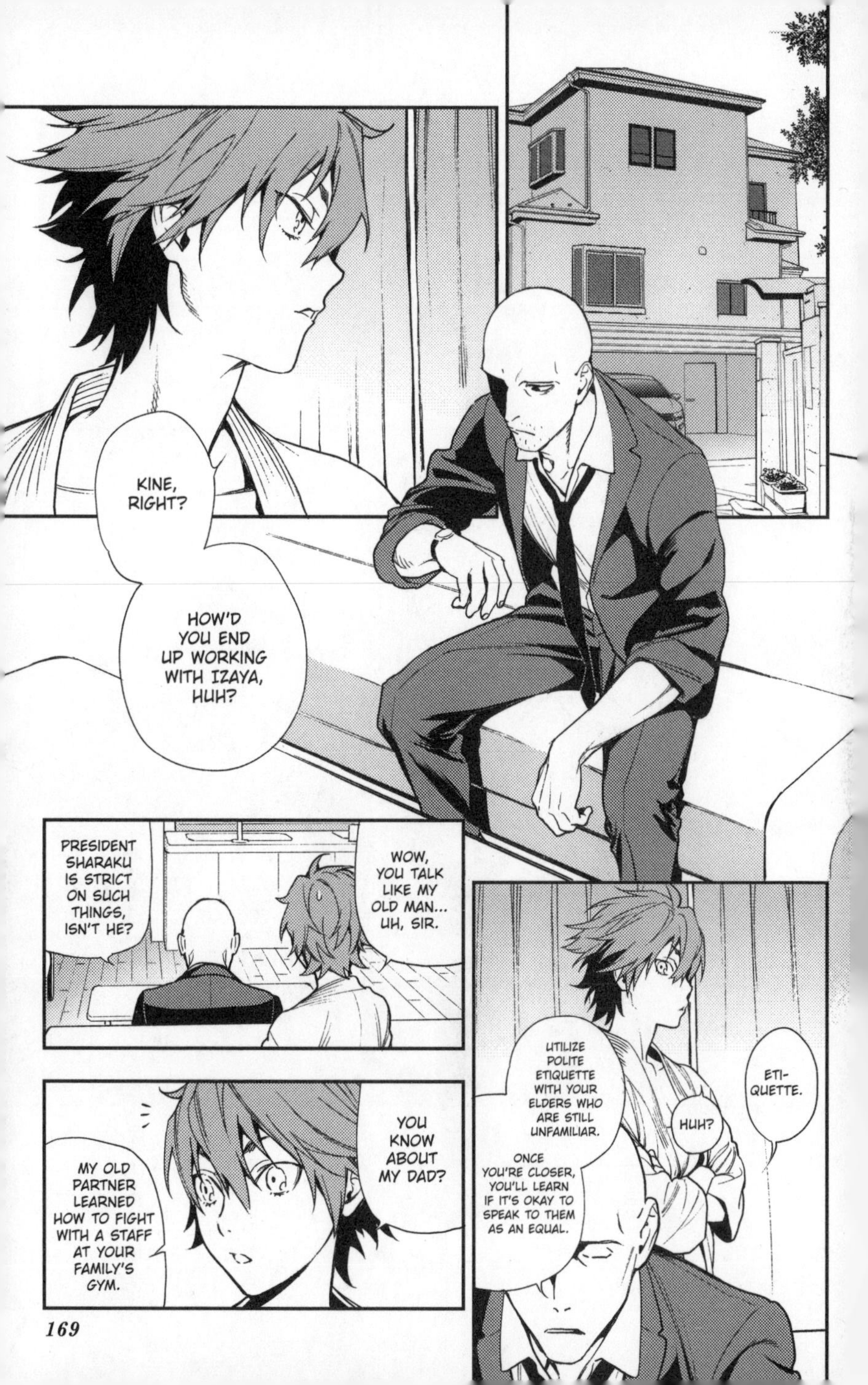
KINE, RIGHT?
HOW'D YOU END UP WORKING WITH IZAYA, HUH?
ETI-QUETTE.
HUH?
UTILIZE POLITE ETIQUETTE WITH YOUR ELDERS WHO ARE STILL UNFAMILIAR.
ONCE YOU'RE CLOSER, YOU'LL LEARN IF IT'S OKAY TO SPEAK TO THEM AS AN EQUAL.
WOW, YOU TALK LIKE MY OLD MAN... UH, SIR.
PRESIDENT SHARAKU IS STRICT ON SUCH THINGS, ISN'T HE?
YOU KNOW ABOUT MY DAD?
MY OLD PARTNER LEARNED HOW TO FIGHT WITH A STAFF AT YOUR FAMILY'S GYM.

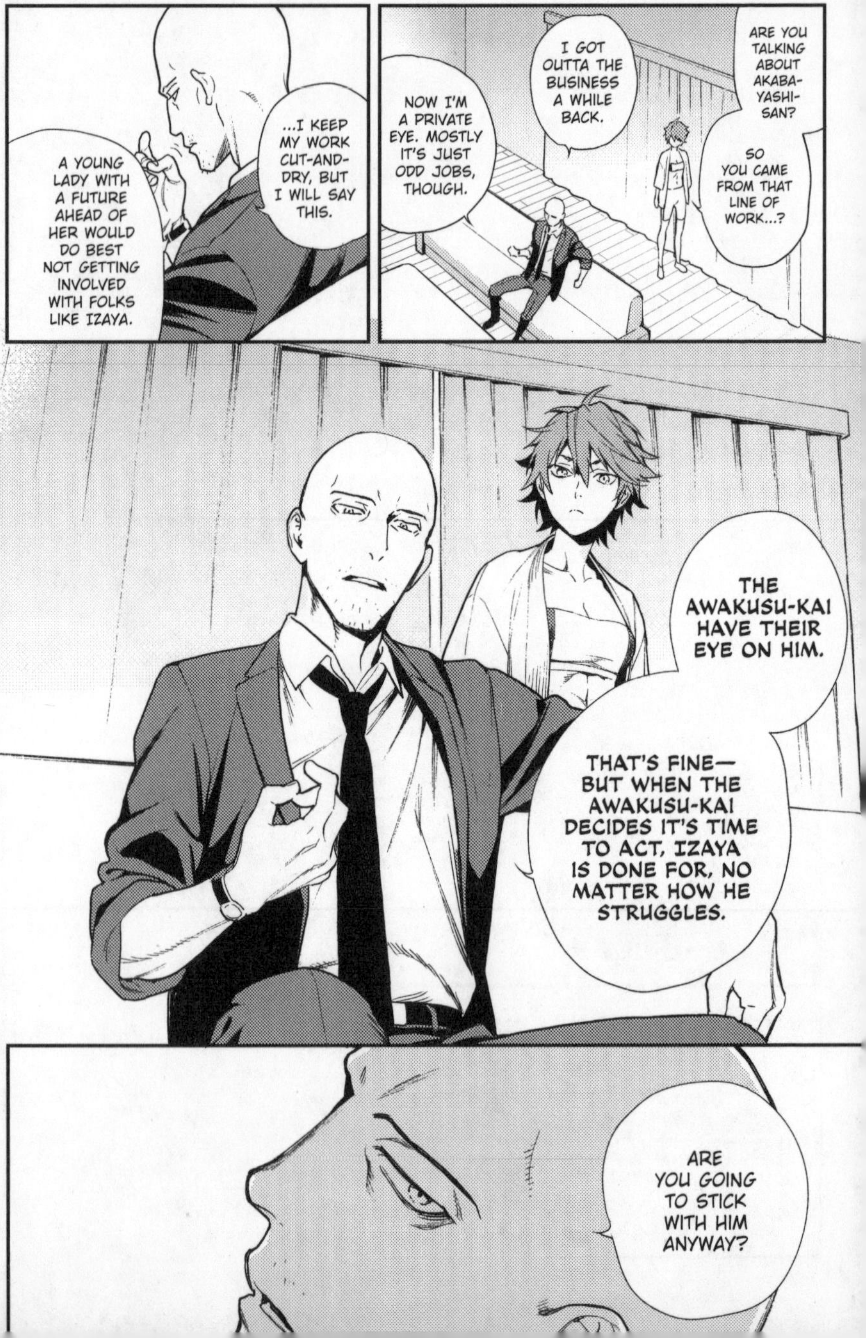
ARE YOU TALKING ABOUT AKABA-YASHI-SAN?
SO YOU CAME FROM THAT LINE OF WORK...?
I GOT OUTTA THE BUSINESS A WHILE BACK.
NOW I'M A PRIVATE EYE. MOSTLY IT'S JUST ODD JOBS, THOUGH.
...I KEEP MY WORK CUT-AND-DRY, BUT I WILL SAY THIS.
A YOUNG LADY WITH A FUTURE AHEAD OF HER WOULD DO BEST NOT GETTING INVOLVED WITH FOLKS LIKE IZAYA.
THE AWAKUSU-KAI HAVE THEIR EYE ON HIM.
THAT'S FINE—BUT WHEN THE AWAKUSU-KAI DECIDES IT'S TIME TO ACT, IZAYA IS DONE FOR, NO MATTER HOW HE STRUGGLES.
ARE YOU GOING TO STICK WITH HIM ANYWAY?

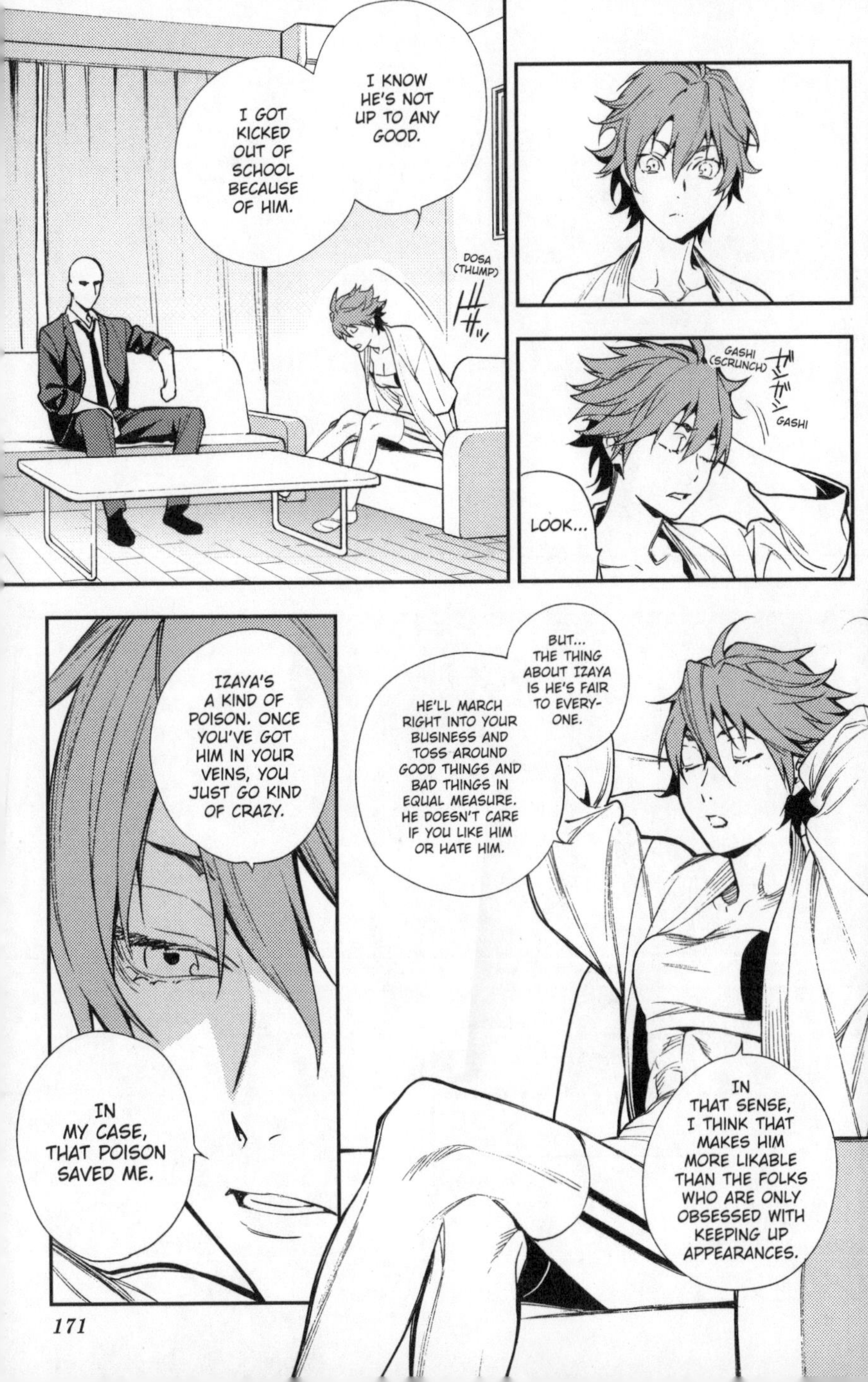
GASHI (SCRUNCH)
GASHI
LOOK...
I KNOW HE'S NOT UP TO ANY GOOD.
I GOT KICKED OUT OF SCHOOL BECAUSE OF HIM.
DOSA (THUMP)
BUT... THE THING ABOUT IZAYA IS HE'S FAIR TO EVERY-ONE.
HE'LL MARCH RIGHT INTO YOUR BUSINESS AND TOSS AROUND GOOD THINGS AND BAD THINGS IN EQUAL MEASURE. HE DOESN'T CARE IF YOU LIKE HIM OR HATE HIM.
IN THAT SENSE, I THINK THAT MAKES HIM MORE LIKABLE THAN THE FOLKS WHO ARE ONLY OBSESSED WITH KEEPING UP APPEARANCES.
IZAYA'S A KIND OF POISON. ONCE YOU'VE GOT HIM IN YOUR VEINS, YOU JUST GO KIND OF CRAZY.
IN MY CASE, THAT POISON SAVED ME.

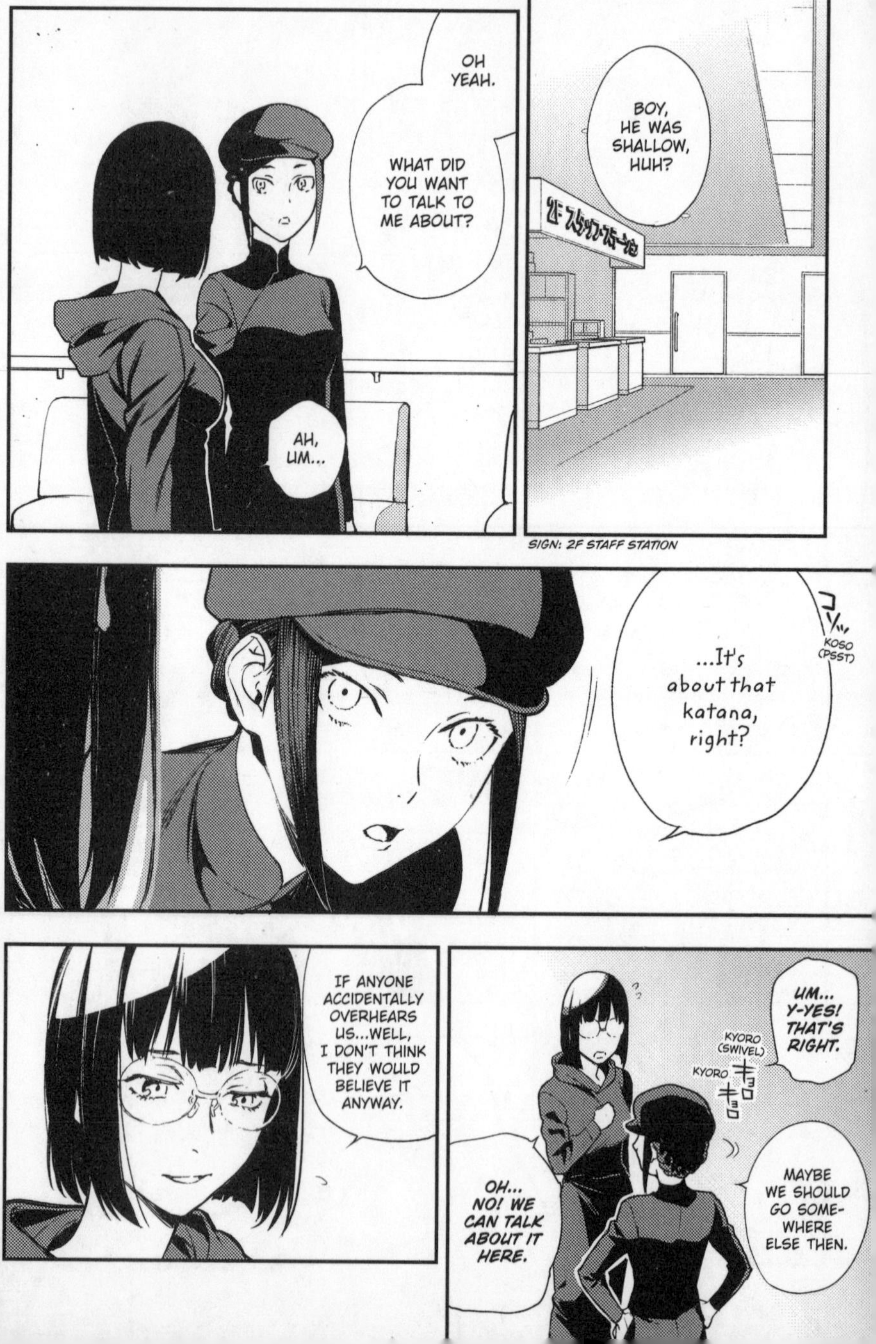
BOY, HE WAS SHALLOW, HUH?
SIGN: 2F STAFF STATION
OH YEAH.
WHAT DID YOU WANT TO TALK TO ME ABOUT?
AH, UM...
KOSO (PSST)
...It's about that katana, right?
UM... Y-YES! THAT'S RIGHT.
KYORO (SWIVEL) KYORO
MAYBE WE SHOULD GO SOME-WHERE ELSE THEN.
OH... NO! WE CAN TALK ABOUT IT HERE.
IF ANYONE ACCIDENTALLY OVERHEARS US...WELL, I DON'T THINK THEY WOULD BELIEVE IT ANYWAY.

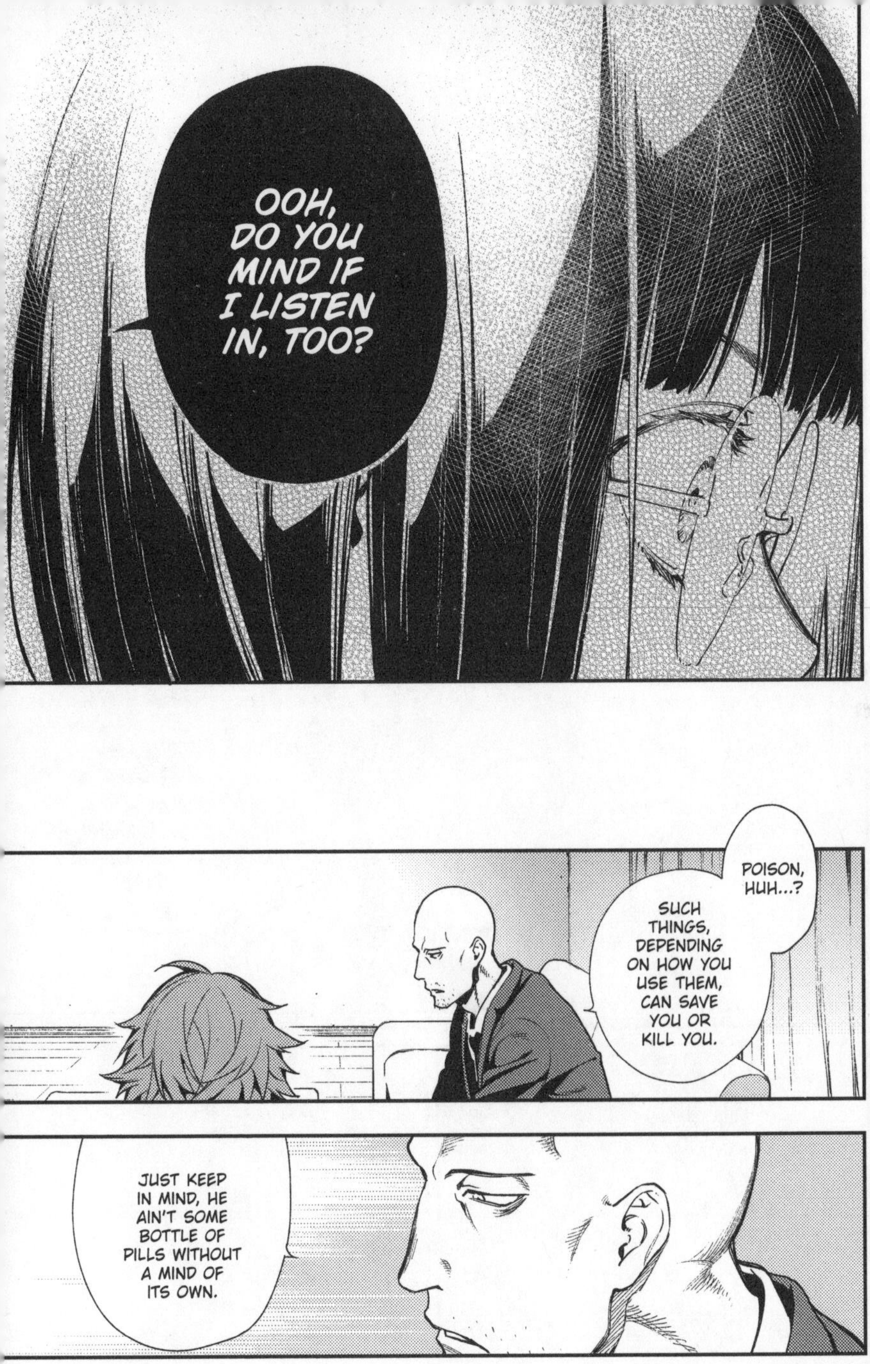
OOH, DO YOU MIND IF I LISTEN IN, TOO?
POISON, HUH...?
SUCH THINGS, DEPENDING ON HOW YOU USE THEM, CAN SAVE YOU OR KILL YOU.
JUST KEEP IN MIND, HE AIN'T SOME BOTTLE OF PILLS WITHOUT A MIND OF ITS OWN.

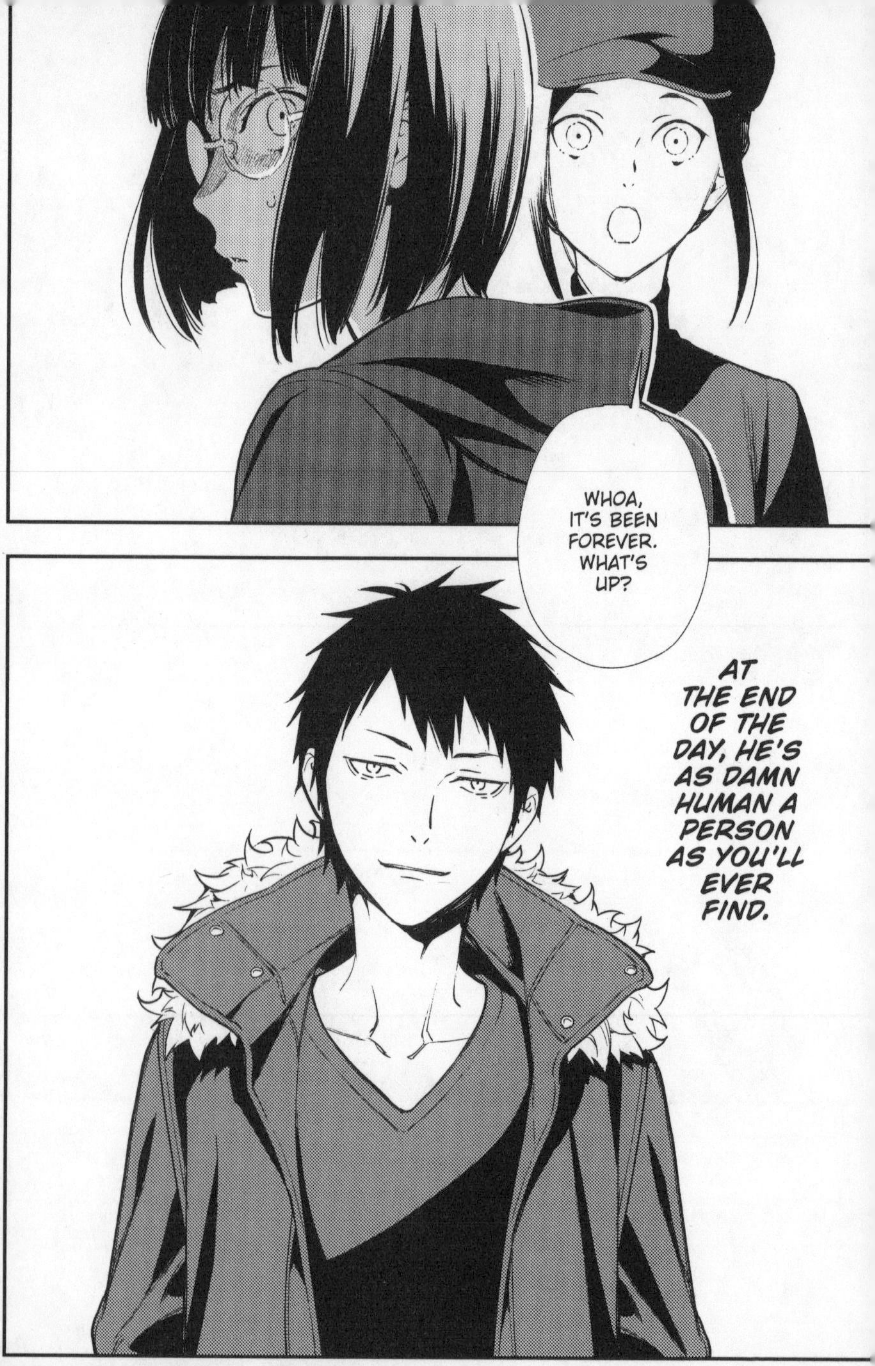
WHOA, IT'S BEEN FOREVER. WHAT'S UP?
AT THE END OF THE DAY, HE'S AS DAMN HUMAN A PERSON AS YOU'LL EVER FIND.

DURARARA!! RE;DOLLARS ARC 7 END

DURARARA!! Re;Dollars Arc

TRANSLATION NOTES

Common Honorifics

no honorific: Indicates familiarity or closeness; if used without permission or reason, addressing someone in this manner would constitute an insult.

-san: The Japanese equivalent of Mr./Mrs./Miss. If a situation calls for politeness, this is the fail-safe honorific.

-sama: Conveys great respect; may also indicate that the social status of the speaker is lower than that of the addressee.

-kun: Used most often when referring to boys, this indicates affection or familiarity. Occasionally used by older men among their peers, but it may also be used by anyone referring to a person of lower standing.

-chan: An affectionate honorific indicating familiarity used mostly in reference to girls; also used in reference to cute persons or animals of either gender.

-sensei: A respectful term for teachers, artists, or high-level professionals.

-senpai: A suffix used to address upperclassmen or more experienced coworkers.

-kouhai: A suffix used to address underclassmen or less experienced coworkers.

-niisan, nii-san, anki, etc.: A term of endearment meaning "big brother" that may be more widely used to address any young man who is like a brother, regardless of whether he is related or not.

-neesan, nee-san, aneki, etc.: The female counterpart of the above, meaning "big sister."

PAGE 47

oden soup: A comforting Japanese dish composed of *oden*, or fish cakes, in warm seafood broth made using ingredients such as dried anchovies, seaweed, etc.

PAGE 131

Akechi: Kogoro Akechi is a fictional detective created by lauded Japanese mystery writer Ranpo Edogawa. Inspired by the character of Sherlock Holmes, one of Akechi's foes is the infamous Fiend with Twenty Faces.

PAGE 135

shamisen: A traditional Japanese instrument that used to be constructed using cat skin.

DURARARA!! Re;Dollars Arc

DRRR!! RE;DOLLARS ARC 07

ART
AOGIRI ✕

CREATOR
RYOHGO NARITA ✕

CHARACTER DESIGN
SUZUHITO YASUDA ✕

TRANSLATION
STEPHEN PAUL ✕

LETTERING
CHIO CHRISTIE ✕

DURARARA!! RE;DOLLARS-HEN Vol. 7
© 2021 Ryohgo Narita
© 2021 Aogiri / SQUARE ENIX CO., LTD.
© 2021 SQUARE ENIX CO., LTD.
DURARARA!! SQUARE ENIX ASCII MEDIA WORKS

First published in Japan in 2021 by SQUARE ENIX CO., LTD.
English translation rights arranged with SQUARE ENIX CO., LTD.
and Yen Press, LLC through Tuttle-Mori Agency, Inc.

English translation © 2022 by SQUARE ENIX CO., LTD.

Yen Press
150 West 30th Street, 19th Floor
New York, NY 10001

Visit us at yenpress.com
facebook.com/yenpress
twitter.com/yenpress
yenpress.tumblr.com
instagram.com/yenpress

First Yen Press Edition: June 2022
Edited by Yen Press Editorial: Won Young Seo
Designed by Yen Press Design: Andy Swist

Yen Press is an imprint of Yen Press, LLC.
The Yen Press name and logo are trademarks of Yen Press, LLC.

Library of Congress Control Number: 2016931000

ISBNs: 978-1-9753-4722-2 (paperback)
978-1-9753-4751-2 (ebook)

10 9 8 7 6 5 4 3 2 1

LSC-C

Printed in the United States of America

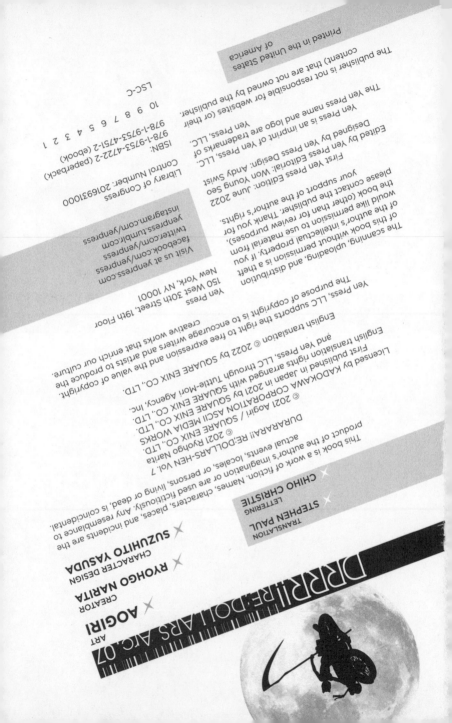